READINGS IN
WORLD CIVILIZATIONS

Volume 2: The Development of the Modern World

Third Edition

KEVIN REILLY

ST. MARTIN'S PRESS / New York

For my friends in the World History Association

Editor: Louise H. Waller
Manager, publishing services: Emily Berleth
Publishing services associate: Kalea Chapman
Project management: Richard Steins
Photo research: Inge King
Cover design: Rod Hernandez
Cover art: Maryland Cartographics

Manufactured in the United States of America.
98765
fedcba

For information, write:
St. Martin's Press, Inc.
175 Fifth Avenue
New York, NY 10010

ISBN: 0-312-09648-8

Acknowledgments

It is a violation of the law to reproduce these selections by any means whatsoever
without the written permission of the copyright holder.

1. European Renaissance and Reformation
   1. From *The Prince* by Niccolò Machiavelli, translated by Luigi Ricci, revised by E. R. P.
Vincent. Copyright © 1935 Oxford University Press.
   2. From the translation based on Wace and Buchheim, *Luther's Primary Works* (London,
1896), edited in B. J. Kidd, *Documents Illustrative of the Continental Reformation* (Oxford,
1911).
   3. Reprinted from *Society and Culture in Early Modern France* by Natalie Zemon Davis with
the permission of the publishers, Stanford University Press. Copyright © 1985 by the Board
of Trustees of the Leland Stanford Junior University.
2. American Civilizations and the Columbian Exchange
   4. From *Germs, Seeds, and Animals* by Alfred W. Crosby, pp. 45–49, 60–61. Reprinted by
permission of M. E. Sharpe, Inc., Armonk, New York 10504.
   5.1. From *The Memoirs of the Conquistador Bernal Diaz de Castillo*, translated by I. I.
Lockhard. London: J. Hatchard, 1844.

Acknowledgments and copyrights are continued at the back of the book on pages 362–
365, which constitute an extension of the copyright page.

READINGS IN
WORLD CIVILIZATIONS

Volume 2: The Development
of the Modern World

Third Edition

CONTENTS

Topical Contents

Philosophy, Literature, and the Arts

Religion

Geographical Contents

PREFACE

When I began my teaching career at Rutgers University in the 1960s, there was no course in world history. We taught a course called "Western Civilization" that had developed in American universities between World War I and World War II. It was a course that identified America's fate with that of Europe; the idea of "Europe" or "the West" made more sense to Americans swept up in European wars than it did to many Europeans (who taught their national histories). A course in Western civilization also seemed the appropriate way for an American population largely descended from Europeans to find its roots.

There were problems with this idea from the beginning. One was that it ignored the heritage of Americans whose ancestors came from Africa, Asia, and other parts of the world. Another was that the world was becoming a much smaller place. Transoceanic journeys that formerly took a week or more had been reduced by jet planes to a few hours. Since the 1960s, the importance of the non-European world for Americans has increased even more. Trade with Japan has become larger than that with European countries. More new American immigrants have come from Asia and Latin American than from Europe. The daily newspaper carries more stories concerning the Middle East, Asia, Africa, and Latin America than Europe. The interests of the United States are more global than ever. For these good reasons, an increasing number of colleges and universities (including Rutgers) are now offering courses in global or world history.

Compiling an anthology for use in such introductory world history classes is a task that requires many decisions and that benefits from the input of many friends. The instructor who considers using the result should be apprised of both.

First the decisions. These two volumes are intended for introductory courses. For me, that consideration prescribes a survey format that encompasses all of world history. (The two volumes of this work divide roughly at the year 1500.) It also mandates that the readings be understandable, at least in their essentials, by typical first-year college students.

In nearly every chapter I have included both primary and secondary sources. Primary sources were selected partly to represent "great works" and cultural legacies and partly to provide students with an authentic glimpse of a particular historical time and place. Some readings do both. The epic of Gilgamesh in Volume One, for example, is a "great work" that also opens a window on Sumer. From it students can learn about Sumerian religion, gender roles, and ideas of kingship and also acquire a basis for making important historical comparisons—the Biblical account of the flood is often compared with the flood in Gilgamesh. The selection in Volume Two from Gabriel García Márquez's *One Hundred Years of Solitude,* one of the "great works" of modern literature, releases an explosion of images, characters, settings, and scenes in a magical confection of hypnotic dream and detail that reveals a good deal about Latin America.

Secondary sources were chosen for their capacity to challenge students with information and points of view probably not found in their survey texts, as well as, of course, for their interest and accessibility. Some readings will introduce students to the work of leading modern historians—such as William H. McNeill, Philip Curtin, Natalie Zemon Davis, Alfred W. Crosby, and Jonathan Spence—and perhaps even induce them to read further in the writings of these great scholars. In some cases the selections may lead students to look at additional primary sources beyond what I have been able to include here. In Volume One, for example, S. G. Brandon's "Paul and His Opponents" should encourage students to examine the New Testament letters of Paul with a keener eye. In Volume Two, the secondary readings on "Dependence and Independence" in Asia, Africa, the Middle East, and Latin America will enable students to get more out of their daily newspaper.

For the third edition I have added more interesting primary sources and newer interpretations. I have also tried to make the collection more global (adding selections, for instance, from Southeast Asia) and more universal (for example, with additional selections on women, technology, and on daily life).

I wanted each reading to be able to stand on its own. I know how frustrating it can be to find that a favorite selection or passage has been so condensed as to become almost worthless. Although space considerations have dictated that some abridging be done, I have tried very hard to be as sensitive as possible to this concern.

I also wanted the students *to read the readings.* Therefore the readings are not preceded by lengthy introductions that, in students' minds, may make the selections seem superfluous. For each reading I have provided an introduction that establishes a context but that principally directs students with a series of questions. These questions ask: What is said? What is the evidence? What conclusion or judgment can be drawn? They are intended to aid students in developing critical thinking skills—recall, analysis and evaluation, and self-expression—and to illustrate how historians work.

The historical understanding that, I am hopeful, will develop from the study of these volumes is qualitative. Different students will remember different specifics. All, however, should gain an increased understanding of past civilizations and ways of life and a greater awareness of the connections and contrasts between past and present. My ultimate goal for these two volumes is that they help students to live in a broader world, both temporally and spatially.

Now for the friends. A work like this would not have been possible without many historian friends and colleagues. As president of the World History Association, I have been fortunate in having many people who are both. Many members of the association—too many to name—offered suggestions, read drafts, sent me favorite selections, and in general helped me improve this work. But I am especially indebted to Lynda Shaffer of Tufts University; Stephen Gosch of the University of Wisconsin-Eau Claire; Marc Gilbert of North Georgia College; Jerry Bentley of the University of Hawaii; Ross Dunn of San Diego State; Ray Lorantas of Drexel University; and Ernest Menze of Iona College. Their criticisms and also, of course, the work of an earlier generation of world historians, especially William H. McNeill, Philip Curtin, and Leften Stavrianos, have been invaluable.

I also want to thank my friends and colleagues where I have learned and taught: at Rutgers—Traian Stoianovich, Michael Adas, Allen Howard, Virginia Yans, Robert Rosen (now at UCLA), and Roger Cranse (now at Vermont College of Norwich University); at Princeton—Robert Tignor, Gyan Prakash, and Robert J. Wright; and at Raritan—Brock Haussamen, Bud McKinley, Mark Bezanson, Tom Valasek, and my Humanities colleagues.

Many others have commented, suggested selections, or reviewed the previous edition. Among them are Linda Addo, North Carolina Agriculture and Technical State University; Andrew Clark, University of North Carolina, Wilmington; Eugene Hermitte, Johnson C. Smith University; Ted Kluz, Auburn University, Montgomery; Bogwa Lorence-Kot, California College of Arts and Crafts; William M. McBride, James Madison University; Stephen Morillo, Wabash College; Gary R. Olsen, New Mexico Tech; Patricia O'Malley, Bradford College; V. Padmavathy, University of Wisconsin-La Crosse; and Allen Wittenborn, University of San Diego.

I want to give special thanks to all of the people at St. Martin's Press. Louise Waller, my editor and friend, has been a superb successor to Michael Weber, who helped me create the first edition. The work of Lynette Blevins and Richard Steins was invaluable. And I want to thank Emily Berleth, manager of publishing services of this edition but also my first "agent," for encouraging me to write history some years ago.

And again I thank Pearl for her loving help and support.

KEVIN REILLY

A NOTE ABOUT THE COVER

St. Martin's Press and I have chosen maps for the covers of these volumes that are both historically valuable and, we hope, attractive. On Volume One, courtesy of Biblioteca Estense Modena/Scala, we have reproduced a Catalan world map from about 1450, not one of the most accurate of the period (especially in its drawing of Asia) but one of the more vivid renderings of history geographically, with its inclusion of legendary rulers of Asia and Africa. For Volume Two, Maryland Cartographics produced a "cartogram" in which each country's size is drawn so as to indicate the world population in 1994. Thus, China and India, for example, appear to be quite large on the map, while Russia and Canada are relatively small.

INTRODUCTION

This is a collection of readings from and about the human past. Those that are from the past are usually called *primary sources*. They can be anything from an old parking ticket to an ancient poem. Those that are about the past we call *secondary sources*, interpretations, or just plain "histories." They can be written immediately after the events they describe or centuries later, by professional historians or by other interested parties.

We read primary sources and histories for the same reason: to find out what happened in the past. People have different motivations for finding out about the past. Some people are curious about everything. Some are interested in knowing what it was like to live in a particular time or be a particular kind of person. Some people are interested in how things change, or how the world got to where it is. Some wonder about human variety, trying to figure out how different or similar people have been throughout history. I hope this book will answer all these questions.

The reading selections are what is important in this book. Each reading is preceded by an introduction that poses some questions. These questions are designed to guide your reading and to suggest approaches to the reading. There are no particular ideas or pieces of information that everyone should get from a particular reading. What you learn from a reading depends very much on who you are, what you already know, and how much attention you give it. My hope is that you get as much from each reading as you can. Each reading should affect you in some way. Some you will like more than others, but each should open a world previously closed.

Treat these readings, especially the primary sources, as openings to a lost world. Keep your eyes and ears open. Notice everything you can. But don't worry if you miss a sign, a name, or even the meaning people attach to some things. This is your discovery. In some cases, I have added explanatory notes, but I have tried to keep these to a bare minimum. Ultimately there are never enough explanations. But more important, I do not want my explanations to become the information that is read, remembered, and studied for an exam. The readings should bring you your own insights, discoveries, and questions. Like a good travel guide they should help you see, not tell you what you saw.

PART ONE

THE EARLY MODERN WORLD: 1500 TO 1750

Statue of Moses by Michelangelo, Rome (Bettmann Archive)

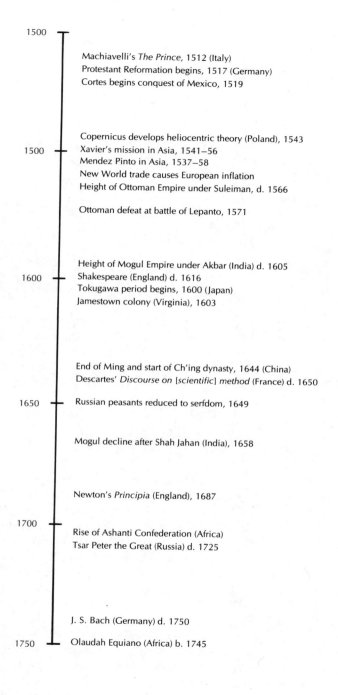

1500 —

Machiavelli's *The Prince*, 1512 (Italy)
Protestant Reformation begins, 1517 (Germany)
Cortes begins conquest of Mexico, 1519

1500 —

Copernicus develops heliocentric theory (Poland), 1543
Xavier's mission in Asia, 1541–56
Mendez Pinto in Asia, 1537–58
New World trade causes European inflation
Height of Ottoman Empire under Suleiman, d. 1566

Ottoman defeat at battle of Lepanto, 1571

1600 —

Height of Mogul Empire under Akbar (India) d. 1605
Shakespeare (England) d. 1616
Tokugawa period begins, 1600 (Japan)
Jamestown colony (Virginia), 1603

End of Ming and start of Ch'ing dynasty, 1644 (China)
Descartes' *Discourse on [scientific] method* (France) d. 1650

1650 —

Russian peasants reduced to serfdom, 1649

Mogul decline after Shah Jahan (India), 1658

Newton's *Principia* (England), 1687

1700 —

Rise of Ashanti Confederation (Africa)
Tsar Peter the Great (Russia) d. 1725

J. S. Bach (Germany) d. 1750

1750 —

Olaudah Equiano (Africa) b. 1745

CHAPTER ONE

European Renaissance and Reformation

1. *THE PRINCE*

Niccolò Machiavelli

Machiavelli's The Prince, *written in 1512 for Prince Lorenzo de Medici, who had just regained control over the city of Florence after a period of relative democracy, is a very modern book. Paying only lip service to traditional religious and ethical concerns, it advises rulers to ask only what works.*

This little book has been called the work of the devil, the first essay in political science, the burial of political morality, the beginning of the modern "religion" of the state, and the first breath of nationalism. Which, if any, of these characterizations seems most accurate? What is "modern" about the book? Do we, or do politicians, think this way today?

NICCOLÒ MACHIAVELLI TO LORENZO
THE MAGNIFICENT SON OF PIERO DI MEDICI

It is customary for those who wish to gain the favour of a prince to endeavour to do so by offering him gifts of those things which they hold most precious, or in which they know him to take especial delight. In this way princes are often presented with horses, arms, cloth of gold, gems, and suchlike ornaments worthy of their grandeur. In my desire, however, to offer to Your Highness some humble testimony of my devotion, I have been unable to find among my possessions anything which I hold so dear or esteem so highly as that knowledge of the deeds of great men which I acquired through a long experience of modern events and a constant study of the past.

With the utmost diligence I have long pondered and scrutinised the actions of the great, and now I offer the results to Your Highness within the compass of a small volume: and although I deem this work unworthy of Your Highness's acceptance, yet my confidence in your humanity assures me that you will receive it with favour, knowing that it is not in my power to offer you a greater gift than that of enabling you to understand in a very short time all those things which I have learnt at the cost of privation and danger in the course of many years. I have not sought to adorn my work with long phrases or high-sounding words or any of those superficial attractions and ornaments with which many writers seek to embellish their material, as I desire no honour for my work but such as the novelty and gravity of its subject may justly deserve. Nor will it, I trust, be deemed presumptuous on the part of a man of humble and obscure condition to attempt to discuss and direct the government of princes; for in the same way that landscape painters station themselves in the valleys in order to draw mountains or high ground, and ascend an eminence in order to get a good view of the plains, so it is necessary to be a prince to know thoroughly the nature of the people, and one of the populace to know the nature of princes.

May I trust, therefore, that Your Highness will accept this little gift in the spirit in which it is offered; and if Your Highness will deign to peruse it, you will recognize in it my ardent desire that you may attain to that grandeur which fortune and your own merits presage for you.

And should Your Highness gaze down from the summit of your lofty position towards this humble spot, you will recognize the great and unmerited sufferings inflicted on me by a cruel fate.

1: The Various Kinds of Government and the Ways by Which They Are Established

All states and dominions which hold or have held sway over mankind are either republics or monarchies. Monarchies are either hereditary in which the rulers have been for many years of the same family, or else they are of recent foundation. The newly founded ones are either entirely new, as was Milan to Francesco Sforza, or else they are, as it were, new members grafted on to the hereditary possessions of the prince that annexes them, as is the kingdom of Naples to the King of Spain. The dominions thus acquired have either been previously accustomed to the rule of another prince, or else have been free states, and they are annexed either by force of arms of the prince himself, or of others, or else fall to him by good fortune or special ability. . . .

5: The Way to Govern Cities or Dominions That, Previous to Being Occupied, Lived under Their Own Laws

When those states which have been acquired are accustomed to live at liberty under their own laws, there are three ways of holding them. The first is to despoil them; the second is to go and live there in person; the third is to allow them to live under their own laws, taking tribute of them, and creating within the country a government composed of a few who will keep it friendly to you. Because this government, being created by the prince, knows that it cannot exist without his friendship and protection, and will do all it can to keep them. What is more, a city used to liberty can be more easily held by means of its citizens than in any other way, if you wish to preserve it.

There is the example of the Spartans and the Romans. The Spartans held Athens and Thebes by creating within them a government of a few; nevertheless they lost them. The Romans, in order to hold Capua, Carthage, and Numantia, ravaged them, but did not lose them. They wanted to hold Greece in almost the same way as the Spartans held it, leaving it free and under its own laws, but they did not succeed; so that they were compelled to lay waste many cities in that province in order to keep it, because in truth there is no sure method of holding them except by despoiling them. And whoever becomes the ruler of a free city and does not destroy it, can expect to be destroyed by it, for it can always find a motive for rebellion in the name of liberty and of its ancient usages, which are forgotten neither by lapse of time nor by benefits received; and whatever one does or provides, so long as the inhabitants are not separated or dispersed, they do not forget that name and those usages, but appeal to them at once in every emergency, as did Pisa after so many years held in servitude by the Florentines. But when cities or provinces have been accustomed to live under a prince, and the family of that prince is extinguished, being on the one hand used to obey, and on the other not having their old prince, they cannot unite in choosing one from among themselves, and they do not know how to live in freedom, so that they are slower to take arms, and a prince can win them over with greater facility and establish himself securely. But in republics there is greater life, greater hatred, and more desire for vengeance; they do not and cannot cast aside the memory of their ancient liberty, so that the surest way is either to lay them waste or reside in them. . . .

8: Of Those Who Have Attained the Position of Prince by Villainy

But as there are still two ways of becoming prince which cannot be attributed entirely either to fortune or to ability, they must not be passed over, although one of them could be more fully discussed if we were treating of republics. These are when one becomes prince by some nefarious or villainous means, or when a private citizen becomes the prince of his country through the favour of his fellow-citizens. And in speaking of the former means, I will give two examples, one ancient, the other modern, without entering further into the merits of this method, and I judge them to be sufficient for any one obliged to imitate them.

Agathocles the Sicilian rose not only from private life but from the lowest and most abject position to be King of Syracuse. The son of a potter, he led a life of the utmost wickedness through all the stages of his fortune. Nevertheless, his wickedness was accompanied by such vigour of mind and body that, having joined the militia, he rose through its ranks to be praetor of Syracuse. Having been appointed to this position, and having decided to become prince, and to hold with violence and without the support of others that which had been constitutionally granted him; and having imparted his design to Hamilcar the Carthaginian, who was fighting with his armies in Sicily, he called together one morning the people and senate of Syracuse, as if he had to deliberate on matters of importance to the republic, and at a given signal had all the senators and the richest men of the people killed by his soldiers. After their death he occupied and held rule over the city without any civil strife. And although he was twice beaten by the Carthaginians and ultimately besieged, he was able not only to defend the city, but leaving a portion of his forces for its defence, with the remainder he invaded Africa, and in a short time liberated Syracuse from the siege and brought the Carthaginians to great extremities, so that they were obliged to come to terms with him, and remain contented with the possession of Africa, leaving Sicily to Agathocles. Whoever considers, therefore, the actions and qualities of this man, will see few if any things which can be attributed to fortune; for, as above stated, it was not by the favour of any person, but through the grades of the militia, in which he had advanced with a thousand hardships and perils, that he arrived at the position of prince, which he afterwards maintained by so many courageous and perilous expedients. It cannot be called virtue to kill one's fellow-citizens, betray one's friends, be without faith, without pity, and without religion; by these methods one may indeed gain power, but not glory. For if the virtues of Agathocles in braving and overcoming perils, and his greatness of soul in supporting and surmounting obstacles be considered, one sees no reason for holding him inferior to any of the most renowned captains. Nevertheless his barbarous cruelty and inhumanity, together with his countless atrocities, do not permit of his being named among the most famous men. We cannot attribute to fortune or virtue that which he achieved without either.

Some may wonder how it came about that Agathocles, and others like him, could, after infinite treachery and cruelty, live secure for many years in their country and defend themselves from external enemies without being conspired against by their subjects; although many others have, owing to their cruelty, been unable to maintain their position in times of peace, not to speak of the uncertain times of war. I believe this arises from the cruelties being exploited well or badly. Well committed may be called those (if it is permissible to use the word well of evil) which are perpetrated once for the need of securing one's self, and which afterwards are not persisted in, but are exchanged for measures as useful to the subjects as possible. Cruelties ill committed are those which, although at first few, increase rather than diminish with time. Those who follow the former method may remedy in some measure their condition, both with God and man; as did Agathocles. As to the others, it is impossible for them to maintain themselves.

Whence it is to be noted, that in taking a state the conqueror must arrange to commit all his cruelties at once, so as not to have to recur to them every day, and so as to be able, by not making fresh changes, to reassure people and win them over by benefiting them. Whoever acts otherwise, either through timidity or bad counsel, is always obliged to stand with knife in hand, and can never depend on his subjects, because they, owing to continually fresh injuries, are unable to depend upon him. For injuries should be done all together, so that being less tasted, they will give less offence. Benefits should be granted little by little, so that they may be better enjoyed. And above all, a prince must live with his subjects in such a way that no accident of good or evil fortune can deflect him from his course; for necessity arising in adverse times, you are not in time with severity, and the good that you do does not profit, as it is judged to be forced upon you, and you will derive no benefit whatever from it.

17: Of Cruelty and Clemency, and Whether It Is Better to Be Loved or Feared

Proceeding to the other qualities before named, I say that every prince must desire to be considered merciful and not cruel. He must, however, take care not to misuse this mercifulness. Cesare Borgia was considered cruel, but his cruelty had brought order to the Romagna, united it, and reduced it to peace and fealty. If this is considered well, it will be seen that he was really much more merciful than the Florentine people, who, to avoid the name of cruelty, allowed Pistoia to be destroyed. A prince, therefore, must not mind incurring the charge of cruelty for the purpose of keeping his subjects united and faithful; for, with a very few examples, he will be more merciful than those who, from excess of tenderness, allow disorders to arise, from whence spring bloodshed and rapine; for these as a rule injure the whole community, while the executions carried out by the prince injure only individuals. And of all princes, it is impossible for a new prince to escape the reputation of cruelty, new states being always full of dangers.

Nevertheless, he must be cautious in believing and acting, and must not be afraid of his own shadow, and must proceed in a temperate manner with prudence and humanity, so that too much confidence does not render him incautious, and too much diffidence does not render him intolerant.

From this arises the question whether it is better to be loved more than feared, or feared more than loved. The reply is, that one ought to be both feared and loved, but as it is difficult for the two to go together, it is much safer to be feared than loved, if one of the two has to be wanting. For it may be said of men in general that they are ungrateful, voluble, dissemblers, anxious to avoid danger, and covetous of gain; as long as you benefit them, they are entirely yours; they offer you their blood, their goods, their life, and their children, as I have before said, when the necessity is remote; but when it approaches, they revolt. And the prince who has relied solely on their words, without making other preparations, is ruined; for the friendship which is gained by purchase and not through grandeur and nobility of spirit is bought but not secured, and at a pinch is not to be expended in your service. And men have less scruple in offending one who makes himself loved than one who makes himself feared; for love is held by a chain of obligation which, men being selfish, is broken whenever it serves their purpose; but fear is maintained by a dread of punishment which never fails.

Still, a prince should make himself feared in such a way that if he does not gain love, he at any rate avoids hatred; for fear and the absence of hatred may well go together, and will be always attained by one who abstains from interfering with the property of his citizens and subjects or with their women. And when he is obliged to take the life of any one, let him do so when there is a proper justification and manifest reason for it; but above all he must abstain from taking the property of others, for men forget more easily the death of their father than the loss of their patrimony. Then also pretexts for seizing property are never wanting, and one who begins to live by rapine will always find some reason for taking the goods of others, whereas causes for taking life are rarer and more fleeting.

26: Exhortation to Liberate Italy from the Barbarians

Having now considered all the things we have spoken of, and thought within myself whether at present the time was not propitious in Italy for a new prince, and if there was not a state of things which offered an opportunity to a prudent and capable man to introduce a new system that would do honour to himself and good to the mass of the people, it seems to me that so many things concur to favour a new ruler that I do not know of any time more fitting for such an enterprise.

2.   APPEAL TO THE GERMAN NOBILITY

Martin Luther

In 1517 Martin Luther posted 95 theses on a church door at Wittenberg to challenge the sale of indulgences by representatives of the Pope. In this letter of 1520, Luther broadened his attack on the Roman papacy. The appeal was addressed to all the German nobility and especially their newly elected emperor, Charles V, who Luther hoped would be sympathetic. Where did Luther disagree with the papacy? What did he want the German nobility and the emperor to do? Were the goals expressed here more political or religious? Could Luther's goals have been accomplished without the Protestant Reformation?

Dr. Martin Luther, to his Most Serene and Mighty Imperial Majesty, and to the Christian Nobility of the German Nation:

The grace and strength of God be with you, Most Serene Majesty! And you, most gracious and well-beloved lords!

It is not out of mere arrogance and perversity that I, an individual, poor and insignificant, have taken it upon me to address your lordships. The distress and misery which oppress all ranks of Christendom, especially in Germany, have moved not me alone, but everybody, to cry aloud for help; this it is that now compels me to cry out and call upon God to send down his Spirit upon some one who shall reach out a hand to this wretched people. Councils have often put about some remedy, which has always been promptly frustrated by the cunning of certain men, so that the evils have only grown worse; which malice and wickedness I now intend, God helping me, to expose, so that, being known, they may cease to effect such scandal and injury. God has given us a young[1] and noble sovereign for our leader, thereby stirring up fresh hope in our hearts; our duty is to do our best to help him and to avail ourselves to the full of this opportunity and his gracious favour.

The Romanists have, with great adroitness, drawn three walls round themselves, with which they have hitherto protected themselves, so that no one could reform them, whereby all Christendom has suffered terribly.

First, if pressed by the temporal power, they have affirmed and maintained that the temporal power has no jurisdiction over them, but, on the contrary, that the spiritual power is above the temporal.

Secondly, if it were proposed to admonish them with the Scriptures, they objected that no one may interpret the Scriptures but the Pope.

---

1. Charles V was nineteen at this time.

Thirdly, if they are threatened with a council, they invented the notion that no one may call a council but the Pope.

Thus they have privily stolen from us our three sticks, so that they may not be beaten. And they have dug themselves in securely behind their three walls, so that they can carry on all the knavish tricks which we now observe. . . .

Now may God help us, and give us one of those trumpets that over-threw the walls of Jericho, so that we may blow down these walls of straw and paper, and that we may have a chance to use Christian rods for the chastisement of sin, and expose the craft and deceit of the devil; thus we may amend ourselves by punishment and again obtain God's favour.

Let us, in the first place, attack the first wall.

There has been a fiction by which the Pope, bishops, priests, and monks are called the 'spiritual estate'; princes, lords, artisans, and peas-ants are the 'temporal estate.' This is an artful lie and hypocritical inven-tion, but let no one be made afraid by it, and that for this reason: that all Christians are truly of the spiritual estate, and there is no difference among them, save of office. As St Paul says (1 Cor. xii), we are all one body, though each member does its own work so as to serve the others. This is because we have one baptism, one Gospel, one faith, and are all Christians alike; for baptism, Gospel, and faith, these alone make spiri-tual and Christian people.

As for the unction by a pope or a bishop, tonsure, ordination, consecra-tion, and clothes differing from those of laymen—all this may make a hypocrite or an anointed puppet, but never a Christian or a spiritual man. Thus we are all consecrated as priests by baptism, as St Peter says: 'Ye are a royal priesthood, a holy nation' (1 Pet. ii. 9); and in the Book of Revelation: 'and hast made us unto our God (by Thy blood) kings and priests' (Rev. v. 10). For, if we had not a higher consecration in us than pope or bishop can give, no priest could ever be made by the consecra-tion of pope or bishop, nor could he say the mass or preach or absolve. Therefore the bishop's consecration is just as if in the name of the whole congregation he took one person out of the community, each member of which has equal power, and commanded him to exercise this power for the rest; just as if ten brothers, co-heirs as king's sons, were to choose one from among them to rule over their inheritance, they would all of them still remain kings and have equal power, although one is appointed to govern.

And to put the matter more plainly, if a little company of pious Chris-tian laymen were taken prisoners and carried away to a desert, and had not among them a priest consecrated by a bishop, and were there to agree to elect one of them . . . and were to order him to baptize, to celebrate the mass, to absolve and to preach, this man would as truly be a priest, as if all the bishops and all the popes had consecrated him. That is why, in cases of necessity, every man can baptize and absolve, which would not be possible if we were not all priests. This great grace and virtue of baptism and of the Christian estate they have annulled and made us forget by their ecclesiastical law. . . .

Since then the 'temporal power' is as much baptized as we, and has the same faith and Gospel, we must allow it to be a priest and bishop, and account its office an office that is proper and useful to the Christian community. For whatever has undergone baptism may boast that it has been consecrated priest, bishop, and pope, although it does not beseem every one to exercise these offices. For, since we are all priests alike, no man may put himself forward, or take upon himself without our consent and election, to do that which we have all alike power to do. For if a thing is common to all, no man may take it to himself without the wish and command of the community. And if it should happen that a man were appointed to one of these offices and deposed for abuses, he would be just what he was before. Therefore a priest should be nothing in Christendom but a functionary; as long as he holds his office, he has precedence; if he is deprived of it, he is a peasant or a citizen like the rest. Therefore a priest is verily no longer a priest after deposition. But now they have invented *characteres indelibiles,* and pretend that a priest after deprivation still differs from a mere layman. They even imagine that a priest can never be anything but a priest—that is, he can never become a layman. All this is nothing but mere talk and a figment of human invention.

It follows, then, that between laymen and priests, princes and bishops, or, as they call it, between 'spiritual' and 'temporal' persons, the only real difference is one of office and function, and not of estate. . . .

But what kind of Christian doctrine is this, that the 'temporal power' is not above the 'spiritual,' and therfore cannot punish it! As if the hand should not help the eye, however much the eye be suffering. . . . Nay, the nobler the member the more bound the others are to help it. . . .

Therefore I say, Forasmuch as the temporal power has been ordained by God for the punishment of the bad and the protection of the good, we must let it do its duty throughout the whole Christian body, without respect of persons, whether it strike popes, bishops, priests, monks, nuns, or whoever it may be. . . .

Whatever the ecclesiastical law has said in opposition to this is merely the invention of Romanist arrogance. . . .

Now, I imagine the first paper wall is overthrown, inasmuch as the 'temporal' power has become a member of the Christian body; although its work relates to the body, yet does it belong to the 'spiritual estate.'. . .

It must indeed have been the archfiend himself who said, as we read in the canon law, 'Were the pope so perniciously wicked as to be dragging hosts of souls to the devil, yet he could not be deposed.'[2] This is the

---

2. If the pope be found to neglect his own salvation and that of his brethren; . . . and if, as hell's chief slave, he should drag with him innumerable multitudes to suffer manifold

accursed, devilish foundation on which they build at Rome, and think the whole world may go to the devil rather than that they should be opposed in their knavery. If a man were to escape punishment simply because he was above his fellows, then no Christian might punish another, since Christ has commanded that each of us esteem himself the lowest and humblest of all (Matt. xviii. 4; Luke ix. 48).

The second wall is even more tottering and weak: namely their claim to be considered masters of the Scriptures. . . . If the article of our faith is right, 'I believe in the holy Christian Church,' the Pope cannot alone be right; else we must say, 'I believe in the Pope of Rome,' and reduce the Christian Church to one man, which is a devilish and damnable heresy. Besides that, we are all priests, as I have said, and have all one faith, one Gospel, one Sacrament; how then should we not have the power of discerning and judging what is right or wrong in matters of faith? . . .

The third wall falls of itself, as soon as the first two have fallen; for if the Pope acts contrary to the Scriptures, we are bound to stand by the Scriptures to punish and to constrain him, according to Christ's commandment . . . 'tell it unto the Church' (Matt. xviii, 15–17). . . . If then I am to accuse him before the Church, I must collect the Church together. . . . Therefore when need requires, and the Pope is a cause of offence to Christendom, in these cases whoever can best do so, as a faithful member of the whole body, must do what he can to procure a true free council. This no one can do so well as the temporal authorities, especially since they are fellow-Christians, fellow-priests. . . .

[Luther proceeds to treat of matters to be discussed at the Council.]

What is the use in Christendom of those who are called 'cardinals'? I will tell you. In Italy and Germany there are many rich convents, endowments, holdings, and benefices; and as the best way of getting these into the hands of Rome they created cardinals, and gave to them the bishoprics, convents, and prelacies, and thus destroyed the service of God. That is why Italy is almost a desert now: the convents are destroyed, the sees consumed, the revenues of the prelacies and of all the churches drawn to Rome; towns are decayed, and the country and the people ruined because there is no more any worship of God or preaching. Why? Because the cardinals must have all the wealth. The Turk himself could not have so desolated Italy and so overthrown the worship of God.

Now that Italy is sucked dry, they come to Germany. They begin in a quiet way, but we shall soon see Germany brought into the same state as Italy. We have a few cardinals already. What the Romanists really mean to do, the 'drunken' Germans are not to see until they have lost everything. . . .

and everlasting torment; still no man may presume to reprove him, for he is appointed judge over all and is judged by none—unless perchance he is found to err from the way of faith (Gratian, *Decretum*, I. xl. 6; *Si papa*, quoted by Robinson). This passage was ascribed to S. Boniface.

Now this devilish state of things is not only open robbery and deceit and the prevailing of the gates of hell, but it is destroying the very life and soul of Christianity; therefore we are bound to use all our diligence to ward off this misery and destruction. If we want to fight Turks, let us begin here—we cannot find worse ones. If we rightly hang thieves and behead robbers, why do we leave the greed of Rome unpunished? for Rome is the greatest thief and robber that has ever appeared on earth, or ever will; and all in the holy names of Church and St Peter. . . .

[Luther proceeds to outline '57 Articles for the Reformation of Christendom,' including restrictions on the sending of contributions to Rome, reduction of the number of monks and mendicants, and the reformation of schools and universities.]

. . . Poor Germans that we are—we have been deceived! We were born to be masters, and we have been compelled to bow the head beneath the yoke of our tyrants, and to become slaves. Name, title, outward signs of royalty, we possess all these; force, power, right, liberty, all these have gone over to the popes, who have robbed us of them. They get the kernel, we get the husk. . . . It is time the glorious Teutonic people should cease to be the puppet of the Roman pontiff. Because the pope crowns the emperor, it does not follow that the pope is superior to the emperor. Samuel, who crowned Saul and David, was not above these kings, nor Nathan above Solomon, whom he consecrated. . . . Let the emperor then be a veritable emperor, and no longer allow himself to be stripped of his sword or of his sceptre! . . .

3.   CITY WOMEN AND RELIGIOUS CHANGE

Natalie Zemon Davis

In this essay a modern historian examines the role of women in the cities of sixteenth-century France because it was in the cities that the appeal of the Protestant Reformation was strongest. Did Protestantism improve the lives of women? In what ways did the Huguenot movement, Calvinism, or the Reformed Church (all expressions of the Protestant Reformation in France) appeal to women or change their lives?

Looking back on the birth and progress of the Calvinist heresy in the course of his own lifetime, the Bordeaux jurist Florimond de Raemond remarked on how much easier it was to entrap women into heresies than men. The Church Fathers had warned us of this long before. Women were weak and imbecile. They could be as precious as pearls or as dangerous as venomous asps. Very often in our religious quarrels, de Raemond went on, their distaffs spun more evils than could ever be wrought by the partisan slash of seditious swords. He knew this from his own experience, for during a few misguided years in the 1560's he had been part of the Huguenot movement himself.

De Raemond was not the only Catholic male to try to discredit the Protestant cause by associating it with the weak will and feeble intellect of the female. Protestant polemicists returned the compliment by characterizing Catholic women as at best ignorant and superstitious and at worst whorish and frenzied. Most modern historians of the Reformation go them one better: they scarcely mention women at all.

Oh yes, there have been and are exceptions. In a tradition of women's history that goes back to Plutarch and Boccaccio, portraits of individual women have been collected—of the wives of Luther and Calvin, for instance, and of Protestant duchesses and queens—which show that, after all, women had something to do with the Reformation. More than a century ago the Scottish pastor James Anderson published his *Ladies of the Reformation, Memoirs of the Distinguished Female Characters Belonging to the Sixteenth Century;* and even today are appearing the charming and useful vignettes by Roland Bainton called *Women of the Reformation.* Furthermore, the great political and literary leaders have been given their due: Marguerite de Navarre, sister of King Francois I of France, whose poetry and patronage were so important in the early days of the French Reformation, and her militant daughter, the Huguenot Jeanne d'Albret, queen of Navarre.

Few social studies exist, however, that try to look systematically at the role of women in religious change in the sixteenth century. Did the Reformation have a distinctive appeal to women? If so, what was it and to what kinds of women? What did Protestant women do to bring about religious change? And what innovations did the Reformation effect in the lives of women of different social classes?

Some hypotheses have been offered. First, there are those that pick out features of a religious movement most likely to attract women. Max Weber has suggested in his *Sociology of Religion* that women are always especially receptive to nonmilitary and nonpolitical prophecy and to religious movements with orgiastic, emotional, or hysterical aspects to them. Weber's assumptions remind us uncomfortably of the Church Fathers and Florimond de Raemond, but in any case we will want to ask whether such criteria could apply to a religion as disciplined as Calvinism. A broader approach is found in Keith Thomas' study of women in the civil war sects of seventeenth-century England. He suggests that the spiritual status and scope of activity—emotional or nonemotional activity—offered to women are what drew them to new religions. The more spiritual equality of the sexes, the more women in the movement.

A second set of hypotheses concerns the state of life of women before religious conversion. Some historians stress a prior sense of uselessness, of imprisonment, from which fresh religious commitment served as an escape. Speaking of the attraction of Protestantism for the women of the English aristocracy, Lawrence Stone comments, "Given the idle and frustrated lives these women lived in the man's world of a great country house, it is hardly surprising that they should have turned in desperation to the comforts of religion." Robert Mandrou attributes the same kind of motivation to the wives of traders, artisans, and unskilled workers in sixteenth-century France: "Stuck in their houses, wholly occupied by their little courtyards and inner world of family and children, these women no doubt found in religious movements a kind of liberation." Other historians, however, talk about this liberation as if it had begun to occur even before women were caught up in religious reform. Nancy Roelker sees the Huguenot noblewomen as strong-minded and already quite independent wives and widows who found in the Reformed cause a way to enhance their activities (by converting their relatives, protecting pastors, giving money and strategic advice to male leaders, and so on) while at the same time preserving their feminine identities. Similarly, Patrick Collinson thinks that it was the education and relative freedom of social life that prepared English gentlewomen and merchants' wives to respond positively to Puritanism in the sixteenth century. "The example of modern Islamic societies," Collinson writes, "leads one to expect the enthusiastic, even violent adoption of political causes by a partially emancipated womanhood. Translated into sixteenth-century categories, we are perhaps witnessing something of the same sort in the vigorous religious partisanship of the women of that time."

Which of these hypotheses best fits the case of the Protestant women in French cities? We will answer this question in the course of this essay. We may note in passing, however, that both of them invoke psychological solutions but do not address themselves to the actual content and organization of the new religious movements. Indeed, Robert Mandrou says that his little housewives might be liberated either by Protestantism or by the transformed Catholicism of the Counter-Reformation; it did not matter which.

A third group of hypotheses has to do with the consequences of the Reformation for women. It is usually argued that it was life within the family that changed most for Protestant women, and for the better. Not only the elimination of clerical celibacy but also the definition of marriage as the school of character is supposed to have led to greater friendship and more equal partnership between Protestant spouses than was possible between Catholic spouses of the same period. Less attention has been paid, however, to the changed roles of women within the life, liturgy, symbolism, and organization of the Reformed Church. Some speculation has been made about the social and psychological origins of Protestant opposition to Mariolatry, but how did banning the cult of Mary affect attitudes toward women and sexual identity?

Let us ask some of these large questions about an important category of women in France—not the great noblewomen already examined by Nancy Roelker, but the women of the cities. Hopefully, some of the conclusions drawn about France may, with appropriate adjustments, be relevant to other parts of Europe.

The growing cities of sixteenth-century France, ranging from ten thousand inhabitants in smaller places to sixty thousand in Lyon and a hundred thousand in Paris, were the centers of organization and dissemination of Protestantism. The decades in question here are especially those up to the Saint Bartholomew's Day Massacre of 1572—the years when it still seemed hopeful, in the words of a female refugee in Geneva, that the new Christians might deliver their cities from the tyranny and cruelty of the papist Pharaohs. For a while they were successful, with the growth of a large Protestant movement and the establishment in 1559 of an official Reformed Church in France. After 1572, the Huguenot party continued to battle for survival, but it was now doomed to remain a zealous but small minority.

Apart from the religious (nuns), almost all adult urban women in the first half of the sixteenth century were married or had once been so. The daughter of a rich merchant, lawyer, or financial officer might find herself betrothed in her late teens. Most women waited until their early twenties, when a dowry could be pieced together from the family or one's wages or extracted from a generous master or mistress.

And then the babies began and kept appearing every two or three years. The wealthy woman, with her full pantry and her country refuge in times of plague, might well raise six or seven children to adulthood. The artisan's wife might bury nearly as many as she bore, while the poor woman was lucky to have even one live through the perils of a sixteenth-century childhood. Then, if she herself had managed to survive the first rounds of childbearing and live into her thirties, she might well find that her husband had not. Remarriage was common, of course, and until certain restrictive edicts of the French king in the 1560's a widow could contract it quite freely. If she then survived her husband into her forties, chances are she would remain a widow. At this stage of life, women outnumbered and outlived men, and even the widow sought after for her wealth might prefer independence to the relative tutelage of marriage.

With the death rate so high, the cities of sixteenth-century France depended heavily on immigration for their increasing populations. Here, however, we find an interesting difference between the sexes: men made up a much larger percentage of the young immigrants to the cities. The male immigrants contributed to every level of the vocational hierarchy—from notaries, judges, and merchants to craftsmen and unskilled day laborers. And although most of the men came from nearby provinces, some were also drawn from faraway cities and from regions outside the kingdom of France. The female immigrants, on the other hand, clustered near the bottom of the social ladder and came mostly from villages and hamlets in surrounding provinces to seek domestic service in the city.

Almost all the women took part in one way or another in the economic life of the city. The picture drawn in Renaissance courtesy books and suggested by the quotation from Robert Mandrou—that of women remaining privily in their homes—is rather far from the facts revealed by judicial records and private contracts. The wife of the wealthy lawyer, royal officer, or prosperous merchant supervised the productive activities of a large household but might also rent out and sell rural and urban properties in her own name, in her husband's name, or as a widow. The wives of tradesmen and master craftsmen had some part in running the shops, not just when they were widowed but also while their husbands were alive: a wife might discipline apprentices (who sometimes resented being beaten by a woman's hand), might help the journeymen at the large looms, might retail meats while her husband and his workers slaughtered cattle, might borrow money with her husband for printing ventures, and so on.

In addition, a significant proportion of women in artisanal families had employ on their own. They worked especially in the textile, clothing, leather, and provisioning trades, although we can also find girls apprenticed to pinmakers and gilders. They sold fish and tripe; they ran inns and taverns. They were painters and, of course, midwives. In Paris they made linen; in Lyon they prepared silk. They made shoes and gloves, belts and collars. In Paris, one Perette Aubertin sold fruit at a stall near the Eglise des Mathurins while her husband worked as a printer. In Lyon, one Pernette Morilier made and sold wimples while her husband worked as a goldsmith. And in an extraordinary document from Lyon, a successful merchant-shoemaker confesses that his prosperity was due not so much to his own profits as to those made by his wife over the preceding 25 years in her separate trade as a linen merchant.

Finally, there were the various semiskilled or unskilled jobs done by women. Domestic service involved a surprisingly high number of girls and women. Even a modest artisanal family was likely to have a wretchedly paid serving girl, perhaps acquired from within the walls of one of the orphan-hospitals recently set up in many urban centers. There was service in the bath-houses, which sometimes slid into prostitution. Every city had its *filles de joie*, whom the town council tried to restrict to certain streets and to stop from brazenly soliciting clients right in front of the parish church. And there was heavy work, such as ferrying people across the Saône and other rivers, the boatwomen trying to argue up their fares as they rowed. If all else failed, a woman could dig ditches and carry things at the municipal construction sites. For this last, she worked shoulder to shoulder with unskilled male day workers, being paid about one-half or two-thirds as much as they for her pains.

The public life of urban women did not, however, extend to the civic assembly or council chamber. Women who were heads of households do appear on tax lists and even on militia rolls and were expected to supply money or men as the city government required. But that was the extent of political participation for them. Male artisans and traders also had little say in these oligarchical city governments, but at least the more prosperous among them might have hoped to influence town councillors through their positions as guild representatives. The guild life of women, however, was limited and already weaker than it had been in the later Middle Ages. In short, the political activity of women on all levels of urban society was indirect or informal only. The wives of royal officers or town councillors might have hoped to influence powerful men at their dining tables. The wives of poor and powerless journeymen and day laborers, when their tables were bare because the city fathers had failed to provide the town with grain, might have tried to change things by joining with their husbands and children in a well-timed grain riot.

What of the literacy of urban women in the century after the introduction of printing to Europe? In the families of the urban elite the women had at least a vernacular education—usually at the hands of private tutors—in French, perhaps in Italian, in music, and in arithmetic. A Latin education among nonnoble city women was rare enough that it was remarked—"learned beyond her sex," the saying went—and a girl like Louise Sarrasin of Lyon, whose physician-father had started her in Hebrew, Greek, and Latin by the time she was eight, was considered a wondrous prodigy. It was women from these wealthy families of bankers and jurists who organized the important literary salons in Paris, Lyon, Poitiers, and elsewhere.

Once outside these restricted social circles, however, there was a dramatic drop in the level of education and of mere literacy among city women. An examination of contracts involving some 1,200 people in Lyon in the 1560's and 1570's to see whether those people could simply sign their names reveals that, of the women, only 28 percent could sign their names. These were almost all from the elite families of well-off merchants and publishers, plus a few wives of surgeons and goldsmiths. All the other women in the group—the wives of mercers, or artisans in skilled trades, and even of a few notaries—could not sign. This is in contrast to their husbands and to male artisans generally, whose ability to sign ranged from high among groups like printers, surgeons, and goldsmiths, to moderate among men in the leather and textile trades, to low—although still well above zero—among men in the food and construction trades. Thus, in the populous middle rank of urban society, although both male and female literacy may have risen from the mid-fifteenth century under the impact of economic growth and the invention of printing, the literacy of the men increased much more than that of the women. Tradesmen might have done business with written accounts; tradeswomen more often had to use finger reckoning, the abacus, or counting stones. Only at the bottom of the social hierarchy, among the unskilled workers and urban gardeners, were men and women alike. As with peasants, there were few of either sex who were literate.

And where would women of artisanal families learn to read and write if their fathers and husbands did not teach them? Nunnery schools received only a small number of lay girls, and these only from fine families. The municipal colleges set up in the first half of the sixteenth century in Toulouse, Nîmes, and Lyon were for boys only; so were most of the little vernacular schools that mushroomed in even quite modest city neighborhoods during these years. To be sure, a few schoolmistresses were licensed in Paris, and there were always some Parisian schoolmasters being chided for illegally receiving girls along with their boy pupils. But in Lyon, where I have found only five female teachers from the 1490's to the 1560's, I have come upon 87 schoolmasters for the same decades.

Thus, in the first half of the sixteenth century, the wealthy and well-born woman was being encouraged to read and study by the availability to her of printed books; by the strengthening of the image of the learned lady, as the writings of Christine de Pisan and Marguerite de Navarre appeared in print; and by the attitude of some fathers, who took seriously the modest educational programs for women being urged by Christian humanists like Erasmus and Juan Luis Vives. Reading and writing for women of the common people was more likely to be ridiculous, a subject for farce.

Into this picture of city women separated from their parish clergy and from male religious organizations, one new element was to enter, even before the Reformation. Women who could read or who were part of circles where reading was done aloud were being prompted by vernacular devotional literature and the Bible to speculate on theology. "Why, they're half theologians," said the Franciscan preachers contemptuously. They own Bibles the way they own love stories and romances. They get carried away by questions on transubstantiation, and they go "running around from . . . one (female) religious house to another, seeking advice and making much ado about nothing." What the good brothers expected from city women was not silly reasoning but the tears and repentance that would properly follow a Lenten sermon replete with all the rhetorical devices and dramatic gestures of which the Franciscans were masters.

Even a man who was more sympathetic than the Franciscans to

lettered females had his reservations about how far their learning should take them. A male poet praised the noble dame Gabrielle de Bourbon in the 1520's for reading vernacular books on moral and doctrinal questions and for composing little treatises to the honor of God and the Virgin Mary. But she knew her limits, for "women must not apply their minds to curious questions of theology and the secret matters of divinity, the knowledge of which belongs to prelates, rectors and doctors."

The Christian humanist Erasmus was one of the few men of his time who sensed the depths of resentment accumulating in women whose efforts to think about doctrine were not taken seriously by the clergy. In one of his *Colloquies,* a lady learned in Latin and Greek is being twitted by an asinine abbot (the phrase is Erasmus'). She finally bursts out, "If you keep on as you've begun, geese may do the preaching sooner than put up with you tongue-tied pastors. The world's a stage that's topsy-turvy now, as you see. Every man must play his part—or exit."

The world was indeed topsy-turvy. The Catholic Church, which Erasmus had tried to reform from within, was being split by Protestants who believed that man was saved by faith in Christ alone and that human work had nothing to do with it, who were changing the sacramental system all around and overthrowing the order of the priesthood.

After 1562 the Reformed Church of France started to settle into its new institutional structures and the promise of Protestantism began to be realized for city women. Special catechism classes in French were set up for women, and in towns under Huguenot control efforts were made to encourage literacy, even among all the poor girls in the orphanages, not just the gifted few. In certain Reformed families the literate husbands finally began teaching their wives to read.

Some Protestant females, however, had more ambitious goals. The image of the new Christian woman with her Bible had beckoned them to more than catechism classes or reading the Scriptures with their husbands. Consider Marie Dentière. One-time abbess in Tournai, but expelled from her convent in the 1520's because of heresy, Dentière married a pastor and found her way to Geneva during its years of religious revolution. There, according to the report of a nun of the Poor Clare order, Marie got "mixed up with preaching," coming, for instance, to the convent to persuade the poor creatures to leave their miserable life. She also published two religious works, one of them an epistle on religious matters addressed to Queen Marguerite de Navarre. Here Dentière inserted a "Defense for Women" against calumnies, not only by Catholic adversaries but also by some of the Protestant faithful. The latter were saying that it was rash for women to publish works to each other on Scriptural matters. Dentière disagreed: "If God has done the grace to some poor women to reveal to them by His Holy Scriptures some good and holy thing, dare they not write about it, speak about it, and declare it, one to the other? . . . Is it not foolishly done to hide the talent that God has given us?"

Dentière maintained the modest fiction that she was addressing herself only to other females. Later women did not. Some of the women prisoners in the French jails preached to "the great consolation" of both male and female listeners. Our ex-Calvinist jurist Florimond de Raemond gave several examples, both from the Protestant conventicles and from the regular Reformed services as late as 1572, of women who while waiting for a preacher to arrive had gone up to pulpits and read from the Bible. One *théologienne* even took public issue with her pastor. Finally, in some of the Reformed churches southwest of Paris—in areas where weavers and women had been early converts—a movement started to permit lay persons to prophesy. This would have allowed both women and unlearned men to get up in church and speak on holy things.

An examination of a few other areas of Protestant reform reveals the same pattern as in reading Scripture and preaching: city women revolted against priests and entered new religious relations that brought them together with men or likened them to men but left them unequal.

The new Calvinist liturgy, with its stress on the concerted fellowship of the congregation, used the vernacular—the language of women and the unlearned—and included Psalms sung jointly by men and women. Nothing shocked Catholic observers more than this. When they heard the music of male and female voices filtering from a house where a conventicle was assembled, all they could imagine were lewd activities with the candles extinguished. It was no better when the Protestant movement came into the open. After the rich ceremony of the mass, performed by the clergy with due sanctity and grandeur, the Reformed service seemed, in the words of a Catholic in Paris in the 1560's, "without law, without order, without harmony." "The minister begins. Everybody follows—men, women, children, servants, chambermaids. . . . No one is on the same verse. . . . The fine-voiced maidens let loose their hums and trills . . . so the young men will be sure to listen. How wrong of Calvin to let women sing in Church."

To Protestant ears, it was very different. For laymen and laywomen in the service the common voice in praise of the Lord expressed the lack of distance between pastor and congregation. The Catholic priests had stolen the Psalms; now they had been returned. As for the participants in the conventicles, the songs gave them courage and affirmed their sense of purity over the hypocritical papists, who no sooner left the mass than they were singing love songs. The Protestant faithful were firmly in control of their sexual impulses, they believed, their dark and sober clothes a testimonial to their sincerity. And when the women and men sang together in the great armed street marches of the 1560's, the songs were a militant challenge to the hardened Catholics and an invitation to the wavering listeners to join the elect.

CHAPTER TWO

American Civilizations and the Columbian Exchange

4. THE COLUMBIAN EXCHANGE

Alfred W. Crosby

In this essay, a modern historian discusses the many ways in which Mexico was transformed by the Spanish conquest. Notice the variety of changes—ecological, biological, and cultural. How was Mexico different a hundred years after the conquest? Which of these changes was the most important? On balance, was the Spanish conquest a benefit or a disaster?

Chimalpahin Cuauhlehuanitzin, one of our best sources of information on Mexico in the years immediately before and after the Spanish conquest, was an Indian historian whom the invaders trained in the reading and writing of the Roman alphabet in the sixteenth century. His writings (in Nahuatl) inform us that the year 13-Flint before the invasion was a grim one in the Valley of Mexico. There was sickness, hunger, and an eclipse of the sun; an eruption of some sort between the volcanoes Iztaccíhuatl and Popocatépetl; "and many ferocious beasts devoured the children." But 13-Flint, Chimalpahin makes clear, was an exception in what was an era of triumph for the Aztecs. They, who within recorded memory had been wanderers from the savage north, now exacted tributes of food, gold, quetzal feathers, and human hearts from vassal states all the way from the remote dry lands from which they had emerged to the rain forests of the south and east. The stiff-necked Tarascos, at the cost of perennial war, retained their independence, as did—precariously—the anciently civilized Mayas, and there were a few others who survived in the chinks of the Aztec Empire. Otherwise, central Mexico lay under the hegemony of the Aztecs.

Lord Ahuitzotl, who was ruler of the Aztecs in 13-Flint, used the legions and wealth under his command to improve and adorn his capital, the incomparable Tenochtitlán. He built a new aqueduct to bring fresh water to its scores of thousands of inhabitants. He rebuilt and reconsecrated the gigantic temple to the Aztec tribal deities, Huitzilopochtli and Tezcatlipoca. He did not—how could he have?—see in the strange events of 13-Flint portents of the end of his empire and of his world.

A decade later, in 10-Rabbit, his nephew Motecuhzoma Xocoyotzin, known to us as Montezuma, succeeded him as leader of the Aztecs. Montezuma's subjects numbered in the millions, and, so far as he or they knew, the empire had no equal in power and riches under the sky. Montezuma made plans to rebuild the great temple once more, higher and more extravagantly than any of his predecessors.

Reports drifted in from the eastern coast of pale, hairy visitors in boats "like towers or small mountains." There were only a few of them, and invaders traditionally came from the north, as had the Aztecs themselves, not from the east and never from the sea. Gods, however, might come from the sea.

THE ONSLAUGHT

In the year 1-Reed the visitors came to invade and to stay forever. The invaders proved to be humans, not gods, but they were incomprehensibly alien and powerful. They had light skin and much hair on their lips and chins; some of them had yellow hair. They dressed in metal and brought weapons of metal. They had huge animals allied with them. The invaders had at their sides dogs bigger and fiercer than any seen before: "The color of their eyes is a burning yellow; their eyes flash fire and shoot off sparks." They had, also, man-animals that ran faster than any man and were more powerful than any creature the Aztecs had ever known. Then these creatures split, and the Aztecs saw that the invaders had "deer to carry them on their backs wherever they wish to go. These deer, our lord, are as tall as the roof of a house."

Most hideous of all the invaders' allies was a pestilence, a *hueyzahuatl*, that swept all the land immediately after the Aztecs, quickened by atrocities, turned on the invaders, killing half of them as they fought their way out of Tenochtitlán. The pestilence spared the invaders but was a thing of agony, disfigurement, and death for the peoples of Mexico. There was no defense against it nor cure for it. Bernardino de Sahagún learned how it struck in the month of Tepeilhuitl and

> spread over the people as great destruction. Some it quite covered on all parts—their faces, their heads, their breasts, and so on. There was a great havoc. Very many died of it. They could not walk; they only lay in their resting places and beds. They could not move; they could not stir; they could not change position, nor lie on one side; nor face down, nor on their backs. And if they stirred, much did they cry out. Great was its destruction. Covered, mantled with pustules, very many people died of them.

One-third, one half—no one knows how many—of the Aztecs and the other peoples of Mexico died.

Then the invaders and their human allies, the Aztecs' former vassals and enemies, diminished by the epidemic but emboldened by the presence of the invaders, fought their way down the causeways and across Lake Texcoco into Tenochtitlán. Seventy-five days later, on the day 1-Serpent of the year 3-House, the siege of Tenochtitlán ended. Aztec poets expressed the grief of those who, somehow, had survived:

> Weep my people:
> know that with these disasters
> we have lost the Mexica nation.
> The water has turned bitter,
> our food is bitter.

The invaders' chief, Hernán Cortés, ordered that stones from the temple of which Lord Ahuitzotl had been so proud should be gathered up, and that a Christian cathedral should be made of them in the center of what had become, by his victory, Mexico City. The vanquished learned that the ominous year 13-Flint was more properly designated as the year 1492 of a deity both more imperialistic and more merciful than Huitzilopochtli or Tezcatlipoca, and that Tenochtitlán had fallen in the year 1521, not 3-House.

The fall of Tenochtitlán in the year 3-House was the worst discrete event in the Aztecs' history. Worse, however, was this: 3-House was the beginning of the most tragic century of their history. Their civilization suffered massive amputations and survived at the root only by accepting alien graftings in the branch, as the conquistadores and the friars replaced their ancient noble and priestly classes. There were advantages that came with the defeat: an alphabet, a more supple instrument for expression than their own logo-syllabic system of writing; the true arch to replace the corbel; tools with an iron edge that did not shatter like an obsidian edge when it struck the rock hidden in the leaves. But the magnitude of the change, good and bad, was almost greater than the mind could encompass or the heart endure. The metamorphosis was more than political or religious or intellectual or technological; it was biological. The biota of Mexico—its *life*—and, in time, that of the entire Western Hemisphere changed.

THE CHANGE

If Lord Ahuitzotl had returned to Mexico (now New Spain) a hundred years after 13-Flint he would have found much the same as in his lifetime. He would have recognized the profiles of the mountains, all the wild birds, and most of the plants. The basic and holy food of his people was still maize. But he would have been stunned by the sight of plants and creatures he had never seen or dreamed of during his days on earth. Alien plants grew alongside the old plants in Mexico, and its 1592 fauna, in its large animals, as as different from that of 1492 as the native fauna of Zimbabwe is from that of Spain.

The invaders had brought in wheat and other Eurasian and African grains; peach, pear, orange, and lemon trees; chick-peas, grape vines, melons, onions, radishes, and much more. A Spanish nobleman come to America could require his *indios* to furnish his table with the foods of his ancestors. Along with the Old World crops had come Old World weeds. European clover was by now so common that the Aztecs had a word of their own for it. They called it Castilian *ocoxochitl*, naming it after a low native plant that also prefers shade and moisture.

Of all the new sights of 1592—the cathedrals, the fields of wheat, wheeled vehicles, brigantines with sails and lounging sailors on Lake Texcoco where there had once been only canoes and sweating paddlers— nothing could have amazed Ahuitzotl more than the new animals: pigs, sheep, goats, burros, and others. Now there were cattle everywhere, and ranches with more than a hundred thousand each in the north. Now there were thousands upon thousands of horses, and they were available to any European (and, despite the law, the Indian, too) with a few coins or the skill to rope them. The horsemanship of the Mexican *vaquero* was already legendary on both sides of the Atlantic.

During Lord Ahuitzotl's lifetime the best way to move four hundred ears of maize in Mexico was on the bent back of a man, and the fastest means to deliver a message was by a runner. Now the bent man loaded four thousand ears onto a wheeled wagon pulled by a burro, and the messenger vaulted onto a horse and set off at several times the fastest pace of the fastest sprinter.

But Lord Ahuitzotl was an Aztec, an *indio*, and what would have put a catch in his breath a century after 13-Flint was not so much the new animals, for all their number, but his own kind of people, in their meager number. War, brutality, hunger, social and family disarray, loss of farm- land to the invading humans and their flocks, and exploitation in general had taken their toll, but disease was the worst enemy. The *hueyzahuatl* of 1520–21, like the fall of Tenochtitlán, may have been the worst of its kind, but, more important, it was the beginning of a series of pestilential onslaughts. The worst of the worst of the times of *cocoliztli* were 1545– 48, a time of bleeding from the nose and eyes, and 1576–81, when, again, many bled from the nose and windrows of Indians fell, but few Spaniards. If Lord Ahuitzotl had returned a century after his death, he would have found one for every ten or even twenty *indios* who had lived in his time.

Some of the survivors were *mestizos*, children of European men and Indian women. The mestizo, with his Indian skin and Visigothic eyes, proffering a cup of cocoa, a mixture of *chocolatl* and Old World sugar;

the wild Chichimec on his Berber mare; the Zapotec herder with his sheep; the Aztec, perhaps the last of the line of Ahuitzotl, receiving the final rites of the Christian faith as he slipped into the terminal coma of an infection newly arrived from Seville—in so many ways New Spain was *new,* a combination, crossing, and concoction of entities that had never before existed on the same continent.

And on and on to the present day. Alaska's and Canada's most remote Eskimos and Indians and South America's last tribes of hunter-gatherers and horticulturists have been decimated by tuberculosis, measles, and influenza within living memory. In 1990 the Yanomamö of the borderland of Brazil and Venezuela were decreasing rapidly under the attack not only or even primarily of the encroaching gold miners, but of malaria, influenza, measles, and chicken pox. The best ally of the invaders continues to be disease.

An avalanche of exotic organisms from the Eastern Hemisphere has been pouring onto the shores of the Americas for five hundred years. It continues, altering the ecosystems in all parts of the Western Hemisphere and the fates of Americans of every ethnicity and generation. The more recent immigrant organisms have often, like the wheat and peach trees that arrived in the sixteenth century, had positive effects. The Far East's soybean, for instance, has become a major crop and source of nourishment in the Americas since World War II, but the nastiest newcomers, like the Japanese beetle and Dutch elm disease, are the ones that get the most attention. Kudzu, a vine introduced from the Far East about a hundred years ago, was a decorous sort of a plant until the 1930s; since then it has been spreading cancerously through the Gulf and southern Atlantic states. The notorious "killer bees," aggressive African bees first released in Brazil in 1957, have spread in spite of every effort to hold them back and in the early 1990s are advancing into the United States. Flying Asian cockroaches, newly arrived, infest Florida. Significant and infamous above all recent imports is the AIDS virus, which probably first appeared in the Western Hemisphere in the 1970s. By sea and by air, by mammoth container ship and by jet aircraft, by diplomatic pouch and by impromptu encounter, the homogenizing process accelerates.

Native Americans often object to the name "New World," a European term for the lands of the Western Hemisphere. They point out that those lands were familiar to them long before Christopher Columbus was born, and their argument is one the rest of us owe respectful consideration. But we all are justified in the use of the title for the Americas since 1492. Until Columbus found his way across the Atlantic, the biota of the two sets of continents on either side were markedly different, the products of what, through time, had usually been divergent evolution. Since then the biota of both, most undeniably of the Americas, have in significant part been the product of revolution, that is, the abrupt addition and explosive propagation of exotic species from the lands on the other side of the waters that Columbus crossed in 1492. The great Genovese navigated, administered, crusaded, enslaved, but above all he mixed, mingled, jumbled, and homogenized the biota of our planet.

5. THE AZTEC CIVILIZATION OF MEXICO:
5.1. A SPANISH DESCRIPTION
Bernal Diaz

Aztec civilization was the last of a long line of native American civilizations that had sprung up in the central highlands of Mexico. In this selection it is described by Bernal Diaz, a conquistador who accompanied Cortes to Mexico in 1519. In what ways was the Aztec civilization like that of Spain? In what ways was it different?

When it was announced to Cortes that Motecusuma [Montezuma]·himself was approaching, he alighted from his horse and advanced to meet him. Many compliments were now passed on both sides. Motecusuma bid Cortes welcome, who, through Marina, said, in return, he hoped his majesty was in good health. If I still remember rightly, Cortes, who had Marina next to him, wished to concede the place of honor to the monarch, who, however, would not accept of it, but conceded it to Cortes, who now brought forth a necklace of precious stones, of the most beautiful colours and shapes, strung upon gold wire, and perfumed with musk, which he hung about the neck of Motecusuma. Our commander was then going to embrace him, but the grandees by whom he was surrounded held back his arms, as they considered it improper. Our general then desired Marina to tell the monarch how exceedingly he congratulated himself upon his good fortune of having seen such a powerful monarch face to face, and of the honour he had done us by coming out to meet us himself. To all this Motecusuma answered in very appropriate terms, and ordered his two nephews, the princes of Tetzuco and Cohohuacan, to conduct us to our quarters. He himself returned to the city, accompanied by his two other relatives, the princes of Cuitlahuac and Tlacupa, with the other grandees of his numerous suite. As they passed by, we perceived how all those who composed his majesty's retinue held their heads bent forward, no one daring to lift up his eyes in his presence; and altogether what deep veneration was paid him.

The road before us now became less crowded, and yet who would have been able to count the vast numbers of men, women, and children who filled the streets, crowded the balconies, and the canoes in the canals, merely to gaze upon us? . . .

We were quartered in a large building where there was room enough for us all, and which had been occupied by Axayacatl, father of Motecusuma, during his lifetime. Here the latter had likewise a secret room full of treasures, and where the gold he had inherited from his father was hid, which he had never touched up to this moment. The apartments and halls were very spacious, and those set apart for our general were furnished with carpets. There were separate beds for each of us, which could not have been better fitted up for a gentleman of the first rank! Every place was swept clean, and the walls had been newly plastered and decorated.

When we had arrived in the great courtyard adjoining this palace, Motecusuma came up to Cortes, and, taking him by the hand, conducted him himself into the apartments where he was to lodge, which had been beautifully decorated after the fashion of the country. He then hung about his neck a chaste necklace of gold, most curiously worked with figures all representing crabs. The Mexican grandees were greatly astonished at all these uncommon favours which their monarch bestowed upon our general.

Cortes returned the monarch many thanks for so much kindness, and the latter took leave of him with these words: "Malinche, you and your brothers must now do as if you were at home, and take some rest after the fatigues of the journey," then returned to his own palace, which was close at hand.

We allotted the apartments according to the several companies, placed our cannon in an advantageous position, and made such arrangements that our cavalry, as well as the infantry, might be ready at a moment's notice. We then sat down to a plentiful repast, which had been previously spread out for us, and made a sumptuous meal.

This our bold and memorable entry into the large city of Temixtitlan, Mexico took place on the 8th of November, 1519. Praise be to the Lord Jesus Christ for all this. . . .

The mighty Motecusuma may have been about this time in the fortieth year of his age. He was tall of stature, of slender make, and rather thin, but the symmetry of his body was beautiful. His complexion was not very brown, merely approaching to that of the inhabitants in general. The hair of his head was not very long, excepting where it hung thickly down over his ears, which were quite hidden by it. His black beard, though thin, looked handsome. His countenance was rather of an elongated form, but cheerful; and his fine eyes had the expression of love or severity, at the proper moments. He was particularly clean in his person, and took a bath every evening. Besides a number of concubines, who were all daughters of persons of rank and quality, he had two lawful wives of royal extraction, whom, however, he visited secretly without any one daring to observe it, save his most confidential servants. He was perfectly innocent of any unnatural crimes. The dress he had on one day was not worn again until four days had elapsed. In the halls adjoining his own private apartments there was always a guard of 2000 men of quality, in waiting: with whom, however, he never held any conversation unless to give them orders or to receive some intelligence from them. Whenever for this purpose they entered his apartment, they had first to take off their rich costumes and put on meaner garments, though these were always neat and clean; and were only allowed to enter into his presence barefooted, with eyes cast down. No person durst look at him full in the face, and during the three prostrations which they were obliged to make before they could approach him, they pronounced these words: "Lord! my Lord! sublime Lord!" Everything that was communicated to him was to be said in few words, the eyes of the speaker being constantly cast down, and on leaving the monarch's presence he walked backwards out of the room. I also remarked that even princes and other great personages who come to Mexico respecting lawsuits, or on other business from the interior of the country, always took off their shoes and changed their whole dress for one of a meaner appearance when they entered his palace. Neither were they allowed to enter the palace straightway, but had to show themselves for a considerable time outside the doors; as it would have been considered want of respect to the monarch if this had been omitted.

Above 300 kinds of dishes were served up for Motecusuma's dinner from his kitchen, underneath which were placed pans of porcelain filled with fire, to keep them warm. Three hundred dishes of various kinds were served up for him alone, and above 1000 for the persons in waiting. He sometimes, but very seldom, accompanied by the chief officers of his household, ordered the dinner himself, and desired that the best dishes and various kinds of birds should be called over to him. We were told that the flesh of young children as a very dainty bit, were also set before him sometimes by way of a relish. Whether there was any truth in this we could not possibly discover; on account of the great variety of dishes, consisting in fowls, turkeys, pheasants, partridges, quails, tame and wild geese, venison, musk swine, pigeons, hares, rabbits, and of numerous other birds and beasts; besides which there were various other kinds of provisions, indeed it would have been no easy task to call them all over by name.

I had almost forgotten to mention, that during dinnertime, two other young women of great beauty brought the monarch small cakes, as white as snow, made of eggs and other very nourishing ingredients, on plates covered with clean napkins; also a kind of long-shaped bread, likewise made of very substantial things, and some pachol, which is a kind of wafer-cake. They then presented him with three beautifully painted and gilt tubes, which were filled with liquid amber, and a herb called by the Indians tabaco. After the dinner had been cleared away and the singing and dancing done, one of the tubes was lighted, and the monarch took the smoke into his mouth, and after he had done this a short time, he fell asleep.

About this time a celebrated cazique [or cacique, a native Indian chief—Ed.], whom we called Tapia, was Motecusuma's chief steward: he kept an account of the whole of Motecusuma's revenue, in large books of paper which the Mexicans call *Amatl*. A whole house was filled with such large books of accounts.

Motecusuma had also two arsenals filled with arms of every description, of which many were ornamented with gold and precious stones. These arms consisted in shields of different sizes, sabres, and a species of broadsword, which is wielded with both hands, the edge furnished with flint stones, so extremely sharp that they cut much better than our Spanish swords: further, lances of greater length than ours, with spikes at their end, full one fathom in length, likewise furnished with several sharp flint stones. The pikes are so very sharp and hard that they will pierce the strongest shield, and cut like a razor; so that the Mexicans even shave themselves with these stones. Then there were excellent bows and arrows, pikes with single and double points, and the proper thongs to throw them with; slings with round stones purposely made for them; also a species of large shield, so ingeniously constructed that it could be rolled up when not wanted: they are only unrolled on the field of battle, and completely cover the whole body from the head to the feet. Further, we saw here a great variety of cuirasses made of quilted cotton, which were outwardly adorned with soft feathers of different colours, and looked like uniforms. . . .

I will now, however, turn to another subject, and rather acquaint my readers with the skilful arts practised among the Mexicans: among which I will first mention the sculptors, and the gold and silversmiths, who were clever in working and smelting gold, and would have astonished the most celebrated of our Spanish goldsmiths: the number of these was very great, and the most skilful lived at a place called Ezcapuzalco, about four miles from Mexico. After these came the very skilful masters in cutting and polishing precious stones, and the calchihuis, which resemble the emerald. Then follow the great masters in painting, and decorators in feathers, and the wonderful sculptors. Even at this day there are living in Mexico three Indian artists, named Marcos de Aguino, Juan de la Cruz, and El Crespello, who have severally reached to such great proficiency in the art of painting and sculpture, that they may be compared to an Apelles, or our contemporaries Michael Angelo and Berruguete. . . .

The powerful Motecusuma had also a number of dancers and clowns: some danced in stilts, tumbled, and performed a variety of other antics for the monarch's entertainment: a whole quarter of the city was inhabited by these performers, and their only occupation consisted in such like performances. Last, Motecusuma had in his service great numbers of stone-cutters, masons, and carpenters who were solely employed in the royal palaces. Above all, I must not forget to mention here his gardens for the culture of flowers, trees, and vegetables, of which there were various kinds. In these gardens were also numerous baths, wells, basins, and ponds full of limpid water, which regularly ebbed and flowed. All this was enlivened by endless varieties of small birds, which sang among the trees. Also the plantations of medical plants and vegetables are well worthy of our notice: these were kept in proper order by a large body of gardeners. All the baths, wells, ponds, and buildings were substantially constructed of stonework, as also the theatres where the singers and dancers performed. There were upon the whole so many remarkable things for my observation in these gardens and throughout the whole town, that I can scarcely find words to express the astonishment I felt at the pomp and splendour of the Mexican monarch. . . .

We had already been four days in the city of Mexico, and neither our commander nor any of us had, during that time, left our quarters, excepting to visit the gardens and buildings adjoining the palace. Cortes now, therefore, determined to view the city, and visit the great market, and the chief temple of Huitzilopochtli. . . . The moment we arrived in this immense market, we were perfectly astonished at the vast numbers of people, the profusion of merchandise which was there exposed for sale, and at the good police and order that reigned throughout. The grandees who accompanied us drew our attention to the smallest circumstance, and gave us full explanation of all we saw. Every species of merchandise had a separate spot for its sale. We first of all visited those divisions of the market appropriated for the sale of gold and silver wares, of jewels, of cloths interwoven with feathers, and of other manufactured goods; besides slaves of both sexes. This slave market was upon as great a scale as the Portuguese market for negro slaves at Guinea. To prevent these from running away, they were fastened with halters about their neck, though some were allowed to walk at large. Next to these came the dealers in coarser wares—cotton, twisted thread, and cacao. In short, every species of goods which New Spain produces were here to be found and everything put me in mind of my native town Medino del Campo during fair time, where every merchandise had a separate street assigned for its sale. In one place were sold the stuffs manufactured of nequen; ropes, and sandals; in another place, the sweet maguey root, ready cooked, and various other things made from this plant. In another division of the market were exposed the skins of tigers, lions, jackals, otters, red deer, wild cats, and of other beasts of prey, some of which were tanned. In another place were sold beans and sage, with other herbs and vegetables. A particular market was assigned for the merchants in fowls, turkeys, ducks, rabbits, hares, deer, and dogs; also for fruit-sellers, pastry-cooks, and tripe-sellers. Not far from these were exposed all manner of earthenware, from the large earthen cauldron to the smallest pitchers. Then came the dealers in honey and honey-cakes, and other sweetmeats. Next to these, the timber-merchants, furniture-dealers, with their stores of tables, benches, cradles, and all sorts of wooden implements, all separately arranged. What can I further add? If I am to note everything down, I must also mention human excrements, which are exposed for sale in canoes lying in the canals near this square, and are used for the tanning of leather; for, according to the assurances of the Mexicans, it is impossible to tan well without it. I can easily imagine that many of my readers will laugh at this; however, what I have stated is a fact, and, as further proof of this, I must acquaint the reader that along every road accommodations were built of reeds, straw, or grass, by which those who made use of them were hidden from the view of the passers-by, so that great care was taken that none of the last mentioned treasures should be lost. But why should I so minutely detail every article exposed for sale in this great market? If I had to enumerate everything singly, I should not so easily get to the end. And yet I have not mentioned the paper, which in this country is called amatl; the tubes filled with liquid amber and tobacco; the various sweet-scented salves, and similar things; nor the various seeds which were exposed for sale in the porticoes of this market, nor the medicinal herbs.

In this marketplace there were also courts of justice, to which three judges and several constables were appointed, who inspected the goods exposed for sale. I had almost forgotten to mention the salt, and those who made the flint knives; also the fish, and a species of bread made of a kind of mud or slime collected from the surface of this lake, and eaten in that form, and has a similar taste to our cheese. Further, instruments of brass, copper, and tin; cups, and painted pitchers of wood; indeed, I wish I had completed the enumeration of all this profusion of merchandize. The variety was so great that it would occupy more space than I can well spare to note them down in; besides which, the market was so crowded with people, and the thronging so excessive in the porticoes, that it was quite impossible to see all in one day. . . .

On quitting the market, we entered the spacious yards which surrounded the chief temple. These appeared to encompass more ground than the marketplace at Salamanca, and were surrounded by a double wall, constructed of stone and lime: these yards were paved with large white flagstones, extremely smooth; and where these were wanting, a kind of brown plaster had been used instead, and all was kept so very clean that there was not the smallest particle of dust or straw to be seen anywhere.

Before we mounted the steps of the great temple, Motecusuma, who was sacrificing on the top to his idols, sent six papas and two of his principal officers to conduct Cortes up the steps. There were 114 steps to the summit. . . . Indeed, this infernal temple, from its great height, commanded a view of the whole surrounding neighbourhood. From this place we could likewise see the three causeways which led into Mexico,—that from Iztapalapan, by which we had entered the city four days ago; that from Tlacupa, along which we took our flight eight months after, when we were beaten out of the city by the new monarch Cuitlahuatzin; the third was that of Tepeaquilla. We also observed the aqueduct which ran from Chapultepec, and provided the whole town with sweet water. We could also distinctly see the bridges across the openings, by which these causeways were intersected, and through which the waters of the lake ebbed and flowed. The lake itself was crowded with canoes, which were bringing provisions, manufactures, and other merchandize to the city. From here we also discovered that the only communication of the houses in this city, and of all the other towns built in the lake, was by means of drawbridges or canoes. In all these towns the beautiful white plastered temples rose above the smaller ones, like so many towers and castles in our Spanish towns, and this, it may be imagined, was a splendid sight.

After we had sufficiently gazed upon this magnificent picture, we again turned our eyes toward the great market, and beheld the vast numbers of buyers and sellers who thronged there. The bustle and noise occasioned by this multitude of human beings was so great that it could be heard at a distance of more than four miles. Some of our men, who had been at Constantinople and Rome, and travelled through the whole of Italy, said that they never had seen a marketplace of such large dimensions, or which was so well regulated, or so crowded with people as this one at Mexico.

On this occasion Cortes said to father Olmedo, who had accompanied us: "I have just been thinking that we should take this opportunity, and apply to Motecusuma for permission to build a church here."

To which father Olmedo replied, that it would, no doubt, be an excellent thing if the monarch would grant this; but that it would be acting overhasty to make a proposition of that nature to him now, whose consent would not easily be gained at any time.

Cortes then turned to Motecusuma, and said to him, by means of our interpretress, Doña Marina: "Your majesty is, indeed, a great monarch, and you merit to be still greater! It has been a real delight to us to view all your cities. I have now one favour to beg of you, that you would allow us to see your gods and teules."

To which Motecusuma answered, that he must first consult the chief papas, to whom he then addressed a few words. Upon this, we were led into a kind of small tower, with one room, in which we saw two basements resembling altars, decked with coverings of extreme beauty. On each of these basements stood a gigantic, fat-looking figure, of which the one on the right hand represented the god of war Huitzilopochtli. This idol had a very broad face, with distorted and furious-looking eyes, and was covered all over with jewels, gold, and pearls, which were stuck to it by means of a species of paste, which, in this country, is prepared from a certain root. Large serpents, likewise, covered with gold and precious stones, wound round the body of this monster, which held in one hand a bow, and in the other a bunch of arrows. Another small idol which stood by its side, representing its page, carried this monster's short spear, and its golden shield studded with precious stones. Around Huitzilopochtli's neck were figures representing human faces and hearts made of gold and silver, and decorated with blue stones. In front of him stood several perfuming pans with copal, the incense of the country; also the hearts of three Indians, who had that day been slaughtered, were now consuming before him as a burnt-offering. Every wall of this chapel and the whole floor had become almost black with human blood, and the stench was abominable.

Respecting the abominable human sacrifices of these people, the following was communicated to us: The breast of the unhappy victim destined to be sacrificed was ripped open with a knife made of sharp flint; the throbbing heart was then torn out, and immediately offered to the idol-god in whose honour the sacrifice had been instituted. After this, the head, arms and legs were cut off and eaten at their banquets, with the exception of the head, which was saved, and hung to a beam appropriated for that purpose. No other part of the body was eaten, but the remainder was thrown to the beasts which were kept in those abominable dens, in which there were also vipers and other poisonous serpents, and, among the latter in particular, a species at the end of whose tail there was a kind of rattle. This last mentioned serpent, which is the most dangerous, was kept in a cabin of a diversified form, in which a quantity of feathers had been strewed: here it laid its eggs, and it was fed with the flesh of dogs and of human beings who had been sacrificed. We were positively told that, after we had been beaten out of the city of Mexico, and had lost 850 of our men, these horrible beasts were fed for many successive days with the bodies of our unfortunate countrymen. Indeed, when all the tigers and lions roared together, with the howlings of the jackals and foxes, and hissing of the serpents, it was quite fearful, and you could not suppose otherwise than that you were in hell.

Our commander here said smilingly, to Motecusuma: "I cannot imagine that such a powerful and wise monarch as you are should not have yourself discovered by this time that these idols are not divinities, but evil spirits, called devils. In order that you may be convinced of this, and that your papas may satisfy themselves of this truth, allow me to erect a cross on the summit of this temple; and, in the chapel, where stand your Huitzilopochtli and Tetzcatlipuca, give us a small space that I may place there the image of the holy Virgin; then you will see what terror will seize these idols by which you have been so long deluded."

Motecusuma knew what the image of the Virgin Mary was, yet he was very much displeased with Cortes' offer, and replied, in presence of two papas, whose anger was not less conspicuous, "Malinche, could I have conjectured that you would have used such reviling language as you have just done, I would certainly not have shown you my gods. In our eyes these are good divinities: they preserve our lives, give us nourishment, water, and good harvests, healthy and growing weather, and victory whenever we pray to them for it. Therefore we offer up our prayers to them, and make them sacrifices. I earnestly beg of you not to say another word to insult the profound veneration in which we hold these gods."

As soon as Cortes heard these words and perceived the great excitement under which they were pronounced, he said nothing in return, but merely remarked to the monarch with a cheerful smile: "It is time for us both to depart hence." To which Motecusuma answered, that he would not detain him any longer, but he himself was now obliged to stay some time to atone to his gods by prayer and sacrifice for having committed *gratlatlacol,* by allowing us to ascend the great temple, and thereby occasioning the affronts which we had offered them.

5.2. AZTEC ACCOUNT OF THE CONQUEST

The following is a Mexican account of the Spanish conquest of Mexico in 1519. The account was translated from records and memories in the Mexican Nahuatl language with the help of Spanish missionaries in the years after the conquest. What does this account suggest about the goals and motives of the Spanish? How did the Spanish capture the Aztec king, Montezuma (Motecuhzoma), and the capital city? How is this account similar to, and different from, the Spanish account by Diaz?

SPEECHES OF MOTECUHZOMA AND CORTES

When Motecuhzoma had given necklaces to each one, Cortes asked him: "Are you Motecuhzoma? Are you the king? Is it true that you are the king Motecuhzoma?"

And the king said: "Yes, I am Motecuhzoma." Then he stood up to welcome Cortes; he came forward, bowed his head low and addressed him in these words: "Our lord, you are weary. The journey has tired you, but now you have arrived on the earth. You have come to your city, Mexico. You have come here to sit on your throne, to sit under its canopy.

"The kings who have gone before, your representatives, guarded it and preserved it for your coming. The kings Itzcoatl, Motecuhzoma the Elder, Axayacatl, Tizoc and Ahuitzol ruled for you in the City of Mexico. The people were protected by their swords and sheltered by their shields.

"Do the kings know the destiny of those they left behind, their posterity? If only they are watching! If only they can see what I see!

"No, it is not a dream. I am not walking in my sleep. I am not seeing you in my dreams. . . . I have seen you at last! I have met you face to face! I was in agony for five days, for ten days, with my eyes fixed on the Region of the Mystery. And now you have come out of the clouds and mists to sit on your throne again.

"This was foretold by the kings who governed your city, and now it has taken place. You have come back to us; you have come down from the sky. Rest now, and take possession of your royal houses. Welcome to your land, my lords!"

When Motecuhzoma had finished, La Malinche translated his address into Spanish so that the Captain could understand it. Cortes replied in his strange and savage tongue, speaking first to La Malinche: "Tell Motecuhzoma that we are his friends. There is nothing to fear. We have wanted to see him for a long time, and now we have seen his face and heard his words. Tell him that we love him well and that our hearts are contented."

Then he said to Motecuhzoma: "We have come to your house in Mexico as friends. There is nothing to fear."

La Malinche translated this speech and the Spaniards grasped Motecuhzoma's hands and patted his back to show their affection for him.

ATTITUDES OF THE SPANIARDS AND THE NATIVE LORDS

The Spaniards examined everything they saw. They dismounted from their horses, and mounted them again, and dismounted again, so as not to miss anything of interest.

The chiefs who accompanied Motecuhzoma were: Cacama, king of Tezcoco; Tetlepanquetzaltzin, king of Tlacopan; Itzcuauhtzin the Tlacochcalcatl, lord of Tlatelolco; and Topantemoc, Motecuhzoma's treasurer in Tlatelolco. These four chiefs were standing in a file.

The other princes were: Atlixcatzin [chief who has taken captives][1]; Tepeoatzin, The Tlacochcalcatl; Quetzalaztatzin, the keeper of the chalk; Totomotzin; Hecateupatiltzin; and Cuappiatzin.

When Motecuhzoma was imprisoned, they all went into hiding. They ran away to hide and treacherously abandoned him!

THE SPANIARDS TAKE POSSESSION OF THE CITY

When the Spaniards entered the Royal House, they placed Motecuhzoma under guard and kept him under their vigilance. They also placed a guard over Itzcuauhtzin, but the other lords were permitted to depart.

Then the Spaniards fired one of their cannons, and this caused great confusion in the city. The people scattered in every direction; they fled without rhyme or reason; they ran off as if they were being pursued. It was as if they had eaten the mushrooms that confuse the mind, or had seen some dreadful apparition. They were all overcome by terror, as if their hearts had fainted. And when night fell, the panic spread through the city and their fears would not let them sleep.

In the morning the Spaniards told Motecuhzoma what they needed in the way of supplies: tortillas, fried chickens, hens' eggs, pure water, firewood and charcoal. Also: large, clean cooking pots, water jars, pitchers, dishes and other pottery. Motecuhzoma ordered that it be sent to them. The chiefs who received this order were angry with the king and no longer revered or respected him. But they furnished the Spaniards with all the provisions they needed—food, beverages and water, and fodder for the horses.

THE SPANIARDS REVEAL THEIR GREED

When the Spaniards were installed in the palace, they asked Motecuhzoma about the city's resources and reserves and about the warriors' ensigns and shields. They questioned him closely and then demanded gold.

Motecuhzoma guided them to it. They surrounded him and crowded close with their weapons. He walked in the center, while they formed a circle around him.

When they arrived at the treasure house called Teucalco, the riches of gold and feathers were brought out to them: ornaments made of quetzal feathers, richly worked shields, disks of gold, the necklaces of the idols, gold nose plugs, gold greaves and bracelets and crowns.

The Spaniards immediately stripped the feathers from the gold shields and ensigns. They gathered all the gold into a great mound and

---

1. Military title given to a warrior who had captured four enemies.

set fire to everything else, regardless of its value. Then they melted down the gold into ingots. As for the precious green stones, they took only the best of them; the rest were snatched up by the Tlaxcaltecas. The Spaniards searched through the whole treasure house, questioning and quarreling, and seized every object they thought was beautiful.

THE SEIZURE OF MOTECUHZOMA'S TREASURES

Next they went to Motecuhzoma's storehouse, in the place called Totocalco [Place of the Palace of the Birds],[2] where his personal treasures were kept. The Spaniards grinned like little beasts and patted each other with delight.

When they entered the hall of treasures, it was as if they had arrived in Paradise. They searched everywhere and coveted everything; they were slaves to their own greed. All of Motecuhzoma's possessions were brought out: fine bracelets, necklaces with large stones, ankle rings with little gold bells, the royal crowns and all the royal finery—everything that belonged to the king and was reserved to him only. They seized these treasures as if they were their own, as if this plunder were merely a stroke of good luck. And when they had taken all the gold, they heaped up everything else in the middle of the patio.

La Malinche called the nobles together. She climbed up to the palace roof and cried: "Mexicanos, come forward! The Spaniards need your help! Bring them food and pure water. They are tired and hungry; they are almost fainting from exhaustion! Why do you not come forward? Are you angry with them?"

The Mexicans were too frightened to approach. They were crushed by terror and would not risk coming forward. They shied away as if the Spaniards were wild beasts, as if the hour were midnight on the blackest night of the year. Yet they did not abandon the Spaniards to hunger and thirst. They brought them whatever they needed, but shook with fear as they did so. They delivered the supplies to the Spaniards with trembling hands, then turned and hurried away.

THE PREPARATIONS FOR THE FIESTA

The Aztecs begged permission of their king to hold the fiesta of Huitzilopochtli. The Spaniards wanted to see this fiesta to learn how it was celebrated. A delegation of the celebrants came to the palace where Motecuhzoma was a prisoner, and when their spokesman asked his permission, he granted it to them.

2. The zoological garden attached to the royal palaces.

As soon as the delegation returned, the women began to grind seeds of the chicalote.[3] These women had fasted for a whole year. They ground the seeds in the patio of the temple.

The Spaniards came out of the palace together, dressed in armor and carrying their weapons with them. They stalked among the women and looked at them one by one; they stared into the faces of the women who were grinding seeds. After this cold inspection, they went back into the palace. It is said that they planned to kill the celebrants if the men entered the patio.

THE STATUE OF HUITZILOPOCHTLI

On the evening before the fiesta of Toxcatl, the celebrants began to model a statue of Huitzilopochtli. They gave it such a human appearance that it seemed the body of a living man. Yet they made the statue with nothing but a paste made of the ground seeds of the chicalote, which they shaped over an armature of sticks.

When the statue was finished, they dressed it in rich feathers, and they painted crossbars over and under its eyes. They also clipped on its earrings of turquoise mosaic; these were in the shape of serpents, with gold rings hanging from them. Its nose plug, in the shape of an arrow, was made of gold and was inlaid with fine stones.

They placed the magic headdress of hummingbird feathers on its head. They also adorned it with an *anecuyotl,* which was a belt made of feathers, with a cone at the back. Then they hung around its neck an ornament of yellow parrot feathers, fringed like the locks of a young boy. Over this they put its nettle-leaf cape, which was painted black and decorated with five clusters of eagle feathers.

Next they wrapped it in its cloak, which was painted with skull and bones, and over this they fastened its vest. The vest was painted with dismembered human parts: skulls, ears, hearts, intestines, torsos, breasts, hands and feet. They also put on its *maxtlatl,* or loincloth, which was decorated with images of dissevered limbs and fringed with amate paper. This *maxtlatl* was painted with vertical stripes of bright blue.

They fastened a red paper flag at its shoulder and placed on its head what looked like a sacrificial flint knife. This too was made of red paper; it seemed to have been steeped in blood.

The statue carried a *tehuehuelli,* a bamboo shield decorated with four clusters of fine eagle feathers. The pendant of this shield was blood-red, like the knife and the shoulder flag. The statue also carried four arrows.

Finally, they put the wristbands on its arms. These bands, made of coyote skin, were fringed with paper cut into little strips.

3. Edible plants also used in medicines.

THE BEGINNING OF THE FIESTA

Early the next morning, the statue's face was uncovered by those who had been chosen for that ceremony. They gathered in front of the idol in single file and offered it gifts of food, such as round seedcakes or perhaps human flesh. But they did not carry it up to its temple on top of the pyramid.

All the young warriors were eager for the fiesta to begin. They had sworn to dance and sing with all their hearts, so that the Spaniards would marvel at the beauty of the rituals.

The procession began, and the celebrants filed into the temple patio to dance the Dance of the Serpent. When they were all together in the patio, the songs and the dance began. Those who had fasted for twenty days and those who had fasted for a year were in command of the others; they kept the dancers in file with their pine wands. (If anyone wished to urinate, he did not stop dancing, but simply opened his clothing at the hips and separated his clusters of heron feathers.)

If anyone disobeyed the leaders or was not in his proper place they struck him on the hips and shoulders. Then they drove him out of the patio, beating him and shoving him from behind. They pushed him so hard that he sprawled to the ground, and they dragged him outside by the ears. No one dared to say a word about this punishment, for those who had fasted during the year were feared and venerated; they had earned the exclusive title "Brothers of Huitzilopochtli."

The great captains, the bravest warriors, danced at the head of the files to guide the others. The youths followed at a slight distance. Some of the youths wore their hair gathered into large locks, a sign that they had never taken any captives. Others carried their headdresses on their shoulders; they had taken captives, but only with help.

Then came the recruits, who were called "the young warriors." They had each captured an enemy or two. The others called to them: "Come, comrades, show us how brave you are! Dance with all your hearts!"

THE SPANIARDS ATTACK THE CELEBRANTS

At this moment in the fiesta, when the dance was loveliest and when song was linked to song, the Spaniards were siezed with an urge to kill the celebrants. They all ran forward, armed as if for battle. They closed the entrances and passageways, all the gates of the patio: the Eagle Gate in the lesser palace, the Gate of the Canestalk and the Gate of the Serpent of Mirrors. They posted guards so that no one could escape, and then rushed into the Sacred Patio to slaughter the celebrants. They came on foot, carrying their swords and their wooden or metal shields.

They ran in among the dancers, forcing their way to the place where the drums were played. They attacked the man who was drumming and cut off his arms. Then they cut off his head, and it rolled across the floor.

They attacked all the celebrants, stabbing them, spearing them, striking them with their swords. They attacked some of them from behind, and these fell instantly to the ground with their entrails hanging out. Others they beheaded: they cut off their heads, or split their heads to pieces.

They struck others in the shoulders, and their arms were torn from their bodies. They wounded some in the thigh and some in the calf. They slashed others in the abdomen, and their entrails all spilled to the ground. Some attempted to run away, but their intestines dragged as they ran; they seemed to tangle their feet in their own entrails. No matter how they tried to save themselves, they could find no escape.

Some attempted to force their way out, but the Spaniards murdered them at the gates. Others climbed the walls, but they could not save themselves. Those who ran into the communal houses were safe there for a while; so were those who lay down among the victims and pretended to be dead. But if they stood up again, the Spaniards saw them and killed them.

The blood of the warriors flowed like water and gathered into pools. The pools widened, and the stench of blood and entrails filled the air. The Spaniards ran into the communal houses to kill those who were hiding. They ran everywhere and searched everywhere; they invaded every room, hunting and killing.

6. A DUTCH MASSACRE OF THE ALGONQUINS

David Pieterzen DeVries

David Pieterzen DeVries was a ship's captain who became a landlord or "patroonship" holder in the Dutch colony of New Amsterdam (now New York). After a disastrous venture to establish a farming and whaling colony, Swanendael, on the Delaware River (near modern Philadelphia), he was granted the first patroonship on Staten Island. There he had frequent contact with the Algonquin and Raritan Indians. He was a member of the Board of Directors (the Twelve Men), responsible to the Dutch West India Company for the governance of New Amsterdam. When in 1642, a new governor, Dutch merchant Willem Kieft, urged increased settlement and Indian removal, DeVries attempted to urge caution. He described what happened in February 1643 in his book, Voyages from Holland to America.

Why did DeVries oppose the governor's plan to attack the Algonquins? What does this story suggest about Dutch-Indian relations before 1643? What were the consequences of the massacre?

The 24th of February, sitting at a table with the Governor, he began to state his intentions, that he had a mind to *wipe the mouths* of the savages; that he had been dining at the house of Jan Claesen Damen, where Maryn Adriaensen and Jan Claesen Damen, together with Jacob Planck, had presented a petition to him to begin this work. I answered him that they were not wise to request this; that such work could not be done without the approbation of the Twelve Men; that it could not take place without my assent, who was one of the Twelve Men; that moreover I was the first patroon, and no one else hitherto had risked there so many thousands, and also his person, as I was the first to come from Holland or Zeeland to plant a colony; and that he should consider what profit he could derive from this business, as he well knew that on account of trifling with the Indians we had lost our colony in the South River at Swanendael, in the Hoere-kil, with thirty-two men, who were murdered in the year 1630; and that in the year 1640, the cause of my people being murdered on Staten Island was a difficulty which he had brought on with the Raritan Indians, where his soldiers had for some trifling thing killed some savages. . . . But it appeared that my speaking was of no avail. He had, with his comurderers, determined to commit the murder, deeming it a Roman deed, and to do it without warning the inhabitants in the open lands that each one might take care of himself against the retaliation of the savages, for he could not kill all the Indians. When I had expressed all these things in full, sitting at the table, and the meal was over, he told me he wished me to go to the large hall, which he had been lately adding to his house. Coming to it, there stood all his soldiers ready to cross the river to Pavonia to commit the murder. Then spoke I again to Governor Willem Kieft: "Let this work alone; you wish to break the mouths of the Indians, but you will also murder our own nation, for there are none of the settlers in the open country who are aware of it. My own dwelling, my people, cattle, corn, and tobacco will be lost." He answered me, assuring me that there would be no danger; that some soldiers should go to my house to protect it. But that was not done. So was this business begun between the 25th and 26th of February in the year 1643. I remained that night at the Governor's, sitting up. I went and sat by the kitchen fire, when about midnight I heard a great shrieking, and I ran to the ramparts of the fort, and looked over to Pavonia. Saw nothing but firing, and heard the shrieks of the savages murdered in their sleep. I returned again to the house by the fire. Having sat there awhile, there came an Indian with his squaw, whom I knew well, and who lived about an hour's walk from my house, and told me that they two had fled in a small skiff, which they had taken from the shore at Pavonia; that the Indians from Fort Orange had surprised them; and that they had come to conceal themselves in the fort. I told them that they must go away immediately; that this was no time for them to come to the fort to conceal themselves; that they who had killed their people at Pavonia were not Indians, but the Swannekens, as they call the Dutch, had done it. They then asked me how they should get out of the fort. I took them to the door, and there was no sentry there, and so they betook themselves to the woods. When it was day the soldiers returned to the fort, having massacred or murdered eighty Indians, and considering they had done a deed of Roman valor, in murdering so many in their sleep; where infants were torn from their mothers' breasts, and hacked to pieces in the presence of the parents, and the pieces thrown into the fire and in the water, and other sucklings, being bound to small boards, were cut, stuck, and pierced, and miserably massacred in a manner to move a heart of stone. Some were thown into the river, and when the fathers and mothers endeavored to save them, the soldiers would not let them come on land but made both parents and children drown—children from five to six years of age, and also some old and decrepit persons. Those who fled from this onslaught, and concealed themselves in the neighboring sedge, and when it was morning, came out to beg a piece of bread, and to be permitted to warm themselves, were murdered in cold blood and tossed into the fire or the water. Some came to our people in the country with their hands, some with their legs cut off, and some holding their entrails in their arms, and others had such horrible cuts and gashes, that worse than they were could never happen. And these poor simple creatures, as also many of our own people, did not know any better than that they had been attacked by a party of other Indians—the Maquas. After this exploit, the soldiers were rewarded for their services, and Director Kieft thanked them by taking them by the hand and congratulating them. At another place, on the same night, on Corler's Hook near Corler's plantation, forty Indians were in the same manner attacked in their sleep, and massacred there in the same manner. Did the Duke of Alva in the Netherlands ever do anything more cruel? This is indeed a disgrace to our nation, who have so generous a governor in our Fatherland as the Prince of Orange, who has always endeavored in his wars to spill as little blood as possible. As soon as the savages understood that the Swannekens had so treated them, all the men whom they could surprise on the farmlands, they killed; but we have never heard that they have ever permitted women or children to be killed. They burned all the houses, farms, barns, grain, haystacks, and destroyed everything they could get hold of. So there was an open destructive war begun. They also burnt my farm, cattle, corn, barn, tobacco-house, and all the tobacco. My people saved themselves in the house where I alone lived, which was made with embrasures, through which they defended themselves. Whilst my people were in alarm the savage whom I had aided to escape from the fort in the night came there, and told the other Indians that I was a good chief, that I had helped him out of the fort, and that the killing of the Indians took place contrary to my wish. Then they all cried out together to my people that they would not shoot them; that if they had not destroyed my cattle they would not do it, nor burn my house; that they would let my little brewery stand, though they wished to get the copper kettle, in order to make darts for their arrows; but hearing now that it had been done contrary to my wish, they all went away, and left my house unbesieged. When now the Indians had destroyed so many farms and men in revenge for their people, I went to Governor Willem Kieft, and asked him if it was not as I had said it would be, that he would only effect the spilling of Christian blood. Who would now compensate us for our losses? But he gave me no answer. He said he wondered that no Indians came to the fort. I told him that I did not wonder at it; "why should the Indians come here where you have so treated them?"

7. THE SLAVE TRADE

Olaudah Equiano

The consequences of the European arrival in the Americas were devastating for the human inhabitants of three continents: North America, South America, and Africa. The inhabitants of the Americas were decimated by diseases, especially smallpox, from which they had no immunities. The inhabitants of Africa, especially western Africa, were decimated by the European slave trade.

This selection is part of the autobiography of one of the Africans who was enslaved, Olaudah Equiano. He was born in 1745 in what is today Nigeria, sold to British slavers at the age of eleven, and shipped off to the British West Indies. In 1766 he was able to buy his freedom and became involved in the antislavery movement in England. What was slavery in Africa like, and how was it different from slavery in the Americas? For those, like Equiano, who survived, what were the worst aspects of the Atlantic slave trade? What do you think of Equiano's criticism of "nominal Christians"?

I hope the reader will not think I have trespassed on his patience in introducing myself to him with some account of the manners and customs of my country. They had been implanted in me with great care, and made an impression on my mind, which time could not erase, and which all the adversity and variety of fortune I have since experienced served only to rivet and record; for, whether the love of one's country be real or imaginary, or a lesson of reason, or an instinct of nature, I still look back with pleasure on the first scenes of my life, though that pleasure has been for the most part mingled with sorrow.

My father, besides many slaves, had a numerous family, of which seven lived to grow up, including myself and a sister, who was the only daughter. As I was the youngest of the sons, I became, of course, the greatest favourite with my mother, and was always with her; and she used to take particular pains to form my mind. I was trained up from my earliest years in the arts of agriculture and war: my daily exercise was shooting and throwing javelins; and my mother adorned me with emblems, after the manner of our greatest warriors. In this way I grew up till I was turned the age of eleven, when an end was put to my happiness in the following manner:—Generally, when the grown people in the neighbourhood were gone far in the fields to labour, the children assembled together in some of the neighbour's premises to play; and commonly some of us used to get up a tree to look out for any assailant, or kidnapper, that might come upon us; for they sometimes took those opportunities of our parents' absence, to attack and carry off as many as they could seize. One day, as I was watching at the top of a tree in our yard, I saw one of those people come into the yard of our next neighbour but one, to kidnap, there being many stout young people in it. Immediately, on this, I gave the alarm of the rogue, and he was surrounded by the stoutest of them, who entangled him with cords, so that he could not escape till some of the grown people came and secured him. But alas! ere long, it was my fate to be thus attacked, and to be carried off, when none of the grown people were nigh. One day, when all our people were gone out to their works as usual, and only I and my dear sister were left to mind the house, two men and a woman got over our walls, and in a moment seized us both; and, without giving us time to cry out, or make resistance, they stopped our mouths, and ran off with us into the nearest wood. Here they tied our hands, and continued to carry us as far as they could, till night came on, when we reached a small house, where the robbers halted for refreshment, and spent the night. We were then unbound; but were unable to take any food; and, being quite overpowered by fatigue and grief, our only relief was some sleep, which allayed our misfortune for a short time. The next morning we left the house, and continued travelling all the day. For a long time we had kept the woods, but at last we came into a road which I believed I knew. I had now some hopes of being delivered; for we had advanced but a little way before I discovered some people at a distance, on which I began to cry out for their assistance, but my cries had no other effect than to make them tie me faster and stop my mouth, and then they put me into a large sack. They also stopped my sister's mouth, and tied her hands; and in this manner we proceeded till we were out of sight of these people. When we went to rest the following night they offered us some victuals; but we refused them; and the only comfort we had was in being in one another's arms all that night, and bathing each other with our tears. But alas! we were soon deprived of even the smallest comfort of weeping together. The next day proved a day of greater sorrow than I had yet experienced; for my sister and I were then separated, while we lay clasped in each other's arms: it was in vain that we besought them not to part us: she was torn from me, and immediately carried away, while I was left in a state of distraction not to be described. I cried and grieved continually; and for several days did not eat any thing but what they forced into my mouth. At length, after many days travelling, during which I had often changed masters, I got into the hands of a chieftain, in a very pleasant country. This man had two wives and some children, and they all used me extremely well, and did all they could to comfort me; particularly the first wife, who was something like my mother. Although I was a great many days journey from my father's house, yet these people spoke exactly the same language with us. This first master of mine, as I may call him, was a smith; and my principal employment was working his bellows, which were the same kind as I had seen in my vicinity. They were in some respects not unlike the stoves here in gentlemen's kitchens; and were covered over with leather; and in the middle of that leather a stick was fixed, and a person stood up, and worked it, in the same manner as is done to pump water out of a cask with a hand pump. I believe it was gold he worked, for it was of a lovely bright yellow colour, and was worn by the women on their wrists and ankles. . . .

Soon after this my master's only daughter and child by his first wife sickened and died, which affected him so much that for some time he was almost frantic, and really would have killed himself, had he not been watched and prevented. However, in a small time afterwards he recovered; and I was again sold. I was now carried to the left of the sun's rising, through many dreary wastes and dismal woods, amidst the hideous roarings of wild beasts. The people I was sold to used to carry me very often, when I was tired, either on their shoulders or on their backs. I saw many convenient well-built sheds along the roads, at proper distances, to accommodate the merchants and travellers, who lay in those buildings along with their wives, who often accompany them; and they always go well armed.

From the time I left my own nation I always found somebody that understood me till I came to the sea coast. The languages of different nations did not totally differ, nor were they so copious as those of the Europeans, particularly the English. They were therefore easily learned;

and, while I was journeying thus through Africa, I acquired two or three different tongues. . . .

I came to a town called Timnah, in the most beautiful country I had yet seen in Africa. It was extremely rich, and there were many rivulets which flowed through it, and supplied a large pond in the centre of the town, where the people washed. Here I first saw and tasted cocoa nuts, which I thought superior to any nuts I had ever tasted before; and the trees, which were loaded, were also interspersed amongst the houses, which had commodious shades adjoining, and were in the same manner as ours, the insides being neatly plastered and whitewashed. Here I also saw and tasted for the first time sugar-cane. Their money consisted of little white shells, the size of the fingernail: they were known in this country by the name of core.[1] I was sold here for one hundred and seventy-two of them by a merchant who lived and brought me there. I had been about two or three days at his house, when a wealthy widow, a neighbour of his, came there one evening, and brought with her an only son, a young gentleman about my own age and size. Here they saw me; and, having taken a fancy to me, I was bought of the merchant, and went home with them. Her house and premises were situated close to one of those rivulets I have mentioned, and were the finest I ever saw in Africa: they were very extensive, and she had a number of slaves to attend her. The next day I was washed and perfumed, and when mealtime came, I was led into the presence of my mistress, and ate and drank before her with her son. This filled me with astonishment; and I could scarce help expressing my surprise that the young gentleman should suffer me, who was bound, to eat with him who was free; and not only so, but that he would not at any time either eat or drink till I had taken first, because I was the eldest, which was agreeable to our custom. Indeed every thing here, and all their treatment of me, made me forget that I was a slave. The language of these people resembled ours so nearly, that we understood each other perfectly. They had also the very same customs as we. There were likewise slaves daily to attend us, while my young master and I, with other boys, sported with our darts and bows and arrows, as I had been used to do at home. In this resemblance to my former happy state, I passed about two months, and I now began to think I was to be adopted into the family, and was beginning to be reconciled to my situation, and to forget by degrees my misfortunes, when all at once the delusion vanished; for, without the least previous knowledge, one morning early, while my dear master and companion was still asleep, I was awakened out of my reverie to fresh sorrow, and hurried away even amongst the uncircumcised.

Thus, at the very moment I dreamed of the greatest happiness, I found myself most miserable; and it seemed as if fortune wished to give me this

1. Cowrie, a seashell obtained from the Maldive Islands and used as currency in many parts of West Africa.

taste of joy only to render the reverse more poignant. The change I now experienced was as painful as it was sudden and unexpected. It was a change indeed from a state of bliss to a scene which is inexpressible by me, as it discovered to me an element I had never before beheld, and till then had no idea of, and wherein such instances of hardship and fatigue continually occurred as I can never reflect on but with horror.

The first object which saluted my eyes when I arrived on the coast was the sea, and a slaveship, which was then riding at anchor, and waiting for its cargo. These filled me with astonishment, which was soon converted into terror, which I am yet at a loss to describe, nor the then feelings of my mind. When I was carried on board I was immediately handled, and tossed up, to see if I were sound, by some of the crew; and I was now persuaded that I had got into a world of bad spirits, and that they were going to kill me. Their complexions too differing so much from ours, their long hair, and the language they spoke, which was very different from any I had ever heard, united to confirm me in this belief. Indeed, such were the horrors of my views and fears at the moment, that, if ten thousand worlds had been my own, I would have freely parted with them all to have exchanged my condition with that of the meanest slave in my own country. When I looked round the ship too, and saw a large furnace of copper boiling, and a multitude of black people of every description chained together, every one of their countenances expressing dejection and sorrow, I no longer doubted of my fate; and, quite overpowered with horror and anguish, I fell motionless on the deck and fainted. When I recovered a little, I found some black people about me, who I believed were some of those who brought me on board, and had been receiving their pay; they talked to me in order to cheer me, but all in vain. I asked them if we were not to be eaten by those white men with horrible looks, red faces, and long hair. They told me I was not; and one of the crew brought me a small portion of spirituous liquor in a wine-glass; but, being afraid of him, I would not take it out of his hand. One of the blacks therefore took it from him, and gave it to me, and I took a little down my palate, which, instead of reviving me, as they thought it would, threw me into the greatest consternation at the strange feeling it produced having never tasted any such liquor before. Soon after this, the blacks who brought me on board went off, and left me abandoned to despair. I now saw myself deprived of all chance of returning to my native country, or even the least glimpse of hope of gaining the shore, which I now considered as friendly; and I even wished for my former slavery, in preference to my present situation, which was filled with horrors of every kind, still heightened by my ignorance of what I was to undergo. I was not long suffered to indulge my grief; I was soon put down under the decks, and there I received such a salutation in my nostrils as I had never experienced in my life; so that, with the loathsomeness of the stench, and crying together, I became so sick and low that I was not able to eat, nor had I the least desire to taste any thing. I now wished for the last friend, death, to relieve me; but soon, to my grief, two of the white men offered me eatables; and, on my refusing to eat, one of them held me fast by the hands, and laid me across, I think, the windlass, and tied my feet while the other flogged me severely. I had never experienced any thing of this kind before; and, although not being used to the water, I naturally feared that element the first time I saw it; yet, nevertheless, could I have got over the nettings, I would have jumped over the side; but I could not; and, besides, the crew used to watch us very closely who were not chained down to the decks, lest we should leap into the water: and I have seen some of these poor African prisoners most severely cut for attempting to do so, and hourly whipped for not eating. This indeed was often the case with myself. In a little time after, amongst the poor chained men, I found some of my own nation, which in a small degree gave ease to my mind. I inquired of them what was to be done with us? they gave me to understand we were to be carried to these white people's country to work for them. I then was a little revived, and thought, if it were no worse than working, my situation was not so desperate: but still I feared I should be put to death, the white people looked and acted, as I thought, in so savage a manner; for I had never seen among any people such instances of brutal cruelty; and this not only shown towards us blacks, but also to some of the whites themselves. One white man in particular I saw, when we were permitted to be on deck, flogged[2] so unmercifully with a large rope near the foremast, that he died in consequence of it; and they tossed him over the side as they would have done a brute. This made me fear these people the more; and I expected nothing less than to be treated in the same manner. I could not help expressing my fears and apprehensions to some of my countrymen: I asked them if these people had no country, but lived in this hollow place the ship? they told me they did not, but came from a distant one. "Then," said I, "how comes it in all our country we never heard of them?" They told me, because they lived so very far off. I then asked, where were their women? had they any like themselves? I was told they had. "And why," said I, "do we not see them?" they answered, because they were left behind. I asked how the vessel could go? they told me they could not tell; but that there were cloth put upon the masts by the help of the ropes I saw, and then the vessel went on; and the white men had some spell or magic they put in the water when they liked in order to stop the vessel. I was exceedingly amazed at this account, and really thought they were spirits. I therefore wished much to be from amongst them, for I expected they would sacrifice me: but my wishes were

---

2. Such brutal floggings were at this time considered essential to the maintenance of discipline in the British navy and on ships engaged in the slave trade.

vain; for we were so quartered that it was impossible for any of us to make our escape. While we stayed on the coast I was mostly on deck; and one day, to my great astonishment, I saw one of these vessels coming in with the sails up. As soon as the whites saw it, they gave a great shout, at which we were amazed; and the more so as the vessel appeared larger by approaching nearer. At last she came to an anchor in my sight, and when the anchor was let go, I and my countrymen who saw it were lost in astonishment to observe the vessel stop; and were now convinced it was done by magic. Soon after this the other ship got her boats out, and they came on board of us, and the people of both ships seemed very glad to see each other. Several of the strangers also shook hands with us black people, and made motions with their hands, signifying, I suppose, we were to go to their country; but we did not understand them. At last, when the ship we were in had got in all her cargo, they made ready with many fearful noises, and we were all put under deck, so that we could not see how they managed the vessel. But this disappointment was the least of my sorrow. The stench of the hold while we were on the coast was so intolerably loathsome, that it was dangerous to remain there for any time, and some of us had been permitted to stay on the deck for the fresh air; but now that the whole ship's cargo were confined together, it became absolutely pestilential. The closeness of the place, and the heat of the climate, added to the number in the ship, which was so crowded that each had scarcely room to turn himself, almost suffocated us. This produced copious perspirations, so that the air soon became unfit for respiration, from a variety of loathsome smells, and brought on a sickness amongst the slaves, of which many died, thus falling victims to the improvident avarice, as I may call it, of their purchasers. This wretched situation was again aggravated by the galling of the chains, now become insupportable; and the filth of the necessary tubs, into which the children often fell, and were almost suffocated. The shrieks of the women, and the groans of the dying, rendered the whole a scene of horror almost inconceivable. Happily perhaps for myself I was soon reduced so low here that it was thought necessary to keep me almost always on deck; and from my extreme youth I was not put in fetters. In this situation I expected every hour to share the fate of my companions, some of whom were almost daily brought upon deck at the point of death, which I began to hope would soon put an end to my miseries. Often did I think many of the inhabitants of the deep much more happy than myself; I envied them the freedom they enjoyed, and as often wished I could change my condition for theirs. Every circumstance I met with served only to render my state more painful, and heighten my apprehensions and my opinion of the cruelty of the whites. One day they had taken a number of fishes; and when they had killed and satisfied themselves with as many as they thought fit, to our astonishment who were on the deck, rather than give any of them to us to eat, as we expected, they tossed the remaining fish into the sea again, although we begged and prayed for some as well as we could, but in vain; and some of my countrymen, being pressed by hunger, took an opportunity, when they thought no one saw them, of trying to get a little privately; but they were discovered, and the attempt procured them some very severe floggings.

One day, when we had a smooth sea, and moderate wind, two of my wearied countrymen, who were chained together (I was near them at the time), preferring death to such a life of misery, somehow made through the nettings, and jumped into the sea; immediately another quite dejected fellow, who, on account of his illness, was suffered to be out of irons, also followed their example; and I believe many more would very soon have done the same, if they had not been prevented by the ship's crew, who were instantly alarmed. Those of us that were the most active were in a moment put down under the deck; and there was such a noise and confusion amongst the people of the ship as I never heard before, to stop her, and get the boat out to go after the slaves. However, two of the wretches were drowned, but they got the other, and afterwards flogged him unmercifully, for thus attempting to prefer death to slavery. In this manner we continued to undergo more hardships than I can now relate; hardships which are inseparable from this accursed trade. Many a time we were near suffocation, from the want of fresh air, which we were often without for whole days together. This, and the stench of the necessary tubs, carried off many. During our passage I first saw flying fishes, which surprised me very much: they used frequently to fly across the ship, and many of them fell on the deck. I also now first saw the use of the quadrant. I had often with astonishment seen the mariners make observations with it, and I could not think what it meant. They at last took notice of my surprise; and one of them, willing to increase it, as well as to gratify my curiosity, made me one day look through it. The clouds appeared to me to be land, which disappeared as they passed along. This heightened my wonder: and I was now more persuaded than ever that I was in another world, and that every thing about me was magic. At last, we came in sight of the island of Barbadoes, at which the whites on board gave a great shout, and made many signs of joy to us. We did not know what to think of this; but, as the vessel drew nearer, we plainly saw the harbour, and other ships of different kinds and sizes: and we soon anchored amongst them off Bridge Town. Many merchants and planters now come on board, though it was in the evening. They put us in separate parcels, and examined us attentively. They also made us jump, and pointed to the land, signifying we were to go there. We thought by this we should be eaten by these ugly men, as they appeared to us; and when, soon after we were all put down under the deck again, there was much dread and trembling among us, and nothing but bitter cries to be heard all the night from these apprehensions, insomuch that at last the white people got some old slaves from the land to pacify us. They told us we were not to be eaten, but to work, and were soon to go on land where we should see many of our country people. This report eased us much; and sure enough, soon after we landed, there came to us Africans of all languages. We were conducted immediately to the merchant's yard, where we were all pent up together like so many sheep in a fold, without regard to sex or age. As every object was new to me, everything I saw filled me with surprise. What struck me first was, that the houses were built with bricks, in stories, and in every other respect different from those I have seen in Africa: but I was still more astonished on seeing people on horseback. I did not know what this could mean; and indeed I thought these people were full of nothing but magical arts. While I was in this astonishment, one of my fellow prisoners spoke to a countryman of his about the horses, who said they were the same kind they had in their country. I understood them, though they were from a distant part of Africa, and I thought it odd I had not seen any horses there; but afterwards, when I came to converse with different Africans, I found they had many horses amongst them, and much larger than those I then saw. We were not many days in the merchant's custody, before we were sold after their usual manner, which is this: on a signal given (as the beat of a drum), the buyers rush at once into the yard where the slaves are confined, and make choice of that parcel they like best. The noise and clamour with which this is attended, and the eagerness visible in the countenances of the buyers, serve not a little to increase the apprehension of the terrified Africans, who may well be supposed to consider them as the ministers of that destruction to which they think themselves devoted. In this manner, without scruple, are relations and friends separated, most of them never to see each other again. I remember in the vessel in which I was brought over, in the men's apartment, there were several brothers who, in the sale, were sold in different lots; and it was very moving on this occasion to see and hear their cries at parting. O, ye nominal Christians! might not an African ask you, learned you this from your God? who says unto you, Do unto all men as you would men should do unto you. Is it not enough that we are torn from our country and friends to toil for your luxury and lust of gain? Must every tender feeling be likewise sacrificed to your avarice? Are the dearest friends and relations, now rendered more dear by their separation from their kindred, still to be parted from each other, and thus preventing from cheering the gloom of slavery with the small comfort of being together, and mingling their sufferings and sorrows? Why are parents to love their children, brothers their sisters, or husbands their wives? Surely this is a new refinement in cruelty, which, while it has no advantage to atone for it, thus aggravates distress, and adds fresh horrors even to the wretchedness of slavery.

CHAPTER THREE

Commerce, Colonies, and Converts in Southeast Asia

8. THE EXPANSION OF ISLAM

Jerry H. Bentley

By 1500 Islam had lost its footing in Spain but was advancing in eastern Europe and Southeast Asia. In this selection, a modern historian explains why Islamic expansion was so successful. How did Islam win converts, even among Christians? What explains the success of Islam in Melaka (on the Malay peninsula)?

While Chinese fleets reconnoitered the Indian Ocean under imperial auspices, the house of Islam continued to expand as a result of both state policies and commercial relationships. In Spain, the *reconquista* gradually but relentlessly pressured the Muslim kingdom of Granada toward its final collapse in 1492. Elsewhere, however, the realm of Islam stretched its boundaries, even in Europe. The Ottoman Turks consolidated the Islamic conquest of Anatolia and used the resulting momentum to expand into Egypt, the Balkans, and eastern Europe as far as Hungary. In India, Islam spread more slowly, but there too Muslim rulers strengthened their positions especially in the Sind, Gujarat, and Bengal. In all these lands, Islam became established largely by a continuing process of conversion induced by political, social, and economic pressures, as Turkish rulers and conquerors provided official sponsorship and support of their faith.

Several contemporary accounts by travelers to these regions illustrate pressures brought on nonbelievers to convert to Islam if they sojourned for very long in these lands. Johann Schiltberger, for example, who fell captive at the battle of Nicopolis (1396), left an account describing his experiences during almost thirty years in Ottoman service. Schiltberger despised Islam, which he called a "wicked religion," and he himself resisted continuous pressure to abandon his native faith in its favor. Yet it seems that conversions to Islam were by no means uncommon: Schiltberger described an elaborate ritual that he said registered an individual's conversion from Christianity to Islam. The convert publicly recognized Allah as God and Muhammad as his messenger, then received new clothes and participated in a parade of celebration. Poor converts also received large gifts of money as inducements to conversion. Schiltberger's experience shows that it was possible to rebuff the pressures and resist the temptations to convert to Islam. Indeed, after years of planning, he ultimately escaped captivity and returned to his native Bavaria.

Others, however, felt greater pressure to join the cultural majority. The Russian merchant Athanasius Nikitin visited Arabia, Persia, and India in the late fifteenth century. About the time of his fourth Easter away from home, he composed an account of his travels and experiences. Despite intense pressure to convert, he reported that he had diligently observed Christian holy days—but he frankly admitted that he did not know how much longer he could refrain from apostasy. The Italian merchant Niccolò Conti ultimately succumbed to pressures to convert. His case became quite well known because he sought absolution for his apostasy from Pope Eugenius IV, and his story intrigued Poggio Bracciolini, the famous humanist and papal secretary, who wrote an account of it in his widely read work on fortune. Conti had begun his mercantile career in Damascus, where he learned some Arabic; later he traveled to Persia, India, and Sumatra, among other places. On his return trip to Europe, he passed through Egypt, where he faced such intense pressure that he renounced Christianity and accepted Islam. In seeking absolution, he explained that he took this step out of fear and concern for his wife and two children, who had accompanied him on all his travels. Niccolò eventually returned safely to Italy, but his wife and children perished at Cairo in an outbreak of the plague.

Despite the different attitudes and experiences of the authors, all of these accounts throw some light on the process of conversion induced by political, social, and economic pressures. All make it clear that in Islamic lands there was abundant opportunity and considerable incentive for Christians to renounce their faith and convert to Islam. It was possible to retain another faith—but also difficult, especially over a long term, in the absence of regular services and communication with cultural authorities. It certainly required more than usual discipline and determination to resist the various pressures and inducements to accept Islam. Meanwhile, formal acceptance of Islam, for whatever reason, was an event common enough that established rituals and ceremonies marked its occurrence.

Surviving western accounts reflect the experiences of those who resisted Islam to a far greater degree than those who converted. The autobiography of Anselmo Turmeda stands as a rather lonely witness to the fact that Christians sometimes voluntarily converted to Islam. Turmeda was a Franciscan from Mallorca who studied theology at Lérida and Bologna. According to his account, his conversion came after a discussion of New Testament passages concerning the paraclete, who Jesus promised would come in the future and comfort his flock (John 14:16–17, 14:26, 15:26, 16:7–14). Christians identified this comforter as the Holy Spirit, but Islamic theologians had held since the eighth century that the paraclete was none other than Muhammad. Modern scholars have suggested that Turmeda might well have had other reasons for turning to Islam: disillusionment with the decadence of the late medieval church, desire to escape punishment for political activites, or evasion of the Inquisition, since it is possible that he came from a Jewish family. In any case, he made his way to Tunis about 1386, publicly renounced Christianity, and converted to Islam. The sultan showered him with gold dinars and provided him with a new set of clothes, a post as customs official, and a wife, by whom he had a son. About 1420 he composed a work that offered a brief autobiography with an account of his conversion, a history of the sultans at Tunis, and a lengthy attack on Christianity.

How many other medieval Europeans abandoned Christianity and turned to Islam? Their numbers and experiences are lost to history, although it is certainly safe to say that Turmeda was not the only Christian who found opportunities to pursue in the house of Islam. In any case, Turmeda's experience demonstrates that conversion to Islam was a practical alternative for Christians at odds with their inherited society and culture.

The western regions of the Islamic world thus played host to cross-cultural encounters of some intensity, but equally dramatic developments took place as Islam established an enduring presence in southeast Asia. Gujarati merchants had already introduced their faith into the trading centers of Sumatra at least by the thirteenth century, but only in the fifteenth century did Islam gain expansive momentum in southeast Asia. As in other lands where merchants introduced foreign cultural and religious traditions, a process of conversion through voluntary association promoted the expansion of Islam in southeast Asia. The rapid spread of the faith had much to do with the rise of Melaka as the principal entrepôt of southeast Asia. Since a variety of source materials survive to illuminate the development of Melaka, its experience bears investigation.

The origins of Melaka trace to the late fourteenth century and the actions of Paramesvara, a prince of the Hindu trading state at Palembang. During the 1390s, Paramesvara mounted a rebellion at Palembang but had to flee his homeland when the uprising failed. He went to a point near modern Singapore on the Malay peninsula, where he killed the local ruler, a vassal of the king of Siam, and usurped his position. Later he moved up the coast with a band of seaborne retainers and established his presence at Melaka. The early rulers sent out fleets that forced trading vessels to call at Melaka and pay duties there; meanwhile, they either conquered neighboring states or established alliances with them, so that they controlled an increasingly large portion of trade passing through southeast Asian waters. As a result of these policies, Melaka had become a bustling port already by 1403, and it grew rapidly for the next century and more. When the Portuguese conquered the city in

1511, its population approached fifty thousand, and the Portuguese merchant Tomé Pires reported that eighty-four languages could be heard in Melakan streets.

The rapid development of Melaka strongly favored the expansion of Islam in southeast Asia. The rulers of Melaka had tense relations with the Buddhist kingdom of Siam, prompting them to seek external support for their rule. Paramesvara and his two successors each journeyed to the Ming court in order to establish and maintain a Chinese alliance. Meanwhile, they also made common cause with the region's increasingly prominent Muslim traders, who themselves had difficult dealings with Buddhist Siam. As the Muslim community grew in Melaka, *qadis, mullahs,* Sufis, and other cultural authorities joined the merchants there. By the middle of the fifteenth century, Melaka had become a center of Islamic studies and a source of missionaries who worked to spread Islam throughout southeast Asia.

The concentrated presence of Muslims brought political repercussions also in the Melakan ruling class. During his reign, Paramesvara maintained his court on the outskirts of Melaka. He had few dealings with foreigners, but entrusted administration of Melaka to his son. When he assumed the throne in his own right, the son moved his court to the city center of Melaka, converted to Islam, and took a new name, Megat Iskandar Shah. It looks as though Iskandar Shah underwent a classic case of voluntary conversion—one that associated his rule with the traditions and values of the larger world of Islam but that did not necessarily indicate rejection of his inherited culture. Instead, Iskandar Shah and later Muslim rulers of Melaka continued to observe the Hindu and Buddhist traditions that they had brought with them from Palembang. They retained Hindu and Buddhist ceremonials at court, and they relied on the political traditions of Srivijaya to legitimize their rule. Indeed, they never completely abandoned the idea of returning to rule in their ancestral homeland.

The term *conversion through voluntary association* suggests a calculated and somewhat cerebral process, but the experience of Melaka shows that it could lead to considerable internal tension and even violence in communities where it took effect. Before the conversion of Iskandar Shah, elites at Melaka fell into one of two classes: the Malay ruling nobility and the wealthy Muslim merchants. After his conversion, the ruling house itself divided into two camps: those favoring retention of Hindu and Buddhist traditions and those accepting Islam as a cultural foundation for commercial and political alliances. The resulting tensions came to a head in 1445, when the regent for the third ruler of Melaka attempted to stage a reaction in favor of the Hundu and Buddhist traditions. His efforts not only failed but provoked a coup organized by the Islamic faction at court. The coup ended with the victory of Muzaffir Shah, who consolidated his hold on Melaka, established Islam as the state religion, and based his rule on Islamic principles. He then proceeded to extend Melakan influence throughout the region, seize control of the Strait of Singapore, conquer and convert rulers in both the Malay peninsula and Sumatra. As a result of these achievements, Muzaffir Shah's fame spread widely—he became well known as far away as China, India, and Arabia—and he became the first of Melaka's rulers recognized throughout the Islamic world as sultan.

As in other lands, the voluntary conversion of elites facilitated the establishment of Islam at all levels of Melakan and southeast Asian society. The elites themselves served as links between the established local society and the larger world of the Indian Ocean basin, but they also served as conduits through which Islam could enter the local society. Following the conversion of elites, Muslim *qadis* and teachers became increasingly influential as cultural authorities in southeast Asian courts and cities. Meanwhile, Indian Sufis, organized in trade guilds, spread their faith on a more popular level: thanks to their doctrinal flexibility, the Sufis built bridges between the established and the new cultural traditions by absorbing Malay pantheism and animism into Islamic mysticism.

This observation points up the survival of indigenous cultural traditions and the significance of syncretism: as elsewhere, conversion to Islam in southeast Asia resulted not in the extinction of an established cultural tradition and its replacement by another but, rather, in a syncretic blend of cultural alternatives. Shadow plays continued to represent episodes from the Hindu epics, and incantations to Siva and Visnu survived alongside prayers to Allah. Indeed, in some cases ritual Hindu incantations were baptized by the simple addition of the Islamic confession of faith as a conclusion. Not until the eighteenth century did cultural and political authorities undertake zealously to root out pre-Islamic cultural elements and to enforce a more orthodox Islamic faith in southeast Asia.

Meanwhile, though, the house of Islam clearly displayed its potential for further expansion during the fifteenth century. Whether by means of conquest and conversion induced by pressure, as in Anatolia and eastern Europe, or through trade and voluntary conversion, as in southeast Asia, the Islamic community continued to grow rapidly. By century's end, as mosques began to dominate urban landscapes in Java, Sumatra, and the Malay peninsula, the faith had made its first appearance in the Moluccan Islands and even in the southern Philippines. Indeed, on the basis of cultural developments in the preceding five centuries, an impartial observer in the year 1500 might well have predicted that Islam would soon become the world's dominant faith, its principal source of beliefs, values, culture, and human consciousness.

9. CHRISTIAN AND MUSLIM COMMERCE

Mendes Pinto

Mendes Pinto was a Portuguese trader and adventurer who traveled from Portuguese Africa to South Asia, China, and Japan between 1537 and 1558. This selection from his Travels *(one of the most popular books in Europe in the early 1600s) describes some of his activities. The account begins with a voyage up the east coast of the Malay peninsula in what is today Thailand. Notice there are at least three political powers in the area: the Buddhist kingdom of Siam, Muslim Malacca [Melaka], and the Portuguese. How are these three powers similar and different? What is the relationship between trade and political power in Southeast Asia? What does this selection tell you about the role of women in Southeast Asian trade? What is the relationship between trade and piracy? How important are religious differences in these trading conflicts?*

I had been here in Patani for twenty-six days and had just finished expediting a small cargo of goods from China in preparation for my return, when a foist arrived from Malacca. Her captain was a certain Antonio de Faria e Sousa who had been sent there by Pero de Faria to discuss some business with the king as well as to renew the peace treaty he had long maintained with Malacca, and to thank him for the good treatment the Portuguese were getting from him in his kingdom, plus a few other things of that sort designed to build up friendly relations that were of vital importance to our trade, which, frankly speaking, was our chief concern at the time. However, our real intentions were masked by a letter, delivered under the guise of an embassy, along with a costly gift, presented in the name of His Majesty the king and purchased at the expense of his treasury, as is the custom with all the captains in those parts of Asia.

This Antonio de Faria arrived with a cargo of Indian calicoes that were worth about ten or twelve thousand *cruzados*, which he had borrowed in Malacca; but since there was so little demand for them locally, not a single offer came his way. In desperate straits, with hardly any prospects in view, he decided to lay up for the winter and try his best, some way or other, to dispose of them. Some longtime residents in the area advised him to send the goods to *Lugor*, a rich, heavily trafficked seaport in Siam,* a hundred leagues to the north, that was always crowded with junks from the island of Java and from the ports of *Laué, Tanjampura,*

*Modern Nakhon Sri Thammarit, on the east coast of the Malay peninsula, on the Gulf of Siam.

Japara, Demak, Panaruca, Sidayo, Pasuruan, Solor, and Borneo, because they usually paid well there, in gold and precious stones, for that kind of merchandise.

Acting promptly on this advice, which he found to his liking, Antonio de Faria made arrangements to send a local vessel up there because the foist he had come on was not suitable for that purpose, and as his agent he chose a Cristóvão Borralho, who was a good businessman. He was joined by a group of sixteen other men, both merchants and soldiers, who had goods to sell, all of whom went along expecting to turn over a profit of at least six or seven hundred percent, not only on what they were taking with them, but on what they would be returning with as well. And poor me, I happened to be one of them.

Departing from here on a Saturday morning, we navigated all the way along the coast under fair winds, and on the following Thursday morning, we arrived at the bar of *Lugor*. We dropped anchor at the mouth of the river and remained there for the rest of the day, making detailed inquiries that were important, not only for the sale of the merchandise, but for our own personal safety as well. And the news we heard was good, for we found out that the market was so favorable that we could easily expect to make a profit of almost 600 percent. As for the rest, ample security was provided for all, along with free port privileges and customs exemptions that were to remain in effect for the entire month of September, as decreed by the king of Siam for the period of the royal *zumbaias*. But in order to appreciate what this is all about, some explanation is called for.

There is a great king who rules over the entire coastal region and interior of Malaysia. Of all his titles, the one by which he is best known is *Prechau Saleu*, emperor of all the *Sornau*, which is a province comprising thirteen separate kingdoms, otherwise known as Siam. Subject to him are fourteen lesser kings who are required to pay him tribute every year. According to ancient custom, they were forced to make an annual journey to the city of Ayuthia [Ayudhya], capital of the *Sornau* empire and kingdom of Siam, in order to deliver the required tribute personally and perform the *zumbaia*, a ceremony that consists of kissing the sword at his side. Since this city is fifty leagues inland and is accessible only by a rapidly flowing river, it was not unusual for these petty kings to be left stranded for the entire winter, entailing vast expenditures for them. As a result, the fourteen kings got together and petitioned the *prechau*, king of Siam, to relieve them of such an onerous burden and to find a less costly method of paying the tribute. He responded with a decree to the effect that a viceroy, called *poyho* in their language, should represent him in the city of *Lugor*, and that every three years the fourteen kings should pay homage to him in person, as they had done formerly to the emperor himself, and deliver to him in one lump sum the total tribute assessed for the three-year period. Moreover, during the month in which they came to pay homage, they were to be granted customs exemptions on all their goods, the same privilege being extended to all other merchants entering or leaving the harbor, whether native or foreign.

And since the duty-free regulations were in effect at the time we arrived, as I said before, the city was so crowded with merchants from everywhere that it was said that well over fifteen hundred richly laden vessels had entered the harbor with an enormous variety of cargo from many different places. That was the news we heard when we anchored in the mouth of the river, and we were all so happy and excited about it that we decided to enter the river as soon as the sea breeze shifted.

But it was our misfortune, sinners that we were, that what we had been looking forward to with such great anticipation, never came to pass, for shortly before ten o'clock, just as we were sitting down to dinner, with the hawser [mooring rope] at short stay and everything made ready for us to sail when we had finished eating, we saw a huge junk coming out of the river with only her foresail and mizzen set. As she came alongside, she dropped anchor a little to windward of us, but once they had anchored, it did not take them long to notice that we were Portuguese, that there were very few of us, and that our ship was very small. They slackened their lines, letting the junk drift till it lay on our starboard, and as soon as it was even with our bow, they threw out a pair of grappling hooks attached to two very long iron chains, dragging us alongside; and since their ship was much larger than ours, we lay aboard, held fast beneath the curve of their prow, right below the hawse.

Then, about seventy or eighty Moors,* including some Turks, came bursting out of the deckhouse where they had been hiding, screaming widly and hurling stones, javelins, lances, and spears in such profusion that it looked like rain from heaven; and in less time than it takes to recite the Credo, twelve out of the sixteen Portuguese on board were dead, as well as thirty-six of the slaves and sailors. Four of us escaped by plunging into the sea, where one drowned immediately, but the three remaining survivors managed to reach the shore and take cover in the jungle, all battered and bruised, and sinking in mud up to our waists.

The Moors on the junk quickly boarded our ship and finished off six or seven of the boys they found lying wounded on deck, sparing none. Working rapidly, they transferred all the cargo they could find to their junk, then smashed a huge hole in the side of our ship, sending it to the bottom; next, they cut the grappling irons they had secured us with, clapped on all sail and quickly sped away out of fear of being discovered.

*Referred to Muslims or Africans.—Ed.

LADY OF THE SWAMP

Finding ourselves wounded and destitute, the three of us who survived the disaster suddenly broke down and cried; and we began hitting ourselves like madmen, for we nearly went out of our minds at the thought of what we had witnessed less than half an hour before. We carried on that way for the rest of the day, and having noticed that the terrain all around us was swampy and teeming with lizards and snakes, we decided that we had better stay there for the night also, which we spent almost shoulder deep in the slime.

At daybreak the next morning we followed the river until we came to a small tributary which we were afraid to cross, not only because it was too deep but also because it was swarming with lizards. And so another night went by in agony, which continued unabated for five more days without our being able to make any progress either backwards or forwards, for no matter which way we turned we encountered nothing but swamp and tall grass. It was about this time that one of our companions died, a rich, honorable man by the name of Bastião Henriques, who had lost eight thousand *cruzados* on the *lanchara*. And the two remaining companions, Cristóvão Borralho and I, broke down and cried over his half-buried body, too exhausted to speak, yet fully determined to spend what we thought were our last few hours of life right there, without moving from the edge of the river.

The following day, the seventh since our misfortune, just before sundown we saw a barge laden with salt, coming up the river by oar. As it came alongside, we asked the rowers on bended knee to please take us on board. They stopped and stared for a moment, amazed by the sight of us there on our knees with upraised arms, as though we were praying. Without a word they made as if to move off, throwing us into a panic. We both started shouting, and with the tears streaming down our cheeks we pleaded with them again not to leave us there to die. Upon hearing our cries, a woman came out from under the awning. She was somewhat advanced in years and appeared to be as kindly and noble a person as indeed she later turned out to be. She was moved to pity by our plight the moment she saw us there displaying our wounds. Acting in compassion, she reached for a pole and brought the barge nearer to shore, cracking it three or four times over the backs of the sailors for refusing to help; after which, six of them jumped ashore and carried us aboard on their shoulders. Appalled by our condition and the extent of our wounds, with our shirts and trousers all muddied and bloodied, this noble woman saw to it that we were promptly washed with many buckets of water, and that each of us received one of her sarongs to cover ourselves with in the meantime; and then she made us sit down beside her while she sent for food, which she herself placed in front of us.

"Come now, eat, eat up, you poor strangers," she urged us, "and do not despair at finding yourselves in such a sad state. Look at me. Here I am, a woman, barely fifty years of age, and less than six years ago I found myself suddenly taken captive, robbed of a personal fortune worth over 100,000 *cruzados*, and stricken by the death of three sons; and I saw my husband, who was dearer to me than life itself, and my whole family—father and sons, two brothers, and son-in-law—all torn to pieces in front of my eyes by the trunks of the elephants of the king of Siam. Though sick at heart and weary of life, I endured all these misfortunes and many others almost as bad when, in the same manner, I saw three virgin daughters, my mother and father, and thirty-two members of my family—nephews, nieces, and cousins—thrown alive into flaming ovens, uttering screams to pierce the very gates of heaven, calling on God to avail them in that hour of unbearable pain and torment. But I had committed too many sins for their cries to be heard in the court of His infinite mercy, and the Lord of Lords turned a deaf ear to what I thought were their just pleas; but the truth is that whatsoever God ordains is the best for us and we must accept it."

We responded to this by telling her that it was because we too had sinned that God had permitted this calamity to befall us.

"In the face of adversity," she said, mingling her tears with ours, "when we feel the hand of the Lord, it is always best to acknowledge the reason for it and to confess to the truth of it with our own mouths; but you must believe it sincerely, deep down in your heart, with a pure and steadfast faith; for therein often lies the reward for our suffering."

And after speaking in this manner for a while, she asked us how our misfortune had come about and what had occurred to bring us to such a sorry pass. We told her everything that had happened but that we did not know who had done it to us or why. Hearing this, some of the men in her crew volunteered the information that the huge junk we were talking about belonged to a Gujerati Moor [Indian Muslim] by the name of *Khoja* Hassim, who had sailed out of the river that morning, bound for Hainan with a cargo of brazilwood.

"Well, strike me dead, if that isn't so!" this dignified woman exclaimed, beating her breast in amazement, "because that same Moor has been heard boasting in public to all who would listen that he had slain quite a number of those men from Malacca on several different occasions, and that he hated them with such a passion that he had vowed to his Mohammed that he would yet kill as many more."

Astounded by such unheard-of news we asked her to tell us more about this man and why he went around telling everyone that he hated us so. As for the reason why, she said that all she knew was that she had once heard him say that a great captain of ours by the name of Heitor da Silveira had killed his father and two of his brothers on a *nao* he had captured in the Straits of Mecca, that was bound from Jidda to Dabul. And for the rest of the journey she continued talking about the Moor, going into great detail about the deep hatred he had for us and the terrible things he said about us.

ANTONIO DE FARIA SWEARS VENGEANCE

Departing from where she had found us, this honorable woman proceeded up the river under sail and oar for about two leagues, stopping overnight at a little village; and early the next morning she departed for the city of *Lugor,* five leagues further, arriving close to midday. After landing, she went straight to her house where she took us and kept us for twenty-three days, nursing us back to health and providing for all our needs with the utmost generosity.

This woman was a member of a distinguished family, as we learned later, and the widow of the *shahbandar* of *Prevedim* who, in 1538, in the city of *Banchá,* had been slain by the *pate* of *Lasapará,* king of *Quaijuão,* on the island of Java; and at the time she rescued us in the manner described, she was returning from a junk she owned that was anchored outside the bar, laden with salt; and since it was too heavy a vessel to cross the sandbank, she had been unloading it little by little onto the river barge.

And at the end of the twenty-three days I referred to, when, with God's help, we had recovered completely and were well enough to travel, she recommended us to a kinsman of hers, a merchant bound [south] for Patani, about eighty-five leagues from there, who took us aboard the oar-propelled *calaluz* that he himself was traveling on, and seven days later we reached Patani, after navigating along a wide, freshwater river called *Sumèhitão.* And since Antonio de Faria was searching the horizon, watching and waiting for us or for some word of his merchandise, as soon as he saw us and heard what had happened he was so upset that it was more than half an hour before he could speak.

By this time our lodgings could not hold all the Portuguese who came crowding in, most of whom had invested their money on the ill-fated *lanchara* that had been carrying a cargo worth more than sixty thousand *cruzados* in her hold, the bulk of it in the form of minted silver to be traded for gold. And when some well-meaning people there tried to console him for the loss of the twelve thousand *cruzados* he had borrowed in Malacca, Antonio de Faria, who had been left destitute, replied quite candidly that he did not dare to face his creditors in Malacca for fear that they would force him to honor the notes he had signed, which he was in no position to do at the time, and that it made more sense to him to go after the ones who had stolen his money than be in default with the ones who had lent it to him. And right then and there, in front of everyone, he swore on the holy Gospels, and said that, apart from the oath he was taking, he was also promising God that he would immediately go in search of the thief who had stolen his property and make him pay dearly one way or another, by fair means or foul, though he felt that fair play alone was too good for someone like that who had murdered sixteen of his Portuguese soldiers as well as thirty-six of the Christian slaves and sailors, and that it would not be right to let him off so easily without some kind of punishment, for otherwise, with each passing day we would see another atrocity of the same sort, and then another, and so on, until a hundred had been committed.

All the bystanders praised him highly for the stand he had taken, and a lot of young men, and good soldiers too, offered him their services, and still others offered to lend him money to buy arms and whatever else he needed. He immediately accepted all the offers made by his friends and went about making preparations as fast as he could; and within eighteen days he had enlisted a company of fifty-five soldiers.

As for poor me, I was forced to join him too, because I had not a farthing to my name, nor anyone who would so much as give me or lend me one; besides, I owed more than five hundred *cruzados* to some friends in Malacca, which together with five hundred of my own had been carried off—for my sins—by that dog, in one fell swoop, with the rest of the stolen booty mentioned above; and out of it all, the only thing I was able to save was my skin, and even that was in not too good a shape after having received three spear wounds and the blow of a stone to the head, which had left me hovering between life and death three or four times; and even here in Patani I still had to have a bone removed before I recovered completely. As for my companion Cristóvão Borralho, he was in far worse condition than I from an equal number of wounds he had received in return for the twenty-five hundred *cruzados* that were stolen from him along with the rest.

10. XAVIER'S LETTER
FROM INDIA

Saint Francis Xavier (1506–52) was one of the original members of the Society of Jesus, or the Jesuits, founded by Saint Ignatius of Loyola (1491–1556) in 1534. Sent by Loyola as a missionary to the Portuguese empire in Asia in 1541, Xavier was the first to introduce the Western world including Christianity to many people in India, Malacca [Melaka], and Japan. This selection is from a letter that Xavier sent to Loyola from India, probably in 1549. How extensive were the Jesuit missions in Asia by 1549? How suc-

*cessful had they been? What obstacles to the spread of Christianity did
Xavier face in India and Southeast Asia?*

My own and only Father in the Heart of Christ, I think that the many
letters from this place which have lately been sent to Rome will inform
you how prosperously the affairs of religion go on in these parts,
through your prayers and the good bounty of God. But there seem to be
certain things which I ought myself to speak about to you; so I will just
touch on a few points relating to these parts of the world which are so
distant from Rome. In the first place, the whole race of the Indians, as
far as I have been able to see, is very barbarous; and it does not like to
listen to anything that is not agreeable to its own manners and customs,
which, as I say, are barbarous. It troubles itself very little to learn anything about divine things and things which concern salvation. Most of
the Indians are of vicious disposition, and are adverse to virtue. Their
instability, levity, and inconstancy of mind are incredible; they have
hardly any honesty, so inveterate are their habits of sin and cheating. We
have hard work here, both in keeping the Christians up the mark and in
converting the heathen. And, as we are your children, it is fair that on
this account you should take great care of us and help us continually by
your prayers to God. You know very well what a hard business it is to
teach people who neither have any knowledge of God nor follow reason,
but think it a strange and intolerable thing to be told to give up their
habits of sin, which have now gained all the force of nature by long
possession. . . .

The experience which I have of these countries makes me think that I
can affirm with truth, that there is no prospect of perpetuating our
Society out here by means of the natives themselves, and that the Christian religion will hardly survive us who are now in the country; so that it
is quite necessary that continual supplies of ours should be sent out from
Europe. We have now some of the Society in all parts of India where
there are Christians. Four are in the Moluccas, two at Malacca, six in the
Comorin Promontory, two at Coulan, as many at Bazain, four at Socotra.
The distances between these places are immense; for instance, the
Moluccas are more than a thousand leagues from Goa, Malacca five
hundred, Cape Comorin two hundred, Coulan one hundred and twenty,
Bazain sixty, and Socotra three hundred. In each place there is one of the
Society who is Superior of the rest. As these Superiors are men of re-
markable prudence and virtue, the others are very well content.

The Portuguese in these countries are masters only of the sea and of
the coast. On the mainland they have only the towns in which they live.
The natives themselves are so enormously addicted to vice as to be little
adapted to receive the Christian religion. They so dislike it that it is most
difficult to get them to hear us if we begin to preach about it, and they
think it like death to be asked to become Christians. So for the present we

devote ourselves to keeping the Christians whom we have. Certainly, if the Portuguese were more remarkable for their kindness to the new converts, a great number would become Christians; as it is, the heathen see that the converts are despised and looked down upon by the Portuguese, and so, as is natural, they are unwilling to become converts themselves. For all these reasons there is no need for me to labour in these countries, and as I have learnt from good authorities that there is a country near China called Japan, the inhabitants of which are all heathen, quite untouched by Mussulmans or Jews, and very eager to learn what they do not know both in things divine and things natural, I have determined to go thither as soon as I can. . . .

11. COMMERCE AND GENDER IN SOUTHEAST ASIA

Anthony Reid

This selection is from a modern historian's study of Southeast Asia between 1450 and 1680. The Southeast Asian culture Reid found was different from the neighboring cultures of India and China and had not been completely changed by the successive waves of Buddhist, Muslim, and Christian missionaries. Here, the author discusses distinctive Southeast Asian cultural traditions regarding sexual relations and the role of women. What are some of these traditions? How and why did Vietnam depart from this pattern? How would a Christian missionary like Saint Francis Xavier respond to this culture? What evidence do you see here (and in other readings) of the role of women in Southeast Asian commerce? What institutions have empowered women, and what institutions have limited them in Southeast Asia?

SEXUAL RELATIONS

Relations between the sexes represented one aspect of the social system in which a distinctive Southeast Asian pattern was especially evident. Even the gradual strengthening of the influence of Islam, Christianity, Buddhism, and Confucianism in their respective spheres over the last four centuries has by no means eliminated a common pattern of relatively high female autonomy and economic importance. In the sixteenth and seventeenth centuries the region probably represented one extreme of human experience on these issues. It would be wrong to say that women were *equal* to men—indeed, there were very few areas in which they competed directly. Women had different functions from men, but these included transplanting and harvesting rice, weaving, and marketing. Their reproductive role gave them magical and ritual powers which it was difficult for men to match. These factors may explain why the value of daughters was never questioned in Southeast Asia as it was in China, India, and the Middle East; on the contrary, [it was believed that] "the more daughters a man has, the richer he is."

Throughout Southeast Asia wealth passed from the male to the female side in marriage—the reverse of European dowry. Vietnam in modern times has been the exception to this pattern as to many others, because of the progressive imposition of the sternly patriarchal Confucian system beginning in the fifteenth century. Yet in southern Vietnam as late as the seventeenth century men continued what must have been an older Southeast Asian pattern, giving bride-wealth at marriage and even residing with the families of their brides.

To some early Christian missionaries the practice of paying bride-wealth was disapproved as a form of buying a wife. Although the terminology of the market was occasionally used in this as in other transactions, the practice of bride-wealth in fact demonstrated the high economic value of women and contributed to their autonomy. In contrast to the other major area of bride-price, Africa, where the wealth went to the bride's father and was eventually inherited through the male line, Southeast Asian women benefited directly from the system. Tomé Pires put it strongly for the Malays he knew [in 1515]: "The man must give the woman ten *tahil* and six *mas* of gold as dowry which must always be actually in her power." In other cases bride-wealth was paid to the bride's parents, who transferred some property to their daughter.

In sharp contrast to the Chinese pattern, the married couple more frequently resided in the wife's than in the husband's village. In Thailand, Burma, and Malaya that was the rule. Southeast Asian legal codes differed markedly from their supposed Indian or Chinese (in Vietnam) models in their common insistence that property be held jointly by the married couple and administered together. In inheritance all children had an equal claim regardless of sex, though favoured children or those caring for the aged might obtain a larger share. Islamic law, which required that sons receive double the inheritance of daughters, was never effectively implemented. The stern Chinese legal principle that wives had no say in the disposal of family property found its way into some nineteenth-century Vietnamese law codes, but never into Vietnamese practice.

The relative autonomy enjoyed by women extended to sexual relations. Southeast Asian literature of the period leaves us in little doubt that women took a very active part in courtship and lovemaking, and demanded as much as they gave by way of sexual and emotional gratification. The literature describes the physical attractiveness of male heroes and their appeal to women as enthusiastically as it does the reverse. One of the themes of classical Malay and Javanese literature is the physical attraction of such heroes as Panji and Hang Tuah: "If Hang Tuah passed, married women tore themselves from the embraces of their husbands so that they could go out and see him. . . ."

As usual, Chou Ta-kuan [in the 1200s] had a colourful way of describing the expectations the Cambodian women of his day had of their men. "If the husband is called away for more than ten days, the wife is apt to say, 'I am not a spirit; how am I supposed to sleep alone?' " The idea of the ever faithful wife left behind during her husband's travels was upheld in the pages of Indian-derived epics, but not in everyday life. At Javanese marriages, according to [Stamford] Raffles [in 1815], the groom was solemnly warned, "If you should happen to be absent from her for the space of seven months on shore, or one year at sea, without giving her any subsistence . . . your marriage shall be dissolved, if your wife desires it, without any further form or process." Vietnamese law as promulgated in the fifteenth century (once again diverging sharply from Chinese practice) set a similar period of five months' absence, or twelve months if the marriage had produced children.

The most graphic demonstration of the strong position women enjoyed in sexual matters was the painful surgery men endured on their penis to increase the erotic pleasure of women. Once again, this is a phenomenon whose dispersion throughout Southeast Asia is very striking, though it appears to be absent in other parts of the world. Although it is the Indian *Kama Sutra* which makes the earliest reference to such surgery, this probably refers to Southeast Asian practice. A careful recent survey of the ethnographic evidence suggests that the phenomenon may best be understood as a symptom of the power and autonomy enjoyed by Southeast Asian women. . . .

The most draconian surgery was the insertion of a metal pin, complemented by a variety of wheels, spurs, or studs, in the central and southern Philippines and parts of Borneo. Pigafetta [in 1524] was the first of the astonished Europeans to describe the practice:

The males, large and small, have their penis pierced from one side to the other near the head with a gold or tin bolt as large as a goose quill. In both ends of the same bolt some have what resembles a spur, with points upon the ends; others are like the head of a cart nail. I very often asked many, both old and young, to see their penis, because I could not credit it. In the middle of the bolt is a hole, through which they urinate. . . . They say their women wish it so, and that if they did otherwise they would not have communication with them. When the men wish to have communication with their women, the latter themselves take the penis not in the regular way and commence very gently to introduce it, with the spur on top first, and then the other part. When it is inside it takes its regular position; and thus the penis always stays inside until it gets soft, for otherwise they could not pull it out.

The same phenomenon is described by many others, in different Visayan islands and in Mindanao, who agree that its purpose was always explained as enhancing sexual pleasure, especially for the women. Some peoples of northwest Borneo, notably the Iban and the Kayan, continued this practice until modern times, and their oral tradition attributes its origins to a legendary woman who found sexual intercourse without such an aid less satisfying than masturbation.

The same result was obtained in other parts of Southeast Asia by the less painful but probably more delicate operation of inserting small balls or bells under the loose skin of the penis. The earliest report is from the Chinese Muslim Ma Huan [in 1433]. He reported that in Siam,

> when a man has attained his twentieth year, they take the skin which surrounds the *membrum virile,* and with a fine knife . . . they open it up and insert a dozen tin beads inside the skin; they close it up and protect it with medicinal herbs. . . . The beads look like a cluster of grapes. . . . If it is the king . . . or a great chief or a wealthy man, they use gold to make hollow beads, inside which a grain of sand is placed. . . . They make a tinkling sound, and this is regarded as beautiful.

Numerous European writers note the same phenomenon in Pegu during the fifteenth and sixteenth centuries, and Tomé Pires described it as a special feature of the Pegu men among all the varied traders visiting Melaka. "The Pegu lords wear as many as nine gold ones, with beautiful trebble, contralto and tenor tones, the size of the Alvares plums in our country; and those who are too poor . . . have them in lead." Pires adds, perhaps with tongue in cheek, "Our Malay women rejoice greatly when the Pegu men come to their country, and they are very fond of them. The reason for this must be their sweet harmony." The primary purpose seems again the pleasure of the female. When the Dutch admiral Jacob van Neck asked in some astonishment what purpose was served by the sweet-sounding little golden bells the wealthy Thais of Patani carried in their penises, they replied that "the women obtain inexpressible pleasure from it." . . .

That the majority Muslim population of Indonesia and Malaysia had divorce rates in excess of 50 percent as late as the 1960s is sometimes attributed to the influence of Islam in sanctioning easy divorce for men. Much more important, however, was the pan-Southeast-Asian pattern of female autonomy, which meant that divorce did not markedly reduce a woman's livelihood, status, or network of kin support. In noting the acceptance the Javanese gave to women of twenty-two or twenty-three living with their fourth or fifth husband, [G. W.] Earl attributed this attitude entirely to the freedom and economic independence enjoyed by women.

Christian Europe was until the eighteenth century a very "chaste" society in comparative terms, with an exceptionally late average age of marriage (in the twenties), with high proportions never marrying and with a low rate of extramarital conceptions by later standards. (In England this rate rose from only 12 percent of births in 1680 to 50 percent by 1800). Southeast Asia was in many respects the complete antithesis of that chaste pattern, and it seemed to European observers of the time that its inhabitants were preoccupied with sex. The Portuguese liked to say that the Malays were "fond of music and given to love," while Javanese, like Burmese, Thais, and Filipinos, were characterized as "very lasciviously given, both men and women." What this meant was that premarital sexual relations were regarded indulgently, and virginity at marriage was not expected of either party. If pregnancy resulted from these pre-marital activities, the couple were expected to marry, and failing that, resort might be had to abortion or (at least in the Philippines) to infanticide.

FEMALE ROLES

It is already clear that women had a relatively high degree of economic autonomy in premodern Southeast Asia. Nevertheless, it was taken for granted that the opposition of male and female characteristics was a fundamental part of the cosmic dualism. Perhaps for this very reason it was not thought necessary to create artificial markers of gender through dress, hairstyle, or speech patterns, none of which stressed the male-female distinction. A rash of recent studies on the anthropology of gender in Indonesia has uncovered a variety of expressions of the complementary opposition of male and female. Maleness is typically associated with white (semen), warmth, sky, form, control, and deliberate creativity; the female with red (blood), coolness, earth, substance, spontaneity, and natural creativity. The male feature is often seen (at least by males) as preferred, but both are necessary and the union of the two is a powerful ideal.

Such theoretical distinctions help explain the clear boundaries between male and female domains in the house, the fields, and the marketplace. Since everyday activities formed part of this cosmic dualism, especially when they affected plant and animal life, it was not a matter of indifference whether men or women performed them. Male work included all that pertained to metals and animals—ploughing, felling the jungle, hunting, metalworking, woodworking, and house building—as well as statecraft and formal (international) religion. The female domain included transplanting, harvesting, vegetable growing, food preparation, weaving, pottery making (in most areas), and marketing, as well as ancestor cults and mediation with the spirits.

At village level these dichotomies have not changed greatly in the last four centuries. The male domain has expanded enormously, however, through the greater role of statecraft and formal religion, and the ability of larger sections of the population to imitate aristocratic mores which portray women as dependent, decorous, and loyal. In the age of commerce, assumptions of male superiority already affected the courts and the urban elite, who listened to Indian epics of Rama and Sita, studied Chinese Confucian classics (in Vietnam), or were tutored by the theologians of Theravada Buddhism, Islam, or Christianity. In 1399, for example, the Thai queen of Sukhothai prayed that through her merit she might be "reborn as a male," thus moving up the Buddhist hierarchy.

That there was a discrepancy between courtly ideals and everyday reality there is no doubt. What requires examination is the extent to which women in that period were still able to extend their spheres of action into those larger events which are the normal subjects for historians. By examining successively trade, diplomacy, warfare, entertainment, literature, and statecraft we shall see that Southeast Asian women were playing an unusually influential role by comparison with later periods or with other parts of the world.

Since marketing was a female domain par excellence, this is the place to start. Even today Southeast Asian countries top the comparative statistics assembled by Ester Boserup for female participation in trade and marketing. Fifty-six percent of those so listed in Thailand were women, 51 percent in the Philippines, 47 percent in Burma, and 46 percent in Cambodia. Although Indonesia had a lower rate, 31 percent, this still contrasted sharply with other Muslim countries, particularly in the Middle East (1 to 5 percent). In Bangkok at the time of the 1947 census, three times as many Thai women as men were registered as owners or managers of businesses. A famous Minangkabau poem first written down in the 1820s exhorted mothers to teach their daughters "to judge the rise and fall of prices." Southeast Asian women are still expected to show more commercially shrewd and thrifty attitudes than men, and male Chinese and European traders are apt to be derided for having the mean spirit of a woman on such matters.

Although the casual visitor to Southeast Asia today might not be aware of the female trading role, which is now restricted to rural and small-scale markets, this has not always been the case. Early European and Chinese traders were constantly surprised to find themselves dealing with women.

CHAPTER FOUR

Asian Continental Empires

12.　THE LATE MING EMPIRE

Jonathan Spence

Spence, a modern historian of China, examines here the end of the Ming dynasty, which fell in 1644. How was China different from the rest of the world in 1600? How was Ming China organized and governed? How would you describe Ming culture? How did life differ between cities and the countryside? How was life in the north different from that in the south? What were the social and economic threats to Ming prosperity in the early 1600s?

In the year A.D. 1600, the empire of China was the largest and most sophisticated of all the unified realms on earth. The extent of its territorial domains was unparalleled at a time when Russia was only just beginning to coalesce as a country, India was fragmented between Mughal and Hindu rulers, and a grim combination of infectious disease and Spanish conquerors had laid low the once great empires of Mexico and Peru. And China's population of some 120 million was far larger than that of all the European countries combined.

There was certainly pomp and stately ritual in capitals from Kyoto to Prague, from Delhi to Paris, but none of these cities could boast of a palace complex like that in Peking, where, nestled behind immense walls, the gleaming yellow roofs and spacious marble courts of the Forbidden City symbolized the majesty of the Chinese emperor. Laid out in a meticulous geometrical order, the grand stairways and mighty doors of each successive palace building and throne hall were precisely aligned with the arches leading out of Peking to the south, speaking to all comers of the connectedness of things personified in this man the Chinese termed the Son of Heaven.

Rulers in Europe, India, Japan, Russia, and the Ottoman Empire were all struggling to develop systematic bureaucracies that would expand their tax base and manage their swelling territories effectively, as well as draw to new royal power centers the resources of agriculture and trade. But China's massive bureaucracy was already firmly in place, harmonized by a millennium of tradition and bonded by an immense body of statutory laws and provisions that, in theory at least, could offer pertinent advice on any problem that might arise in the daily life of China's people.

One segment of this bureaucracy lived in Peking, serving the emperor in an elaborate hierarchy that divided the country's business among six ministries dealing respectively with finance and personnel, rituals and laws, military affairs and public works. Also in Peking were the senior scholars and academicians who advised the emperor on ritual matters, wrote the official histories, and supervised the education of the imperial children. This concourse of official functionaries worked in uneasy proximity with the enormous palace staff who attended to the emperor's more personal needs: the court women and their eunuch watchmen, the imperial children and their nurses, the elite bodyguards, the banquet-hall and kitchen staffs, the grooms, the sweepers and the water carriers.

The other segment of the Chinese bureaucracy consisted of those assigned to posts in the fifteen major provinces into which China was divided during the Ming dynasty. These posts also were arranged in elaborate hierarchies, running from the provincial governor at the top, down through the prefects in major cities to the magistrates in the counties. Below the magistrates were the police, couriers, militiamen, and tax gatherers who extracted a regular flow of revenue from China's farmers. A group of officials known as censors kept watch over the integrity of the bureaucracy both in Peking and in the provinces.

The towns and cities of China did not, in most cases, display the imposing solidity in stone and brick of the larger urban centers in post-Renaissance Europe. Nor, with the exception of a few famous pagodas, were Chinese skylines pierced by towers as soaring as those of the greatest Christian cathedrals or the minarets of Muslim cities. But this low architectural profile did not signify an absence of wealth or religion. There were many prosperous Buddhist temples in China, just as there were Daoist temples dedicated to the natural forces of the cosmos, ancestral meeting halls, and shrines to Confucius, the founding father of China's ethical system who had lived in the fifth century B.C. A scattering of mosques dotted some eastern cities and the far western areas, where most of China's Muslims lived. There were also some synagogues, where descendants of early Jewish travelers still congregated, and dispersed small groups with hazy memories of the teachings of Nestorian Christianity, which had reached China a millenium earlier. The lesser grandeur of China's city architecture and religious centers represented not any absence of civic pride or disesteem of religion, but rather a political fact: the Chinese state was more effectively centralized than those elsewhere in the world; its religions were more effectively controlled; and the growth of powerful, independent cities was prevented by a watchful government that would not tolerate rival centers of authority.

With hindsight we can see that the Ming dynasty, whose emperors had ruled China since 1368, was past its political peak by the early seventeenth century; yet in the years around 1600, China's cultural life was in an ebullient condition that few, if any, other countries could match. If one points to the figures of exceptional brilliance or insight in late sixteenth-century European society, one will easily find their near equivalents in genius and imagination working away in China at just the same time. There was no Chinese dramatist with quite the range of Shakespeare, but in the 1590s Tang Xianzu was writing plays of thwarted, youthful love, of family drama and social dissonance, that were every bit as rich and complex as *A Midsummer Night's Dream* or *Romeo and Juliet*. And if there was no precise equal to Miguel de Cervantes, whose *Don Quixote* was to become a central work of Western culture, it was in the 1590s that China's most beloved novel of religious quest and picaresque adventure, *The Journey to the West*, was published. This novel's central hero, a mischievous monkey with human traits who accompanies the monk-hero on his action-filled travels to India in search of Buddhist scriptures, has remained a central part of Chinese folk culture to this day. Without pushing further for near parallels, within this same period in China, essayists, philosophers, nature poets, landscape painters, religious theorists, historians, and medical scholars all produced a profusion of significant works, many of which are now regarded as classics of the civilization.

Perhaps in all this outpouring, it is the works of the short-story writers and the popular novelists that make the most important commentary about the vitality of Ming society, for they point to a new readership in the towns, to new levels of literacy, and to a new focus on the details of daily life. In a society that was largely male-dominated, they also indicate a growing audience of literate women. The larger implications of expanding female literacy in China were suggested in the writings of late Ming social theorists, who argued that educating women would enhance the general life of society by bringing improvements in morals, child rearing, and household management.

These many themes run together in another of China's greatest novels, *Golden Lotus*, which was published anonymously in the early 1600s. In this socially elaborate and sexually explicit tale, the central character (who draws his income both from commerce and from his official connections) is analyzed through his relationships with his five consorts, each of whom speaks for a different facet of human nature. In many senses, *Golden Lotus* can be read as allegory, as a moral fable of the way greed and selfishness destroy those with the richest opportunities for happiness; yet it also has a deeply realistic side, and illuminates the tensions and cruelties within elite Chinese family life as few other works have ever done.

Novels, paintings, plays, along with the imperial compendia on court life and bureaucratic practice, all suggest the splendors—for the wealthy—of China in the late Ming. Living mainly in the larger commercial towns rather than out in the countryside, the wealthy were bonded together in elaborate clan or lineage organizations based on family descent through the male line. These lineages often held large amounts of land that provided income for support of their own schools, charity to those fallen on hard times, and the maintenance of ancestral halls in which family members offered sacrifices to the dead. The spacious compounds of the rich, protected by massive gates and high walls, were filled with the products of Chinese artisans, who were sometimes employed in state-directed manufactories but more often grouped in small, guild-controlled workshops. Embroidered silks that brought luster to the female form were always in demand by the rich, along with the exquisite blue and white porcelain that graced the elaborate dinner parties so beloved at the time. Glimmering lacquer, ornamental jade, feathery latticework, delicate ivory, cloisonné and shining rosewood furniture made the homes of the rich places of beauty. And the elaborately carved brush holders of wood or stone, the luxurious paper, even the ink sticks and the stones on which they were rubbed and mixed with water to produce the best and blackest ink, all combined to make of every scholar's desk a ritual and an aesthetic world before he had even written a word.

Complementing the domestic decor, the food and drink of these wealthier Chinese would be a constant delight: pungent shrimp and bean curd, crisp duck and water chestnuts, sweetmeats, clear teas, smooth alcohol of grain or grape, fresh and preserved fruits and juices— all of these followed in stately sequence at parties during which literature, religion, and poetry were discussed over the courses. After the meal, as wine continued to flow, prize scroll paintings might be produced from the family collection, and new works of art, seeking to capture the essence of some old master, would be created by the skimming brushes of the inebriated guests.

At its upper social and economic levels, this was a highly educated society, held together intellectually by a common group of texts that reached back before the time of Confucius to the early days of the unification of a northern Chinese state in the second millennium B.C. While theorists debated its merits for women, education was rigorous and protracted for the boys of wealthy families, introducing them to the rhythms of classical Chinese around the age of six. They then kept at their studies in school or with private tutors every day, memorizing, translating, drilling until, in their late twenties or early thirties, they might be ready to tackle the state examinations. Success in these examinations, which rose in a hierarchy of difficulty from those held locally to those conducted in the capital of Peking, allegedly under the supervision of the emperor himself, brought access to lucrative bureaucratic office and immense social prestige. Women were barred by law from taking the state examinations; but those of good family often learned to write classical poetry from their parents or brothers, and courtesans in the city pleasure quarters were frequently well trained in poetry and song, skills that heightened their charms in the eyes of their educated male patrons. Since book printing with wooden blocks had been developing in China since the tenth century, the maintenance of extensive private libraries was feasible, and the wide distribution of works of philosophy, poetry, history, and moral exhortation was taken for granted.

Though frowned on by some purists, the dissemination of popular works of entertainment was also accelerating in the late sixteenth century, making for a rich and elaborate cultural mix. City dwellers could call on new images of tamed nature to contrast with their own noise and bustle, and find a sense of order in works of art that interpreted the world for them. The possibilities for this sense of contentment were caught to perfection by the dramatist Tang Xianzu in his play *The Peony Pavilion* of 1598. Tang puts his words into the mouth of a scholar and provincial bureaucrat named Du Bao. One side of Du Bao's happiness comes from the fact that administrative business is running smoothly:

> The mountains are at their loveliest
> and court cases dwindle,
> "The birds I saw off at dawn,
> at dusk I watch return,"
> petals from the vase cover my seal box,
> the curtains hang undisturbed.

This sense of peace and order, in turn, prompts a more direct response to nature, when official duties can be put aside altogether, the literary overlays forgotten, and nature and the simple pleasures enjoyed on their own terms:

> Pink of almond fully open,
> iris blades unsheathed,
> fields of spring warming to season's life.
> Over thatched hut by bamboo fence juts a tavern flag,
> rain clears, and the smoke spirals from kitchen stoves.

It was a fine vision, and for many these were indeed glorious days. As long as the country's borders remained quiet, as long as the bureaucracy worked smoothly, as long as the peasants who did the hard work in the fields and the artisans who made all the beautiful objects remained content with their lot—then perhaps the splendors of the Ming would endure.

TOWN AND FARM

The towns and cities of Ming China, especially in the more heavily populated eastern part of the country, had a bustling and thriving air. Some were busy bureaucratic centers, where the local provincial officials had their offices and carried out their tax gathering and administrative tasks.

Others were purely commercial centers, where trade and local markets dictated the patterns of daily life. Most were walled, closed their gates at night, and imposed some form of curfew.

As with towns and cities elsewhere in the world, those in China could be distinguished by their services and their levels of specialization. Local market towns, for instance, were the bases for coffinmakers, iron-workers, tailors, and noodle makers. Their retail shops offered for sale such semispecial goods as tools, wine, headgear, and religious supplies, including incense, candles, and special paper money to burn at sacrifices. Such market towns also offered winehouses for customers to relax in. Larger market towns, which drew on a flow of traders and wealthy purchasers from a wider region, could support cloth-dyeing establishments, shoemakers, iron foundries, firecracker makers, and sellers of bamboo, fine cloth, and teas. Travelers here found bathhouses and inns, and could buy the services of local prostitutes. Rising up the hierarchy to the local cities that coordinated the trade of several regional market towns, there were shops selling expensive stationery, leather goods, ornamental lanterns, altar carvings, flour, and the services of tinsmiths, seal cutters, and lacquer-ware sellers. Here, too, visitors could find pawnshops and local "banks" to handle money exchanges, rent a sedan chair, and visit a comfortably appointed brothel. As the cities grew larger and their clientele richer, one found ever more specialized luxury goods and services, along with the kinds of ambience in which wealth edged—sometimes dramatically, sometimes unobtrusively—into the realms of decadence, snobbery, and exploitation.

At the base of the urban hierarchy, below the market towns, there were the small local townships where the population was too poor and scattered to support many shops and artisans, and where most goods were sold only by traveling peddlers at periodic markets. Such townships housed neither the wealthy nor any government officials; as a result, the simplest of teahouses, or perhaps a roadside stall, or an occasional temple fair would be the sole focus for relaxation. Nevertheless, such smaller townships performed a vast array of important functions, for they served as the bases for news and gossip, matchmaking, simple schooling, local religious festivals, traveling theater groups, tax collection, and the distribution of famine relief in times of emergency.

Just as the towns and cities of Ming China represented a whole spectrum of goods and services, architecture, levels of sophistication, and administrative staffing, making any simple generalization about them risky, so, too, was the countryside apparently endless in its variety. Indeed the distinction between town and country was blurred in China, for suburban areas of intensive farming lay just outside and sometimes even within the city walls, and artisans might work on farms in peak periods, or farmers work temporarily in towns during times of dearth.

It was south of the Huai River, which cuts across China between the

Yellow River and the Yangzi, that the country was most prosperous, for here climate and soil combined to make intensive rice cultivation possible. The region was crisscrossed by myriad rivers, canals, and irrigation streams that fed lush market gardens and paddies in which the young rice shoots grew, or flowed into lakes and ponds where fish and ducks were raised. Here the seasonal flooding of the paddy fields returned needed nutrients to the soil. In the regions just south of the Yangzi River, farmers cultivated mulberry trees for the leaves on which silk worms fed, as well as tea bushes and a host of other products that created extra resources and allowed for a richly diversified rural economy. Farther to the south, sugarcane and citrus were added to the basic crops; and in the mountainous southwest, forests of bamboo and valuable hardwood lumber brought in extra revenue. Water transport was fast, easy, and cheap in south China. Its villages boasted strong lineage organizations that helped to bond communities together.

Although there were many prosperous farming villages north of the Huai River, life there was harsher. The cold in winter was extreme, as icy winds blew in from Mongolia, eroding the land, filling the rivers with silt, and swirling fine dust into the eyes and noses of those who could not afford to shelter behind closed doors. The main crops were wheat and millet, grown with much toil on overworked land, which the scattered farming communities painstakingly fertilized with every scrap of human and animal waste they could recycle. Fruit trees such as apple and pear grew well, as did soybeans and cotton; but by the end of the sixteenth century, much of the land was deforested, and the Yellow River was an unpredictable force as its silt-laden waters meandered across the wide plains to the sea. Unhindered by the dikes, paddies, and canals of the South, bandit armies could move men and equipment easily across the northern countryside, while cavalry forces could race ahead and to the flanks, returning to warn the slower foot soldiers of any danger from opposing forces or sorties from garrison towns. Lineage organizations were weaker here, villages more isolated, social life often more fragmented, and the tough-minded owner-cultivator, living not far above subsistence level, more common than either the prosperous landlord or the tenant farmer.

China's rural diversity meant that "landlords" could not be entirely distinguished from "peasants." For every wealthy absentee landlord living in one of the larger towns, for example, there might be scores of smaller-scale local landlords living in the countryside, perhaps renting out some of their land or hiring part-time labor to till it. Similarly, there were millions of peasant proprietors who owned a little more land than they needed for subsistence, and they might farm their own land with the help of some seasonal laborers. Others, owning a little *less* land than they needed for subsistence, might rent an extra fraction of an acre or hire themselves out as casual labor in the busy seasons. And in most

peasant homes, there was some form of handicraft industry that connected the rural family to a commercial network.

The social structure was further complicated by the bewildering variety of land-sale agreements and rental contracts used in China. While the
state sought extra revenue by levying a tax on each land deal, in return
for which it granted an official contract with a red seal, many farmers—
not surprisingly—tried to avoid these surcharges by drawing up their
own unofficial contracts. The definition of a land sale, furthermore, was
profoundly ambiguous. Most land sales were conducted on the general
understanding that the seller might at some later date reclaim the land
from the buyer at the original purchase price, or that the seller retained
"subsurface" rights to the soil while the purchaser could till the land for a
specified period. If land rose in price, went out of cultivation, became
waterlogged, or was built upon, a maze of legal and financial problems
resulted, leading often to family feuds and even to murder.

For centuries, whether in the north or the south, the peasantry of
China had shown their ability to work hard and to survive even when
sudden natural calamities brought extreme deprivation. In times of
drought or flood, there were various forms of mutual aid, loans, or relief
grain supplies that could help to tide them and their families over. Perhaps some sort of part-time labor could be secured, as a porter, an
irrigation worker, or barge puller. Children could be indentured, on
short- or long-term contracts, for domestic service with the rich. Female
children could be sold in the cities; and even if they ended up in brothels,
at least they were alive and the family freed of an extra mouth to feed.
But if, on top of all the other hardships, the whole fabric of law and
order within the society began to unravel, then the situation became
hopeless indeed. If the market towns closed their gates, if bands of
desperate men began to roam the countryside, seizing the few stores that
the rural families had laid in against the coming winter's cold, or stealing
the last seed grain carefully hoarded for the next spring's planting, then
the poor farmers had no choice but to abandon their fields—whether
the land was rented or privately owned—and to swell the armies of the
homeless marchers.

In the early 1600s, despite the apparent prosperity of the wealthier
elite, there were signs that this dangerous unraveling might be at hand.
Without state-sponsored work or relief for their own needy inhabitants,
then the very towns that barred their gates to the rural poor might erupt
from within. Driven to desperation by high taxes and uncertain labor
prospects, thousands of silk weavers in the Yangzi-delta city of Suzhou
went on strike in 1601, burnt down houses, and lynched hated local
tyrants. That same year, southwest of Suzhou, in the Jiangxi province
porcelain-manufacturing city of Jingdezhen, thousands of workers ri-
oted over low wages and the Ming court's demand that they meet heightened production quotas of the exquisite "dragon bowls" made for palace

use. One potter threw himself into a blazing kiln and perished to under-line his fellows' plight. A score of other cities and towns saw some kind of social and economic protest in the same period.

Instability in the urban world was matched by that in the countryside. There were incidents of rural protest in the late Ming, as in earlier periods, that can be seen as having elements of class struggle inherent in them. These incidents, often accompanied by violence, were of two main kinds: protests by indentured laborers or "bondservants" against their masters in attempts to regain their free status as farmers, and strikes by tenants who refused to pay their landlords what they regarded as unjust rents.

Even if they were not common, there were enough such incidents to offer a serious warning to the wealthier Chinese. In that same play, *The Peony Pavilion,* in which he speaks glowingly of the joys of the official's life, Tang Xianzu gently mocks the rustic yokels of China, putting into deliberately inelegant verse the rough-and-ready labor of their days:

> Slippery mud,
> sloppery thud,
> short rake, long plough, clutch 'em as they slide.
> After rainy night sow rice and hemp,
> when sky clears fetch out the muck,
> then a stink like long-pickled fish
> floats on the breeze.

The verses sounded amusing. But Tang's audience had not yet begun to think through the implications of what might happen when those who labored under such conditions sought to overthrow their masters.

13. THE OTTOMAN EMPIRE UNDER SULEIMAN

Ghislain de Busbecq

Suleiman I (r. 1520–66), known as Suleiman the Magnificent in the West and Suleiman the Law Giver by the Turks, was one of the greatest sultans of the Ottoman Empire. His armies brought Muslim rule almost to the gates of Vienna. Ghislain de Busbecq (1522–90), a Flemish nobleman, was sent on a diplomatic mission to Istanbul in 1555 by Ferdinand I, archduke of Austria and king of Hungary and Bohemia (and Holy Roman Emperor from 1556 to 1564). In his letters to a fellow Hapsburg diplomat, published in 1589, Busbecq warned Christian Europe of the Ottoman threat. What does Busbecq see as the source of Turkish strength? Some historians have said Busbecq exaggerated a bit to alarm his European audience. Do you see any signs of this?

On reaching Amasya[1] we were taken to pay our respects to Achmet, the Chief Vizier, and the other Pashas (for the Sultan himself was away), and we opened negotiations with them in accordance with the [King Ferdinand's] injunctions. The Pashas, anxious not to appear at this early stage prejudiced against our cause, displayed no opposition but postponed the matter until their master could express his wishes. On his return we were introduced into his presence; but neither in his attitude nor in his manner did he appear very well disposed to our address, or the arguments, which we used, or the instructions which we brought.

The Sultan was seated on a rather low sofa, not more than a foot from the ground and spread with many costly coverlets and cushions embroidered with exquisite work. Near him were his bow and arrows. His expression, as I have said, is anything but smiling, and has a sternness which, though sad, is full of majesty. On our arrival we were introduced into his presence by his chamberlains, who held our arms—a practice which has always been observed since a Croatian sought an interview and murdered the Sultan Amurath [Murad II] in revenge for the slaughter of his master, Marcus the Despot of Serbia. After going through the pretence of kissing his hand, we were led to the wall facing him backwards, so as not to turn our backs or any part of them towards him. He then listened to the recital of my message, but, as it did not correspond with his expectations (for the demands of my imperial master were full of dignity and independence, and, therefore, far from acceptable to one who thought that his slightest wishes ought to be obeyed), he assumed an expression of disdain, and merely answered "Giusel, Giusel," that is, "Well, Well." We were then dismissed to our lodging.

The Sultan's head-quarters were crowded by numerous attendants, including many high officials. All the cavalry of the guard were there . . . , and a large number of Janissaries.[2] In all that great assembly no single man owed his dignity to anything but his personal merits and bravery; no one is distinguished from the rest by his birth, and honour is paid to each man according to the nature of the duty and offices which he discharges. Thus there is no struggle for precedence, every man having his place

1. April 7, 1555. [Busbecq had to come to this northeastern city while Suleiman was busy stabilizing his eastern border with Safavid Persia, accomplished by the treaty of Amasya, May 29, 1555.—Ed.]
2. An elite military force originally drawn from conquered Christian families, converted to Islam and expected to remain single, celibate, and totally dedicated to the sultan.—Ed.

assigned to him in virtue of the function which he performs. The Sultan himself assigns to all their duties and offices, and in doing so pays no attention to wealth or the empty claims of rank, and takes no account of any influence or popularity which a candidate may possess; he only considers merit and scrutinizes the character, natural ability, and disposition of each. Thus each man is rewarded according to his deserts, and offices are filled by men capable of performing them. In Turkey every man has it in his power to make what he will of the position into which he is born and of his fortune in life. Those who hold the highest posts under the Sultan are very often the sons of shepherds and herdsmen, and, so far from being ashamed of their birth, they make it a subject of boasting, and the less they owe to their forefathers and to the accident of birth, the greater is the pride which they feel. They do not consider that good qualities can be conferred by birth or handed down by inheritance, but regard them partly as the gift of heaven and partly as the product of good training and constant toil and zeal. Just as they consider that an aptitude for the arts, such as music or mathematics or geometry, is not transmitted to a son and heir, so they hold that character is not hereditary, and that a son does not necessarily resemble his father, but his qualities are divinely infused into his bodily frame. Thus, among the Turks, dignities, offices, and administrative posts are the rewards of ability and merit; those who were dishonest, lazy, and slothful never attain to distinction, but remain in obscurity and contempt. This is why the Turks succeed in all that they attempt and are a dominating race and daily extend the bounds of their rule. Our method is very different; there is no room for merit, but everything depends on birth; considerations of which alone open the way to high official position. On this subject I shall perhaps say more in another place, and you must regard these remarks as intended for your ears only.[3]

Now come with me and cast your eye over the immense crowd of turbaned heads, wrapped in countless folds of the whitest silk, and bright raiment of every kind and hue, and everywhere the brilliance of gold, silver, purple, silk, and satin. A detailed description would be a lengthy task, and no mere words could give an adequate idea of the novelty of the sight. A more beautiful spectacle was never presented to my gaze. Yet amid all this luxury there was a great simplicity and economy. The dress of all has the same form whatever the wearer's rank; and no edgings or useless trimmings are sewn on, as is the custom with us, costing a large sum of money and worn out in three days. Their most beautiful garments of silk or satin, even if they are embroidered, as they usually are, cost only a ducat to make.

3. Gradually certain offices tended to become the preserves of certain families or patrons. However a lowly man could rise on the basis of merit. In a system in which the ruler wished to hold the sole allegiance of his officers and officials, a man of slave origin, owing by conquest everything to his master, was an ideal candidate.

The Turks were quite as much astonished at our manner of dress as we at theirs. They wear long robes which reach almost to their ankles, and are not only more imposing but seem to add to the stature; our dress, on the other hand, is so short and tight that it discloses the forms of the body, which would be better hidden, and is thus anything but becoming, and besides, for some reason or other, it takes away from a man's height and gives him a stunted appearance.

What struck me as particularly praiseworthy in that great multitude was the silence and good discipline. There were none of the cries and murmurs which usually proceed from a motley concourse, and there was no crowding. Each man kept his appointed place in the quietest manner possible. The officers, namely, generals, colonels, captains, and lieutenants—to all of whom the Turks themselves give the tile of Aga— were seated; the common soldiers stood up. The most remarkable body of men were several thousand Janissaries, who stood in a long line apart from the rest and so motionless that, as they were at some distance from me, I was for a while doubtful whether they were living men or statues, until, being advised to follow the usual custom of saluting them, I saw them all bow their heads in answer to my salutation. On our departure from that part of the field, we saw another very pleasing sight, namely, the Sultan's bodyguard returning home mounted on horses, which were not only very fine and tall but splendidly groomed and caparisoned.

You will probably wish me to describe the impression which Soleiman made upon me. He is beginning to feel the weight of years, but his dignity of demeanour and his general physical appearance are worthy of the ruler of so vast an empire. He has always been frugal and temperate, and was so even in his youth, when he might have erred without incurring blame in the eyes of the Turks. Even in his earlier years he did not indulge in wine or in those unnatural vices to which the Turks are often addicted. Even his bitterest critics can find nothing more serious to allege against him than his undue submission to his wife[4] and its result in his somewhat precipitate action in putting Mustapha to death, which is generally imputed to her employment of love-potions and incantations. It is generally agreed that, ever since he promoted her to the rank of his lawful wife, he has possessed no concubines, although there is no law to prevent his doing so. He is a strict guardian of his religion and its ceremonies, being not less desirous of upholding his faith than of extending his dominions. For his age—he has almost reached his sixtieth year—he enjoys quite good health, though his bad complexion may be due to some hidden malady; and indeed it is generally believed that he has an incurable ulcer or gangrene on his leg. This defect of complexion he

4. Roxalana: a favorite wife of Suleiman, who led him to suspect his first-born (by another wife) son Mustapha, and to have him strangled.

remedies by painting his face with a coating of red powder, when he wishes departing ambassadors to take with them a strong impression of his good health; for he fancies that it contributes to inspire greater fear in foreign potentates if they think that he is well and strong. I noticed a clear indication of this practice on the present occasion; for his appearance when he received me in the final audience was very different from that which he presented when he gave me an interview on my arrival.

The Sultan, when he sets out on a campaign, takes as many as 40,000 camels with him, and almost as many baggage-mules, most of whom, if his destination is Persia, are loaded with cereals of every kind, especially rice. Mules and camels are also employed to carry tents and arms and warlike machines and implements of every kind. The territories called Persia which are ruled by the Sophi,[5] as we call him (the Turkish name being Kizilbash), are much less fertile than our country; and, further, it is the custom of the inhabitants, when their land is invaded, to lay waste and burn everything, and so force the enemy to retire through lack of food. The latter, therefore, are faced with serious peril, unless they bring an abundance of food with them. They are careful, however, to avoid touching the supplies which they carry with them as long as they are marching against their foes, but reserve them, as far as possible, for their return journey, when the moment for retirement comes and they are forced to retrace their steps through regions which the enemy has laid waste, or which the immense multitude of men and baggage animals has, as it were, scraped bare, like a swarm of locusts. It is only then that the Sultan's store of provisions is opened, and just enough food to sustain life is weighed out each day to the Janissaries and the other troops in attendance upon him. The other soldiers are badly off, if they have not provided food for their own use; most of them, having often experienced such difficulties during their campaigns—and this is particularly true of the cavalry—take a horse on a leading-rein loaded with many of the necessities of life.[6] These include a small piece of canvas to use as a tent, which may protect them from the sun or a shower of rain, also some clothing and bedding and a private store of provisions, consisting of a leather sack or two of the finest flour, a small jar of butter, and some spices and salt; on these they support life when they are reduced to the extremes of hunger. They take a few spoonfuls of flour and place them in water, adding a little butter, and then flavour the mixture with salt and spices. This, when it is put on the fire, boils and swells up so as to fill a large bowl. They eat of it once or twice a day, according to the quantity, without any bread, unless they have with them some toasted bread or biscuit. They thus contrive to live on short

5. I.e., Sûfî, Ismâ'îl II, Safavid Shâh. The Turks called the Safavids Kizilbash (red-headed or hatted) because of their distinctive red headgear.
6. This refers to those irregular "feudal" troops called up during a general mobilization and responsible for their own supplies.

rations for a month or even longer, if necessary. Some soldiers take with them a little sack full of beef dried and reduced to a powder, which they employ in the same manner as the flour, and which is of great benefit as a more solid form of nourishment. Sometimes, too, they have recourse to horseflesh; for in a great army a large number of horses necessarily dies, and any that die in good condition furnish a welcome meal to men who are starving. I may add that men whose horses have died, when the Sultan moves his camp, stand in a long row on the road by which he is to pass with their harness or saddles on their heads, as a sign that they have lost their horses, and implore his help to purchase others. The Sultan then assists them with whatever gift he thinks fit.

All this will show you with what patience, sobriety, and economy the Turks struggle against the difficulties which beset them, and wait for better times. How different are our soldiers, who on campaign despise ordinary food and expect dainty dishes (such as thrushes and beccaficoes) and elaborate meals. If these are not supplied, they mutiny and cause their own ruin; and even if they are supplied, they ruin themselves just the same. For each man is his own worst enemy and has no more deadly foe than his own intemperance, which kills him if the enemy is slow to do so. I tremble when I think of what the future must bring when I compare the Turkish system with our own; one army must prevail and the other be destroyed, for certainly both cannot remain unscathed. On their side are the resources of a mighty empire, strength unimpaired, experience and practice in fighting, a veteran soldiery, habituation to victory, endurance of toil, unity, order, discipline, frugality, and watchfulness. On our side is public poverty, private luxury, impaired strength, broken spirit, lack of endurance and training; the soldiers are insubordinate, the officers avaricious; there is contempt for discipline; licence, recklessness, drunkenness, and debauchery are rife; and, worst of all, the enemy is accustomed to victory, and we to defeat. Can we doubt what the result will be? Persia alone interposes in our favour; for the enemy, as he hastens to attack, must keep an eye on this menace in his rear. But Persia is only delaying our fate; it cannot save us. When the Turks have settled with Persia, they will fly at our throats supported by the might of the whole East; how unprepared we are I dare not say!

But to return to the point from which I digressed. I mentioned that baggage animals are employed on campaign to carry the arms and tents, which mainly belong to the Janissaries. The Turks take the utmost care to keep their soldiers in good health and protected from the inclemency of the weather; against the foe they must protect themselves, but their health is a matter for which the State must provide. Hence one sees the Turk better clothed than armed. He is particularly afraid of the cold, against which, even in the summer, he guards himself by wearing three garments, of which the innermost—call it shirt or what you will—is woven of coarse thread and provides much warmth. As a further protection against cold and rain tents are always carried, in which each man is given just enough space to lie down, so that one tent holds twenty-five or thirty Janissaries. The material for the garments to which I have referred is provided at the public expense. To prevent any disputes or suspicion of favour, it is distributed in the following manner. The soldiers are summoned by companies in the darkness to a place chosen for the purpose—the balloting station or whatever name you like to give it—where are laid out ready as many portions of cloth as there are soldiers in the company; they enter and take whatever chance offers them in the darkness, and they can only ascribe it to chance whether they get a good or a bad piece of cloth. For the same reason their pay is not counted out to them but weighed, so that no one can complain that he has received light or chipped coins. Also their pay is given them not on the day on which it falls due but on the day previous.

The armour which is carried is chiefly for the use of the household cavalry, for the Janissaries are lightly armed and do not usually fight at close quarters, but use muskets. When the enemy is at hand and a battle is expected, the armour is brought out, but it consists mostly of old pieces picked up in various battlefields, the spoil of former victories. These are distributed to the household cavalry, who are otherwise protected by only a light shield. You can imagine how badly the armour, thus hurriedly given out, fits its wearers. One man's breastplate is too small, another's helmet is too large, another's coat of mail is too heavy for him to bear. There is something wrong everywhere; but they bear it with equanimity and think that only a coward finds fault with his arms, and vow to distinguish themselves in the fight, whatever their equipment may be; such is the confidence inspired by repeated victories and constant experience of warfare. Hence also they do not hesitate to re-enlist a veteran infantryman in the cavalry, though he has never fought on horseback, since they are convinced that one who has warlike experience and long service will acquit himself well in any kind of fighting. . . .

14. RUSSIAN EMPIRE: TWO LAW CODES:
14.1. PEASANTS REDUCED TO SERFDOM, 1649

The Russian Empire expanded across the continent of Asia in the sixteenth and seventeenth centuries. To escape the burden of increasing rents at home, peasants fled to settle in the new lands. Russian landlords, deprived of many of their peasant laborers, had Tsar Alexis (1645–1676) pass laws like this one of 1649.

How did these laws end the mass migration of peasants? What degree of liberty did it allow peasants? How did the law treat a peasant's wife, family, and property?

Chapter XI. Procedure concerning the Peasants

1. All peasants who have fled from lands belonging to the Tsar and are now living on lands belonging to church officials, hereditary land-owners, and service landowners are to be returned to the Tsar's lands according to the land cadastres of 1627–31 regardless of the fifteen-year limit. These peasants are to be returned with their wives, children, and all movable property.

2. The same applies to peasants who have fled from hereditary land-owners and service landowners to other hereditary landowners and service landowners, or to the towns, to the army, or to lands belonging to the Tsar.

3. Fugitive peasants must be returned with their wives, children, and movable property, plus their standing grain and threshed grain. But the possessions which the fugitive peasants owned in the years prior to this code are not to be claimed. If a fugitive peasant gave his daughter, sister, or niece in marriage to a local peasant, do not break up the marriage. Leave the girl with the local peasant. It was not a crime in the past to receive fugitive peasants—there was only a time limit for recovering them. Therefore the lord of the local peasant should not be deprived of his labor, especially as lands have changed hands frequently so that the present lord may not have been the person who received the fugitives anyway.

4. All hereditary landowners, service landowners, and officials manag-ing the Tsar's lands must have proper documents identifying their peas-ants in case of dispute. Such documents must be written by public scribes. . . . Illiterate landholders must have their documents signed by impartial, trustworthy persons. . . .

12. If a girl flees after the promulgation of this code and marries another landholder's peasant, then her husband and children will be returned with her to her former landholder. The movable property of her husband, however, will not be returned with them.

13. When a widower marries a fugitive peasant girl, any children he had by a previous marriage will not be surrendered with him to the lord of his new wife, but will remain with the lord of his first wife. . . .

15. If a widowed peasant remarries in flight, then both she and her husband will be returned to the lord of her first husband, provided her first husband was registered with a landholder.

16. If the peasant widow's first husband was not registered with a landholder, then she must live on the premises belonging to the lord of the peasant she married.

17. If a peasant in flight marries off his daughter, then his son-in-law will be returned to the landholder of his wife. . . .

18. A peasant woman in flight who marries will be returned with her husband to her former landholder.

19. Peasant women who are permitted to marry another landholder's peasant must be given release documents in which they are precisely described.

20. When peasants arrive in a hereditary estate or in a service estate and say that they are free people and wish to live with the landholder as peasants, the landholder must ascertain the truth of their claim. Within a year such people must be brought to Moscow or another large city for certification.

21. The lord who did not check carefully whether such people were free must pay the plaintiff to whom the peasants rightfully belong ten rubles per year per fugitive to compensate the plaintiff for his lost income and the taxes he paid while the peasant was absent.

22. Peasant children who deny their parents must be tortured. . . .

33. Bondmen and peasants who flee abroad and then return to Russia cannot claim that they are free men, but must be returned to their former hereditary landowners and service landowners.

34. When fugitive peasants of different landowners marry abroad, and then return to Russia, the landholders will cast lots for the couple. The winning service landowner gets the couple and must pay five rubles to the landholder who lost because both of the peasants were in flight abroad.

14.2. WESTERNIZING BY PETER THE GREAT, 1701–1714

Under Tsar Peter the Great (1682–1725), Russia consolidated its empire in the West, regaining some of the territory in the Baltic that had been lost in the expansion to the Pacific. Peter looked to the West for guidance as well as territory. Convinced that Western science, culture, and work habits were all responsible for the advantages he personally witnessed in Europe, Peter determined to "westernize" Russia. In a series of over 3,000 decrees, Peter covered everything from mathematics to mustaches.

Why do you suppose Peter passed decrees to change Russian clothing and shaving habits? What suggests that there might have been resistance to some of his decrees? Which elements in Russian society did Peter try to change? What new social groups or institutions was he trying to develop?

Decree on Western Dress (1701)

Western dress shall be worn by all the boyars, members of our councils and of our court . . . gentry of Moscow, secretaries . . . provincial gentry, gosti, government officials, strel'tsy, members of the guilds purveying for our household, citizens of Moscow of all ranks, and residents of provincial cities . . . excepting the clergy and peasant tillers of the soil.[1] The upper dress shall be of French or Saxon cut, and the lower dress . . .— (including) waistcoat, trousers, boots, shoes, and hats—shall be of the German type. They shall also ride German saddles. Likewise the womenfolk of all ranks, including the priests', deacons', and church attendants' wives, the wives of the dragoons, the soldiers, and the strel'tsy, and their children, shall wear Western dresses, hats, jackets, and underwear— undervests and petticoats—and shoes. From now on no one of the above-mentioned is to wear Russian dress or Circassian coats, sheepskin coats, or Russian peasant coats, trousers, boots, and shoes. It is also forbidden to ride Russian saddles, and the craftsmen shall not manufacture them or sell them at the marketplaces.

Decree on Shaving (1705)

A decree to be published in Moscow and in all the provincial cities: Henceforth, in accordance with this, His Majesty's decree, all court attendants . . . provincial service men, government officials of all ranks, military men, all the gosti, members of the wholesale merchants' guild, and members of the guilds purveying for our household must shave their beards and moustaches. But, if it happens that some of them do not wish to shave their beards and moustaches, let a yearly tax be collected from such persons; from court attendants . . . provincial service men, military men, and government officials of all ranks—60 rubles per person; from the gosti and members of the wholesale merchants' guild of the first class—100 rubles per person; from members of the wholesale merchants' guild of the middle and the lower class (and) . . . from (other) merchants and townsfolk—60 rubles per person; . . . from townsfolk (of the lower rank), boyars' servants, stagecoachmen, waggoners, church attendants (with the exception of priests and deacons), and from Moscow

---

1. "Boyars" were nobles; "gosti" were merchants; and "strel'tsy" were soldiers in the imperial guard.

residents of all ranks—30 rubles per person. Special badges shall be issued to them from the Administrator of Land Affairs of Public Order . . . which they must wear. . . . As for the peasants, let a toll of two half-copecks per beard be collected at the town gates each time they enter or leave a town; and do not let the peasants pass the town gates, into or out of town, without paying this toll.

Decree on Compulsory Education of the Russian Nobility (1714)

Send to every administrative district some persons from mathematical schools to teach the children of the nobility—except those of freeholders and government clerks—mathematics and geometry; as a penalty for evasion establish a rule that no one will be allowed to marry unless he learns these subjects. Inform all prelates to issue no marriage certificates to those who are ordered to go to schools. . . .

The Great Sovereign has decreed; in all administrative districts children between the ages of ten and fifteen of the nobility, of government clerks, and of lesser officials, except those of freeholders, must be taught mathematics and some geometry. Toward that end, students should be sent from mathematical schools as teachers, several into each administrative district to prelates and to renowned monasteries to establish schools. During their instruction these teachers should be given food and financial remuneration . . . from district revenues set aside for that purpose by personal orders of His Imperial Majesty. No fees should be collected from students. When they have mastered the material, they should then be given certificates written in their own handwriting. When the students are released they ought to pay one ruble each for their training. Without these certificates they should not be allowed to marry nor receive marriage certificates.

An Instruction to Russian Students Abroad Studying Navigation (1714)

1. Learn how to draw plans and charts and how to use the compass and other naval indicators.

2. Learn how to navigate a vessel in battle as well as in a simple maneuver, and learn how to use all appropriate tools and instruments; namely, sails, ropes, and oars, and the like matters, on row boats and other vessels.

3. Discover as much as possible how to put ships to sea during a naval battle. Those who cannot succeed in this effort must diligently ascertain what action should be taken by the vessels that do and those that do not put to sea during such a situation (naval battle). Obtain from foreign

naval officers written statements, bearing their signatures and seals, of how adequately you are prepared for naval duties.

4. If, upon his return, anyone wishes to receive from the Tsar greater favors for himself, he should learn, in addition to the above enumerated instructions, how to construct those vessels abroad which he would like to demonstrate his skills.

5. Upon his return to Moscow, every foreign-trained Russian should bring with him at his own expense, for which he will later be reimbursed, at least two experienced masters of naval science. They the returnees will be assigned soldiers, one soldier per returnee, to teach them what they have learned abroad. And if they do not wish to accept soldiers they may teach their acquaintances or their own people. The treasury will pay for transportation and maintenance of soldiers. And if anyone other than soldiers learns the art of navigation the treasury will pay 100 rubles for the maintenance of every such individual.

CHAPTER FIVE

The Scientific Revolution

15. THE SCIENTIFIC REVOLUTION IN THE WEST

Franklin Le Van Baumer

This selection is a brief survey of the elements of the Western scientific revolution by a modern intellectual historian. What are the most important elements described here? What were some of the causes of the scientific revolution? What were some of the effects? Why might this essay be called a social or cultural history of science, instead of an internal history? Is this a revealing perspective?

In his book *The Origins of Modern Science* Professor Butterfield of Cambridge writes that the "scientific revolution" of the sixteenth and seventeenth centuries "outshines everything since the rise of Christianity and reduces the Renaissance and Reformation to the rank of mere episodes, mere internal displacements, within the system of medieval Christendom." "It looms so large as the real origin both of the modern world and of the modern mentality that our customary periodisation of European history has become an anachronism and an encumbrance."[1] This view can no longer be seriously questioned. The scientific achievements of the century and a half between the publication of Copernicus's *De Revolutionibus Orbium Celestium* (1543) and Newton's *Principia* (1687) marked the opening of a new period of intellectual and cultural life in the West, which I shall call the Age of Science. What chiefly distinguished this age from its predecessor was that science—meaning by science a body of knowledge, a method, an attitude of mind, a metaphysic (to be described below)—became the directive force of Western civilization, displacing theology and antique letters. Science made the world of the spirit, of Platonic Ideas, seem unreliable and dim by comparison with the material world. In the seventeenth century it drove revealed Christianity out of the physical universe into the region of history and private morals; to an ever growing number of people in the two succeeding centuries it made religion seem outmoded even there. Science invaded the schools, im-

1. (London, 1950), p. viii.

posed literary canons, altered the world-picture of the philosophers, suggested new techniques to the social theorists. It changed profoundly man's attitude toward custom and tradition, enabling him to declare his independence of the past, to look down condescendingly upon the "ancients," and to envisage a rosy future. The Age of Science made the intoxicating discovery that melioration depends, not upon "change from within" (St. Paul's birth of the new man), but upon "change from without" (scientific and social mechanics).

I

Some people will perhaps object that there was no such thing as "scientific revolution" in the sixteenth and seventeenth centuries. They will say that history does not work that way, that the new science was not "revolutionary," but the cumulative effect of centuries of trial and error among scientists. But if by "scientific revolution" is meant the occasion when science became a real intellectual and cultural force in the West, this objection must surely evaporate. The evidence is rather overwhelming that sometime between 1543 and 1687, certainly by the late seventeenth century, science captured the interest of the intellectuals and upper classes. Francis Bacon's ringing of a bell to call the wits of Europe together to advance scientific learning did not go unheeded. Note the creation of new intellectual institutions to provide a home for science—the *Academia del Cimento* at Florence (1661), the Royal Society at London (1662), the *Académie des Sciences* at Paris (1666), the Berlin Academy (1700), to mention only the most important. These scientific academies signified the advent of science as an organized activity. Note the appearance of a literature of popular science, of which Fontenelle's *Plurality of Worlds* is only one example, and of popular lectures on scientific subjects. Note the movement for educational reform sponsored by Bacon and the Czech John Amos Comenius, who denounced the traditional education for its exclusive emphasis upon "words rather than things" (literature rather than nature itself). Evidently, by the end of the seventeenth century the prejudice against "mechanical" studies as belonging to practical rather than high mental life had all but disappeared. Bacon complained in 1605 that "matters mechanical" were esteemed "a kind of dishonour unto learning to descend to inquiry or meditation upon." But the Royal Society included in its roster a number of ecclesiastics and men of fashion. The second marquis of Worcester maintained a laboratory and published a book of inventions in 1663. Not a few men appear to have been "converted" from an ecclesiastical to a scientific career, and, as Butterfield notes, to have carried the gospel into the byways, with all the zest of the early Christian missionaries.

To account historically for the scientific revolution is no easy task. The problem becomes somewhat more manageable, however, if we exclude from the discussion the specific discoveries of the scientists. Only the internal history of science can explain how Harvey, for example, discovered the circulation of the blood, or Newton the universal law of gravitation.

But certain extrascientific factors were plainly instrumental in causing so many people to be simultaneously interested in "nature," and, moreover, to think about nature in the way they did. Professor Whitehead reminds us that one of these factors was medieval Christianity itself and medieval scholasticism. Medieval Christianity sponsored the Greek, as opposed to the primitive, idea of a rationally ordered universe which made the orderly investigation of nature seem possible. Scholasticism trained western intellectuals in exact thinking. The Renaissance and the Protestant Reformation also prepared the ground for the scientific revolution—not by design, but as an indirect consequence of their thinking. As I have previously noted, humanism and Protestantism represented a movement toward the concrete. Erasmus preferred ethics to the metaphysical debates of the philosophers and theologians. The Protestants reduced the miraculous element in institutional Christianity and emphasized labor in a worldly calling. Furthermore, by attacking scholastic theology with which Aristotle was bound up, they made it easier for scientists to think about physics and astronomy in un-Aristotelian terms. As E. A. Burtt has noted of Copernicus, these men lived in a mental climate in which people generally were seeking new centers of reference. Copernicus, the architect of the heliocentric theory of the universe, was a contemporary of Luther and Archbishop Cranmer, who moved the religious center from Rome to Wittenberg and Canterbury. In the sixteenth century the economic center of gravity was similarly shifting from the Mediterranean to the English Channel and the Atlantic Ocean. The revival of ancient philosophies and ancient texts at the Renaissance also sharpened the scientific appetite. The Platonic and Phythagorean revival in fifteenth-century Italy undoubtedly did a good deal to accustom scientists to think of the universe in mathematical, quantitative terms. The translation of Galen and Archimedes worked the last rich vein of ancient science, and made it abundantly clear that the ancients had frequently disagreed on fundamentals, thus necessitating independent investigation. By their enthusiasm for natural beauty, the humanists helped to remove from nature the medieval stigma of sin, and thus to make possible the confident pronouncement of the scientific movement that God's Word could be read not only in the Bible but in the great book of nature.

But no one of these factors, nor all of them together, could have produced the scientific revolution. One is instantly reminded of Bacon's statement that "by the distant voyages and travels which have become frequent in our times, many things in nature have been laid open and discovered which may let in new light upon philosophy." The expansion of Europe, and increased travel in Europe itself, not only stimulated interest in nature but opened up to the West the vision of a "Kingdom of

Man" upon earth. Much of Bacon's imagery was borrowed from the geographical discoveries: he aspired to be the Columbus of a new intellectual world, to sail through the Pillars of Hercules (symbol of the old knowledge) into the Atlantic Ocean in search of new and more useful knowledge. Bacon, however, failed to detect the coincidence of the scientific revolution with commercial prosperity and the rise of the middle class. Doubtless, the Marxist Professor Hessen greatly oversimplified when he wrote that "Newton was the typical representative of the rising bourgeoisie, and in his philosophy he embodies the characteristic features of his class." The theoretical scientists had mixed motives. Along with a concern for technology, they pursued truth for its own sake, and they sought God in his great creation. All the same, it is not stretching the imagination too far to see a rough correspondence between the mechanical universe of the seventeenth-century philosophers and the bourgeois desire for rational, predictable order. Science and business were a two-way street. If science affected business, so did business affect science—by its businesslike temper and its quantitative thinking, by its interest in "matter" and the rational control of matter.

II

The scientific revolution gave birth to a new conception of knowledge, a new methodology, and a new worldview substantially different from the old Aristotelian-Christian worldview. . . .

Knowledge now meant exact knowledge: what you know for certain, and not what may possibly or even probably be. Knowledge is what can be clearly apprehended by the mind, or measured by mathematics, or demonstrated by experiment. Galileo came close to saying this when he declared that without mathematics "it is impossible to comprehend a single word of (the great book of the universe)"; likewise Descartes when he wrote that "we ought never to allow ourselves to be persuaded of the truth of anything unless on the evidence of our Reason." The distinction between "primary" and "secondary qualities" in seventeenth-century metaphysics carried the same implication. To Galileo, Descartes, and Robert Boyle those mathematical qualities that inhered in objects (size, weight, position, etc.) were "primary," i.e., matters of real knowledge; whereas all the other qualities that our senses tell us are in objects (color, odor, taste, etc.) were "secondary," less real because less amenable to measurement. The inference of all this is plain: knowledge pertains to "natural philosophy" and possibly social theory, but not to theology or the older philosophy or poetry which involve opinion, belief, faith, but not knowledge. The Royal Society actually undertook to renovate the English language, by excluding from it metaphors and pulpit eloquence which conveyed no precise meaning. The "enthusiasm" of the religious man became suspect as did the "sixth sense" of the poet who could convey pleasure but not knowledge.

The odd thing about the scientific revolution is that for all its avowed distrust of hypotheses and systems, it created its own system of nature, or worldview. "I perceive," says the "Countess" in Fontenelle's popular dialogue of 1686, "Philosophy is now become very Mechanical." "I value (this universe) the more since I know it resembles a Watch, and the whole order of Nature the more plain and easy it is, to me it appears the more admirable." Descartes and other philosophers of science in the seventeenth century constructed a mechanical universe which resembled the machines—watches, pendulum clocks, steam engines—currently being built by scientists and artisans. However, it was not the observation of actual machines but the new astronomy and physics that made it possible to picture the universe in this way. The "Copernican revolution" destroyed Aristotle's "celestial world" of planets and stars which, because they were formed of a subtle substance having no weight, behaved differently from bodies on earth and in the "sublunary world." The new laws of motion formulated by a succession of physicists from Kepler to Newton explained the movement of bodies, both celestial and terrestrial, entirely on mechanical and mathematical principles. According to the law of inertia, the "natural" motion of bodies was in a straight line out into Euclidean space. The planets were pulled into their curvilinear orbits by gravitation which could operate at tremendous distances, and which varied inversely as the square of the distance.

Thus, the universe pictured by Fontenelle's Countess was very different from that of Dante in the thirteenth, or Richard Hooker in the sixteenth century. Gone was the Aristotelian-Christian universe of purposes, forms, and final causes. Gone were the spirits and intelligences which had been required to push the skies daily around the earth. The fundamental features of the new universe were numbers (mathematical quantities) and invariable laws. It was an economical universe in which nature did nothing in vain and performed its daily tasks without waste. In such a universe the scientist could delight and the bourgeois could live happily ever after—or at least up to the time of Darwin. The fact that nature appeared to have no spiritual purpose—Descartes said that it would continue to exist regardless of whether there were any human beings to think it—was more than compensated for by its dependability. Philosophy had indeed become very mechanical. Descartes kept God to start his machine going, and Newton did what he could to save the doctrine of providence. But for all practical purposes, God had become the First Cause, "very well skilled in mechanics and geometry." And the rage for mechanical explanation soon spread beyond the confines of physics to encompass the biological and social sciences. Thus did Descartes regard animals as a piece of clockwork, Robert Boyle the human body as a "matchless engine."

Under the circumstances, one would logically expect there to have been warfare between science and religion in the seventeenth century. But such was not the case. To be sure, some theologians expressed dismay at the downfall of Aristotelianism, and the Roman Church took steps to suppress Copernicanism when Giordano Bruno interpreted it to mean an infinite universe and a plurality of worlds. But the majority of the scientists and popularizers of science were sincerely religious men— not a few were actually ecclesiastics—who either saw no conflict or else went to some lengths to resolve it. Science itself was commonly regarded as a religious enterprise. . . .

In the final analysis, however, the new thing in seventeenth-century thought was the dethronement of theology from its proud position as the sun of the intellectual universe. Bacon and Descartes and Newton lived in an age that was finding it increasingly difficult to reconcile science and religion. To save the best features of both they effected a shaky compromise. For all practical purposes they eliminated religious purpose from nature—thus allowing science to get on with its work, while leaving religion in control of private belief and morals. By their insistence that religious truth itself must pass the tests of reason and reliable evidence, John Locke and the rationalists further reduced theology's prerogatives. Bacon was prepared to believe the word of God "though our reason be shocked at it." But not Locke: " 'I believe because it is impossible,' might," he says, "in a good man, pass for a sally of zeal, but would prove a very ill rule for men to choose their opinions or religion by." Good Christian though Locke might be, his teaching had the effect of playing down the supernatural aspects of religion, of equating religion with simple ethics. . . .

16.   WOMEN AND SCIENCE

Bonnie S. Anderson and
Judith P. Zinsser

This selection from a recent history of European women shows how some women, especially the better educated, could participate in the scientific revolution of the seventeenth and eighteenth centuries. But the authors also show how much of the scientific revolution endowed male prejudices with false scientific respectability. What factors seem to have enabled women to participate in the scientific revolution? In what ways was the scientific revolution a new bondage for women?

WOMEN SCIENTISTS

In the same way that women responded to and participated in Humanism, so they were drawn to the intellectual movement known as the Scientific Revolution. The excitement of the new discoveries of the seventeenth and eighteenth centuries, in particular, inspired a few gifted women scientists to formulate their own theories about the natural world, to perform their own experiments and to publish their findings. In contrast to those educated strictly and formally according to Humanist precepts, these women had little formal training, and chose for themselves what they read and studied. Rather than encouraging them, their families at best left them to their excitement with the wonders of the "Scientific Revolution"; at worst, parents criticized their daughters' absorption in such inappropriate, inelegant, and unfeminine endeavors.

All across Europe from the sixteenth to the eighteenth centuries these women found fascination in the natural sciences. They corresponded and studied with the male scientists of their day. They observed, and they formulated practical applications from their new knowledge of botany, horticulture, and chemistry. The Countess of Chinchon, wife of the Viceroy to Peru, brought quinine bark to Spain from Latin America because it had cured her malaria. Some noblewomen, like the German Anna of Saxony (1532–1582), found medical uses for the plants they studied. The most gifted of these early naturalists is remembered not as a scientist but as an artist. Maria Sibylla Merian (1647–1717) learned drawing and probably acquired her interest in plants and insects from her stepfather, a Flemish still-life artist. As a little girl she went with him into the fields to collect specimens. Though she married, bore two daughters, and ran a household, between 1679 and her death in 1717 she also managed to complete and have published six collections of engravings of European flowers and insects. These were more than artist's renderings. For example, her study of caterpillars was unique for the day. Unlike the still life done by her contemporaries, the drawings show the insect at every stage of development as observed from the specimens that she collected and nursed to maturity. She explained:

> From my youth I have been interested in insects, first I started with silkworms in my native Frankfurt-am-Main. After that . . . I started to collect all the caterpillars I could find to observe their changes.

Merian's enthusiasm, patience, and skill brought her to the attention of the director of the Amsterdam Botanical Gardens and other male collectors. When her daughter married and moved to the Dutch colony of Surinam, their support was important when she wanted to raise the money for a new scientific project. In 1699, at the age of fifty-two, Maria Sibylla Merian set off on what became a two-year expedition into the interior of South America. She collected, made notations and sketches. Only yellow fever finally forced her to return to Amsterdam in 1701. The resulting book of sixty engravings established her contemporary reputation as a naturalist.

Mathematics, astronomy, and studies of the universe also interested these self-taught women scientists. In 1566 in Paris Marie de Coste Blanche published *The Nature of the Sun and Earth.* Margaret Cavendish (1617–1673), the seventeenth-century Duchess of Newcastle, though haphazard in her approach to science, produced fourteen books on everything from natural history to atomic physics.

Even more exceptional in the eighteenth century was the French noble-woman and courtier, Emilie du Châtelet (1706–1749). She gained admission to the discussions of the foremost mathematicians and scientists of Paris, earned a reputation as a physicist and as an interpreter of the theories of Leibnitz and Newton. Emilie du Châtelet showed unusual intellectual abilities even as a child. By the age of ten she had read Cicero, studied mathematics and metaphysics. At twelve she could speak English, Italian, Spanish, and German and translated Greek and Latin texts like Aristotle and Vergil. Presentation at court and life as a courtier changed none of her scientific interests and hardly modified her studious habits. She seemed to need no sleep, read incredibly fast, and was said to appear in public with ink stains on her fingers from her note-taking and writing. When she took up the study of Descartes, her father complained to her uncle: "I argued with her in vain; she would not understand that no great lord will marry a woman who is seen reading every day." Her mother despaired of a proper future for such a daugher who "flaunts her mind, and frightens away the suitors her other excesses have not driven off." It was her lover and lifelong friend, the Duke de Richelieu, who encouraged her to continue and to formalize her studies by hiring professors in mathematics and physics from the Sorbonne to tutor her. In 1733 she stormed her way into the Café Gradot, the Parisian coffee-house where the scientists, mathematicians, and philosophers regularly met. Barred because she was a woman, she simply had a suit of men's clothes made for herself and reappeared, her long legs now in breeches and hose, to the delight of cheering colleagues and the consternation of the management.

From the early 1730s until the late 1740s her affair with the *philosophe* Voltaire made possible over ten years of study and writing. He paid for the renovation of her husband's country château in Champagne where they established a life filled with their work and time with each other. They had the windows draped so that shifts from day to night would not distract them. They collected a library of ten thousand volumes, more than the number at most universities. He had his study; she hers.

Emilie du Châtelet usually rose at dawn, breakfasted on fish, bread, stew, and wine, then wrote letters, made the household arrangements for the day, and saw her children. Then she studied. She set up her experiments in the great hall of the château—pipes, rods, and wooden balls hung from the rafters as she set about duplicating the English physicist Newton's experiments. She and Voltaire broke the day with a meal together. Then more study and more writing. When she had trouble staying awake she put her hands in ice water until they were numb, then paced and beat them against her arms to restore the circulation.

Châtelet made her reputation as a scientist with her three-volume work on the German mathematician and philosopher Leibnitz, *The Institutions of Physics,* published in 1740. Contemporaries also knew of her work from her translation of Newton's *Principles of Mathematics,* her book on algebra, and her collaboration with Voltaire on his treatise about Newton.

From the fifteenth to the eighteenth centuries privileged women participated in the new intellectual movements. Like the men of their class, they became humanist scholars, naturalists, and scientists. Unfortunately, many of these women found themselves in conflict with their families and their society. A life devoted to scholarship conflicted with the roles that women, however learned, were still expected to fulfill.

SCIENCE AFFIRMS TRADITION

In the sixteenth and seventeenth centuries Europe's learned men questioned, altered, and dismissed some of the most hallowed precepts of Europe's inherited wisdom. The intellectual upheaval of the Scientific Revolution caused them to examine and describe anew the nature of the universe and its forces, the nature of the human body and its functions. Men used telescopes and rejected the traditional insistence on the smooth surface of the moon. Galileo, Leibnitz, and Newton studied and charted the movement of the planets, discovered gravity and the true relationship between the earth and the sun. Fallopio dissected the human body, Harvey discovered the circulation of the blood, and Leeuwenhoek found spermatozoa with his microscope.

For women, however, there was no Scientific Revolution. When men studied female anatomy, when they spoke of female physiology, of women's reproductive organs, of the female role in procreation, they ceased to be scientific. They suspended reason and did not accept the evidence of their senses. Tradition, prejudice, and imagination, not scientific observation, governed their conclusions about women. The writings of the classical authors like Aristotle and Galen continued to carry the same authority as they had when first written, long after they had been discarded in other areas. Men spoke in the name of the new "science" but mouthed words and phrases from the old misogyny. In the name of "science" they gave a supposed physiological basis to the traditional views of women's nature, function, and role. Science affirmed what men had always known, what custom, law, and religion had postulated and justified. With the authority of their "objective," "rational" inquiry they restated ancient premises and arrived at the same traditional conclusions: the innate superiority of the male and the justifiable subordination of the female.

In the face of such certainty, the challenges of women like Lucrezia Marinella and María de Zayas had little effect. As Marie de Gournay, the French essayist, had discovered at the beginning of the seventeenth century, those engaged in the scientific study of humanity viewed the female as if she were of a different species—less than human, at best; nature's mistake, fit only to "play the fool and serve [the male]."

The standard medical reference work, *Gynaecea,* reprinted throughout the last decades of the sixteenth century, included the old authorities like Aristotle and Galen, and thus the old premises about women's innate physical inferiority. A seventeenth-century examination for a doctor in Paris asked the rhetorical question "Is woman an imperfect work of nature?" All of the Aristotelian ideals about the different "humors" of the female and male survived in the popular press even after they had been rejected by the medical elite. The colder and moister humors of the female meant that women had a passive nature and thus took longer to develop in the womb. Once grown to maturity, they were better able to withstand the pain of childbirth.

Even without reference to the humors, medical and scientific texts supported the limited domestic role for women. Malebranche, a French seventeenth-century philosopher, noted that the delicate fibers of the woman's brain made her overly sensitive to all that came to it; thus she could not deal with ideas or form abstractions. Her body and mind were so relatively weak that she must stay within the protective confines of the home to be safe.

No amount of anatomical dissection dispelled old bits of misinformation or changed the old misconceptions about women's reproductive organs. Illustrations continued to show the uterus shaped like a flask with two horns, and guides for midwives gave the principal role in labor to the fetus. As in Greek and Roman medical texts these new "scientific" works assumed that women's bodies dictated their principal function, procreation. Yet even this role was devalued. All of the evidence of dissection and deductive reasoning reaffirmed the superiority of the male's role in reproduction. Men discovered the spermatazoon, but not the ovum. They believed that semen was the single active agent. Much as Aristotle had done almost two millennia earlier, seventeenth-century scientific study hypothesized that the female supplied the "matter," while the life and essence of the embryo came from the sperm alone.

These denigrating and erroneous conclusions were reaffirmed by the work of the seventeenth-century English scientist William Harvey. Having discovered the circulation of the blood, Harvey turned his considerable talents to the study of human reproduction and published his conclusions in 1651. He dissected female deer at all stages of their cycle, when pregnant and when not. He studied chickens and roosters. With all of this dissection and all of this observation he hypothesized an explanation for procreation and a rhapsody to male semen far more extreme than anything Aristotle had reasoned. The woman, like the hen with her unfertilized egg, supplies the matter, the man gives it form and life. The semen, he explained, had almost magical power to "elaborate, concoct"; it was "vivifying, . . . endowed with force and spirit and generative influence," coming as it did from "vessels so elaborate, and endowed with such vital energy." So powerful was this fluid that it did not even have to reach the woman's uterus or remain in the vagina. Rather he believed it gave off a "fecundating power," leaving the woman's body to play a passive, or secondary, role. Simple contact with this magical elixir of life worked like lightning, or—drawing on another set of his experiments—"in the same way as iron touched by the magnet is endowed with its powers and can attract other iron to it." The woman was but the receiver and the receptacle.

Anatomy and physiology confirmed the innate inferiority of woman and her limited reproductive function. They also proved as "scientific truth" all of the traditional negative images of the female nature. A sixteenth-century Italian anatomist accepted Galen's view and believed the ovaries to be internal testicles. He explained their strange placement so "as to keep her from perceiving and ascertaining her sufficient perfection," and to humble her "continual desire to dominate." An early-seventeenth-century French book on childbirth instructed the midwife to tie the umbilical cord far from the body to assure a long penis and a well-spoken young man for a male child and close to the body to give the female a straighter form and to ensure that she would talk less.

No one questioned the equally ancient and traditional connection between physiology and nature: the role of the uterus in determining a woman's behavior. This organ's potential influence confirmed the female's irrationality and her need to accept a subordinate role to the male. The sixteenth-century Italian anatomist Fallopio repeated Aristotle's idea that the womb lusted for the male in its desire to procreate. The French sixteenth-century doctor and writer Rabelais took Plato's view of the womb as insatiable, like an animal out of control when denied sexual intercourse, the cause of that singularly female ailment, "hysteria." Other sixteenth- and seventeenth-century writers on women and their health adopted all of the most misogynistic explanations of the traditional Greek and Roman authorities. No menstruation meant a diseased womb, an organ suffocating in a kind of female excrement. Only intercourse with a man could prevent or cure the condition. Left untreated the uterus would put pressure on other organs, cause convulsions, or drive the woman crazy. Thus, the male remained the key agent in the woman's life. She was innately inferior, potentially irrational, and lost to ill-health and madness without his timely intervention.

So much changed from the fifteenth to the eighteenth centuries in the ways in which women and men perceived their world, its institutions and attitudes. The Renaissance offered the exhilaration of a society in which the individual could be freed from traditional limitations. In the spirit of Humanistic and scientific inquiry men questioned and reformulated assumptions about the mind's capabilities and the description of the natural universe. New methods of reasoning and discourse, of observation and experimentation, evolved and led to the reorientation of the natural universe and more accurate descriptions of the physical world, including man's own body. Yet when it came to questions and assumptions about women's function and role and to descriptions of her nature and her body, no new answers were formulated. Instead, inspired by the intellectual excitement of the times and the increasing confidence in their own perceptions of the spiritual and material world, men argued even more strongly from traditional premises, embellishing and revitalizing the ancient beliefs. Instead of breaking with tradition, descriptions of the female accumulated traditions: the classical, the religious, the literary, the customary, and the legal—all stated afresh in the secular language of the new age. Instead of being freed, women were ringed with yet more binding and seemingly incontrovertible versions of the traditional attitudes about their inferior nature, their proper function and role, and their subordinate relationship to men.

With the advent of printing, men were able to disseminate these negative conclusions about women as they never could before. From the sixteenth century on the printing presses brought the new tracts, pamphlets, treatises, broadsides, and engravings to increasing numbers of Europeans: pictures of the sperm as a tiny, fully formed infant; works by scholars and jurists explaining the female's "natural" physical and legal incapacity; romances and ballads telling of unchaste damsels and vengeful wives set to plague man.

Although these misogynistic attitudes about women flourished and spread, the defense of women had also begun. In her *Book of the City of Ladies* Christine de Pizan, the fifteenth-century writer, asks why no one had spoken on their behalf before, why the "accusations and slanders" had gone uncontradicted for so long? Her allegorical mentor, "Rectitude," replies, "Let me tell you that in the long run, everything comes to a head at the right time."

The world of the courts had widened the perimeters of women's expectations and given some women increased opportunities. However, for the vast majority of women, still not conscious of their disadvantaged and subordinate status, changes in material circumstances had a far greater impact. From the seventeenth to the twentieth centuries more women were able to live the life restricted in previous ages to the few. In Europe's salons and parlors they found increased comfort, greater security, and new ways to value their traditional roles and functions. For these women, "the right time"—the moment for questioning and rejecting the ancient premises of European society—lay in the future.

17. CHINA, TECHNOLOGY, AND CHANGE

Lynda Norene Shaffer

In this selection a modern historian of China cautions against judging Chinese history by later events in Europe. What was the impact of printing, the compass, and gunpowder in Europe? What was the earlier impact of these inventions in China? To what extent were the effects on China and Europe similar? To what extent were they different?

Francis Bacon (1561–1626), an early advocate of the empirical method, upon which the scientific revolution was based, attributed Western Europe's early modern take-off to three things in particular: printing, the compass, and gunpowder. Bacon had no idea where these things had come from, but historians now know that all three were invented in China. Since, unlike Europe, China did not take off onto a path leading from the scientific to the Industrial Revolution, some historians are now asking why these inventions were so revolutionary in Western Europe and, apparently, so unrevolutionary in China.

In fact, the question has been posed by none other than Joseph Needham, the foremost English-language scholar of Chinese science and technology. It is only because of Needham's work that the Western academic community has become aware that until Europe's take-off, China was the unrivaled world leader in technological development. That is why it is so disturbing that Needham himself has posed this apparent puzzle. The English-speaking academic world relies upon him and repeats him; soon this question and the vision of China that it implies will become dogma. Traditional China will take on supersociety qualities—able to contain the power of printing, to rein in the potential of the compass, even to muffle the blast of gunpowder.

The impact of these inventions on Western Europe is well known. Printing not only eliminated much of the opportunity for human copying errors, it also encouraged the production of more copies of old books and an increasing number of new books. As written material became both cheaper and more easily available, intellectual activity increased. Printing would eventually be held responsible, at least in part, for the spread of classical humanism and other ideas from the Renaissance. It is also said to have stimulated the Protestant Reformation, which urged a return to the Bible as the primary religious authority.

The introduction of gunpowder in Europe made castles and other medieval fortifications obsolete (since it could be used to blow holes in their walls) and thus helped to liberate Western Europe from feudal aristocratic power. As an aid to navigation the compass facilitated the Portuguese- and Spanish-sponsored voyages that led to Atlantic Europe's sole possession of the Western Hemisphere, as well as the Portuguese circumnavigation of Africa, which opened up the first all-sea route from Western Europe to the long-established ports of East Africa and Asia.

Needham's question can thus be understood to mean, Why didn't China use gunpowder to destroy feudal walls? Why didn't China use the compass to cross the Pacific and discover America, or to find an all-sea route to Western Europe? Why didn't China undergo a Renaissance or Reformation? The implication is that even though China possessed these technologies, it did not change much. Essentially Needham's question is asking, What was wrong with China?

Actually, there was nothing wrong with China. China was changed fundamentally by these inventions. But in order to see the changes, one must abandon the search for peculiarly European events in Chinese history, and look instead at China itself before and after these breakthroughs.

To begin, one should note that China possessed all three of these technologies by the latter part of the Tang dynasty (618–906)—between four and six hundred years before they appeared in Europe. And it was during just that time, from about 850, when the Tang dynasty began to falter, until 960, when the Song dynasty (960–1279) was established, that China underwent fundamental changes in all spheres. In fact, historians are now beginning to use the term *revolution* when referring to technological and commercial changes that culminated in the Song dynasty, in the same way that they refer to the changes in eighteenth- and nineteenth-century England as the Industrial Revolution. And the word might well be applied to other sorts of changes in China during this period.

For example, the Tang dynasty elite was aristocratic, but that of the Song was not. No one has ever considered whether the invention of gunpowder contributed to the demise of China's aristocrats, which occurred between 750 and 960, shortly after its invention. Gunpowder may, indeed, have been a factor although it is unlikely that its importance lay in blowing up feudal walls. Tang China enjoyed such internal peace that its aristocratic lineages did not engage in castle-building of the sort typical in Europe. Thus, China did not have many feudal fortifications to blow up.

The only wall of significance in this respect was the Great Wall, which was designed to keep steppe nomads from invading China. In fact, gunpowder may have played a role in blowing holes in this wall, for the Chinese could not monopolize the terrible new weapon, and their nomadic enemies to the north soon learned to use it against them. The Song dynasty ultimately fell to the Mongols, the most formidable force ever to emerge from the Eurasian steppe. Gunpowder may have had a profound effect on China—exposing a united empire to foreign invasion and terrible devastation—but an effect quite opposite to the one it had on Western Europe.

On the other hand, the impact of printing on China was in some ways very similar to its later impact on Europe. For example, printing contributed to a rebirth of classical (that is, preceding the third century A.D.) Confucian learning, helping to revive a fundamentally humanistic outlook that had been pushed aside for several centuries.

After the fall of the Han dynasty (206 B.C.–A.D. 220), Confucianism had lost much of its credibility as a world view, and it eventually lost its central place in the scholarly world. It was replaced by Buddhism, which had come from India. Buddhists believed that much human pain and confusion resulted from the pursuit of illusory pleasures and dubious ambitions: enlightenment and, ultimately, salvation would come from a progressive disengagement from the real world, which they also believed to be illusory. This point of view dominated Chinese intellectual life until the ninth century. Thus the academic and intellectual comeback of classical Confucianism was in essence a return to a more optimistic literature that affirmed the world as humans had made it.

The resurgence of Confucianism within the scholarly community was due to many factors, but printing was certainly one of the most important. Although it was invented by Buddhist monks in China, and at first benefited Buddhism, by the middle of the tenth century, printers were turning out innumerable copies of the classical Confucian corpus. This return of scholars to classical learning was part of a more general movement that shared not only its humanistic features with the later Western European Renaissance, but certain artistic trends as well.

Furthermore, the Protestant Reformation in Western Europe was in some ways reminiscent of the emergence and eventual triumph of Neo-Confucian philosophy. Although the roots of Neo-Confucianism can be found in the ninth century, the man who created what would become its most orthodox synthesis was Zhu Xi (Chu Hsi, 1130–1200). Neo-Confucianism was significantly different from classical Confucianism, for it had undergone an intellectual (and political) confrontation with Buddhism and had emerged profoundly changed. It is of the utmost importance to understand that not only was Neo-Confucianism new, it was also heresy, even during Zhu Xi's lifetime. It did not triumph until the thirteenth century, and it was not until 1313 (when Mongol conquerors ruled China) that Zhu Xi's commentaries on the classics became the single authoritative text against which all academic opinion was judged.

In the same way that Protestantism emerged out of a confrontation with the Roman Catholic establishment and asserted the individual Christian's autonomy, Neo-Confucianism emerged as a critique of Buddhist ideas that had taken hold in China, and it asserted an individual moral capacity totally unrelated to the ascetic practices and prayers of the Buddhist priesthood. In the twelfth century Neo-Confucianists lifted the work of Mencius (Meng Zi, 370–290 B.C.) out of obscurity and assigned it a place in the corpus second only to that of the *Analects of Confucius*. Many facets of Mencius appealed to the Neo-Confucianists, but one of the most important was his argument that humans by nature are fundamentally good. Within the context of the Song dynasty, this was an assertion that morally could be pursued through an engagement in human affairs, and that the Buddhist monk's withdrawal from life's mainstream did not bestow upon them any special virtue.

The importance of these philosophical developments notwithstanding, printing probably had its greatest impact on the Chinese political system. The origin of the civil service examination system in China can be traced back to the Han dynasty, but in the Song dynasty government-administered examinations became the most important route to political power in China. For almost a thousand years (except the early period of Mongol rule), China was governed by men who had come to power simply because they had done exceedingly well in examinations on the Neo-Confucian canon. At any one time thousands of students were studying for the exams, and thousands of inexpensive books were required. Without printing such a system would not have been possible.

The development of this alternative to aristocratic rule was one of the most radical changes in world history. Since the examinations were ultimately open to 98 percent of all males (actors were one of the few groups excluded), it was the most democratic system in the world prior to the development of representative democracy and popular suffrage in Western Europe in the eighteenth and nineteenth centuries. (There were some small-scale systems, such as the classical Greek city-states, which might be considered more democratic, but nothing comparable in size to Song China or even the modern nation-states of Europe.)

Finally we come to the compass. Suffice it to say that during the Song dynasty, China developed the world's largest and most technologically sophisticated merchant marine and navy. By the fifteenth century its ships were sailing from the north Pacific to the east coast of Africa. They could have made the arduous journey around the tip of Africa and on into Portuguese ports; however, they had no reason to do so. Although the Western European economy was prospering, it offered nothing that China could not acquire much closer to home at much less cost. In particular, wool, Western Europe's most important export, could easily be obtained along China's northern frontier.

Certainly, the Portuguese and the Spanish did not make their unprecedented voyages out of idle curiosity. They were trying to go to the Spice Islands, in what is now Indonesia, in order to acquire the most valuable commercial items of the time. In the fifteenth century these islands were the world's sole suppliers of the fine spices, such as cloves, nutmeg, and mace, as well as a source for the more generally available pepper. It was this spice market that lured Columbus westward from Spain and drew Vasco Da Gama around Africa and across the Indian Ocean.

After the invention of the compass, China also wanted to go to the Spice Islands and, in fact, did go, regularly—but Chinese ships did not have to go around the world to get there. The Atlantic nations of Western Europe, on the other hand, had to buy spices from Venice (which controlled the Mediterranean trade routes) or from other Italian city-states; or they had to find a new way to the Spice Islands. It was necessity that mothered those revolutionary routes that ultimately changed the world.

Gunpowder, printing, the compass—clearly these three inventions changed China as much as they changed Europe. And it should come as no surprise that changes wrought in China between the eighth and tenth centuries were different from changes wrought in Western Europe between the thirteenth and fifteenth centuries. It would, of course, be unfair and ahistorical to imply that something was wrong with Western Europe because the technologies appeared there later. It is equally unfair to ask why the Chinese did not accidentally bump into the Western Hemisphere while sailing east across the Pacific to find the wool markets of Spain.

18. A DUTCH ANATOMY LESSON IN JAPAN

Sugita Gempaku

Sugita Gempaku (1733–1817) was a Japanese physician who (as he tells us here) suddenly discovered the value of Western medical science when he chanced to witness a dissection shortly after he obtained a Dutch anatomy book.

What was it that Sugita Gempaku learned on that day in 1771? What

*were the differences between the treatments of anatomy in the Chinese
and the Dutch medical books? What accounts for these differences?*

Somehow, miraculously I obtained a book on anatomy written in [The
Netherlands]. . . . It was a strange and even miraculous happening that I
was able to obtain that book in that particular spring of 1771. Then at the
night of the third day of the third month, I received a letter from a man by
the name of Tokuno, who was in the service of the Town Commissioner.
Tokuno stated in his letter that "A post-mortem examination of the body
of a condemned criminal by a resident physician will be held tomorrow at
Senjukotsugahara. You are welcome to witness it if you so desire."

The next day, when we arrived at the location . . . Ryotaku reached
under his kimono to produce a Dutch book and showed it to us. "This is
a Dutch book of anatomy called *Tabulae Anatomicae*. I bought this a few
years ago when I went to Nagasaki, and kept it." As I examined it, it was
the same book I had and was of the same edition. We held each other's
hands and exclaimed: "What a coincidence!" Ryotaku continued by saying: "When I went to Nagasaki, I learned and heard," and opened this
book. "These are called *long* in Dutch, they are lungs," he taught us.
"This is *hart*, or the heart. When it says *maag* it is the stomach, and when
it says *milt* it is the spleen." However, they did not look like the heart
given in the Chinese medical books, and none of us were sure until we
could actually see the dissection.

Thereafter we went together to the place which was especially set for
us to observe the dissection. . . . That day, the old butcher pointed to this
and that organ. After the heart, liver, gall bladder, and stomach were
identified, he pointed to other parts for which there were no names. "I
don't know their names. But I have dissected quite a few bodies from my
youthful days. Inside of everyone's abdomen there were these parts and
those parts." . . . The old butcher again said, "Every time I had a dissection, I pointed out to those physicians many of these parts, but not a
single one of them questioned 'What was this?' or 'What was that?' " We
compared the body as dissected against the charts both Ryotaku and I
had, and could not find a single variance from the charts. The Chinese
Book of Medicine says that the lungs are like the eight petals of the lotus
flower, with three petals hanging in front, three in back, and two petals
forming like two ears and that the liver has three petals to the left and
four petals to the right. There were no such divisions, and the positions
and shapes of intestines and gastric organs were all different from those
taught by the old theories. The official physicians . . . had witnessed
dissection seven or eight times. Whenever they witnessed the dissection,
they found that the old theories contradicted reality. Each time they were
perplexed and could not resolve their doubts. Every time they wrote
down what they thought was strange. They wrote in their books, "The
more we think of it, there must be fundamental differences in the bodies

of Chinese and of the eastern barbarians." I could see why they wrote this way.

That day, after the dissection was over, we decided that we also should examine the shape of the skeletons left exposed on the execution ground. We collected the bones, and examined a number of them. Again, we were struck by the fact that they all differed from the old theories while conforming to the Dutch charts.

The three of us, Ryotaku, Junan, and I went home together. On the way home we spoke to each other and felt the same way. "How marvelous was our actual experience today. It is a shame that we were ignorant of these things until now. As physicians who serve their masters through medicine, we performed our duties in complete ignorance of the true form of the human body. How disgraceful it is. Somehow, through this experience, let us investigate further the truth about the human body. If we practice medicine with this knowledge behind us, we can make contributions for people under heaven and on this earth." Ryotaku spoke to us. "Indeed, I agree with you wholeheartedly." Then I spoke to my companion. "Somehow if we can translate anew this book called *Tabulae Anatomicae,* we can get a clear notion of the human body inside out. It will have great benefit in the treatment of our patients. Let us do our best to read it and understand it without the help of translators." . . .

The next day, we assembled at the house of Ryotaku and recalled the happenings of the previous day. When we faced that *Tabulae Anatomicae,* we felt as if we were setting sail on a great ocean in a ship without oars or a rudder. With the magnitude of the work before us, we were dumbfounded by our own ignorance. However, Ryotaku had been thinking of this for some time, and he had been in Nagasaki. He knew some Dutch through studying and hearing, and knew some sentence patterns and words. He was also ten years older than I, and we decided to make him head of our group and our teacher. At that time I did not know the twenty-five letters of the Dutch alphabet. I decided to study the language with firm determination, but I had to acquaint myself with letters and words gradually.

PART TWO
THE WORLD OF THE WEST: 1750 TO 1914

Statue of Balzac by Rodin, Rodin Museum, Paris (Arthur Sidofsky/Art Resource, NY)

1750	Industrial Revolution begins (Europe) Hume writes about religion and miracles (Britain), 1740s and 1750s France loses New World empire, 1763
	American Declaration of Independence; Smith's *Wealth of Nations* (Britain), 1776
	French Revolution; U.S. Constitution written, 1789
1800	Louisiana Purchase, 1803
	Latin American revolutions, 1810–24
	Slavery abolished in British Empire, 1807–38
1850	First Opium War (China), 1839–42 European revolutions of 1848; Marx and Engels write *Communist Manifesto* (Germany) Admiral Perry in Japan, 1853–54
	Indian "Mutiny," 1857 Darwin develops evolution theory (Britain), 1859
	U.S. Civil War, 1861–65 Meiji Restoration (Japan), 1868 Suez Canal built, 1859–69
	European participation in Africa begins, 1880
1900	Peak labor migrations, 1875–1914 Freud develops psychoanalytic theory (Vienna) c. 1900 Einstein works on relativity theory (Switzerland) c. 1905
	Mexican revolution, 1910–20 Taisho liberal era (Japan), 1912–26 Chinese Nationalist Revolution, 1911 Panama Canal built, 1904–14
1914	World War I begins, 1914

CHAPTER SIX

Enlightenment and Revolution

19. ON MIRACLES

David Hume

The European "Enlightenment" of the eighteenth century was the expression of a new class of intellectuals, independent of the clergy but allied with the rising middle class. Their favorite words were "reason," "nature," and "progress." They applied the systematic doubt of Descartes and the reasoning method of the scientific revolution to human affairs, including religion and politics. With caustic wit and good humor, they asked new questions and popularized new points of view that eventually revolutionized Western politics and culture. While the French philosophes and Voltaire may be the best known, the Scottish philosopher David Hume (1711–1776) may have been the most brilliant. What is his argument in this selection? Does he prove his argument to your satisfaction? How does he use "reason" and "nature" to make his case? Is this scientific method incompatible with religion?

I flatter myself that I have discovered an argument . . . , which, if just, will, with the wise and learned, be an everlasting check to all kinds of superstitious delusion, and consequently will be useful as long as the world endures; for so long, I presume, will the accounts of miracles and prodigies be found in all history, sacred and profane. . . .

A wise man proportions his belief to the evidence. . . .

A miracle is a violation of the laws of nature; and as a firm and unalterable experience has established these laws, the proof against a miracle, from the very nature of the fact, is as entire as any argument from experience can possibly be imagined. . . . Nothing is esteemed a miracle, if it ever happens in the common course of nature. It is no miracle that a man, seemingly in good health, should die on a sudden; because such a kind of death, though more unusual than any other, has yet been frequently observed to happen. But it is a miracle that a dead man should come to life; because that has never been observed in any age or country. There must, therefore, be an uniform experience against every miraculous event, otherwise the event would not merit that appellation. And as an uniform experience amounts to a proof, there is here a direct and full *proof,* from the nature of the fact, against the existence of any miracle. . . .

(Further) there is not to be found, in all history, any miracle attested by a sufficient number of men, of such unquestioned good sense, education, and learning, as to secure us against all delusion in themselves; of such undoubted integrity, as to place them beyond all suspicion of any design to deceive others; of such credit and reputation in the eyes of mankind, as to have a great deal to lose in case of their being detected in any falsehood. . . .

Secondly, We may observe in human nature a principle which, if strictly examined, will be found to diminish extremely the assurance, which we might, from human testimony, have in any kind of prodigy. . . . The passion of *surprise* and *wonder,* arising from miracles, being an agreeable emotion, gives a sensible tendency towards the belief of those events from which it is derived. . . .

With what greediness are the miraculous accounts of travellers received, their descriptions of sea and land monsters, their relations of wonderful adventures, strange men, and uncouth manners? But if the spirit of religion join itself to the love of wonder, there is an end of common sense; and human testimony, in these circumstances, loses all pretensions to authority. A religionist may be an enthusiast, and imagine he sees what has no reality: He may know his narrative to be false, and yet persevere in it, with the best intentions in the world, for the sake of promoting so holy a cause: Or even where this delusion has not place, vanity, excited by so strong a temptation, operates on him more powerfully than on the rest of mankind in any other circumstances; and self-interest with equal force. . . .

The many instances of forged miracles and prophecies and supernatural events, which, in all ages, have either been detected by contrary evidence, or which detect themselves by their absurdity, prove sufficiently the strong propensity of mankind to the extraordinary and marvellous, and ought reasonably to beget a suspicion against all relations of this kind. . . .

Thirdly, It forms a strong presumption against all supernatural and miraculous relations, that they are observed chiefly to abound among ignorant and barbarous nations; or if a civilized people has ever given admission to any of them, that people will be found to have received them from ignorant and barbarous ancestors, who transmitted them with that inviolable sanction and authority which always attend received opinions. . . .

I may add, as a *fourth* reason, which diminishes the authority of prodigies, that there is no testimony for any, even those which have not been expressly detected, that is not opposed by any infinite number of witnesses; so that not only the miracle destroys the credit of testimony, but the testimony destroys itself. To make this the better understood, let us consider, that in matters of religion, whatever is different is contrary; and that it is impossible the religions of ancient Rome, of Turkey, of Siam, and of China, should all of them be established on any solid foundation. Every miracle, therefore, pretended to have been wrought in any of these religions (and all of them abound in miracles), as its direct scope is to establish the particular system to which it is attributed; so has it the same force, though more indirectly, to overthrow every other system. In destroying a rival system, it likewise destroys the credit of those miracles on which that system was established, so that all the prodigies of different religions are to be regarded as contrary facts, and the evidences of these prodigies, whether weak or strong, as opposite to each other. . . .

Upon the whole, then, it appears, that no testimony for any kind of miracle has ever amounted to a probability, much less to a proof; and that, even supposing it amounted to proof, it would be opposed by another proof, derived from the very nature of the fact which it would endeavour to establish. It is experience only which gives authority to human testimony; and it is the same experience which assures us of the laws of nature. When, therefore, these two kinds of experience are contrary, we have nothing to do but to subtract the one from the other, and embrace an opinion either on one side or the other, with that assurance which arises from the remainder. But according to the principle here explained, this subtraction with regard to all popular religions amounts to an entire annihilation; and therefore we may establish it as a maxim, that no human testimony can have such force as to prove a miracle, and make it a just foundation for any such system of religion.

20.   WHAT IS ENLIGHTENMENT?

Immanuel Kant

Immanuel Kant (1724–1804), a university professor in the small town of Königsberg, East Prussia (now Kaliningrad, in Russia), was one of the most influential philosophers in European history. In this brief selection from his Critique of Practical Reason *he shows us how the Enlightenment's quest for scientific reason meant a demand, sometimes revolutionary, for political freedom. Do we, as Kant suggests, impose restrictions on our intellectual freedom? Do we need courage to use our own reason? What does he mean by "the freedom to make public use of one's reason"? Why is this so important?*

Enlightenment is man's release from his self-incurred tutelage. Tutelage is man's inability to make use of his understanding without direction from another. Self-incurred is this tutelage when its cause lies not in lack of reason but in lack of resolution and courage to use it without direction from another. *Sapere aude!* "Have courage to use your own reason!"—that is the motto of enlightenment.

Laziness and cowardice are the reasons why so great a portion of mankind, after nature has long since discharged them from external direction, nevertheless remains under lifelong tutelage, and why it is so easy for others to set themselves up as their guardians. It is so easy not to be of age. If I have a book which understands for me, a pastor who has a conscience for me, a physician who decides my diet, and so forth, I need not trouble myself. I need not think, if I can only pay—others will readily undertake the irksome work for me.

That the step to competence is held to be very dangerous by the far greater portion of mankind (and by the entire fair sex)—quite apart from its being arduous—is seen to by those guardians who have so kindly assumed superintendence over them. After the guardians have first made their domestic cattle dumb and have made sure that these placid creatures will not dare take a single step without the harness of the cart to which they are confined, the guardians then show them the danger which threatens if they try to go alone. Actually, however, this danger is not so great, for by falling a few times they would finally learn to walk alone. But an example of this failure makes them timid and ordinarily frightens them away from all further trials.

For any single individual to work himself out of the life under tutelage which has become almost his nature is very difficult. He has come to be fond of this state, and he is for the present really incapable of making use of his reason, for no one has ever let him try it out. Statutes and formulas, those mechanical tools of the rational employment or rather mis-employment of his natural gifts, are the fetters of an everlasting tutelage. Whoever throws them off makes only an uncertain leap over the narrowest ditch because he is not accustomed to that kind of free motion. Therefore, there are only few who have succeeded by their own exercise of mind both in freeing themselves from incompetence and in achieving a steady pace.

But that the public should enlighten itself is more possible; indeed, if only freedom is granted, enlightenment is almost sure to follow. For there will always be some independent thinkers, even among the established guardians of the great masses, who, after throwing off the yoke of tutelage from their own shoulders, will disseminate the spirit of the rational appreciation of both their own worth and every man's vocation for thinking for himself. But be it noted that the public, which has first been brought under this yoke by their guardians, forces the guardians themselves to remain bound when it is incited to do so by some of the guardians who are themselves capable of some enlightenment—so harmful is it to implant prejudices, for they later take vengeance on their cultivators or on their descendants. Thus the public can only slowly attain enlightenment. Perhaps a fall of personal despotism or of avaricious or tyrannical oppression may be accomplished by revolution, but never a true reform in ways of thinking. Rather, new prejudices will serve as well as old ones to harness the great unthinking masses.

For this enlightenment, however, nothing is required but freedom, and indeed the most harmless among all the things to which this term can properly be applied. It is the freedom to make public use of one's reason at every point. But I hear on all sides, "Do not argue!" The officer says: "Do not argue but drill!" The tax-collector: "Do not argue but pay!" The cleric: "Do not argue but believe!" Everywhere freedom is restricted.

21. TWO REVOLUTIONARY DECLARATIONS

The American Declaration of Independence and the French Declaration of the Rights of Man and Citizen are similar products of the Enlightenment. Whether the French document of 1789 that served as a summary of the philosophy of the French Revolution was based on Thomas Jefferson's American Declaration of 1776, the debt of both to the Enlightenment ideas of John Locke, the French philosophes, and the emerging consensus of middle-class goals is evident. In what ways are the declarations similar and different? Have we broadened or lessened our idea of freedom since then?

21.1. THE AMERICAN DECLARATION OF INDEPENDENCE

In Congress, July 4, 1776 the Unanimous Declaration of the Thirteen United States of America

When in the course of human events, it becomes necessary for one people to dissolve the political bands which have connected them with another, and to assume among the powers of the earth, the separate and equal station to which the Laws of Nature and of Nature's God entitle them, a decent respect to the opinions of mankind requires that they should declare the causes which impel them to the separation.

We hold these truths to be self-evident, that all men are created equal, that they are endowed by their Creator with certain unalienable rights, that among these are life, liberty and the pursuit of happiness. That to secure these rights, governments are instituted among men, deriving their just powers from the consent of the governed. That whenever any form of government becomes destructive of these ends, it is the right of the people to alter or to abolish it, and to institute new government, laying its foundation on such principles and organizing its powers in such form, as to them shall seem most likely to effect their safety and happiness. Prudence, indeed, will dictate that governments long established should not be changed for light and transient causes; and accordingly all experience hath shown, that mankind are more disposed to suffer, while evils are sufferable, than to right themselves by abolishing the forms to which they are accustomed. But when a long train of abuses and usurpations, pursuing invariably the same object evinces a design to reduce them under absolute despotism, it is their right, it is their duty, to throw off such government, and to provide new guards for their future security. Such has been the patient sufferance of these Colonies; and such is now the necessity which constrains them to alter their former systems of government. The history of the present King of Great Britain is a history of repeated injuries and usurpations, all having in direct object the establishment of an absolute tyranny over these States. To prove this, let facts be submitted to a candid world.

He has refused his assent to laws, the most wholesome and necessary for the public good.

He has forbidden his Governors to pass laws of immediate and pressing importance, unless suspended in their operation till his assent should be obtained; and when so suspended, he has utterly neglected to attend to them.

He has refused to pass other laws for the accommodation of large districts of people, unless those people would relinquish the right of representation in the Legislature, a right inestimable to them and formidable to tyrants only.

He has called together legislative bodies at places unusual, uncomfortable, and distant from the depository of their public records, for the sole purpose of fatiguing them into compliance with his measures.

He has dissolved representative houses repeatedly, for opposing with manly firmness his invasions on the rights of the people.

He has refused for a long time, after such dissolutions, to cause others to be elected; whereby the legislative powers, incapable of annihilation, have returned to the people at large for their exercise; the State remaining in the meantime exposed to all the dangers of invasion from without and convulsions within.

He has endeavoured to prevent the population of these states; for that purpose obstructing the laws of naturalization of foreigners; refusing to pass others to encourage their migration hither, and raising the conditions of new appropriations of lands.

He has obstructed the administration of justice, by refusing his assent to laws for establishing judiciary powers.

He has made judges dependent on his will alone, for the tenure of their offices, and the amount and payment of their salaries.

He has erected a multitude of new offices, and sent hither swarms of officers to harass our people, and eat out their substance.

He has kept among us, in times of peace, standing armies without the consent of our legislatures.

He has affected to render the military independent of and superior to the civil power.

He has combined with others to subject us to a jurisdiction foreign to our constitution, and unacknowledged by our laws; giving his assent to their acts of pretended legislation:

For quartering large bodies of armed troops among us:

For protecting them, by a mock trial, from punishment for any murders which they should commit on the inhabitants of these States:

For cutting off our trade with all parts of the world:

For imposing taxes on us without our consent:

For depriving us in many cases, of the benefits of trial by jury:

For transporting us beyond seas to be tried for pretended offences:

For abolishing the free system of English laws in a neighbouring Province, establishing therein an arbitrary government, and enlarging its boundaries so as to render it at once an example and fit instrument for introducing the same absolute rule into these Colonies:

For taking away our Charters, abolishing our most valuable laws, and altering fundamentally the forms of our governments:

For suspending our own Legislatures, and declaring themselves invested with power to legislate for us in all cases whatsoever.

He has abdicated government here, by declaring us out of his protection and waging war against us.

He has plundered our seas, ravaged our coasts, burnt our towns, and destroyed the lives of our people.

He is at this time transporting large armies of foreign mercenaries to complete the works of death, desolation and tyranny, already begun with circumstances of cruelty and perfidy scarcely paralleled in the most barbarous ages, and totally unworthy the head of a civilized nation.

He has constrained our fellow citizens taken captive on the high seas to bear arms against their country, to become the executioners of their friends and brethren, or to fall themselves by their hands.

He has excited domestic insurrections amongst us, and has endeavoured to bring on the inhabitants of our frontiers, the merciless Indian savages, whose known rule of warfare, is an undistinguished destruction of all ages, sexes, and conditions.

In every state of these oppressions we have petitioned for redress in the most humble terms: our repeated petitions have been answered only be repeated injury. A prince whose character is thus marked by every act which may define a tyrant is unfit to be the ruler of a free people.

Nor have we been wanting in attention to our British brethren. We have warned them from time to time of attempts by their legislature to extend an unwarrantable jurisdiction over us. We have reminded them of the circumstances of our emigration and settlement here. We have appealed to their native justice and magnanimity, and we have conjured them by the ties of our common kindred to disavow these usurpations, which would inevitably interrupt our connections and correspondence. They too have been deaf to the voice of justice and of consanguinity. We must, therefore, acquiesce in the necessity, which denounces our separation, and hold them, as we hold the rest of mankind, enemies in war, in peace friends.

We, therefore, the Representatives of the United States of America, in General Congress assembled, appealing to the Supreme Judge of the world for the rectitude of our intentions, do, in the name, and by authority of the good people of these Colonies, solemnly publish and declare, That these United Colonies are, and of right ought to be Free and Independent States; that they are absolved from all allegiance to the British Crown, and that all political connection between them and the State of Great Britain, is and ought to be totally dissolved; and that as Free and Independent States, they have full power to levy war, conclude peace, contract alliances, establish commerce, and to do all other acts and things which Independent States may of right do. And for the support of this declaration, with a firm reliance on the protection of Divine Providence, we mutually pledge to each other our lives, our fortunes, and our sacred honor.

21.2. THE FRENCH DECLARATION OF THE RIGHTS OF MAN AND CITIZEN

The representatives of the French people, organized in National Assembly, considering that ignorance, forgetfulness, or contempt of the rights of man are the sole causes of public misfortunes and of the corruption of governments, have resolved to set forth in a solemn declaration the natural, inalienable, and sacred rights of man, in order that such declaration, continually before all members of the social body, may be a perpetual reminder of their rights and duties; in order that the acts of the legislative power and those of the executive power may constantly be compared with the aim of every political institution and may accordingly be more respected; in order that the demands of the citizens, founded henceforth upon simple and incontestable principles, may always be directed towards the maintenance of the Constitution and the welfare of all.

Accordingly, the National Assembly recognizes and proclaims, in the presence and under the auspices of the Supreme Being, the following rights of man and citizen.

1. Men are born and remain free and equal in rights; social distinctions may be based only upon general usefulness.

2. The aim of every political association is the preservation of the natural and inalienable rights of man; these rights are liberty, property, security, and resistance to oppression.

3. The source of all sovereignty resides essentially in the nation; no group, no individual may exercise authority not emanating expressly therefrom.

4. Liberty consists of the power to do whatever is not injurious to others; thus the enjoyment of the natural rights of every man has for its limits only those that assure other members of society the enjoyment of those same rights; such limits may be determined only by law.

5. The law has the right to forbid only actions which are injurious to society. Whatever is not forbidden by law may not be prevented, and no one may be constrained to do what it does not prescribe.

6. Law is the expression of the general will; all citizens have the right to concur personally, or through their representatives, in its formation; it must be the same for all, whether it protects or punishes. All citizens, being equal before it, are equally admissible to all public offices, positions, and employments, according to their capacity, and without other distinction than that of virtues and talents.

7. No man may be accused, arrested, or detained except in the cases determined by law, and according to the forms prescribed thereby. Whoever solicit, expedite, or execute arbitrary orders, or have them executed, must be punished; but every citizen summoned or apprehended in pursuance of the law must obey immediately; he renders himself culpable by resistance.

8. The law is to establish only penalties that are absolutely and obviously necessary; and no one may be punished except by virtue of a law established and promulgated prior to the offence and legally applied.

9. Since every man is presumed innocent until declared guilty, if ar-

rest be deemed indispensable, all unnecessary severity for securing the person of the accused must be severely repressed by law.

10. No one is to be disquieted because of his opinions, even religious, provided their manifestation does not disturb the public order established by law.

11. Free communication of ideas and opinions is one of the most precious of the rights of man. Consequently, every citizen may speak, write, and print freely, subject to responsibility for the abuse of such liberty in the cases determined by law.

12. The guarantee of the rights of man and citizen necessitates a public force; such a force, therefore, is instituted for the advantage of all and not for the particular benefit of those to whom it is entrusted.

13. For the maintenance of the public force and for the expenses of administration a common tax is indispensable; it must be assessed equally on all citizens in proportion to their means.

14. Citizens have the right to ascertain, by themselves or through their representatives, the necessity of the public tax, to consent to it freely, to supervise its use, and to determine its quota, assessment, payment, and duration.

15. Society has the right to require of every public agent an accounting of his administration.

16. Every society in which the guarantee of rights is not assured or the separation of powers not determined has no constitution at all.

17. Since property is a sacred and inviolate right, no one may be deprived thereof unless a legally established public necessity obviously requires it, and upon condition of a just and previous indemnity.

22.   THE U.S. BILL OF RIGHTS

The Bill of Rights is the first ten amendments to the U.S. Constitution. It was officially adopted in 1791, shortly after the Constitution went into effect. What rights are protected by these amendments? Why were they important? Are they still important? Compare the Bill of Rights with the declarations you have just read.

AMENDMENT I

Congress shall make no law respecting an establishment of religion, or prohibiting the free exercise thereof; or abridging the freedom of speech, or of the press; or the right of the people peaceably to assemble, and to petition the Government for a redress of grievances.

AMENDMENT II

A well-regulated Militia, being necessary to the security of a free State, the right of the people to keep and bear Arms, shall not be infringed.

AMENDMENT III

No Soldier shall, in time of peace, be quartered in any house without the consent of the Owner, nor in time of war, but in a manner to be prescribed by law.

AMENDMENT IV

The right of the people to be secure in their persons, houses, papers, and effects, against unreasonable searches and seizures, shall not be violated, and no Warrants shall issue, but upon probable cause, supported by Oath or affirmation, and particularly describing the place to be searched, and the persons or things to be seized.

AMENDMENT V

No person shall be held to answer for a capital, or otherwise infamous crime, unless on a presentment or indictment of a Grand Jury, except in cases arising in the land or naval forces, or in the Militia, when an actual service in time of War or public danger; nor shall any person be subject for the same offence to be twice put in jeopardy of life or limb; nor shall be compelled in any criminal case to be a witness against himself, nor be deprived of life, liberty, or property, without due process of law; nor shall private property be taken for public use, without just compensation.

AMENDMENT VI

In all criminal prosecutions, the accused shall enjoy the right to a speedy and public trial, by an impartial jury of the State and district wherein the crime shall have been committed, which district shall have been previously ascertained by law, and to be informed of the nature and cause of the accusation; to be confronted with the witness against him; to have compulsory process for obtaining witness in his favor, and to have the Assistance of Counsel for his defence.

AMENDMENT VII

In Suits at common law, where the value in controversy shall exceed twenty dollars, the right of trial by jury shall be preserved, and no fact tried by a jury, shall be otherwise reexamined in any Court of the United States, than according to the rules of the common law.

AMENDMENT VIII

Excessive bail shall not be required, nor excessive fines imposed, nor cruel and unusual punishments inflicted.

AMENDMENT IX

The enumeration in the Constitution, of certain rights, shall not be construed to deny or disparage others retained by the people.

AMENDMENT X

The powers not delegated to the United States by the Constitution, nor prohibited by it to the States, are reserved to the States respectively, or to the people.

23. A CONSTITUTION FOR VENEZUELA

Simón Bolívar

Simón Bolívar (1783–1830), called "the Liberator," successfully led the Latin American revolution for independence from Spain between 1810 and 1824. In 1819 he became president of Venezuela and of what is today Colombia, Ecuador, and Panama. In that year he gave the following speech on the Constitution of Venezuela.

What does he see as the difference between the independence of Spanish-American colonies and that of the United States? What does he mean when he says that Latin Americans have been denied "domestic tyranny"? Would you call Bolívar a "democrat"? Is he more or less democratic than the French or North American revolutionaries? What kind of society do you think would result from the constitution he envisions?

Let us review the past to discover the base upon which the Republic of Venezuela is founded.

America, in separating from the Spanish monarchy, found herself in a situation similar to that of the Roman Empire when its enormous framework fell to pieces in the midst of the ancient world. Each Roman division then formed an independent nation in keeping with its location or interests; but this situation differed from America's in that those members proceeded to reestablish their former associations. We, on the contrary, do not even retain the vestiges of our original being. We are not Europeans; we are not Indians; we are but a mixed species of aborigines and Spaniards. Americans by birth and Europeans by law, we find ourselves engaged in a dual conflict: we are disputing with the natives for titles of ownership, and at the same time we are struggling to maintain ourselves in the country that gave us birth against the opposition of the invaders. Thus our position is most extraordinary and complicated. But there is more. As our role has always been strictly passive and political existence nil, we find that our quest for liberty is now even more difficult of accomplishment; for we, having been placed in a state lower than slavery, had been robbed not only of our freedom but also of the right to exercise an active domestic tyranny. Permit me to explain this paradox.

In absolute systems, the central power is unlimited. The will of the despot is the supreme law, arbitrarily enforced by subordinates who take part in the organized oppression in proportion to the authority that they wield. They are charged with civil, political, military, and religious functions; but, in the final analysis, the satraps of Persia are Persian, the pashas of the Grand Turk are Turks, and the sultans of Tartary are Tartars. China does not seek her mandarins in the homeland of Genghis Khan, her conqueror. America, on the contrary, received everything from Spain, who, in effect, deprived her of the experience that she would have gained from the exercise of an active tyranny by not allowing her to take part in her own domestic affairs and administration. This exclusion made it impossible for us to acquaint ourselves with the management of public affairs; nor did we enjoy that personal consideration, of such great value in major revolutions, that the brilliance of power inspires in the eyes of the multitude. In brief, Gentlemen, we were deliberately kept in ignorance and cut off from the world in all matters relating to the science of government.

Subject to the three-fold yoke of ignorance, tyranny, and vice, the

American people have been unable to acquire knowledge, power, or [civic] virtue. The lessons we received and the models we studied, as pupils of such pernicious teachers, were most destructive. We have been ruled more by deceit than by force, and we have been degraded more by vice than by superstition. Slavery is the daughter of darkness: an ignorant people is a blind instrument of its own destruction. Ambition and intrigue abuse the credulity and experience of men lacking all political, economic, and civic knowledge; they adopt pure illusion as reality; they take license for liberty, treachery for patriotism, and vengeance for justice. This situation is similar to that of the robust blind man who, beguiled by his strength, strides forward with all the assurance of one who can see, but, upon hitting every variety of obstacle, finds himself unable to retrace his steps.

If a people, perverted by their training, succeed in achieving their liberty, they will soon lose it, for it would be of no avail to endeavor to explain to them that happiness consists in the practice of virtue; that the rule of law is more powerful than the rule of tyrants, because, as the laws are more inflexible, every one should submit to their beneficent austerity; that proper morals, and not force, are the bases of law; and that to practice justice is to practice liberty. Therefore, Legislators, your work is so much the more arduous, inasmuch as you have to reeducate men who have been corrupted by erroneous illusions and false incentives. Liberty, says Rousseau, is a succulent morsel, but one difficult to digest. Our weak fellow-citizens will have to strengthen their spirit greatly before they can digest the wholesome nutriment of freedom. Their limbs benumbed by chains, their sight dimmed by the darkness of dungeons, and their strength sapped by the pestilence of servitude, are they capable of marching toward the august temple of Liberty without faltering? Can they come near enough to bask in its brilliant rays and to breathe freely the pure air which reigns therein? . . .

The more I admire the excellence of the federal Constitution of Venezuela, the more I am convinced of the impossibility of its application to our state. And to my way of thinking, it is a marvel that its prototype in North America endures so successfully and has not been overthrown at the first sign of adversity or danger. Although the people of North America are a singular model of political virtue and moral rectitude; although that nation was cradled in liberty, reared on freedom, and maintained by liberty alone; and—I must reveal everything—although those people, so lacking in many respects, are unique in the history of mankind, it is a marvel, I repeat, that so weak and complicated a government as the federal system has managed to govern them in the difficult and trying circumstances of their past. But, regardless of the effectiveness of this form of government with respect to North America, I must say that it has never for a moment entered my mind to compare the position and character of two states as dissimilar as the English-American and the Spanish-American. Would it not be most difficult to apply to Spain the English system of political, civil, and religious liberty: Hence, it would be even more difficult to adapt to Venezuela the laws of North America. Does not *L'Esprit des Lois* state that laws should be suited to the people for whom they are made; that it would be a major coincidence if those of one nation could be adapted to another; that laws must take into account the physical conditions of the country, climate, character of the land, location, size, and mode of living of the people; that they should be in keeping with the degree of liberty that the Constitution can sanction respecting the religion of the inhabitants, their inclinations, resources, number, commerce, habits, and customs? This is the code we must consult, not the code of Washington! . . .

Venezuela had, has, and should have a republican government. Its principles should be the sovereignty of the people, division of powers, civil liberty, proscription of slavery, and the abolition of monarchy and privileges. We need equality to recast, so to speak, into a unified nation, the classes of men, political opinions, and public customs.

Among the ancient and modern nations, Rome and Great Britain are the most outstanding. Both were born to govern and to be free and both were built not on ostentatious forms of freedom, but upon solid institutions. Thus I recommend to you, Representatives, the study of the British Constitution, for that body of laws appears destined to bring about the greatest possible good for the peoples that adopt it; but, however perfect it may be, I am by no means proposing that you imitate it slavishly. When I speak of the British government, I only refer to its republican features; and, indeed, can a political system be labelled a monarchy when it recognizes popular sovereignty, division and balance of powers, civil liberty, freedom of conscience and of press, and all that is politically sublime? Can there be more liberty in any other type of republic? Can more be asked of any society? I commend this Constitution to you as that most worthy of serving as model for those who aspire to the enjoyment of the rights of man and who seek all the political happiness which is compatible with the frailty of human nature.

Nothing in our fundamental laws would have to be altered were we to adopt a legislative power similar to that held by the British Parliament. Like the North Americans, we have divided national representation into two chambers; that of Representatives and the Senate. The first is very wisely constituted. It enjoys all its proper functions, and it requires no essential revision, because the Constitution, in creating it, gave it the form and powers which the people deemed necessary in order that they might be legally and properly represented. If the Senate were hereditary rather than elective, it would, in my opinion, be the basis, the tie, the very soul of our republic. In political storms this body would arrest the thunderbolts of the government and would repel any violent popular reaction. Devoted to the government because of a natural interest in its own preservation, a hereditary senate would always oppose any attempt on the part of the people to infringe upon the jurisdiction and authority of their magistrates. It must be confessed that most men are unaware of their best interests, and that they constantly endeavor to assail them in the hands of their custodians—the individual clashes with the mass, and the mass with authority. It is necessary, therefore, that in all governments there be a neutral body to protect the injured and disarm the offender. To be neutral, this body must not owe its origin to appointment by the government or to election by the people, if it is to enjoy a full measure of independence which neither fears nor expects anything from these two sources of authority. The hereditary senate, as a part of the people, shares its interests, its sentiments, and its spirit. For this reason it should not be presumed that a hereditary senate would ignore the interests of the people or forget its legislative duties. The senators in Rome and in the House of Lords in London have been the strongest pillars upon which the edifice of political and civil liberty has rested.

At the outset, these senators should be elected by Congress. The successors to this Senate must command the initial attention of the government, which should educate them in a *colegio* designed especially to train these guardians and future legislators of the nation. They ought to learn the arts, sciences, and letters that enrich the mind of a public figure. From childhood they should understand the career for which they have been destined by Providence, and from earliest youth they should prepare their minds for the dignity that awaits them.

The creation of a hereditary senate would in no way be a violation of political equality. I do not solicit the establishment of a nobility, for as a celebrated republican has said, that would simultaneously destroy equality and liberty. What I propose is an office for which the candidates must prepare themselves, an office that demands great knowledge and the ability to acquire such knowledge. All should not be left to chance and the outcome of elections. The people are more easily deceived than is Nature perfected by art; and, although these senators, it is true, would not be bred in an environment that is all virtue, it is equally true that they would be raised in an atmosphere of enlightened education. Furthermore, the liberators of Venezuela are entitled to occupy forever a high rank in the Republic that they have brought into existence. I believe that posterity would view with regret the effacement of the illustrious names of its first benefactors. I say, moreover, that it is a matter of public interest and national honor, of gratitude on Venezuela's part, to honor gloriously, until the end of time, a race of virtuous, prudent, and persevering men who, overcoming every obstacle, have founded the Republic at the price of the most heroic sacrifices. And if the people of Venezuela do not applaud the elevation of their benefactors, then they are unworthy to be free, and they will never be free.

A hereditary senate, I repeat, will be the fundamental basis of the legislative power, and therefore the foundation of the entire government. It will also serve as a counterweight to both government and people; and as a neutral power it will weaken the mutual attacks of these two eternally rival powers. In all conflicts the calm reasoning of a third party will serve as the means of reconciliation. Thus the Venezuelan senate will give strength to this delicate political structure, so sensitive to violent repercussions; it will be the mediator that will lull the storms and it will maintain harmony between the head and the other parts of the political body.

CHAPTER SEVEN

Capitalism and the Industrial Revolution

24. ASIA AND THE INDUSTRIAL REVOLUTION

Arnold Pacey

According to this modern historian of technology, Asian techniques and inventions played a significant role in the Industrial Revolution of Europe. The author also argues that British industrialization depended as much on the military conquest of India as it did on Indian technology. What evidence does the author provide for these arguments? What do you think of that evidence?

DEINDUSTRIALIZATION

During the eighteenth century, India participated in the European industrial revolution through the influence of its textile trade, and through the investments in shipping made by Indian bankers and merchants. Developments in textiles and shipbuilding constituted a significant industrial movement, but it would be wrong to suggest that India was on the verge of its own industrial revolution. There was no steam engine in India, no coal mines and few machines. . . . [E]xpanding industries were mostly in coastal areas. Much of the interior was in economic decline, with irrigation works damaged and neglected as a result of the breakup of the Mughal Empire and the disruption of war. Though political weakness in the empire had been evident since 1707, and a Persian army heavily defeated Mughal forces at Delhi in 1739, it was the British who most fully took advantage of the collapse of the empire. Between 1757 and 1803, they took control of most of India except the Northwest. The result was that the East India Company now administered major sectors of the economy, and quickly reduced the role of the big Indian bankers by changes in taxes and methods of collecting them.

Meanwhile, India's markets in Europe were being eroded by competition from machine-spun yarns and printed calicoes made in Lancashire, and high customs duties were directed against Indian imports into Britain. Restrictions were also placed on the use of Indian-built ships for voyages to England. From 1812, there were extra duties on any imports they delivered, and that must be one factor in the decline in shipbuilding. A few Indian ships continued to make the voyage to Britain, however, and there was one in Liverpool Docks in 1839 when Herman Melville arrived from America. It was the *Irrawaddy* from Bombay and Melville commented: 'Forty years ago, these merchantmen were nearly the largest in the world; and they still exceed the generality.' They were 'wholly built by the native shipwrights of India, who . . . surpassed the European artisans'. Melville further commented on a point which an Indian historian confirms, that the coconut fibre rope used for rigging on most Indian ships was too elastic and needed constant attention. Thus the rigging on the *Irrawaddy* was being changed for hemp rope while it was in Liverpool. Sisal rope was an alternative in India, used with advantage on some ships based at Calcutta.

Attitudes to India changed markedly after the subcontinent had fallen into British hands. Before this, travellers found much to admire in technologies ranging from agriculture to metallurgy. After 1803, however, the arrogance of conquest was reinforced by the rapid development of British industry. This meant that Indian techniques which a few years earlier seemed remarkable could now be equalled at much lower cost by British factories. India was then made to appear rather primitive, and the idea grew that its proper role was to provide raw materials for western industry, including raw cotton and indigo dye, and to function as a market for British goods. This policy was reflected in 1813 by a relaxation of the East India Company's monopoly of trade so that other British companies could now bring in manufactured goods freely for sale in India. Thus the textile industry, iron production and shipbuilding were all eroded by cheap imports from Britain, and by handicaps placed on Indian merchants.

By 1830, the situation had become so bad that even some of the British in India began to protest. One exclaimed, 'We have destroyed the manufactures of India', pleading that there should be some protection for silk weaving, 'the last of the expiring manufactures of India'. Another observer was alarmed by a 'commercial revolution' which produced 'so much present suffering to numerous classes in India'.

The question that remains is the speculative one of what might have happened if a strong Mughal government had survived. Fernand Braudel argues that although there was no lack of 'capitalism' in India, the economy was not moving in the direction of home-grown industrialization. The historian of technology inevitably notes the lack of development of machines, even though there had been some increase in the use of water-wheels during the eighteenth century both in the iron industry and at gunpowder mills. However, it is impossible not to be struck by the achievements of the shipbuilding industry, which produced skilled carpenters and a model of large-scale organization. It also trained up draughtsmen and people with mechanical interests. It is striking that one of the Wadia shipbuilders installed gas lighting in his home in 1834 and built a small foundry in which he made parts for steam engines. Given an independent and more prosperous India, it is difficult not to believe that a response to British industrialization might well have taken the form of a spread of skill and innovation from the shipyards into other industries.

As it was, such developments were delayed until the 1850s and later, when the first mechanized cotton mill opened. It is significant that some of the entrepreneurs who backed the development of this industry were from the same Parsi families as had built ships in Bombay and invested in overseas trade in the eighteenth century.

GUNS AND RAILS: ASIA, BRITAIN AND AMERICA

Asian Stimulus

Britain's 'conquest' of India cannot be attributed to superior armaments. Indian armies were also well equipped. More significant was the prior breakdown of Mughal government and the collaboration of many Indians. Some victories were also the result of good discipline and bold strategy, especially when Arthur Wellesley, the future Duke of Wellington, was in command. Wellesley's contribution also illustrates the distinctive western approach to the organizational aspect of technology. Indian armies might have had good armament, but because their guns were made in a great variety of different sizes, precise weapons drill was impossible and the supply of shot to the battlefield was unnecessarily complicated. By contrast, Wellesley's forces standardized on just three sizes of field gun, and the commander himself paid close attention to the design of gun carriages and to the bullocks which hauled them, so that his artillery could move as fast as his infantry, and without delays due to wheel breakages.

Significantly, the one major criticism regularly made of Indian artillery concerned the poor design of gun carriages. Many, particularly before 1760, were little better than four-wheeled trolleys. But the guns themselves were often of excellent design and workmanship. Whilst some were imported and others were made with the assistance of foreign craftworkers, there was many a brass cannon and mortar of Indian design, as well as heavy muskets for camel-mounted troops. Captured field guns were often taken over for use by the British, and after capturing 90 guns in one crucial battle, Wellesley wrote that 70 were 'the finest brass ordnance I have ever seen'. They were probably made in northern India, perhaps at the great Mughal arsenal at Agra.

Whilst Indians had been making guns from brass since the sixteenth century, Europeans could at first only produce this alloy in relatively small quantities because they had no technique for smelting zinc. By the eighteenth century, however, brass was being produced in large quantities in Europe, and brass cannon were being cast at Woolwich Arsenal near London. Several European countries were importing metallic zinc from China for this purpose. However, from 1743 there was a smelter near Britsol in England producing zinc, using coke as fuel, and zinc smelters were also developed in Germany. At the end of the century, Britain's imports of zinc from the Far East were only about 40 tons per year. Nevertheless, a British party which visited China in 1797 took particular note of zinc smelting methods. These were similar to the process used in India, which involved vaporizing the metal and then condensing it. There is a suspicion that the Bristol smelting works of 1743 was based on Indian practice, although the possibility of independent invention cannot be excluded.

A much clearer example of the transfer of technology from India occurred when British armies on the subcontinent encountered rockets, a type of weapon of which they had no previous experience. The basic technology had come from the Ottoman Turks or from Syria before 1500, although the Chinese had invented rockets even earlier. In the 1790s, some Indian armies included very large infantry units equipped with rockets. French mercenaries in Mysore had learned to make them, and the British Ordnance Office was enquiring for somebody with expertise on the subject. In response, William Congreve, whose father was head of the laboratory at Woolwich Arsenal, undertook to design a rocket on Indian lines. After a successful demonstration, about 200 of his rockets were used by the British in an attack on Boulogne in 1806. Fired from over a kilometre away, they set fire to the town. After this success, rockets were adopted quite widely by European armies, though some commanders, notably the Duke of Wellington, frowned on such imprecise weapons, and they tended to drop out of use later in the century. What happened next, however, was typical of the whole British relationship with India. William Congreve set up a factory to manufacture the weapons in 1817, and part of its output was exported to India to equip rocket troops operating there under British command.

Yet another aspect of Asian technology in which eighteenth-century Europeans were interested was the design of farm implements. Reports on seed drills and ploughs were sent to the British Board of Agriculture from India in 1795. A century earlier the Dutch had found much of interest in ploughs and winnowing machines of a Chinese type which they saw in Java. Then a Swedish party visiting Guangzhou (Canton) took a winnowing machine back home with them. Indeed, several of these machines were imported into different parts of Europe, and similar devices for cleaning threshed grain were soon being made there. The inventor of one of them, Jonas Norberg, admitted that he got 'the initial idea' from three machines 'brought here from China', but had to create a new type because the Chinese machines 'do not suit our kinds of grain'. Similarly, the Dutch saw that the Chinese plough did not suit their type of soil, but it stimulated them to produce new designs with curved metal mould-boards in contrast to the less efficient flat wooden boards used in Europe hitherto.

In most of these cases, and especially with zinc smelting, rockets and winnowing machines, we have clear evidence of Europeans studying Asian technology in detail. With rockets and winnowers, though perhaps not with zinc, there was an element of imitation in the European inventions which followed. In other instances, however, the more usual course of technological dialogue between Europe and Asia was that European innovation was challenged by the quality or scale of Asian output, but took a different direction, as we have seen in many aspects of the textile industry. Sometimes, the dialogue was even more limited, and served mainly to give confidence in a technique that was already known. Such was the case with occasional references to China in the writings of engineers designing suspension bridges in Britain. The Chinese had a reputation for bridge construction, and before 1700 Peter the Great had asked for bridge-builders to be sent from China to work in Russia. Later, several books published in Europe described a variety of Chinese bridges, notably a long-span suspension bridge made with iron chains.

Among those who developed the suspension bridge in the West were James Finley in America, beginning in 1801, and Samuel Brown and Thomas Telford in Britain. About 1814, Brown devised a flat, wrought-iron chain link which Telford later used to form the main structural chains in his suspension bridges. But beyond borrowing this specific technique, what Telford needed was evidence that the suspension principle was applicable to the problem he was then tackling. Finley's two longest bridges had spanned 74 and 93 metres, over the Merrimac and Schuylkill rivers in the eastern United States. Telford was aiming to span almost twice the larger distance with his 176-metre Menai Bridge. Experiments at a Shropshire ironworks gave confidence in the strength of the chains. But Telford may have looked for reassurance even further afield. One of his notebooks contains the reminder, 'Examine Chinese bridges.' It is clear from the wording which follows that he had seen a recent booklet advocating a 'bridge of chains', partly based on a Chinese example, to cross the Firth of Forth in Scotland.

25. THE WEALTH OF NATIONS

Adam Smith

The Wealth of Nations, *published the year of the American Declaration of Independence, is also a work of the Enlightenment. Smith (1723–1790) applied scientific principles to economic behavior and came up with some startling conclusions for his age, and possibly ours too. Informing his conclusions was the conviction that people acted principally out of self-interest and that allowing them the freedom to do so resulted in a natural social harmony and economic productivity. "It is not from the benevolence of the butcher, the brewer, or the baker, that we expect our dinner," he says, "but from their regard of their own interest. We address ourselves not to their humanity, but to their self-love, and never talk to them of our own necessities, but of their advantage."*

In the following selections, Smith discusses the division of labor, the market, the relation between labor and prices, supply and demand, money, and free trade. What does he say about these topics? How is his position different from that held by people in his day? Do most people today accept Smith's ideas?

BOOK I: OF THE CAUSES OF IMPROVEMENT IN THE PRODUCTIVE POWERS OF LABOUR, AND OF THE ORDER ACCORDING TO WHICH ITS PRODUCE IS NATURALLY DISTRIBUTED AMONG THE DIFFERENT RANKS OF THE PEOPLE

Chapter I: Of the Division of Labour

The greatest improvement in the productive powers of labour, and the greater part of the skill, dexterity, and judgment with which it is anywhere directed, or applied, seem to have been the effects of the division of labour.

The effects of the division of labour, in the general business of society, will be more easily understood by considering in what manner it operates in some particular manufactures. It is commonly supposed to be carried furthest in some very trifling ones; not perhaps that it really is carried further in them than in others of more importance: but in those trifling manufactures which are destined to supply the small wants of but a small number of people, the whole number of workmen must necessarily be small; and those employed in every different branch of the work can often be collected into the same workhouse, and placed at once under the view of the spectator. In those great manufactures, on the contrary, which are destined to supply the great wants of the great body of the people, every different branch of the work employs so great a number of workmen that it is impossible to collect them all into the same workhouse. We can seldom see more, at one time, than those employed in one single branch. Though in such manufactures, therefore, the work may really be divided into a much greater number of parts than in those of a more trifling nature, the division is not near so obvious, and has accordingly been much less observed.

To take an example, therefore, from a very trifling manufacture; but one in which the division of labour has been very often taken notice of, the trade of the pin-maker; a workman not educated to this business (which the division of labour has rendered a distinct trade), nor acquainted with the use of the machinery employed in it (to the invention of which the same division of labour has probably given occasion), could scarce, perhaps, with his utmost industry, make one pin in a day, and certainly could not make twenty. But in the way in which this business is now carried on, not only the whole work is a peculiar trade, but it is divided into a number of branches, of which the greater part are likewise peculiar trades. One man draws out the wire, another straights it, a third cuts it, a fourth points it, a fifth grinds it at the top for receiving the head; to make the head requires two or three distinct operations; to put it on is a peculiar business, to whiten the pins is another; it is even a trade by itself to put them into the paper; and the important business of making a pin is, in this manner, divided into about eighteen distinct operations, which, in some manufactories, are all performed by distinct hands, though in others the same man will sometimes perform two or three of them. I have seen a small manufactory of this kind where ten men only were employed, and where some of them consequently performed two or three distinct operations. But though they were very poor, and therefore but indifferently accommodated with the necessary machinery, they could, when they exerted themselves, make among them about twelve pounds of pins in a day. There are in a pound upwards of four thousand pins of a middling size. Those ten persons, therefore, could make among them upwards of forty-eight thousand pins in a day. Each person, therefore, making a tenth part of forty-eight thousand pins, might be considered as making four thousand eight hundred pins in a day. But if they had all wrought separately and independently, and without any of them having been educated to this peculiar business, they certainly could not each of them have made twenty, perhaps not one pin in a day; that is, certainly, not the two hundred and fortieth, perhaps not the four thousand eight hundredth part of what they are at present capable of performing, in consequence of a proper division and combination of their different operations.

In every other art and manufacture, the effects of the division of labour are similar to what they are in this very trifling one; though, in many of them, the labour can neither be so much subdivided, nor reduced to so great a simplicity of operation.

Chapter III: That the Division of Labour Is Limited by the Extent of the Market

As it is the power of exchanging that gives occasion to the division of labour, so the extent of this division must always be limited by the extent of that power, or, in other words, by the extent of the market. When the market is very small, no person can have any encouragement to dedicate himself entirely to one employment, for want of the power to exchange all that surplus part of the produce of his own labour, which is over and above his own consumption, for such parts of the produce of other men's labour as he has occasion for.

There are some sorts of industry, even of the lowest kind, which can be carried on nowhere but in a great town. A porter, for example, can find employment and subsistence in no other place. A village is by too much narrow a sphere for him.

Chapter V: Of the Real and Nominal Price of Commodities, or Their Price in Labour, and Their Price in Money

Every man is rich or poor according to the degree in which he can afford to enjoy the necessaries, conveniences, and amusements of human life. But after the division of labour has once thoroughly taken place, it is but a very small part of these with which a man's own labour can supply him. The far greater part of them he must derive from the labour of other people, and he must be rich or poor according to the quantity of that labour which he can command, or which he can afford to purchase. The value of any commodity, therefore, to the person who possesses it, and who means not to use or consume it himself, but to exchange it for other commodities, is equal to the quantity of labour which it enables him to purchase or command. Labour, therefore, is the real measure of the exchangeable value of all commodities.

The real price of everything, what everything really costs to the man who wants to acquire it, is the toil and trouble of acquiring it. What everything is really worth to the man who has acquired it, and who wants to dispose of it or exchange it for something else, is the toil and trouble which it can save to himself, and which it can impose upon other people. What is bought with money or with goods is purchased by labour as much as what we acquire by the toil of our own body. That money or those goods indeed save us this toil. They contain the value of a certain quantity of labour which we exchange for what is supposed at the time to contain the value of an equal quantity. Labour was the first price, the original purchase-money that was paid for all things. It was not by gold or by silver, but by labour, that all the wealth of the world was originally purchased; and its value, to those who possess it, and who want to exchange it for some new productions, is precisely equal to the quantity of labour which it can enable them to purchase or command.

Chapter VII: Of the Natural and Market Price of Commodities

. . . When the quantity of any commodity which is brought to market falls short of the effectual demand, all those who are willing to pay the whole value of the rent, wages, and profit, which must be paid in order to bring it thither, cannot be supplied with the quantity which they want. Rather than want it altogether, some of them will be willing to give more. A competition will immediately begin among them, and the market price will rise more or less above the natural price, according as either the greatness of the deficiency, or the wealth and wanton luxury of the competitors, happen to animate more or less the eagerness of the competition. Among competitors of equal wealth and luxury the same deficiency will generally occasion a more or less eager competition, according as the acquisition of the commodity happens to be of more or less importance to them. Hence the exorbitant price of the necessaries of life during the blockade of a town or in a famine.

When the quantity brought to market exceeds the effectual demand, it cannot be all sold to those who are willing to pay the whole value of the rent, wages, and profit, which must be paid in order to bring it thither. Some part must be sold to those who are willing to pay less, and the low price which they give for it must reduce the price of the whole. The market price will sink more or less below the natural price, according as the greatness of the excess increases more or less the competition of the sellers, or according as it happens to be more or less important to them to get immediately rid of the commodity. The same excess in the importation of perishables will occasion a much greater competition than in that of durable commodities; in the importation of oranges, for example, than in that of old iron.

When the quantity brought to market is just sufficient to supply the effectual demand, and no more, the market price naturally comes to be either exactly, or as nearly as can be judged of, the same with the natural price. The whole quantity upon hand can be disposed of for this price, and cannot be disposed of for more. The competition of the different dealers obliges them all to accept of this price, but does not oblige them to accept of less.

The quantity of every commodity brought to market naturally suits itself to the effectual demand. It is the interest of all those who employ their land, labour, or stock, in bringing any commodity to market, that the quantity never should exceed the effectual demand; and it is the interest of all other people that it never should fall short of that demand.

I thought it necessary, though at the hazard of being tedious, to examine at full length this popular notion that wealth consists in money, or in gold and silver. Money is common language, as I have already observed, frequently signifies wealth, and this ambiguity of expression has rendered this popular notion so familiar to us that even they who are convinced of its absurdity are very apt to forget their own principles, and in the course of their reasonings to take it for granted as a certain and undeniable truth. Some of the best English writers upon commerce set out with observing that the wealth of a country consists, not in its gold and silver only, but in its lands, houses, and consumable goods of all different kinds. In the course of their reasonings, however, the lands, houses, and consumable goods seem to slip out of their memory, and the strain of their argument frequently supposes that all wealth consists in gold and silver, and that to multiply those metals is the great object of national industry and commerce.

The produce of industry is what it adds to the subject or materials upon which it is employed. In proportion as the value of this produce is great or small, so will likewise be the profits of the employer. But it is only for the sake of profit that any man employs a capital in the support of industry; and he will always, therefore, endeavour to employ it in the support of that industry of which the produce is likely to be of the greatest value, or to exchange for the greatest quantity either of money or of other goods.

But the annual revenue of every society is always precisely equal to the exchangeable value of the whole annual produce of its industry, or rather is precisely the same thing with that exchangeable value. As every individual, therefore, endeavours as much as he can both to employ his capital in the support of domestic industry, and so to direct that industry that its produce may be of the greatest value; every individual necessarily labours to render the annual revenue of the society as great as he can. He generally, indeed, neither intends to promote the public interest, nor knows how much he is promoting it. By preferring the support of domestic to that of foreign industry, he intends only his own security; and by directing that industry in such a manner as its produce may be of the greatest value, he intends only his own gain, and he is in this, as in many other cases, led by an invisible hand to promote an end which was no part of his intention. Nor is it always the worse for the society that it was no part of it. By pursuing his own interest he frequently promotes that of the society more effectually than when he really intends to promote it. I have never known much good done by those who affected to trade for the public good. It is an affectation, indeed, not very common among merchants, and very few words need be employed in dissuading them from it.

What is the species of domestic industry which his capital can employ, and of which the produce is likely to be of the greatest value, every individual, it is evident, can, in his local situation, judge much better than any statesman or lawgiver can do for him. The statesman who should attempt to direct private people in what manner they ought to employ their capitals would not only load himself with a most unnecessary attention, but assume an authority which could safely be trusted, not only to no single person, but to no council or senate whatever, and which would nowhere be so dangerous as in the hands of a man who had folly and presumption enough to fancy himself fit to exercise it.

To give the monopoly of the home market to the produce of domestic industry, in any particular art or manufacture, is in some measure to direct private people in what manner they ought to employ their capitals, and must, in almost all cases, be either a useless or a hurtful regulation. If the produce of domestic can be brought there as cheap as that of foreign industry, the regulation is evidently useless. If it cannot, it must generally be hurtful. It is the maxim of every prudent master of a family never to attempt to make at home what it will cost him more to make than to buy. The tailor does not attempt to make his own shoes, but buys them of the shoemaker. The shoemaker does not attempt to make his own clothes, but employs a tailor. The farmer attempts to make neither the one nor the other, but employs those different artificers. All of them find it for their interest to employ their whole industry in a way in which they have some advantage over their neighbours, and to purchase with a part of its produce, or what is the same thing, with the price of a part of it, whatever else they have occasion for.

What is prudence in the conduct of every private family can scarce be folly in that of a great kingdom. If a foreign country can supply us with a commodity cheaper than we ourselves can make it, better buy it of them with some part of the produce of our own industry employed in a way in which we have some advantage. The general industry of the country, being always in proportion to the capital which employs it, will not thereby be diminished, no more than that of the above-mentioned artificers; but only left to find out the way in which it can be employed with the greatest advantage. It is certainly not employed to the greatest advantage when it is thus directed towards an object which it can buy cheaper than it can make.

26.   THE FACTORY SYSTEM OF PRODUCTION

Andrew Ure

Andrew Ure was one of the leading spokesmen for the development of the factory system. Notice the way he describes, from the vantage of the 1830s, the factories of the early Industrial Revolution. Might some of the workers in these factories use different words to describe them? What are the advantages of factory production, according to Ure? Does he see any

disadvantages? What does he think of Smith's comments on the division
of labor? Will the factory continue to make use of the division of labor?
What does he think of skilled workers? Who are the ideal workers for the
factory, according to Ure?

The term *Factory System*, in technology, designates the combined operation of many orders of work-people, adult and young, in tending with
assiduous skill a series of productive machines continuously impelled by
a central power. This definition includes such organizations as cotton-
mills, flax-mills, silk-mills, woollen-mills, and certain engineering works;
but it excludes those in which the mechanisms do not form a connected
series, nor are dependent on one prime mover. Of the latter class,
examples occur in iron-works, dye-works, soap-works, brass-founderies,
&c. Some authors, indeed, have comprehended under the title *factory*,
all extensive establishments wherein a number of people cooperate towards a common purpose of art; and would therefore rank breweries,
distilleries, as well as the workshops of carpenters, turners, coopers,
&c., under the factory system. But I conceive that this title, in its strictest sense, involves the idea of a vast automaton, composed of various
mechanical and intellectual organs, acting in uninterrupted concert for
the production of a common object, all of them being subordinated to a
self-regulated moving force. If the marshalling of human beings in
systematic order for the execution of any technical enterprise were
allowed to constitute a factory, this term might embrace every department of civil and military engineering,—a latitude of application quite
inadmissible.

In its precise acceptation, the Factory system is of recent origin, and may
claim England for its birthplace. The mills for throwing silk, or making
organzine, which were mounted centuries ago in several of the Italian
states, and furtively transferred to this country by Sir Thomas Lombe in
1718, contained indeed certain elements of a factory, and probably suggested some hints of those grander and more complex combinations of
self-acting machines, which were first embodied half a century later in our
cotton manufacture by Richard Arkwright, assisted by gentlemen of
Derby, well acquainted with its celebrated silk establishment. But the spinning of an entangled flock of fibres into a smooth thread, which consti-
tutes the main operation with cotton, is in silk superfluous; being already
performed by the unerring instinct of a worm, which leaves to human art
the simple task of doubling and twisting its regular filaments. The apparatus requisite for this purpose is more elementary, and calls for few of those
gradations of machinery which are needed in the carding, drawing, rov-
ing, and spinning processes of a cotton-mill.

In my recent tour, continued during several months, through the
manufacturing districts, I have seen tens of thousands of old, young, and

middle-aged of both sexes, many of them too feeble to get their daily bread by any of the former modes of industry, earning abundant food, raiment, and domestic accommodation, without perspiring at a single pore, screened meanwhile from the summer's sun and the winter's frost, in apartments more airy and salubrious than those of the metropolis in which our legislative and fashionable aristocracies assemble.

In those spacious halls the benignant power of steam summons around him his myriads of willing menials, and assigns to each the regulated task, substituting for painful muscular effort on their part, the energies of his own gigantic arm, and demanding in return only attention and dexterity to correct such little aberrations as casually occur in his workmanship. The gentle docility of this moving force qualifies it for impelling the tiny bobbins of the lace-machine with a precision and speed inimitable by the most dexterous hands, directed by the sharpest eyes. Hence, under its auspices, and in obedience to Arkwright's polity, magnificent edifices, surpassing far in number, value, usefulness, and ingenuity of construction, the boasted monuments of Asiatic, Egyptian, and Roman despotism, have, within the short period of fifty years, risen up in this kingdom, to show to what extent capital, industry, and science may augment the resources of a state, while they meliorate the condition of its citizens. Such is the factory system, replete with prodigies in mechanics and political economy, which promises in its future growth to become the great minister of civilization to the terraqueous globe, enabling this country, as its heart, to diffuse along with its commerce the life-blood of science and religion to myriads of people still lying "in the region and shadow of death."

When Adam Smith wrote his immortal elements of economics, automatic machinery being hardly known, he was properly led to regard the division of labor as the grand principle of manufacturing improvement; and he showed, in the example of pin-making, how each handicraftsman, being thereby enabled to perfect himself by practice in one point, became a quicker and cheaper workman. In each branch of manufacture he saw that some parts were, on that principle, of easy execution, like the cutting of pin wires into uniform lengths, and some were comparatively difficult, like the formation and fixation of their heads; and therefore he concluded that to each a workman of appropriate value and cost was naturally assigned. This appropriation forms the very essence of the division of labour, and has been constantly made since the origin of society. The ploughman, with powerful hand and skilful eye, has been always hired at high wages to form the furrow, and the ploughboy at low wages, to lead the team. But what was in Dr. Smith's time a topic of useful illustration, cannot now be used without risk of misleading the public mind as to the right principle of manufacturing industry. In fact, the division, or rather adaptation of labour to the different talents of men, is little thought of in factory employment. On the contrary, wherever a process requires peculiar dexterity and steadiness of hand, it is withdrawn as soon as possible from the *cunning* workman, who is prone to irregularities of many kinds, and it is placed in charge of a peculiar mechanism, so self-regulating, that a child may superintend it. . . .

Mr. Anthony Strutt, who conducts the mechanical department of the great cotton factories of Belper and Milford, has so thoroughly departed from the old routine of the schools, that he will employ no man who has learned his craft by regular apprenticeship; but in contempt, as it were, of the division of labour principle, he sets a ploughboy to turn a shaft of perhaps several tons weight, and never has reason to repent his preference, because he infuses into the turning apparatus a precision of action, equal, if not superior, to the skill of the most experienced journeyman.

An eminent mechanician in Manchester told me that he does not choose to make any steam engines at present, because, with his existing means, he would need to resort to the old principle of the division of labour, so fruitful of jealousies and strikes among workmen; but he intends to prosecute that branch of business whenever he has prepared suitable arrangements on the equalization of labour, or automatic plan. On the graduation system, a man must serve an apprenticeship of many years before his hand and eye become skilled enough for certain mechanical feats; but on the system of decomposing a process into its constituents, and embodying each part in an automatic machine, a person of common care and capacity may be intrusted with any of the said elementary parts after a short probation, and may be transferred from one to another, on any emergency, at the discretion of the master. Such translations are utterly at variance with the old practice of the division of labour, which fixed one man to shaping the head of a pin, and another to sharpening its point, with most irksome and spirit-wasting uniformity, for a whole life. . . .

It is, in fact, the constant aim and tendency of every improvement in machinery to supersede human labour altogether, or to diminish its cost, by substituting the industry of women and children for that of men; or that of ordinary labourers for trained artisans. In most of the water-twist, or throstle cotton-mills, the spinning is entirely managed by females of sixteen years and upwards. The effect of substituting the self-acting mule for the common mule, is to discharge the greater part of the men spinners, and to retain adolescents and children. The proprietor of a factory near Stockport states, in evidence to the commissioners, that, by such substitution, he would save 50*l.* a week in wages, in consequence of dispensing with nearly forty male spinners, at about 25*s.* of wages each. This tendency to employ merely children with watchful eyes and nimble fingers, instead of journeymen of long experience, shows how the scholastic dogma of the division of labour into degrees of skill has been exploded by our enlightened manufacturers.

27. THE COMMUNIST MANIFESTO

Karl Marx and Friedrich Engels

The impact of The Communist Manifesto *was slight when it was first published by Karl Marx and Friedrich Engels in the midst of the revolutionary upheaval in Europe in 1848, but it later became one of the most revolutionary declarations in the world. As you read the* Manifesto, *you might notice the differences in tone, content, and style, between it and the earlier declarations of the American and French revolutions. What accounts for some of these differences?*

Among other things, the Manifesto *is an interpretation of history. What is that interpretation? What do the authors mean when they say that the history of past societies is the history of class struggle? How is that different from other interpretations? What, according to them, are the most distinctive features of modern society, and how did this modern society come about? What do you think of their characterization of modern bourgeois society? Where do you agree or disagree with their descriptions of bourgeois society? What, according to Marx and Engels, are the forces which will destroy bourgeois society?*

A specter is haunting Europe—the specter of communism. All the powers of old Europe have entered into a holy alliance to exorcise this specter: Pope and Czar, Metternich and Guizot, French Radicals and German police spies.

Where is the party in opposition that has not been decried as communistic by its opponents in power? Where the Opposition that has not hurled back the branding reproach of communism, against the more advanced opposition parties, as well as against its reactionary adversaries?

Two things result from this fact: I. Communism is already acknowledged by all European powers to be itself a power.

II. It is high time that Communists should openly, in the face of the whole world, publish their views, their aims, their tendencies, and meet their nursery tale of the specter of communism with a manifesto of the party itself.

To this end, Communists of various nationalities have assembled in London and sketched the following manifesto, to be published in the English, French, German, Italian, Flemish, and Danish languages.

BOURGEOIS AND PROLETARIANS[1]

The history of all hitherto existing society is the history of class struggles.

Freeman and slave, patrician and plebeian, lord and serf, guildmaster and journeyman, in a word, oppressor and oppressed, stood in constant opposition to one another, carried on an uninterrupted, now hidden, now open fight, a fight that each time ended, either in a revolutionary reconstitution of society at large, or in the common ruin of the contending classes.

In the earlier epochs of history, we find almost everywhere a complicated arrangement of society into various orders, a manifold gradation of social rank. In ancient Rome we have patricians, knights, plebeians, slaves; in the Middle Ages, feudal lords, vassals, guild-masters, journeymen, apprentices, serfs; in almost all of these classes, again, subordinate gradations.

The modern bourgeois society that has sprouted from the ruins of feudal society, has not done away with class antagonisms. It has but established new classes, new conditions of oppression, new forms of struggle in place of the old ones.

Our epoch, the epoch of the bourgeoisie, possesses, however, this distinctive feature: It has simplified the class antagonisms. Society as a whole is more and more splitting up into the two great hostile camps, into two great classes directly facing each other—bourgeoisie and proletariat.

From the serfs of the Middle Ages sprang the chartered burghers of the earliest towns. From these burgesses the first elements of the bourgeoisie were developed.

The discovery of America, the rounding of the Cape, opened up fresh ground for the rising bourgeoisie. The East-Indian and Chinese markets, the colonization of America, trade with the colonies, the increase in the means of exchange and in commodities generally, gave to commerce, to navigation, to industry, an impulse never before known, and thereby, to the revolutionary element in the tottering feudal society, a rapid development.

The feudal system of industry, in which industrial production was monopolized by closed guilds, now no longer sufficed for the growing wants of the new markets. The manufacturing system took its place. The guildmasters were pushed aside by the manufacturing middle class; division of labor between the different corporate guilds vanished in the face of division of labor in each single workshop.

Meantime the markets kept ever growing, the demand ever rising.

1. In French *bourgeois* means a town-dweller. "Proletarian" comes from the Latin, *proletarius*, which meant a person whose sole wealth was his offspring (*proles*).

(Note by Engels) By "bourgeoisie" is meant the class of modern capitalists, owners of the means of social production and employers of wage-labor; by "proletariat," the class of modern wage-laborers who, having no means of production of their own, are reduced to selling their labor power in order to live.

Even manufacture[2] no longer sufficed. Thereupon, steam and machinery revolutionized industrial production. The place of manufacture was taken by the giant, modern industry, the place of the industrial middle class, by industrial millionaires—the leaders of whole industrial armies, the modern bourgeois.

Modern industry has established the world market, for which the discovery of America paved the way. This market has given an immense development to commerce, to navigation, to communication by land. This development has, in its turn, reacted on the extension of industry; and in proportion as industry, commerce, navigation, railways extended, in the same proportion the bourgeoisie developed, increased its capital, and pushed into the background every class handed down from the Middle Ages.

We see, therefore, how the modern bourgeoisie is itself the product of a long course of development, of a series of revolutions in the modes of production and of exchange.

Each step in the development of the bourgeoisie was accompanied by a corresponding political advance of that class. An oppressed class under the sway of the feudal nobility, it became an armed and self-governing association in the medieval commune; here independent urban republic (as in Italy and Germany), there taxable "third estate" of the monarchy (as in France); afterwards, in the period of manufacture proper, serving either the semifeudal or the absolute monarchy as a counterpoise against the nobility, and, in fact, cornerstone of the great monarchies in general—the bourgeoisie has at last, since the establishment of modern industry and of the world market, conquered for itself, in the modern representative state, exclusive political sway. The executive of the modern state is but a committee for managing the common affairs of the whole bourgeoisie.

The bourgeoisie has played a most revolutionary role in history.

The bourgeoisie, wherever it has got the upper hand, has put an end to all feudal, patriarchal, idyllic relations. It has pitilessly torn asunder the motley feudal ties that bound man to his "natural superiors," and has left no other bond between man and man than naked self-interest, than callous "cash payment." It has drowned the most heavenly ecstasies of religious fervor, of chivalrous enthusiasm, of philistine sentimentalism, in the icy water of egotistical calculation. It has resolved personal worth into exchange value, and in place of the numberless indefeasible chartered freedoms, has set up that single, unconscionable freedom—Free Trade. In one word, for exploitation, veiled by religious and political illusions, it has substituted naked, shameless, direct, brutal exploitation.

2. By *manufacture* Marx meant the system of production which succeeded the guild system but which still relied mainly upon direct human labor for power. He distinguished it from modern industry which arose when machinery driven by water and steam was introduced.

The bourgeoisie has stripped of its halo every occupation hitherto honored and looked up to with reverent awe. It has converted the physician, the lawyer, the priest, the poet, the man of science, into its paid wage-laborers.

The bourgeoisie has torn away from the family its sentimental veil, and has reduced the family relation to a mere money relation.

The bourgeoisie has disclosed how it came to pass that the brutal display of vigor in the Middle Ages, which reactionaries so much admire, found its fitting complement in the most slothful indolence. It has been the first to show what man's activity can bring about. It has accomplished wonders far surpassing Egyptian pyramids, Roman aqueducts, and Gothic cathedrals; it has conducted expeditions that put in the shade all former migrations of nations and crusades.

The bourgeoisie cannot exist without constantly revolutionizing the instruments of production, and thereby the relations of production, and with them the whole relations of society. Conservation of the old modes of production in unaltered form, was, on the contrary, the first condition of existence for all earlier industrial classes. Constant revolutionizing of production, uninterrupted disturbance of all social conditions, everlasting uncertainty and agitation distinguished the bourgeois epoch from all earlier ones. All fixed, fast-frozen relations, with their train of ancient and venerable prejudices and opinions, are swept away, all new-formed ones become antiquated before they can ossify. All that is solid melts into air, all that is holy is profaned, and man is at last compelled to face with sober senses his real conditions of life and his relations with his kind.

The need of a constantly expanding market for its products chases the bourgeoisie over the whole surface of the globe. It must nestle everywhere, settle everywhere, establish connections everywhere.

The bourgeoisie has through its exploitation of the world market given a cosmopolitan character to production and consumption in every country. To the great chagrin of reactionaries, it has drawn from under the feet of industry the national ground on which it stood. All old-established national industries have been destroyed or are daily being destroyed. They are dislodged by new industries, whose introduction becomes a life and death question for all civilized nations, by industries that no longer work up indigenous raw material, but raw material drawn from the remotest zones; industries whose products are consumed, not only at home, but in every quarter of the globe. In place of the old wants, satisfied by the production of the country, we find new wants, requiring for their satisfaction the products of distant lands and climes. In place of the old local and national seclusion and self-sufficiency, we have intercourse in every direction, universal interdependence of nations. And as in material, so also in intellectual production. The intellectual creations of individual nations become common property. National one-sidedness and narrow-mindedness become more and more impossible, and from the numerous national and local literatures there arises a world literature.

The bourgeoisie, by the rapid improvement of all instruments of production, by the immensely facilitated means of communication, draws all nations, even the most barbarian, into civilization. The cheap prices of its commodities are the heavy artillery with which it batters down all Chinese walls, with which it forces the barbarians' intensely obstinate hatred for foreigners to capitulate. It compels all nations, on pain of extinction, to adopt the bourgeois mode of production; it compels them to introduce what it calls civilization into their midst, i.e., to become bourgeois themselves. In a word, it creates a world after its own image.

The bourgeoisie has subjected the country to the rule of the towns. It has created enormous cities, has greatly increased the urban population as compared with the rural, and has thus rescued a considerable part of the population from the idiocy of rural life. Just as it has made the country dependent on the towns, so it has made barbarian and semi-barbarian countries dependent on the civilized ones, nations of peasants on nations of bourgeois, the East on the West.

More and more the bourgeoisie keeps doing away with the scattered state of the population, of the means of production, and of property. It has agglomerated population, centralized means of production, and has concentrated property in a few hands. The necessary consequence of this was political centralization. Independent, or but loosely connected provinces, with separate interests, laws, governments and systems of taxation, became lumped together into one nation, with one government, one code of laws, one national class interest, one frontier and one customs tariff.

The bourgeoisie, during its rule of scarce one hundred years, has created more massive and more colossal productive forces than have all preceding generations together. Subjection of nature's forces to man, machinery, application of chemistry to industry and agriculture, steam-navigation, railways, electric telegraphs, clearing of whole continents for cultivation, canalization of rivers, whole populations conjured out of the ground—what earlier century had even a presentiment that such productive forces slumbered in the lap of social labor?

We see then that the means of production and of exchange, which served as the foundation for the growth of the bourgeoisie, were generated in feudal society. At a certain stage in the development of these means of production and of exchange, the conditions under which feudal society produced and exchanged, the feudal organization of agriculture and manufacturing industry, in a word, the feudal relations of property became no longer compatible with the already developed productive forces; they became so many fetters. They had to be burst asunder; they were burst asunder.

Into their place stepped free competition, accompanied by a social and political constitution adapted to it, and by the economic and political sway of the bourgeois class.

A similar movement is going on before our own eyes. Modern bourgeois society with its relations of production, of exchange and of property, a society that has conjured up such gigantic means of production and exchange, is like the sorcerer who is no longer able to control the powers of the nether world whom he has called up by his spells. For many a decade past the history of industry and commerce is but the history of the revolt of modern productive forces against modern conditions of productions, against the property relations that are the conditions for the existence of the bourgeoisie and of its rule. It is enough to mention the commercial crises that by their periodical return put the existence of the entire bourgeois society on trial, each time more threateningly. In these crises a great part not only of the existing products, but also of the previously created productive forces, are periodically destroyed. In these crises there breaks out an epidemic that, in all earlier epochs, would have seemed an absurdity—the epidemic of overproduction. Society suddenly finds itself put back into a state of momentary barbarism; it appears as if a famine, a universal war of devastation had cut off the supply of every means of subsistence; industry and commerce seem to be destroyed. And why? Because there is too much civilization, too much means of subsistence, too much industry, too much commerce. The productive forces at the disposal of society no longer tend to further the development of the conditions of bourgeois property; on the contrary, they have become too powerful for these conditions, by which they are fettered, and no sooner do they overcome these fetters than they bring disorder into the whole of bourgeois society, endanger the existence of bourgeois property. The conditions of bourgeois society are too narrow to comprise the wealth created by them. And how does the bourgeoisie get over these crises? On the one hand by enforced destruction of a mass of productive forces; on the other, by the conquest of new markets, and by the more thorough exploitation of the old ones. That is to say, by paving the way for more extensive and more destructive crises, and by diminishing the means whereby crises are prevented.

The weapons with which the bourgeoisie felled feudalism to the ground are now turned against the bourgeoisie itself.

But not only has the bourgeoisie forged the weapons that bring death to itself; it has also called into existence the men who are to wield those weapons—the modern working class—the proletarians.

CHAPTER EIGHT

Western Economic Expansion

28. THE IMPERIALISM OF FREE TRADE

John Gallagher and
Ronald Robinson

The period from 1840 to 1880 in Britain (the mid-Victorian period) was one in which the doctrine of "free trade" was very popular. Groups like the "Manchester school" and economic liberals (influenced by Adam Smith) advocated "free trade" as against tariffs, protection, and political empire. That fact has led many historians to interpret British policy in this period as anti-imperialist.

Nonsense, say these modern authors. The British did not oppose empire in this period. They just did not want to own one. They believed that Britain could dominate the rest of the world, without having to pay for the occupation and administration of colonies, through free trade. If Britain could convince the weak governments of Asia, Africa, and South America to eliminate trade barriers, the superiority of British industry would bring Britain cheaper "informal empire." How do Robinson and Gallagher support this argument? Are you convinced?

It ought to be a commonplace that Great Britain during the nineteenth century expanded overseas by means of "informal empire" as much as by acquiring dominion in the strict constitutional sense. For purposes of economic analysis it would clearly be unreal to define imperial history exclusively as the history of those colonies coloured red on the map. Nevertheless, almost all imperial history has been written on the assumption that the empire of formal dominion is historically comprehensible in itself and can be cut out of its context in British expansion and world politics. The conventional interpretation of the nineteenth-century empire continues to rest upon study of the formal empire alone, which is rather like judging the size and character of icebergs solely from the parts above the water-line.

The most striking fact about British history in the nineteenth century, as Seeley pointed out, is that it is the history of an expanding society. The exports of capital and manufacturers, the migration of citizens, the dissemination of the English language, ideas and constitutional forms, were all of them radiations of the social energies of the British peoples. Between 1812 and 1914 over twenty million persons emigrated from the British Isles, and nearly 70 per cent of them went outside the Empire. Between 1815 and 1880, it is estimated, £1,187,000,000 in credit had accumulated abroad, but no more than one-sixth was placed in the formal empire. Even by 1913, something less than half of the £3,975,000,000 of foreign investment lay inside the Empire. Similarly, in no year of the century did the Empire buy much more than one-third of Britain's exports. The basic fact is that British industrialization caused an ever-extending and intensifying development of overseas regions. Whether they were formally British or not, was a secondary consideration.

As the British industrial revolution grew, so new markets and sources of supply were linked to it at different times, and the degree of imperialist action accompanying that process varied accordingly. Thus mercantilist techniques of formal empire were being employed to develop India in the mid-Victorian age at the same time as informal techniques of free trade were being used in Latin America for the same purpose. It is for this reason that attempts to make phases of imperialism correspond directly to phases in the economic growth of the metropolitan economy are likely to prove in vain. The fundamental continuity of British expansion is only obscured by arguing that changes in the terms of trade or in the character of British exports necessitated a sharp change in the process.

From this vantage point the many-sided expansion of British industrial society can be viewed as a whole of which both the formal and informal empires are only parts. Both of them then appear as variable political functions of the extending pattern of overseas trade, investment, migration and culture. If this is accepted, it follows that formal and informal empires are essentially interconnected and to some extent interchangeable. Then not only is the old, legalistic, narrow idea of empire unsatisfactory, but so is the old idea of informal empire as a separate, nonpolitical category of expansion. A concept of informal empire which fails to bring out the underlying unity between it and the formal empire is sterile. Only within the total framework of expansion is nineteenth-century empire intelligible.

Let us now attempt, tentatively, to use the concept of the totality of British expansion described above to restate the main themes of the history of modern British expansion. We have seen that interpretations of this process fall into contradictions when based upon formal political criteria alone. If expansion both formal and informal is examined as a single process, will these contradictions disappear?

The growth of British industry made new demands upon British policy. It necessitated linking undeveloped areas with British foreign trade and, in so doing, moved the political arm to force an entry into markets closed by the power of foreign monopolies.

British policy . . . was active in this way before the American colonies had been lost, but its greatest opportunities came during the Napoleonic Wars. The seizure of the French and Spanish West Indies, the filibustering expedition to Buenos Aires in 1806, the taking of Java in 1811, were all efforts to break into new regions and to tap new resources by means of political action. But the policy went further than simple housebreaking, for once the door was opened and British imports with their political implications were pouring in, they might stop the door from being shut again. Raffles,* for example, temporarily broke the Dutch monopoly of the spice trade in Java and opened the island to free trade. Later, he began the informal British paramountcy over the Malacca trade routes and the Malay peninsula by founding Singapore. In South America, at the same time, British policy was aiming at indirect political hegemony over new regions for the purposes of trade. The British navy carried the Portuguese royal family to Brazil after the breach with Napoleon, and the British representative there extorted from his grateful clients the trade treaty of 1810 which left British imports paying a lower tariff than the goods of the mother country. The thoughtful stipulation was added "that the Present Treaty shall be unlimited in point of duration, and that the obligations and conditions expressed or implied in it shall be perpetual and immutable." . . .

In both the formal and informal dependencies in the mid-Victorian age there was much effort to open the continental interiors and to extend the British influence inland from the ports and to develop the hinterlands. The general strategy of this development was to convert these areas into complementary satellite economies, which would provide raw materials and food for Great Britain, and also provide widening markets for its manufactures. This was the period, the orthodox interpretation would have us believe, in which the political arm of expansion was dormant or even withered. In fact, that alleged inactivity is seen to be a delusion if we take into account the development in the informal aspect. Once entry had been forced into Latin America, China and the Balkans, the task was to encourage stable governments as good investment risks, just as in weaker or unsatisfactory states it was considered necessary to coerce them into more cooperative attitudes.

The types of informal empire and the situations it attempted to exploit were as various as the success which it achieved. Although commercial and capital penetration tended to lead to political cooperation and hegemony, there are striking exceptions. In the United States, for example, British business turned the cotton South into a colonial economy, and the British investor hoped to do the same with the Midwest. But the political

---

*Sir Thomas Stamford Bingley Raffles (1781–1826), an administrator of the British East India Company.—Ed.

strength of the country stood in his way. It was impossible to stop American industrialization, and the industrialized sections successfully campaigned for tariffs, despite the opposition of those sections which depended on the British trade connexion. In the same way, American political strength thwarted British attempts to establish Texas, Mexico and Central America as informal dependencies.

Conversely, British expansion sometimes failed, if it gained political supremacy without effecting a successful commercial penetration. There were spectacular exertions of British policy in China, but they did little to produce new customers. Britain's political hold upon China failed to break down Chinese economic self-sufficiency. The Opium War of 1840, the renewal of war in 1857, widened the inlets for British trade but they did not get Chinese exports moving. Their main effect was an unfortunate one from the British point of view, for such foreign pressures put Chinese society under great strains as the Taiping Rebellion unmistakably showed. It is important to note that this weakness was regarded in London as an embarrassment, and not as a lever for extracting further concessions. In fact, the British worked to prop up the tottering Pekin regime, for as Lord Clarendon put it in 1870, "British interests in China are strictly commercial, or at all events only so far political as they may be for the protection of commerce." The value of this self-denial became clear in the following decades when the Pekin government, threatened with a scramble for China, leaned more and more on the diplomatic support of the honest British broker.

The simple recital of these cases of economic expansion, aided and abetted by political action in one form or other, is enough to expose the inadequacy of the conventional theory that free trade could dispense with empire. We have seen that it did not do so. Economic expansion in the mid-Victorian age was matched by a corresponding political expansion which has been overlooked because it could not be seen by that study of maps which, it has been said, drives sane men mad. It is absurd to deduce from the harmony between London and the colonies of white settlement in the mid-Victorian age any British reluctance to intervene in the fields of British interests. The warships at Canton are as much a part of the period as responsible government for Canada; the battlefields of the Punjab are as real as the abolition of suttee.

Far from being an era of "indifference," the mid-Victorian years were the decisive stage in the history of British expansion overseas, in that the combination of commercial penetration and political influence allowed the United Kingdom to command those economies which could be made to fit best into her own. A variety of techniques adapted to diverse conditions and beginning at different dates were employed to effect this domination. A paramountcy was set up in Malaya centred on Singapore; a suzerainty over much of West Africa reached out from the port of

Lagos and was backed up by the African squadron. On the east coast of Africa British influence at Zanzibar, dominant thanks to the exertions of Consul Kirk, placed the heritage of Arab command on the mainland at British disposal.

But perhaps the most common political technique of British expansion was the treaty of free trade and friendship made with or imposed upon a weaker state. The treaties with Persia of 1836 and 1857, the Turkish treaties of 1838 and 1861, the Japanese treaty of 1858, the favours extracted from Zanzibar, Siam and Morocco, the hundreds of anti-slavery treaties signed with crosses by African chiefs—all these treaties enabled the British government to carry forward trade with these regions.

29. BRITISH RULE IN INDIA

Jawaharlal Nehru

British rule in India was an example of how what began as "informal" commercial administration (that of the East India Company) became increasingly a matter of formal, government policy. Finally the shock of the Indian mutiny in 1857 forced the government to take over officially.

Jawaharlal Nehru was a leader in the Indian struggle for independence and became India's first prime minister. The Discovery of India, from which this selection was taken, was written from prison in 1946, the year before Indian independence. This is obviously a work written in the heat of the struggle. That gives it a directness and clarity but also an uncompromising sharpness. Do you find it convincing, or overstated? Can you explain why?

Looking back over (the 18th century), it almost seems that the British succeeded in dominating India by a succession of fortuitous circumstances and lucky flukes. With remarkably little effort, considering the glittering prize, they won a great empire and enormous wealth which helped to make them the leading power in the world. It seems easy for a slight turn in events to have taken place which would have dashed their hopes and ended their ambitions. They were defeated on many occasions—by Haider Ali and Tipu, by the Marathas, by the Sikhs and by the Gurkhas. A little less of good fortune and they might have lost their foothold in India, or at the most, held on to certain coastal territories only.

And yet a closer scrutiny reveals, in the circumstances then existing, a certain inevitability in what happened. Good fortune there certainly was, but there must be an ability to profit by good fortune.

India was then exporting her manufactured products to Europe and other countries. Her banking system was efficient and well organized throughout the country, and the hundis or bills of exchange issued by the great business or financial houses were honored everywhere in India, as well as in Iran, and Kabul and Herat and Tashkent and other places in central Asia. Merchant capital had evolved, and there was an elaborate network of agents, jobbers, brokers, and middlemen. The shipbuilding industry was flourishing; one of the flagships of an English admiral during the Napoleonic wars had been built by an Indian firm in India. India was, in fact, as advanced industrially, commercially, and financially as any country prior to the Industrial Revolution. No such development could have taken place unless the country had enjoyed long periods of stable and peaceful government and the highways were safe for traffic and trade.

Foreign adventurers originally came to India because of the excellence of her manufacturers, which had a big market in Europe. The chief business of the British East India Company in its early days was to trade with Indian goods in Europe, and very profitable trading it was, yielding enormous dividends. So efficient and highly organized were Indian methods of production, and such was the skill of India's artisans and craftsmen, that they could compete successfully even with the higher techniques of production which were being established in England. When the big machine age began in England, Indian goods continued to pour in and had to be stopped by very heavy duties, and in some cases by outright prohibition.

Clive described Murshidabad in Bengal in 1757, the very year of Plassey,* as a city "as extensive, populous, and rich as the city of London, with this difference that there are individuals in the first possessing infinitely greater property than in the last." The city of Dacca in eastern Bengal was famous for its fine muslins. These two cities, important as they were, were near the periphery of Hindustan. All over the vast land there were greater cities and large numbers of big manufacturing and trading centers, and a very rapid and ingenious system of communicating news and market prices had been evolved. The great business houses often received news, even of the wars that were going on, long before dispatches reached the officials of the East India Company. The economy of India had thus advanced to as high a stage as it could reach prior to the Industrial Revolution. Whether it had the seeds of further progress in it or was too much bound up with the rigid social structure, it is difficult to say. It seems quite possible, however, that under normal conditions it would have undergone that change and begun to adapt itself, in its own way, to the new industrial conditions. And yet, though it was ripe

*Robert Clive gained control of the West Bengal state of Plassey in 1757, thus clearing the way for British rule in North India.—Ed.

for a change, that change itself required a revolution within its own framework. Perhaps some catalytic agent was necessary to bring about that change. It is clear that howsoever highly organized and developed its preindustrial economy was, it could not compete for long with the products of industrialized countries. It had to industrialize itself or submit to foreign economic penetration, which would have led to political interferences. As it happened, foreign political domination came first and this led to a rapid destruction of the economy she had built up, without anything positive or constructive taking its place. The East India Company represented both British political power and British vested interests and economic power. It was supreme, and being a company of merchants, it was intent on making money. Just when it was making money with amazing rapidity and in fantastic quantities, Adam Smith wrote about it in *The Wealth of Nations* in 1776: "The government of an exclusive company of merchants is perhaps the worst of all governments for any country whatever."

Though the Indian merchant and manufacturing classes were rich and spread out all over the country, and even controlled the economic structure, they had no political power. Government was despotic and still largely feudal. In fact, it was probably more feudal than it had been at some previous stages of Indian history. Hence there was no middle class strong enough to seize power, or even consciously thinking of doing so, as in some Western countries. The people gradually had grown apathetic and servile. There was thus a gap which had to be filled before any revolutionary change could take place. Perhaps this gap had been produced by the static nature of Indian society which refused to change in a changing world, for every civilization which resists change declines. That society, as constituted, had no more creative part to play. A change was overdue.

The British, at that time, were politically much more advanced. They had had their political revolution and had established the power of Parliament over that of the king. Their middle classes, conscious of their new power, were full of the impulse to expand. That vitality and energy, proof of a growing and progressive society, are indeed very evident in England. They show themselves in many ways, and most of all in the inventions and discoveries which heralded the Industrial Revolution.

The chief business of the East India Company in its early period, the very object for which it was started, was to carry Indian manufactured goods—textiles, etc., as well as spices and the like—from the East to Europe, where there was a great demand for these articles. With the developments in industrial techniques in England a new class of industrial capitalists rose there demanding a change in this policy. The British market was to be closed to Indian products and the Indian market opened to British manufacturers. The British parliament, influenced by this new class, began to take a greater interest in India and the working of the East India Company. To begin with, Indian goods were excluded from Britain by legislation, and as the company held a monopoly in the Indian export business, this exclusion influenced other foreign markets also. This was followed by vigorous attempts to restrict and crush Indian manufactures by various measures and internal duties which prevented the flow of Indian goods within the country itself. British goods meanwhile had free entry. The Indian textile industry collapsed, affecting vast numbers of weavers and artisans. The process was rapid in Bengal and Bihar; elsewhere it spread gradually with the expansion of British rule and the building of railways. It continued through the nineteenth century, breaking up other old industries also, shipbuilding, metalwork, glass, paper, and many crafts.

To some extent this was inevitable as the older manufacturing came into conflict with the new industrial technique. But it was hastened by political and economic pressure, and no attempt was made to apply the new techniques to India. Indeed every attempt was made to prevent this happening, and thus the growth of the new industry prevented. Machinery could not be imported into India. A vacuum was created in India which could only be filled by British goods, and which also led to rapidly increasing unemployment and poverty. The classic type of modern colonial economy was built up, India becoming an agricultural colony of industrial England, supplying raw materials and providing markets for England's industrial goods.

The liquidation of the artisan class led to unemployment on a prodigious scale. What were all these scores of millions, who had so far been engaged in industry and manufacture, to do now? Where were they to go? Their old profession was no longer open to them; the way to a new one was barred. They could die of course; that way of escape from an intolerable situation is always open. They did die in tens of millions. The English governor-general of India, Lord Bentinck, reported in 1834 that "the misery hardly finds a parallel in the history of commerce. The bones of the cotton-weavers are bleaching the plains of India."

But still vast numbers of them remained, and these increased from year to year as British policy affected remoter areas of the country and created more unemployment. All these hordes of artisans and craftsmen had no jobs, no work, and all their ancient skill was useless. They drifted to the land, for the land was still there. But the land was fully occupied and could not possibly absorb them profitably. So they became a burden on the land and the burden grew, and with it grew the poverty of the country, and the standard of living fell to incredibly low levels. This compulsory back-to-the-land movement of artisans and craftsmen led to an ever-growing disproportion between agriculture and industry; agriculture became more and more the sole business of the people because of the lack of occupations and wealth-producing activities.

India became progressively ruralized. In every progressive country there has been, during the past century, a shift of population from *meanly ag*

agriculture to industry; from village to town; in India this process was reversed, as a result of British policy. The figures are instructive and significant. In the middle of the nineteenth century about 55 per cent of the population is said to have been dependent on agriculture; recently this proportion was estimated to be 74 per cent. This is a prewar figure. Though there has been greater industrial employment during the war, those dependent on agriculture actually went up in the census of 1941, owing to increase of population. The growth of a few large cities (chiefly at the expense of the smaller towns) is apt to mislead the superficial observer and give him a false idea of Indian conditions.

This, then, is the real, the fundamental cause of the appalling poverty of the Indian people, and it is of comparatively recent origin. Other causes that contribute to it are themselves that result of this poverty and chronic starvation and undernourishment—like diseases and illiteracy. Excessive population is unfortunate and steps should be taken to curb it wherever necessary; but the density in India still compares favorably with that of many industrialized countries. It is only excessive for a predominantly agricultural community, and under a proper economic system the entire population can be made productive and should add to the wealth of the country. As a matter of fact, great density of population exists only in special areas, like Bengal and the Gangetic valley, and vast areas are still sparsely populated. It is worth remembering that Great Britain is more than twice as densely populated as India.

Then there was the Indian Army, consisting of British and Indian troops but officered entirely by Englishmen. This was reorganized repeatedly, especially after the mutiny of 1857, and ultimately became organizationally linked up with the British Army. This was so arranged as to balance its different elements and keep the British troops in key positions. "Next to the grand counterpoise of a sufficient European force, comes the counterpoise of natives against natives," says the official report on reorganization in 1858. The primary function of these forces was to serve as an army of occupation—"Internal Security Troops" they were called, and a majority of these were British. The Frontier Province served as a training ground for the British Army at India's expense. The field army (chiefly Indian) was meant for service abroad and it took part in numerous British imperial wars and expeditions, India always bearing the cost. Steps were taken to segregate Indian troops from the rest of the population.

Thus India had to bear the cost of her own conquest, and then of her transfer (or sale) from the East India Company to the British crown, and for the extension of the British empire to Burma and elsewhere, and expeditions to Africa, Persia, etc., and for her defense against Indians themselves. She was not only used as a base for imperial purposes, without any reimbursement for this, but she had further to pay for the training of part of the British Army in England—"capitation" charges these were called. Indeed India was charged for all manner of other expenses incurred by Britain, such as the maintenance of British diplomatic and consular establishments in China and Persia, the entire cost of the telegraph line from England to India, part of the expenses of the British Mediterranean fleet, and even the receptions given to the sultan of Turkey in London.

The building of railways in India, undoubtedly desirable and necessary, was done in an enormously wasteful way. The government of India guaranteed 5 per cent interest on all capital invested, and there was no need to check or estimate what was necessary. All purchases were made in England.

The civil establishment of government was also run on a lavish and extravagant scale, all the highly paid positions being reserved for Europeans. The process of Indianization of the administrative machine was very slow and only became noticeable in the twentieth century. This process, far from transferring any power to Indian hands, proved yet another method of strengthening British rule. The really key positions remained in British hands, and Indians in the administration could only function as the agents of British rule.

To all these methods must be added the deliberate policy, pursued throughout the period of British rule, of creating divisions among Indians, of encouraging one group at the cost of the other. This policy was openly admitted in the early days of their rule, and indeed it was a natural one for an imperial power. With the growth of the nationalist movement, that policy took subtler and more dangerous forms, and though denied, functioned more intensively than ever.

Nearly all our major problems today have grown up during British rule and as a direct result of British policy: the princes; the minority problem; various vested interests, foreign and Indian; the lack of industry and the neglect of agriculture; the extreme backwardness in the social services; and, above all, the tragic poverty of the people. . . .

The modern type of finance imperialism added new kinds of economic exploitation which were unknown in earlier ages. The record of British rule in India during the nineteenth century must necessarily depress and anger an Indian, and yet it illustrates the superiority of the British in many fields, not least in their capacity to profit by our disunity and weaknesses. A people who are weak and who are left behind in the march of time invite trouble and ultimately have only themselves to blame. If British imperialism with all its consequences was, in the circumstances, to be expected in the natural order of events, so also was the growth of opposition to it inevitable, and the final crisis between the two.

30. THE LETTER OF COMMISSIONER LIN TO QUEEN VICTORIA

One of the darkest hours of European commercial imperialism was the British insistence that the Chinese open their ports to the trade of British opium, harvested and shipped from British India. The Chinese Emperor sent Lin Tse-hsu, a distinguished scholar-official who had already proved his ability to halt opium smuggling in his area of jurisdiction, and two other officials to the port of Canton in 1839 to deal with British demands. In the following letter to Queen Victoria, Commissioner Lin and his colleagues tried to explain the reasons for the Chinese ban on opium importation. What reasons do they give? Do you find them convincing? What do you think was the response of the queen and her government?

Lin, high imperial commissioner, a president of the Board of War, viceroy of the two Keäng provinces, &c., Tang, a president of the Board of War, viceroy of the two Kwang provinces, &c., and E, a vice-president of the Board of War, lieut.-governor of Kwangtung, &c., hereby conjointly address this public dispatch to the queen of England for the purpose of giving her clear and distinct information (on the state of affairs) &c.

It is only our high and mighty emperor, who alike supports and cherishes those of the Inner Land, and those from beyond the seas—who looks upon all mankind with equal benevolence—who, if a source of profit exists anywhere, diffuses it over the whole world—who, if the tree of evil takes root anywhere, plucks it up for the benefit of all nations—who, in a word, hath implanted in his breast that heart (by which beneficent nature herself) governs the heavens and the earth! You, the queen of your honorable nation, sit upon a throne occupied through successive generations by predecessors, all of whom have been styled respectful and obedient. Looking over the public documents accompanying the tribute sent (by your predecessors) on various occasions, we find the following—"All the people of my (i.e. the king of England's) country, arriving at the Central Land for purposes of trade, have to feel grateful to the great emperor for the most perfect justice, for the kindest treatment," and other words to that effect. Delighted did we feel that the kings of your honorable nation so clearly understood the great principles of propriety, and were so deeply grateful for the heavenly goodness (of our emperor):—therefore, it was that we of the heavenly dynasty nourished and cherished your people from afar, and bestowed upon them redoubled proofs of our urbanity and kindness. It is merely from these circumstances, that your country—deriving immense advantage from its commercial intercourse with us, which has endured now two hundred years—has become the rich and flourishing kingdom that it is said to be!

But, during the commercial intercourse which has existed so long, among the numerous foreign merchants resorting hither, are wheat and tares, good and bad; and of these latter are some, who, by means of introducing opium by stealth, have seduced our Chinese people, and caused every province of the land to overflow with that poison. These then know merely to advantage themselves, they care not about injuring others! This is a principle which heaven's Providence repugnates; and which mankind conjointly look upon with abhorrence! Moreover, the great emperor hearing of it, actually quivered with indignation, and especially dispatched me, the commissioner, to Canton, that in conjunction with the viceroy and lieut.-governor of the province, means might be taken for its suppression!

Every native of the Inner Land who sells opium, as also all who smoke it, are alike adjudged to death. Were we then to go back and take up the crimes of the foreigners, who, by selling it for many years have induced dreadful calamity and robbed us of enormous wealth, and punish them with equal severity, our laws could not but award to them absolute annihilation! But, considering that these said foreigners did yet repent of their crime, and with a sincere heart beg for mercy; that they took 20,283 chests of opium piled up in their store-ships, and through Elliot, the superintendent of the trade of your said country, petitioned that they might be delivered up to us, when the same were all utterly destroyed, of which we, the imperial commissioner and colleagues, made a duly prepared memorial to his majesty;—considering these circumstances, we have happily received a fresh proof of the extraordinary goodness of the great emperor, inasmuch as he who voluntarily comes forward, may yet be deemed a fit subject for mercy, and his crimes be graciously remitted him. But as for him who again knowingly violates the laws, difficult indeed will it be thus to go on repeatedly pardoning! He or they shall alike be doomed to the penalties of the new statute. We presume that you, the sovereign of your honorable nation, on pouring out your heart before the altar of eternal justice, cannot but command all foreigners with the deepest respect to reverence our laws! If we only lay clearly before your eyes, what is profitable and what is destructive, you will then know that the statutes of the heavenly dynasty cannot but be obeyed with fear and trembling!

We find that your country is distant from us about sixty or seventy thousand miles, that your foreign ships come hither striving the one with the other from our trade, and for the simple reason of their strong desire to reap a profit. Now, out of the wealth of our Inner Land, if we take a part to bestow upon foreigners from afar, it follows, that the immense wealth which the said foreigners amass, ought properly speaking to be portion of our own native Chinese people. By what principle of reason then, should these foreigners send in return a poisonous drug, which involves in destruction those very natives of China? Without meaning to say that the foreigners harbor such destructive intentions in their hearts, we yet positively assert that from their inordinate thirst after gain, they are perfectly careless about the injuries they inflict upon us! And such being the case, we should like to ask what has become of that conscience which heaven has implanted in the breasts of all men?

We have heard that in your own country opium is prohibited with the utmost strictness and severity:—this is a strong proof that you know full well how hurtful it is to mankind. Since then you do not permit it to injure your own country, you ought not to have the injurious drug transferred to another country, and above all others, how much less to the Inner Land! Of the products which China exports to your foreign countries, there is not one which is not beneficial to mankind in some shape or other. There are those which serve for food, those which are useful, and those which are calculated for resale;—but all are beneficial. Has China (we should like to ask) ever yet sent forth a noxious article from its soil? Not to speak of our tea and rhubarb, things which your foreign countries could not exist a single day without, if we of the Central Land were to grudge you what is beneficial, and not to compassionate your wants, then wherewithal could you foreigners manage to exist? And further, as regards your woolens, camlets, and longells, were it not that you get supplied with our native raw silk, you could not get these manufactured! If China were to grudge you those things which yield a profit, how could you foreigners scheme after any profit at all? Our other articles of food, such as sugar, ginger, cinnamon, &c., and our other articles for use, such as silk piece-goods, chinaware, &c., are also many necessaries of life to you; how can we reckon up their number! On the other hand, the things that come from your foreign countries are only calculated to make presents of, or serve for mere amusement. It is quite the same to us if we have them, or if we have them not. If these are of no material consequence to us of the Inner Land, what difficulty would there be in prohibiting and shutting our market against them? It is only that our heavenly dynasty most freely permits you to take off her tea, silk, and other commodities, and convey them for consumption everywhere, without the slightest stint or grudge, for no other reason, but that where a profit exists, we wish that it be diffused abroad for the benefit of all the earth!

Your honorable nation takes away the products of our Central Land, and not only do you thereby obtain food and support for yourselves, but moreover, by reselling these products to other countries you reap a threefold profit. Now if you would only not sell opium, this threefold profit would be secured to you: how can you possibly consent to forgo it for a drug that is hurtful to men, and an unbridled craving after gain that seems to know no bounds! Let us suppose that foreigners came from another country, and brought opium into England, and seduced the people of your country to smoke it, would not you, the sovereign of the said country, look upon such a procedure with anger, and in your just indignation endeavor to get rid of it? Now we have always heard that your highness possesses a most kind and benevolent heart, surely then you are incapable of doing or causing to be done unto another, that which you should not wish another to do unto you! We have at the same time heard that your ships which come to Canton do each and every of them carry a document by your highness' self, on which are written these words "you shall not be permitted to carry contraband goods;" this shows that the laws of your highness are in their origin both distinct and severe, and we can only suppose that because the ships coming here have been very numerous, due attention has not been given to search and examine; and for this reason it is that we now address you this public document, that you may clearly know how stern and severe are the laws of the central dynasty, and most certainly you will cause that they be not again rashly violated!

Moreover, we have heard that in London the metropolis where you dwell, as also in Scotland, Ireland, and other such places, no opium whatever is produced. It is only in sundry parts of your colonial kingdom of Hindostan, such as Bengal, Madras, Bombay, Patna, Malwa, Benares, Malacca, and other places where the very hills are covered with the opium plant, where tanks are made for the preparing of the drug; month by month, and year by year, the volume of the poison increases, its unclean stench ascends upwards, until heaven itself grows angry, and the very gods thereat get indignant! You, the queen of the said honorable nation, ought immediately to have the plant in those parts plucked up by the very root! Cause the land there to be hoed up afresh, sow in its stead the five grains, and if any man dare again to plant in these grounds a single poppy, visit his crime with the most severe punishment. By a truly benevolent system of government such as this, will you indeed reap advantage, and do away with a source of evil. Heaven must support you, and the gods will crown you with felicity! This will get for yourself the blessing of long life, and from this will proceed the security and stability of your descendants!

In reference to the foreign merchants who come to this our Central Land, the food that they eat, and the dwellings that they abide in, proceed entirely from the goodness of our heavenly dynasty:—the profits which they reap, and the fortunes which they amass, have their origin only in that portion of benefit which our heavenly dynasty kindly allots them: and as these pass but little of their time in your country, and the greater part of their time in ours, it is a generally received maxim of old and of modern times, that we should conjointly admonish, and clearly make known the punishment that awaits them.

Suppose the subject of another country were to come to England to trade, he would certainly be required to comply with the laws of England, then how much more does this apply to us of the celestial empire! Now it is a fixed statute of this empire, that any native Chinese who sells opium is punishable with death, and even he who merely smokes it, must not less die. Pause and reflect for a moment: if you foreigners did not bring the opium hither, where should our Chinese people get it to resell? It is you foreigners who involve our simple natives in the pit of death, and are they alone to be permitted to escape alive? If so much as one of those deprive one of our people of his life, he must forfeit his life in requital for that which he has taken:—how much more does this apply to him who by means of opium destroys his fellowmen? Does the havoc which he commits stop with a single life? Therefore it is that those foreigners who now import opium into the Central Land are condemned to be beheaded and strangled by the new statute, and this explains what we said at the beginning about plucking up the tree of evil, wherever it takes root, for the benefit of all nations.

31. AMERICAN EXPANSION FROM THE INDIAN PERSPECTIVE

R. David Edmunds

This article by a modern historian suggests that the expansion of white settlement across what is today the continental United States was similar to the economic expansion of European powers in India and China. By Professor Edmunds's account, the meeting of European and Native American was far more complex than is usually imagined. In what ways was American expansion in the nineteenth century like that of European economic expansion in Asia? How was it different? How did U.S. policy toward the Indians change during the nineteenth century? How did the attitudes and responses of Indians differ over the course of the century? How did some Indians participate in their own extinction or assist in "civilizing" the settlers?

Most Americans have readily accepted the conventional view that the westward expansion of the American frontier marked a similar advance of "civilization" over "savagery." Imbued with an ethnocentric bias, textbooks throughout the late nineteenth and much of the twentieth centuries described Indian people as part of a wilderness habitat to be altered, eradicated, or pushed further west. Indeed, in all editions published prior to the late 1960s, the most widely adopted college textbook focusing upon the history of the American westward movement discussed Indian-white relations in a chapter entitled "The Indian Barrier," while popular accounts of the American West as portrayed in movies and television emphasized the Indians' armed, if futile, resistance to the march of American "progress."

Such an interpretation is markedly simplistic and reflects an ignorance of the interaction of Indian and non-Indian peoples on the American frontier. Of course Indians sometimes resisted white expansion, but more often they interacted peacefully with white frontiersmen, shaping the region's social and economic institutions and modifying their own society to better accommodate both to a changing environment. Moreover, this interaction provides some valuable insights into the attitudes and assumptions of American society. Americans' opinions about Indians not only reflect their beliefs regarding minority groups but also illustrate their appraisal of themselves. For many nineteenth-century Americans, a preconceived and often erroneous conception of Indian or "savage" life provided a welcome contrast to what they envisioned as the "progress of American civilization."

During the first quarter of the nineteenth century, attitudes toward Indians probably differed between American frontiersmen and political leaders in Washington. Most of the Founding Fathers were the products of Enlightenment philosophy; and although they viewed Indian people as lesser beings, they still had been influenced by Rousseau's conceptions of the "noble savage." More ethnocentric than racist, they believed that the Indians could be converted into small yeomen farmers and eventually assimilated into American society. Since most Indians already had been forced from the eastern seaboard, politicians in Washington, D.C., did not view them as a threat. Thomas Jefferson may have encouraged the proprietors of government-sponsored Indian factories (or trading posts) to lure the tribespeople into debt so they would be forced to cede their surplus lands, but he also supported a systematic program to provide the Indians with agents and farm implements so they could learn to be farmers.

American frontiersmen were less willing to assimilate the Indians. Although American historians continue to argue over the reasons frontiersmen moved west, most scholars agree that economic opportunity was of primary importance. Many frontiersmen were economic opportunists, eager to better their lot, and they had no qualms about seizing every advantage that furthered their aspirations. If some of those advantages came at the expense of the Indian people, it caused little concern to frontier entrepreneurs willing to ride roughshod over any group denying them access to riches. To many frontiersmen, the lands and the resources controlled by Indians were "plums ripe for the plucking." At worst, Indians were a threat; at best, they were a nuisance.

Conflicts over Indian policy spurred considerable disagreement between local, state, and federal governments. Many of these disputes reflect a theme familiar to most American historians: the federal government's inability to maintain effective control over its western citizens. Between 1795 and 1809, federal officials signed seventeen treaties with the tribes of Ohio, Indiana, Illinois, and Michigan, but the agreements were honored more in their violation than in their adherence. Imbued with a sense of their own self-righteousness, American frontiersmen ignored the treaty regulations and regularly crossed over onto Indian lands to hunt, trap, or establish homesteads. Although federal officials in Ohio and Indiana made desultory attempts to protect Indian interests, they could not stop the tide of American aggrandizement. White trespass upon Indian lands reached such proportions that in 1808 William Henry Harrison, the governor of Indiana Territory, complained:

> The people of Kentucky . . . make a constant practice of crossing over onto Indian lands . . . to kill deer, bear, and buffaloe [*sic*]. . . . One hunter will destroy more game than five of the common Indians.

And in response to a more serious problem, Harrison added, "A great many of the Inhabitants of the Fronteers [*sic*] consider the murdering of the Indians in the highest degree meritorious." Federal lawmakers in Washington might be willing to differentiate between Indian and white lands, but for many frontiersmen the western territories were a vast cornucopia to be exploited. They disregarded Indian claims to the land and its resources.

American aggression caused considerable problems for the Indian people of Ohio, Indiana, and Illinois. Not only were their homelands overrun by frontiersmen, but the invaders severely depleted the game animals. Moreover, Indian attempts to seek justice brought little recourse since white juries systematically freed most Americans accused of crimes against the tribesmen. Not surprisingly, resentment swelled and the tribes struck back at the Americans. Unwilling to admit that they were the authors of their own misfortune, American frontiersmen in the first decade of the nineteenth century blamed the British, whom they charged with inciting the Indians against the settlements. Although the British did exercise considerable influence among the tribes, a close examination of these events indicates Indian resistance to American expansion was a natural, indigenous act. The British did attempt to manipulate Indian resentment of the Americans for their own purposes; however, in most instances the tribesmen were more militant than the Crown, and British Indian agents often attempted to restrain the warriors rather than precipitate a general conflict with the United States. In these instances, the Indians welcomed the technical and logistical support of the Crown, but their decision to resist the Americans was their own.

Traditionally, historians have championed Tecumseh, the Shawnee war chief, as the architect of the Indian resistance that coalesced prior to the War of 1812. Both British and American authors have been eager to point out that from 1809 through 1811, the Shawnee statesman traveled among the western tribes attempting to enlist the warriors into a pan-Indian political and military organization designed to defend the remaining Indian land base east of the Mississippi. In contrast, Tecumseh's brother, Tenskwatawa, known as the Prophet, usually has been portrayed as a religious charlatan who rode Tecumseh's coattails to a position of minor prominence. Yet throughout American history, during periods of significant stress, Indian people traditionally have turned to religious leaders or revitalization movements for their deliverance. Spiritual spokesmen such as Neolin, the Delaware prophet who emerged prior to Pontiac's rebellion; Handsome Lake of the Senecas, a contemporary of Tenskwatawa; and the Paiute Wovoka and his Ghost Dance are good examples of holy men who arose to meet their people's needs.

It appears from recent scholarship that Tenskwatawa was more instrumental than Tecumseh in forging the Indian coalition in the years preceding the War of 1812. Upon examination of all the primary materials focusing on these events, it is clear that for four years, from 1805 until 1809, the religious teachings of the Prophet were the magnet that attracted thousands of Indians, first to Greenville, in Ohio, then to Prophetstown. Although there are extensive references to the Prophet and his movements in documents from this period, there is no mention of Tecumseh prior to April 1808, when British officials in Canada mention that "the Prophet's brother" visited Amherstburg. William Henry Harrison, Tecumseh's primary antagonist, does not mention the Shawnee chief until August 1810, and then Harrison also refers to him only as "the Prophet's brother," since he evidently had not yet learned Tecumseh's name. Indeed, Tecumseh did not challenge his brother for leadership until after the Treaty of Fort Wayne (1809), which transferred extensive Indian landholdings in Indiana to the United States. The Shawnee war chief then used his brother's religious movement as the base for his ill-fated, political-military confederacy.

White historians have probably championed Tecumseh as the author of the Indian resistance movement since his concepts of political and military unity seemed more logical (by white standards) than the Prophet's religious revitalization. In retrospect, white historians had little understanding of Indian religious doctrines, but they believed that if *they* had been Indians, they also would have attempted to forge the tribes into a multitribal confederacy. Yet the Prophet's doctrines had more appeal to the Indians. Americans have idolized Tecumseh because they believe that he fits their concept of the "noble savage"; since his death both folklorists and historians have enshrouded the Shawnee chief with extensive apocrypha.

Recent inquiry has also illustrated that different socioeconomic groups on the frontier reacted to the Indians in different ways. Historians have indicated, for example, that much of the violence between Indians and whites that occurred in the Far West during the middle decades of the nineteenth century was triggered by miners and other more transient workers, not farmers. Many white farmers who saw themselves as permanent residents of a region were interested in promoting peace and stability between the white and Indian populations. In contrast, miners were eager for the maximum exploitation of mineral resources and had little interest in the long-term development of a region. Preferring to make their "stake" and then retire to more comfortable surroundings, miners and other transients viewed Indians as impediments to their success and were quite willing to eliminate them. In addition, since many miners and other transient laborers often were unemployed, they sometimes welcomed the opportunity to draw rations and wages for service in militia or paramilitary units that were formed to suppress "Indian uprisings." Such earnings hardly matched the riches of a bonanza strike in the gold fields but, for destitute laborers, payment for military services offered ready cash.

The notion that frontier transients formed the backbone of frontier militias suggests an explanation for other Indian-white confrontations. In 1774 Lord Dunmore's War was precipitated when frontier riffraff murdered innocent Shawnees and Delawares along the Ohio. Almost sixty years later, on May 14, 1832, the Black Hawk War probably would have terminated without bloodshed if the drunken militia partially composed of miners from Wisconsin's Fever River District and commanded by Major Isaiah Stillman had not attacked Black Hawk's envoys as the old Sauk war chief prepared to surrender. The resulting Battle of Stillman's Run ended any chance for the hapless Sauks and Foxes to withdraw peacefully to Iowa. On November 28, 1864, ill-trained and drunken militia were also responsible for the slaughter of more than 150 Cheyennes and Arapahos at Sand Creek in Colorado. Many of the volunteers making up this force were unemployed miners lured west by the Colorado gold rush of the late 1850s. Illegal trespass by miners onto Indian lands in the Black Hills also triggered the last of the Sioux wars, culminating in Custer's defeat at the Battle of the Little Big Horn. Other miners organized the mob who murdered 144 Apaches at Camp Grant, near Tucson, Arizona, in April 1871.

In retrospect, if Indian lands held valuable resources, those treasures were exploited. Although the federal government might promise to protect the inviolability of Indian real estate, such promises often were broken. The consequences of this repeating cycle should have a profound message for tribal communities holding valuable mineral or water resources in the twentieth century.

Disputes between Indians and whites over Indian lands in the Southeast also offer some interesting insights into the conflict between frontiersmen and federal officials while illustrating the entrepreneurial values of the Jacksonians. By the 1820s, many Americans were dissatisfied with the established organic economic system that emphasized careful centralized planning (a national bank, tariffs, federal support for internal improvements, etc.), and new entrepreneurs emerged who argued that "the powdered wig set" (the federal government) controlled the nation's resources for their own benefit. After the adoption of the cotton gin spread cotton production across the Gulf plains, Indian lands in the region became the focus of local land speculators. Their complaint was not that the federal government had failed to purchase Indian land holdings (indeed, by the 1820s much of the former tribal holdings already were in the public domain) but that the government did not immediately buy all Indian lands remaining within their respective states and send the tribes packing across the Mississippi.

In contrast, many officials in Washington, as exemplified by President John Quincy Adams, still gave at least lip service to the civilization programs that had been in force since the beginning of the century. In theory, the Indians were to adopt white values and be assimilated into American society. In actuality, Adams also may have favored some type of removal program, but he championed carefully planned and legalistic procedures through which the changing status of the Indians and their tenure of tribal lands could be delineated.

Any delays necessitated by long-term planning were unacceptable to local expansionists. In Georgia a group of these expansionists, led by Governor George M. Troup, negotiated the Treaty of Indian Springs with a faction representing a minority of the Creek Confederacy. The treaty was signed by federal officials, but these men were clearly acting on behalf of Troup. After the treaty was ratified by the Senate in March 1825, the Creeks executed William McIntosh, the leader of the treaty faction. In response, Troup threatened to overrun Creek lands with the Georgia militia. Federal officials interceded, nullifying the Treaty of Indian Springs, but signed the Treaty of Washington with the Creeks one year later. The new treaty also called for the cession of Creek lands in Georgia (already a fait accompli, since settlers had moved into the region); but the terms were more favorable for the Indians, and the federal government promised to guarantee the remaining Creek lands in Alabama. In theory at least, federal officials had interceded to partially protect Indian interests from expansionists at the state and local levels of government.

Whether the Adams regime would (or could) have honored its promises remains doubtful, but in 1828 Andrew Jackson was elected to the presidency and a spokesman for the frontier entrepreneurs was in the White House. Jackson's election also marked an increase in federal pressure to remove the tribespeople to the trans-Mississippi west. Although previous administrations had counseled the Indians to remove, they had appraised the problem from an ethnocentric rather than a racial perspective. Presidents such as John Quincy Adams believed the Indians to be inferior, but from Adams' viewpoint they were inferior because they had not attained the socioeconomic-political level of Europeans or Americans. If Indians would adopt white ways and become civilized, they could be assimilated into American society.

The Jacksonians had no intention of assimilating the Indians into American society. Regardless of the tribespeople's adoption of American institutions, frontier entrepreneurs wanted them removed from their lands and forced beyond the frontier. The Cherokee's "civilization" program, for example, afforded them little protection from white Georgians. After gold was discovered on Cherokee lands, white Americans ignored the tribe's constitution, newspaper, and pious Protestant congregations. Tribal lands were overrun. Regardless of how "civilized" the Cherokees had become, other Americans still saw them as "Indians" and, therefore, not encompassed in the protection that the Constitution extended to white men.

Ironically, however, by the 1820s many of the Cherokees, Choctaws, and other southern tribes were of mixed Indian-white descent. The emergence of these mixed-blood communities on the American frontier indicates that considerable acculturation already had transpired. Still, frontiersmen considered such individuals, regardless of the minority quantum of their Indian descent (one-half blood, one-quarter blood, etc.), to be Indian. On the southern frontier this infusion of white lineage often had occurred in the middle and late eighteenth century, when British and sometimes French traders had married Indian women. The mixed-blood children of these marriages often exerted considerable influence in tribal affairs; and since they were the products of both cultures, they sometimes served as cultural brokers, representing tribal interests (as they defined them) in mediating with the federal government.

The Choctaws provide a telling illustration of the key role that mixed-bloods played in this interchange. Although the Choctaws originally had sustained themselves through hunting and horticulture, by the middle of the eighteenth century they had become so enmeshed in the European trading system that much of their economy was based on their ability to supply deerskins to British merchants. After the American Revolution they shifted to Americans, but by 1800 they had so depleted the deer population in Mississippi that they no longer could provide the hides needed to purchase necessities. Meanwhile, they had grown increasingly in debt to American traders who constantly clamored for payment.

Aware that the deer herds had diminished and that they could no longer maintain their old life-style in Mississippi, some of the traditional Choctaw leaders were willing to exchange the tribe's lands in Mississippi for similar regions in Arkansas. In contrast, many mixed-blood Choctaws opposed such a removal. Adapting to a market economy, they began to raise cattle and eventually to plant cotton on their old Mississippi lands. Although many rank-and-file Choctaws no longer could sustain themselves in Mississippi, they still retained an emotional attachment to their homeland and rallied to the mixed-bloods' leadership.

In response, the mixed-bloods portrayed themselves as Choctaw patriots attempting to defend the tribe's homeland. Federal officials preferred to negotiate with the older, more traditional chiefs, but their leadership was usurped by the mixed-bloods who brought further changes to the tribe. Allying themselves with Protestant missionaries, the mixed-bloods encouraged the work ethic, thrift, the accumulation of capital, and sobriety since they asserted that these qualities would enhance the tribe's ability to retain their homelands. Under the mixed-bloods' leadership, much of Choctaw society was transformed, and growing numbers of tribesmen began to raise cattle and grow cotton. In addition, the political structure of the tribe was altered as mixed-bloods such as Peter Pitchlyn, David Folsum, and Greenwood LeFlore emerged as the new leaders of the Choctaw Nation.

A parallel but different blend of cultures also occurred in the Old Northwest. In 1827, Commissioner of Indian Affairs Thomas McKenney traveled among the tribes of Michigan, Illinois, and Wisconsin. Discouraged over the Indians' lack of "progress," he reported back to Washington that the tribes should be removed beyond the Mississippi because they had rejected federal attempts to transform them into small yeoman farmers. McKenney charged that they still followed the life-style of their fathers: "They catch fish, and plant patches of corn; dance, hunt, and get drunk when they can get liquor, fish and often starve." From McKenney's perspective, tribes such as the Ottawas, Miamis, or Potawatomis seemed hopeless: they still clung to their tribal values and had rejected all tenets of "civilization."

Yet McKenney and most other Americans failed to understand that many of these Indian people had also made great changes from the traditional cultures of their forefathers. Although they generally had rejected American attempts to foster agriculture among them, they had adopted a life-style that resembled those whites with whom they had the closest contact: the Creole French whose ancestors had settled in the region during the previous century. Like the Indians, during the first decades of the nineteenth century many of the Creoles also continued to hunt, trap, and fish; and, like the Indians, they too were seen as improvident and even "uncivilized" by Anglo-Americans. American officials newly arrived at Vincennes, Indiana, described the Creole population as "a rabble whose appearance caused us to doubt whether we had not actually landed among the savages themselves," and at Detroit, Governor Lewis Cass charged that Creole traders:

> spend one half the year in labor, want, and exposure, and the other half in indolence and amusements. Associated with the Indians, they contracted their manners, and gained their confidence. As a necessary consequence, their farms are neglected. . . .

In retrospect, if American observers had been less biased, they would have noted that by the 1820s many Miami, Potawatomi, and other tribesmen were active in the fur trade, working as porters or laborers, or selling merchandise to both whites and Indians. In 1816, when Indiana entered the union, the wealthiest man in the state was reputed to be Jean Baptiste Richardville, a mixed-blood Miami trader. During the 1830s, when frontier artist George Winter painted Miami, Delaware, and Potawatomi residents of the Wabash and Tippecanoe valleys, his portraits indicate that many of these people dressed in ruffled shirts, frock coats, and other clothing similar to that of white frontier residents. Of course not all Indians were as acculturated as Richardville, or the Burnett or Coquillard families among the Potawatomis, but neither were they living in the manner of their forefathers. Indeed, many of these Indians already had adopted tenets of European culture; however, from the American perspective, it was the wrong culture: the Creole French. Ironically, American frontiersmen were almost as biased in their attitudes toward the Creoles as they were toward the Indians. Since the tribespeople had acculturated toward the wrong ethnic group, American observers refused to admit that they had made any significant changes. They were not yeoman farmers, so they should be removed to the West.

The importance of the Indian trade to the economy of the American frontier has often been underestimated. By the third decade of the nineteenth century, almost all of the tribes east of the Great Plains were enmeshed in the American economic system, and were dependent upon traders, both Indian and white, for many of the necessities of life. In addition, because of their annuity payments and other sources of income, they provided an important source of revenue for frontier communities, especially for the merchants. Historians have begun to explore the nature of this relationship, and their inquiries indicate that the Indian trade, if properly manipulated, was so lucrative that frontier merchants vied among themselves to gain a greater share of it. In 1821 John Crowell resigned his seat as the lone congressman from the state of Georgia to accept an appointment as agent to the Creek Indians. He promptly issued trading licenses to members of his family, and Crowell and his kinsmen amassed a fortune.

Because most tribesmen were illiterate, they had little control over the distribution of treaty and annuity payments; and there were few checks upon the traders' practice of selling the Indians goods on credit, then padding the accounts when the payment was due. Sometimes the fraud reached phenomenal proportions. In 1833 treaty goods worth $20,000 and destined for the Ottawas, Chippewas, and Potawatomis were pilfered from government storehouses at Chicago while Governor George B. Porter of Michigan Territory was charged with illegally validating over $100,000 in claims against the tribes for a trading firm composed of his friends. Although federal officials attempted to investigate the frauds, Porter died of cholera and the proceedings were abandoned. Three years later, other bands of Potawatomis in Indiana were alleged to have accumulated debts to frontier merchants totaling over $160,000. Another federal investigation subsequently proved that almost half of these claims were fictitious. Nevertheless, in many other instances the funds were deducted from the Indians' annuities. If the Age of Jackson was a time of economic opportunism, Indian people and their resources played a significant role in the development of the economy in the West.

Not surprisingly, many frontier merchants exercised considerable influence over the tribes. Indian traders such as the Ewing brothers of Indiana, the Kinzie-Forsyth partnership at Chicago, or the Chouteau brothers at St. Louis dabbled in tribal politics and sometimes attempted to prevent the removal of tribes that allegedly owed them money. In 1837 George Ewing warned government officials that certain tribes in northern Indiana would never remove unless he was paid what he claimed the Indians owed to him. In some instances federal agents negotiating for the purchase of tribal lands were forced to work through the traders to ensure the success of the proceedings. Ironically, the traders then removed west with the tribespeople, following the source of their revenue across the Mississippi.

Although much has been written about the hardships encountered by the Indians during the removal process, there is another facet of this forced relocation that we often overlook: the role played by the Indians in bringing changes to the trans-Mississippi West. Ironically, those eastern tribes seeking new homes on the fringe of the Great Plains were agents of the very socioeconomic system they were fleeing. Moreover, their entrance onto lands previously dominated by tribes indigenous to the region posed a substantial threat to western peoples. In many cases the western tribes opposed the resettlement of eastern Indians, and bitter conflicts emerged over hunting lands in Iowa, Kansas, Missouri, and Oklahoma.

The emigrant warriors usually emerged as victors in these conflicts. Although the popular press has touted the military skill of the Plains tribes, the eastern warriors had experienced over a century of intertribal conflict generated by European and American confrontations. Cherokee, Shawnee, and Delaware warriors steadily pushed the Osages from their lands in Missouri and Arkansas, while tribes from the Old Northwest usurped the hunting lands of several Plains tribes in Kansas. Potawatomi, Sauk, and Fox tribesmen may have feigned pleas to federal agents asking for protection against the Sioux, but when the two sides met on the prairie, the newcomers (the Potawatomis) formed ranks and, firing from horseback, easily repulsed the Sioux and their allies. Seeking revenge, one year later another large war party of almost seven hundred Plains warriors attacked about two hundred Sauks and Foxes who were hunting buffalo on the Smoky Hill River in Kansas. In this instance, the Sauks and Foxes dismounted, again formed ranks, and repulsed their enemies' repeated charges. When the Plains Indians withdrew, they had suffered over one hundred casualties. The Sauks and Foxes lost only a handful of warriors.

In frontier Oklahoma, the occupation of the eastern part of the state by the five southern ("civilized") tribes created an oasis of sophistication in an area not known for its gentility. Although full-blood traditionalists may have moved west intending to re-create their old way of life free from American influence, the acculturated mixed-bloods who had dominated the tribes in their ancestral homelands reasserted themselves. Centered around communities such as Atoka, Tahlequah, Muskogee, and Tishomingo, the Choctaws, Cherokees, Creeks, Chickasaws and, later, the Seminoles carved out plantations, planted fields of cotton, and erected fine antebellum homes. Indeed, their adherence to southern values was sufficiently pervasive that during the Civil War so many fought for the Confederate cause that they formed an effective barrier to any Union expeditions against Texas.

The emigrant tribes made significant achievements in other fields. The Cherokees established perhaps the best rural school system west of the Mississippi during the antebellum period. Financed by the tribal government, both male and female seminaries sent their graduates back to the eastern states to attend college, from which they returned to help build the Cherokee Nation. Modeled after Mount Holyoke College at South Hadley, Massachusetts, the Cherokee Female Seminary, established near Tahlequah in 1851, provided its students with a "progressive" nineteenth-century education featuring instruction in subjects ranging from English literature and geography to proper manners.

Further north, in Kansas, acculturated Potawatomis at St. Mary's Mission operated ferries across the Kansas River and sold produce and other supplies to both military expeditions and settlers traveling west to Colorado and California. One western emigrant commented that the Indians at St. Mary's were as "civilized" as most whites on the border, but added that "their head gear ran much to feathers." Other travelers expressed surprise at their sophistication and described the prosperity of their villages. In 1854 these Potawatomis purchased and operated the first McCormick's reaper utilized in Kansas (although they refused an offer by the McCormick Company to provide them with a retail franchise); and when dignitaries visited their mission, they entertained them with band concerts and piano recitals. By any standard, these Indian emigrants did as much to "tame" the frontier as did most non-Indian pioneers.

The economic success of the five southern tribes created another phenomenon that also proliferated in Oklahoma: the continued intermarriage of Indians and whites. Since all members of the tribe or their spouses were eligible to claim potential farmland within tribal territories, many white men married Indian women. Such marriages were celebrated for other reasons. Most frontier whites in Oklahoma were from relatively low socioeconomic classes. When these men married the often more sophisticated, more financially secure Indian women, they were marrying "up." It is not surprising that so many modern Oklahomans claim Cherokee grandmothers. Maternal ancestors such as these Cherokee women were proud additions to non-Indian families struggling to improve themselves on the frontier.

There is another facet of the American experience in the first half of the nineteenth century in which Indians played an important, if sometimes unwitting, role: the attempt by a new nation to establish its own intellectual identity. In this instance, Americans used idealized or popular conceptions of Indians to define their own "progress," or as foils to rationalize American expansion. Indeed, the dual image of the Indian that emerges during this period offers interesting insights into the intellectual life of the new nation.

The concept of the Indian as a "noble savage" did not become popular in the United States until the nineteenth century. Eager to develop a national literature, authors along the eastern seaboard turned to the Indian as a subject uniquely American. Since all Indians had been removed from the region and, therefore, were associated with the past, it was easy for writers to romanticize the tribesmen. Indian leaders such as King Philip (Metacom), Hiawatha, Tecumseh, and Pocahontas emerged from nineteenth-century literature in images that were larger than life. Moreover, the depiction of Indians in heroic, if sometimes tragic, terms also enhanced most Americans' self-esteem, for in their victory over such champions Americans could assure themselves they were worthy to inherit the tribesmen's kingdom.

Other Americans envisioned Indians in less heroic terms. In the decades following the War of 1812, the United States was eager to take its rightful place among the "civilized" nations of the Western world. Although most Americans seemed to be pleased to have broken with a decadent Europe, others were uncertain of the nation's status and sought reassurance that American society had come of age. For Americans unsure of their standing, the triumph of American civilization over the Indian population of the United States seemed to provide one favorable measure of their country's progress. Not only did their "republican virtue" separate them from European corruption, but their achievements assured them that they no longer were "primitives" like the Indians. The Indians symbolized a wilderness that was being transformed and conquered, and the tribespeople's demise was indicative of the "grand dame of progress" sweeping westward across the United States.

Finally, the "civilization" programs fostered by the Bureau of Indian Affairs also offer some useful insights into the value systems of American society. Since many Americans continued to champion small yeoman farmers as the American ideal, federal Indian policy attempted to remold Indians in the yeoman image. Although many tribes had a rich agricultural heritage, such labor traditionally was performed by women; but these individuals were excluded from the government's efforts. In American society, farming was dominated by males, and federal programs expected Indian men to adopt similar roles. Since white Americans did not encourage their wives or daughters to till the soil, Indians were forced to follow a similar pattern.

Viewing the early frontier experience from an Indian perspective enriches and enlivens the story of America's national expansion. Discussions of the "Indian problem" demonstrate that there was a considerable gap in understanding between Washington, D.C., policymakers and enterprising frontiersmen, and that the nation's new federal institutions were exceedingly fragile.

Moreover, the interaction of Indians and whites on the moving western frontier was both fluid and multidimensional. Contacts did not simply involve white male yeomen and befeathered chiefs, but also mixed-blood politicians, fur traders, miners, local merchants, missionaries, tribal religious leaders, war chiefs, and ordinary citizens. The Indian experience on the American frontier both illuminates powerful themes in our past—racism, nationalism, and economic development—and demonstrates the variety of people and interests who contributed to the process we have come to call the "settlement" of the West.

CHAPTER NINE

Migrations and Imperialism

32. LABOR ON THE MOVE
Eric Wolf

"Workers of the world, unite!" was the concluding call of the Communist Manifesto. *In fact, the call of capitalism might have been "workers of the world, disperse." The great age of capitalist industrialization (the last two hundred years) has witnessed one of the greatest mass population movements in world history. Marx and Engels would not have been surprised. The great labor migrations were part of the establishment of the single world market that they described.*

Here a modern anthropologist gives us a sense of the enormous dimensions of those population transfers. We in the United States are particularly aware of the story of North American immigration, but this selection reminds us that it was part of a global story. What, according to the author, are the three stages of migration? Are any of these stages still continuing? What was the relationship between immigration to and the industrialization of the United States? In what ways was South African immigration similar to that of the United States? Why were there so many Indian and Chinese migrants? Was there any connection between migration and the "free-trade empires" discussed in the previous chapter?

People may move for religious, political, ecological, or other reasons; but the migrations of the nineteenth and twentieth centuries were largely labor migrations, movements of the bearers of labor power. These labor migrations, of course, carried with them newspaper editors to publish papers for Polish miners or German metalworkers, shopkeepers to supply their fellow migrants with pasta or red beans, religious specialists to minister to Catholic or Buddhist souls, and others. Each migration involved the transfer to the new geographical location not only of man power but also of services and resources. Each migratory wave generated, in turn, suppliers of services at the point of arrival, whether these were labor agents, merchants, lawyers, or players of percussion instruments.

In the development of capitalism, three waves of migration stand out, each a response to critical changes in the demand for labor, each creating new working classes. The first of these waves was associated with the initial period of European industrialization. Beginning in England, these initial movements toward capitalist industry covered only short distances, since industrial development was itself still localized and limited. Thus, in the cotton town of Preston in Lancashire, where roughly half the population consisted of immigrants in 1851, over 40 percent had come less than ten miles from their birthplaces and only about 30 percent had come more than thirty miles. Fourteen percent of all immigrants had been born in Ireland, however, and came to Preston as part of the rising tide of Irish immigration in the 1840s. Localized as such movements were, they made Lancashire the most urbanized county in Britain by the middle of the nineteenth century, with more than half the people of the county living in fourteen towns with populations of more than 10,000.

Belgium followed Britain in the movement of workers from the countryside, as the industrial towns of the Walloon-speaking southern provinces burgeoned in the 1820s. In the 1830s the Prussian provinces of Westphalia, Rhine, Berlin, and Brandenburg initiated their industrial expansion, attracting a large-scale flow of population from Prussia's eastern agricultural regions. This flow intensified greatly in the last quarter of the century, as dependent cultivators were displaced by the consolidation and mechanization of the large Junker estates.

While the first wave of labor migration under capitalism carried people toward the industrial centers within the European peninsula, a second flow sent Europeans overseas. An estimated 50 million people left Europe permanently between 1800 and 1914. The most important destination of this movement was the United States, which between 1820 and 1915 absorbed about 32 million immigrants, most of them of European origins. This influx of people provided the labor power that underwrote the industrialization of the United States.

A third wave of migration carried contract laborers of diverse origins to the expanding mines and plantations of the tropics. This flow represents a number of developments, such as the establishment of a migratory labor force for the South African mines, the growth of the trade in Indian and Chinese contract labor, and the sponsored migration of Italian laborers to the coffee regions of Brazil. These movements not only laid the basis for a large increase in tropical production but also played a major part in creating an infrastructure of transport and communication, prerequisites for a further acceleration of capitalist development.

THE UNITED STATES

While Britain, Belgium, and Germany recruited their working classes largely through internal and intracontinental migration, the United States imported its working class by sailboat and steamship. Such reliance on immigrant labor, of course, predates the onset of industrialization in the United States. We have discussed the forced movement of Africans to the New World, including the area that was to become, under the impact of British textile development, the Cotton South. European migration before the American War of Independence also included many people who accepted the temporary bondage of indenture in the hope of establishing themselves in the New World; these indentured laborers may have comprised as many as two-thirds of all early migrants. Later in the eighteenth century, there came a quarter of a million Scotch-Irish, transplanted first from the Scottish Lowlands to Ulster, and then forced by rack-renting and rising tithes to abandon Ulster for America. Another group that came in the nineteenth century were Scottish Highlanders, displaced by sheep or driven by rising rents; they were led by their "tacksmen," heads of cadet lines of the chiefly *clann,* who acted as intermediaries between chief and commoners. Another quarter of a million migrants arrived from southwestern Germany, an area of impoverished and parcelized agriculture. Mass immigration into the United States, however, began only after the cessation of the Napoleonic wars.

In the 1820s, 151,000 immigrants came to the United States; in the decade of the 1830s, the number tripled to 599,000. It increased again to 1,713,000 in the 1840s, and to 2,314,000 in the 1850s. The main factors pushing these people out of Europe were the spread of industrial capitalism and the commercialization of agriculture. As industrial capitalism spread, it displaced artisans and destroyed the domestic putting-out system. Transformations in agriculture burdened Irish and southwestern German cultivators with increased rents, mortgages, and indebtedness, and drove Scottish, English, and Scandinavian cultivators off the land to make way for sheep or cattle. In the period between 1820 and 1860, therefore, the main contingents of immigrants came from Ireland (2 million), southwestern Germany (1.5 million), and the British Isles (750,000). Of course, the United States was not the only target of such migrations. Between 1818 and 1828, 250,000 Germans settled in southern Russia. Others went to Brazil, while Irishmen settled in Canada and the Maritime Provinces, or sought new homes in Australia. In the United States, the advent of the new immigrants speeded up capitalist industrialization. "Neither the factory system," says Maldwyn Jones, "nor the great canal and railroad development of the period could have come into existence so quickly without the reservoir of cheap labor provided by immigration." The role of the Irish immigrants, who quickly developed a new monopoly on unskilled labor in construction work and factory employment in this period, in fierce competition with American Blacks, proved especially important in this regard.

More Englishmen, Swedes, and Germans from east of the Elbe arrived between 1860 and 1890. Again, many of them were displaced agriculturalists driven off the land by the disintegration of English, Swedish, and German wheat production between 1865 and 1875, a result of the importation of low-priced American and Russian grain. The Great Depression also affected German and English coal mining, iron and steel production, and textiles; miners, metalworkers, spinners, and weavers came to seek employment in the New World. The cultivators among them could take advantage of land grants offered by the advancing railroads and by the midwestern and western states and territories.

Around 1890 the area of migrant supply shifted from northern and western Europe to southern and eastern Europe. The new immigrants were largely displaced peasants and agricultural laborers from southern Italy, the Austro-Hungarian empire, and the Balkans. In addition, there were Poles, Jews, and Volga-Germans from the Russian empire; Russians themselves migrated mostly to Siberia. The newcomers quickly replaced their predecessors in a number of industrial locations and occupations. The coal miners in Pennsylvania had been largely of British or German origin before 1890, but after that time they were mainly Poles, Slovaks, Italians, and Hungarians. Whereas the New England textile mills had been manned primarily by French-Canadians, English, and Irish, the new textile workers were Portuguese, Greeks, Poles, and Syrians. In the garment trades, Russian Jews and Italians took over from Germans, Czechs, and Irish.

This large-scale influx of European labor had a marked influence on the direction of American technological development. During the first half of the nineteenth century, capitalist entrepreneurs were faced with a relative shortage of labor. There was land available to those who wanted to farm, and there were opportunities for artisan employment, both of which attracted newcomers away from industrial work. Wages were relatively high for all categories of workers. This appears to have fostered the development of labor-saving devices and their early introduction into industry. The later influx of industrially unskilled workers from southern and eastern Europe, in turn, favored the further development of machinery and of rationalized processes of production that did not rely on mechanical skills. In 1908 the U.S. Immigration Commission noted that the new migrants were often drawn into highly capitalized industries, despite their lack of skills:

> As a consequence their employment in the mines and manufacturing plants of the country has been made possible only by the invention of mechanical devices and processes which have eliminated the skill and experience formerly recognized in a large number of occupations.

Most of the foreign-born workers entered the unskilled, lower-paid levels of industrial occupations. While their new employment yielded remuneration substantially higher than they would have earned in Europe, the combination of mechanization and unskilled immigrant labor permitted American entrepreneurs to keep wages down. Without the Italian, Slav, Greek, Portuguese, French-Canadian, and Russian Jewish workers who furnished the bulk of the labor for the leading American industries by 1900, the industrial expansion that took place between 1880 and 1900 would not have been possible.

LABOR FOR THE MINES: SOUTH AFRICA

We have seen that at about the same time the United States moved toward full industrialization, a takeoff into capitalist development also took hold in southern Africa. There, diamonds and gold were discovered in the last third of the nineteenth century, in the areas north of the Orange and Vaal rivers. The core area of South African development shifted correspondingly to these inland areas. At first diamonds and gold were both mined by surface diggers. Sometimes particular tasks were contracted to white entrepreneurs who organized work gangs. While some Africans paid the license fees needed to become full-time diggers, by 1876 the higher-paid skilled jobs were monopolized by white diggers, and African laborers were contracted only for short periods of about three months. By 1892 the skilled workers had formed a trade union to defend their position against any attempt of management to lower labor costs by using African laborers or by sponsoring further immigration from England.

War between Britain and the Afrikaaners for political control of South Africa disrupted mining operations between 1899 and 1902, and cut the available working force in half. By 1906, however, the mines were again in full production, with a labor force of 18,000 whites, 94,000 Africans, and 51,000 Chinese indentured servants. In 1907 there was a strike of white skilled workers who opposed management plans to increase Chinese immigration and to replace white with black labor. It was broken when unemployed Afrikaaners were brought in as strikebreakers. The lasting outcome, however, was the repatriation of Chinese miners and a reinforcement of the color bar in employment.

Most of the white miners, as of 1912, came from outside South Africa—from Britain, Australia, the United States, and elsewhere. These whites made up the skilled labor force. The Africans, in contrast, were unskilled migratory workers, on contracts from six to eighteen months' duration, who received a tenth of the wages paid to the whites.

The idea of employing Africans as temporary laborers became established in the first decade of mining. In the 1880s it was combined with the notion of confining Africans to residential compounds for their contractual period. This practice took root first in the Kimberley diamond mines, in part to stop the illicit sale of diamonds by African miners to dealers, in part to control desertion. This "closed" compound has remained a feature of the diamond mines ever since. Local traders initially protested the company stores set up by the mining companies for their shut-in work force. When the gold mines adopted the compound system somewhat later, compounds were set up in an "open" rather than "closed" form to meet the objections of local storekeepers.

LABOR FOR THE PLANTERS: EAST INDIANS

While Britain, northwestern continental Europe, and the high South African *veld* were importing labor to man the new industrial machinery, other regions of the world were seeking new sources of agricultural labor. The "old" areas of plantation agriculture, most of them growing sugar cane, had lost their supply of slave labor with abolition. On some of the small islands of the Caribbean, such as Barbados and St. Kitts, the freed slaves had no alternative but to work for their former masters. But on the larger islands like Trinidad and Jamaica, and in the mainland sugar colony of Guyana (then Demarara), the ex-slaves could and did take up land beyond the confines of the plantation, and they resisted further work on the old estates. Facing potential ruin, the planters began to agitate for new sources of labor. Sometimes the British intercepted slave ships going to Brazil, nominally freed the slaves, and then sent them to the West Indian sugar islands.

These proved to be only stopgap measures. To the cry for replacement of the old labor supply was soon added the demand for more and more labor as the scale of commercial agriculture expanded. Beyond the old sugar areas, there were sometimes political reasons for importing laborers. In Malaya, for example, the British decided to maintain intact the Malay peasantry and its tributary relationship with village headmen and ruling nobles. The need for plantation labor was therefore met through the organized migration of indentured laborers from India and of contract labor from China.

Whereas Chinese labor came to be utilized primarily in mining and construction work, Indian indentured labor was deployed mainly in plantations, specifically plantations located within the British empire. Already under the Mughals groups of men had taken service as bearers and on ships, and by the end of the eighteenth century there were Indian laborers—hired for periods of two to three years—in all the ports of Southeast Asia. Yet the great stimulus for the development of what Tinker has called "the second slavery" came with the abolition of the slave trade in 1808 and the sudden need for cheap and tractable labor, especially on the sugar-producing plantations of the tropics.

Guyana asked for Indian laborers, as did Jamaica and Trinidad from 1836 on. (At present, East Indians make up more than 50 percent of the population in Guyana, about 40 percent in Trinidad, and about 2 percent in Jamaica.) East Indian labor migration to Mauritius began in 1835; by 1861 East Indians constituted about two-thirds of the population of the island. In 1860 the tea plantations in Assam and Bhutan began to compete for migrants, and between 1870 and the end of the century 700,000–750,000 laborers were recruited for work there. The demand for East Indians in Fiji began in 1879; today, Indians there outnumber native Fijians. After the 1870s Ceylon became a main area of demand; in the 1880s, Burma; after the turn of the century, Malaya. Natal in South Africa began importing East Indian contract labor for its sugar plantations around 1870. All together, Tinker estimates, "over a million Indian laborers went overseas to tropical plantations in the forty years before 1870; though the figure could be as high as two million."

vast migration

LABOR FOR THE PLANTERS: EUROPEANS

Another major source of agricultural labor was European. We have already made mention of the Polish workers who began to replace German tenant-laborers on the Junker estates of eastern Germany after 1870. In the coffee belt of Brazil, the end of slavery also created a labor crisis. It proved impossible to tap the labor of Luso-Brazilian small-scale cultivators, most of whom were held fast in relationships of dependency upon local landlords and other powerholders. For a time, some Brazilian political leaders harbored plans to bring in indentured "Asiatics." Finally, the problem was solved by importing Italian laborers. The government paid for their voyage, and the local planter advanced a year's wages and a subsistence plot, thus subsidizing "free" Italian labor.

The Italian emigration was prompted largely by the crisis of agriculture within Italy beginning in the 1870s. The sale of public-domain land and church holdings had created a situation in which large landowners were able to add to their holdings, while small cultivators were being squeezed out by falling prices for agricultural products. This price decline was in considerable part the result of competition from Russian and American wheat. The increasing flood of manufactured goods also disrupted local handicrafts, while the phylloxera blight destroyed vineyards. Wealthy landowners began to move their liquid wealth into industry but smallholders and laborers could escape the squeeze only by moving elsewhere, either seasonally, temporarily, or permanently.

At first, in the 1860s, Italians took up work in France, Switzerland, Germany, and Austria-Hungary, but only 16,000 emigrated permanently in that decade. In the 1870s the stream of permanent emigration grew to 360,000, with some 12,000 now going to Argentina and Brazil. Then, between 1881 and 1901, the number of permanent emigrants rose sixfold to more than 2 million. In all, more than 4 million left Italy permanently between 1861 and 1911. The majority came from southern Italy, where the agricultural crisis hit most heavily. Four-fifths were agricultural laborers and construction workers. In the 1880s and 1890s

South America was the major target of migration: three times as many went to Brazil and Argentina as went to the United States. By 1901, however, the trend was reversed. In the first decade of the twentieth century, more than twice as many went to the United States as to South America; in the second decade, more than three times as many. By that time, however, the new labor supply had permitted Brazil's coffee planters to lay the basis for rapid industrial growth, with the Brazilian government paying the transportation costs for the new work force.

THE TRADE IN CHINESE LABOR

China proved to be another source of labor for the outside world. In Southeast Asia there had been Chinese before the European expansion. Moslem Chinese of mixed Han, Persian, Arabic, and Central Asian origins, called Hwei or Hui, moved into the southwestern Chinese borderlands during the Mongol period of the thirteenth and fourteenth centuries; many carried on the overland trade to southern Asia. Chinese trading colonies also settled in the islands at this time. In the fifteenth century, however, the Chinese state throttled foreign commerce and created an unpopulated no-man's-land along the coastal fringe in order to prevent foreign contracts with the Han population. This stemmed out-migration. Nevertheless, Chinese laborers were exported by the Portuguese through Macao, while the Dutch East India Company captured Chinese along the China coast in order to populate its headquarters town of Batavia.

The conclusion of treaties at the end of the Opium War in 1842 removed the barrier to emigration and permitted foreign entrepreneurs to tap the Chinese labor market directly through the establishment of the "coolie" trade. Political disorders and economic crises in China, such as the Taiping rebellion, drove many to accept labor contracts abroad. Soon a sophisticated apparatus of traders grew up to facilitate this movement. If an entrepreneur wanted Chinese laborers for use in Malaya, he could contact a "coolie broker" in Singapore or Penang. The coolie broker, in turn, issued the order for labor to "eating-house" keepers in Swatow, Amoy, Hong Kong, or Macao. The eating-house keepers then contacted "headmen" (*khah-taus*), who recruited laborers on the village level. Laborers either paid for their own transportation or else indentured themselves to a "credit-ticket" broker who paid the cost of their travel.

The laborers who had paid their own fare could move about freely in search for work after arrival. The "unpaid passengers," however, were in debt to the broker and indentured to him for the duration of their debt. In Malaya, such indentured arrivals were housed in depots, where they were guarded by "depot keepers" employed by the coolie broker.

Coolie brokers and depot keepers usually held positions in powerful secret societies, which also furnished the depot guards. The secret societies developed a dual function in the context of the labor trade. They maintained social control and coercion over the dependent Chinese population, while at the same time they defended the interests of the Chinese enclave against the dictates and strategies of local governments. The depot system lasted in Malaya until the onset of World War I in 1914.

SINGAPORE

One of the great hubs of this Chinese labor migration was Singapore. Singapore provides an apt example of the ways that the labor trade fitted into the other activities of a major port and commercial center in Asia.

Singapore had been founded in 1819, when England received rights to the site—then inhabited by a few Malay and Chinese fishermen. By 1900 the city had 229,000 inhabitants—two-thirds of them Chinese, the remainder Malays—drawn mainly from the Malay peninsula but also from the island archipelago as far east as Borneo and the Philippines.

From 1867 on, Singapore became a pivot of the British efforts to govern in the peninsula, using British officials, Malay adjutants, and Chinese and Tamil clerks. The British also managed the agency houses charged with handling the European-based trade. Alongside the European traders stood the Chinese merchants, headed by the prestigious Baba families and closely interlinked through kinship ties. As non-Malays they were barred from any access to the formal positions of political authority, but they held much of the real power over capital and men in the city. They advanced money to planters and miners. They managed the labor trade through which workers were funneled to the tin mines of Perak and Selangor and to the plantations. They dominated the powerful secret societies that controlled the immigrant laborers and offered protection and assistance in return for loyalty and service. The British, in turn, used the heads of these secret societies as "captains of the Chinese" to control the Chinese population, until the secret societies themselves accumulated too much power and were declared illegal in 1889. Their place was taken by associations based on common dialect or surname, patterned on the regional associations found in China and fulfilling similar functions of support and welfare. These associations also functioned as religious bodies. In the setting of Singapore, they both embodied the anti-Manchu political stance of the secret societies and offered unorthodox religious expression of individual needs through spirit-medium cults.

Capital in the city thus flowed mainly through British and Chinese hands, while most of the labor was furnished by Chinese.

CHINESE LABOR: OTHER DESTINATIONS

Malaya was not the only destination of Chinese labor. Some 90,000 indentured Chinese laborers were sent to Peru between 1849 and 1874, mostly through Macao, to replace Hawaiians who had died working in the guano beds. Some of these Chinese were assigned to work in the cotton fields of coastal Peru when demand for cotton rose in the wake of the scarcity created by the war between the Union and the Confederacy. Others were employed in railroad construction.

Another 200,000 Chinese were sent to California between 1852 and 1875, where they were employed in fruit growing and processing, in panning for gold, and in building railroads. In the 1860s some 10,000 to 14,000 Chinese laborers built the Central Pacific Railroad of California, which by 1885 linked the West Coast with eastern Utah and thus completed the transcontinental railroad. Five thousand more workers were taken from Hong Kong to Victoria to build the Canadian Pacific Railroad, which opened up the gold placer beds of British Columbia.

In California the movement of Chinese labor was controlled by merchant-brokers who hired out the laborers as needed, while retaining control over them through the operations of secret societies. The secret societies, in turn, were interlinked with the so-called Six Companies, named for their districts of origin in Kwantung province and patterned after the regional associations that developed in China during the Manchu Ch'ing regime. As in Singapore, the Six Companies defended Chinese interests in an antagonistic environment. At the same time, they exercised control over the Chinese population on the West Coast. The Pacific Steamship Company cooperated with them by agreeing not to allow any man to return to China who had not cleared his debts. After the cessation of the labor trade, the Six (later Seven) Companies continued as political, educational, and welfare associations of the Chinese community in the United States.

Gold was discovered not only in California and British Columbia but also in Australia (1853). By 1854 there were 2,000 Chinese miners in the Australian gold fields, with 42,000 there by 1859. Other areas also entered the Chinese labor trade. Cuba contracted for 800 Chinese in 1847, and for some 8,000 to 15,000 in 1852. Between 1856 and 1867, 19,000 Chinese left Hong Kong under contract, of whom 6,630 went to the British West Indies (mostly Guyana), 4,991 to Cuba, 2,370 to Bombay in India, 1,609 to Dutch Guiana, and 1,035 to Tahiti, Hawaii, and other Pacific islands.

In addition to Chinese laborers who stayed abroad only until their contracts expired, there were also migrants who went in search of permanent settlement. One of the major areas of such settlement was Southeast Asia, where the Chinese population in the 1870s was more than 12 million. Early migrant groups were often traders who in time formed a mercantile aristocracy, such as the Babas of Malacca and the Peranakans of Indonesia. Later comers frequently had to contend for power with the earlier arrivals.

Often Chinese merchants would, in their new homeland, build up a dependable following by calling on kinsmen or people from the same home region in China. In employment, close kin were preferred to more distant kin, more distant kin to speakers of the same Chinese dialect, members of the same dialect category to other Chinese, and Chinese to non-Chinese. Such a following, built up on kin or quasi-kin ties, would engage in many different activities, often centering around operations that connected the primary producers in the hinterland with Western commercial enterprises. Chinese were widely active as middlemen, to the point where Indonesians began calling them *bangsa tengah,* "the middle race." Chinese merchants also advanced the credit necessary to oil the circuits of commerce. "The native peasant is in debt to the Chinese trader, the trader to the wholesaler, the wholesaler to the export-import firm. Debt obligations connect all the steps of trade with each other." Unsurprisingly, these middleman and credit functions have often made the Chinese creditor-merchant the target of political attack and persecution in Southeast Asia, where their position has often been compared to that of the Jews in Eastern Europe.

The Chinese laborers, too, faced hostility from workers in the areas to which they were brought. In 1882 the United States passed the Chinese Exclusion Act under pressure from the Knights of Labor, who had even insisted on the ejection of Chinese from the laundry business. The anti-Chinese agitations that broke out on the West Coast of the United States were not merely a California problem but part of an emergent racism in the United States. Restrictions on Chinese immigration constitute merely one phase in a larger movement to divide employment opportunities along racial lines. Similar efforts at excluding the Chinese were made in Australia after their employment in the gold fields came to an end, and in South Africa, where 43,296 Chinese contract laborers worked on the Rand in 1904, only to be repatriated in 1907.

33.   CHINESE LABOR IN CUBA
An Official Inquiry, 1876

As Eric Wolf documented in the previous selection, Chinese laborers were taken to all parts of the world after the British "opened" China with the *Opium War. Chinese had already migrated throughout Southeast Asia, but in the second half of the nineteenth century, they were also taken to the United States to work on the railroads (until they were banned in 1882), to the Pacific Islands to work on plantations, to South America to work in the mines, and to the Caribbean to work on plantations. Many of the Chinese brought to Cuba worked side by side with African slaves on the sugar plantations.*

Slavery was not abolished in Cuba until 1886, but Britain seized Spanish slave ships in the 1840s and the slave trade was effectively suppressed by 1865. Consequently, Cuban sugar planters needed a new source of workers. After a brief experiment with Spanish, Irish, Mayans, Egyptians, and Ethiopians, the planters found an ideal solution. Chinese could be imported in large numbers and paid less than the cost of slaves, and planters did not have to worry about interference from the home country, because China was so weak. The contracts with Chinese workers (mostly Cantonese, from South China) promised free passage to Cuba, housing, food, clothing, and a minimal wage in return for 12-hour workdays, six days a week, for eight years.

Even these minimal inducements were not honored, according to letters the workers sent back to China. As a result, a movement to end the "coolie trade" gained force in China, fanned by rumors (possibly sanctioned by English Protestant missionaries to discredit Spanish Catholics) that Cubans were eating the Chinese. Western powers, eager to end the Spanish advantage in sugar production, suggested the creation of a commission of inquiry. The Chinese emperor agreed, appointing his minister for overseas Chinese to oversee the investigation conducted in 1873. What follows are selections from the commission's report of 1876. The report, based on oral interviews with thousands of Chinese workers, affords a rare opportunity to hear the voices of an underclass that was silenced by poverty and their inability to speak a language other than Chinese.

What did the commission conclude? How were the Chinese workers treated? In what ways did the Cubans violate the rights of Chinese workers? How did the workers respond to their treatment in Cuba? What were the long-term results of this episode of international labor migration?

Translation of Despatch of Commissioners Ch'ên Lanpin, Macpherson and Huber, reporting to the Tsung-li Yamên the results of their enquiry into the condition of Chinese in Cuba.

The Commissioner Ch'ên, and the Commissioners of Customs Macpherson and Huber, address this memorial in reply:—

On the 10th day of the 10th moon of the 12th year of T'ungchih [29th November 1873] was received the communication of the Yamên to the effect that "for the enquiry in regard to Chinese emigrants to the Spanish possession of Cuba, Ch'ên Lanpin, the officer in charge of the Educational Mission abroad, has been selected, that Mr. Macpherson, Commissioner of Customs at Hankow, and Mr. Huber, Commissioner of Customs at Tientsin, are likewise appointed and are to accompany him; that this arrangement has been sanctioned by an Edict of the 30th day of the 7th moon [21st September], that the head of the Commission is to await in the United States the arrival of his associates, and that they are thence to proceed together to their destination, where they are to institute an honest and complete enquiry, of the results of which a full report is to be supplied, as a guide for subsequent action. . . ."

During these investigations, the hours of visiting the dépôts and prisons were always fixed by the local officials, and plantations also were only visited after the assent of the latter had been obtained. Besides, however, in the places where we stayed, as well as on the road, independent enquiries were instituted.

All investigations of Chinese were conducted verbally and in person by ourselves. The depositions and petitions show that $\frac{8}{10}$ths of the entire number declared that they had been kidnapped or decoyed; that the mortality during the voyage from wounds caused by blows, suicide and sickness proves to have exceeded 10 per cent; that on arrival at Havana they were sold into slavery,—a small proportion being disposed of to families and shops, whilst the large majority became the property of sugar planters; that the cruelty displayed even towards those of the former class is great, and that it assumes in the case of those of the latter, proportions that are unendurable. The labour, too, on the plantations is shown to be excessively severe, and the food to be insufficient; the hours of labour are too long, and the chastisements by rods, whips, chains, stocks, &c., &c., productive of suffering and injury. During the past years a large number have been killed by blows, have died from the effects of wounds and have hanged themselves, cut their throats, poisoned themselves with opium, and thrown themselves into wells and sugar caldrons. It was also possible to verify by personal inspection wounds inflicted upon others, the fractured and maimed limbs, blindness, the heads full of sores, the teeth struck out, the ears mutilated, and the skin and flesh lacerated, proofs of cruelty patent to the eyes of all.

On the termination of the contracts the employers, in most cases, withhold the certificates of completion, and insist on renewal of engagements, which may extend to even more than 10 years, and during which the same system of cruelty is adhered to; whilst if the Chinese refuse to assent, they are taken to the dépôts, whence in chains, and watched by guards, they are forced to repair roads, receiving no compensation for their labour, undergoing a treatment exactly similar to that of criminals in jail. Afterwards they are compelled to again enter the service of an employer, and sign a contract, on the completion of which they are once more taken to the dépôts; and as this process is constantly repeated, a return home, and an attempt to gain a livelihood independently, become impossible.

Moreover, since the 2nd moon of the 11th year of Hienfêng [March–April 1861] the issue of Letters of Domicile and Cedulas has ceased, rendering liability to arrest universal, whilst those possessing these papers are constantly, be it on the street or in their own houses, called upon to produce them for inspection, or are even exposed to their being taken away, or torn up, and to themselves being carried away to the endless misery of a dépôt.

Of all these facts the depositions and petitions furnish detailed evidence. . . .

DO THE LAWS PROVIDE ADEQUATELY FOR THE WELL-BEING OF THE COOLIES ON THE VOYAGE?

. . . Of the more than 140,000 Chinese who sailed for Cuba, more than 16,000 died during the voyages, a fact which is sufficient evidence of the absence of effective regulations.

The petition of Li Chao-ch'un and 165 others states, "when, quitting Macao, we proceeded to sea, we were confined in the hold below; some were even shut up in bamboo cages, or chained to iron posts, and a few were indiscriminately selected and flogged as a means of intimidating all others; whilst we cannot estimate the deaths that, in all, took place, from sickness, blows, hunger, thirst, or from suicide by leaping into the sea." The petition of Ch'iu Pi-shan and 35 others states, "If the master be a good man the sufferings are only those produced by grave maladies, but if his disposition be cruel there is no limit to the ill-usage, and there have been cases when more than half the number on board have died. Ten thousand hardships have to be endured during the voyage of several months." The petition of Tiao Mu and 30 others states, "many die from sickness, and many jump into the sea to be devoured by the fish." The petition of Yeh Fu-chün and 52 others states, "the winds and waves on the ocean were great, and three months had passed away, but we had not arrived; as there was no water issued it had to be bought, and for a single cup a dollar was paid. . . ."

ON ARRIVAL WHAT HAPPENS TO THE COOLIE?

By the 13th article of the Spanish Royal Decree of 1860, it is provided that vessels conveying Chinese labourers to Cuba must—save in cases of sudden exigency—land them at Havana. Thence the common practice has been to pass to that port, after undergoing quarantine at Mariello in the neighbourhood of Guanajay.

The petition of Hsieh Shuang-chiu and 11 others states, "on landing, four or five foreigners on horseback, armed with whips, led us like a herd of cattle to the barracoon to be sold." The petition of Ch'iu Pi-shan and 34 others states, "Chinese (in the Havana barracoons) are treated like pigs and dogs, all their movements, even their meals, being watched, until, after the lapse of a few days, they are sold away." The petition of Li Chao-ch'un and 165 others states, "at Havana, after a detention at the quarantine station our queues [pigtails] were cut, and we awaited in the men-market the inspection of a buyer, and the settlement of the price." The petition of Yeh Fu-chün and 52 others states, "when offered for sale in the men-market we were divided into three classes—1st, 2nd and 3rd, and were forced to remove all our clothes, so that our persons might be examined and the price fixed. This covered us with shame." The petition of Chang Ting-chia and 127 others states, "on landing at Havana we were exposed for sale, our persons being examined by intending purchasers, in a manner shameless and before unheard of by us. . . ."

DURING AGREEMENT-TERM, WHAT TIME HAS THE COOLIE AT HIS OWN DISPOSAL—HOW CAN HE USE IT—AND DOES THE LAW PROTECT HIM IN TURNING IT TO PROFITABLE ACCOUNT?

The 10th article of the Emigration Convention of 1866 provides that of every seven days one is to be a day of rest, and that in the 24 hours work during more than 9½ hours cannot be enforced, and that all compulsory additional labour is prohibited. The 5th clause of the contract used in the 10th year of Hienfêng states that besides the specified times of rest, Chinese shall not be compelled to work on Sundays or holidays, and that on these days they shall be permitted to work as they may see fit for their own profit; and the 4th clause of the contracts used in the 3rd, 4th, 10th and 12th years of T'ungchih, prescribes that Sundays shall be days of rest. The article—the 52nd—of the Royal Decree of 1860, which refers to the same point, is however somewhat at variance with the above provisions, as it directs the execution of the ordinary daily tasks even on festival days, when, despite the celebration of the festival, work shall have been permitted by the ecclesiastical authorities.

The contracts for these four years of T'ungchih also stipulate that only 12 hours out of the 24 shall be devoted to labour. The 53rd article of the Decree of 1860 provides that under no circumstances whatever shall employers exact on an average more than 12 hours' work; and the 54th article, that even when an employer is empowered to distribute in the manner most convenient for his interests, the number of hours agreed upon, it shall be understood that no more than 15 hours can be exacted in one day, and that the labourer shall enjoy at least six consecutive hours of rest; and the 45th article authorises their engaging in amusement during their days or hours of leisure. These three clauses, though not altogether in accordance with the Emigration Convention, evince a care for the interests of the class to which they apply, and have been disregarded by the great majority of the Cuban proprietors.

The petition of Ch'iu Pi-shan and 34 others states, "a plantation is a veritable hell; the Chinese are beaten the entire day, and the cruelties of the owner, administrator and overseers are very great. Their bodies are covered with sores, their feet have no rest, and out of the 24 hours they are granted only four for repose." The petition of Wang A-ching and 22 others states, "the work is very hard. We get up at 3 A.M., and labour until noon; at 1 P.M., we resume work until 7 P.M., when we rest half an hour and are allowed a ration of maize, after which work is continued up to midnight. We are struck and flogged, and out of our party of more than 200 men, only over 80 remain." The petition of Wang Hua and of 16 others states, "we have to labour at night nearly until 1 A.M., and we have to recommence work at 4 A.M., and our bodies and our bones cause us so much pain that we cannot work with great activity." Ch'ên Tê-ming declares in his petition, "I was sold to a sugar plantation where I endured every hardship. I and the others got up at 4 A.M. and worked until 1 A.M." The petition of Lin A-ch'ing and 1 other states, "we are in the service of a railway company and have to work night and day. The overseer is very cruel, but whatever he alleges to the superintendent is believed by the latter. Those who have completed their eight years are not allowed to go away. We are constantly flogged by the superintendent at the instigation of the overseer. We get up at 4 A.M., and cease work only at 1 A.M. On Sundays we do not rest." The petition of Yeh Fu-chün and 52 others states, "when sold to sugar plantations, we had to work night and day, having only three hours' sleep." The petition of Ch'ên Ku and 2 others states, "on the sugar plantation we toil daily from 3 A.M. until midnight." The petition of P'an To-li and 2 others states, "we have to labour 19 or 20 hours out of the 24. . . ."

AS COMPARED WITH THEIR FORMER CONDITION IN CHINA, WHAT IS THEIR CONDITION IN CUBA? MORE COMFORTABLE, MORE PROSPEROUS, OR THE REVERSE? DO THEY REGRET HAVING GONE TO CUBA? DO THEY WISH TO GET AWAY? CAN THEY GET AWAY?

Lin A-yung deposes, "on account of the condition of affairs at Cuba I do not desire to remain." Fêng Hui deposes, "the food is insufficient and the labour arduous; my repentence is without limits." Li A-lung deposes, "in China I worked daily during 8 hours, here I have to labour during 20." Liu A-fu deposes, "though I hold a Letter of Domicile and Cedula, and work independently, I am constantly subjected to outrage. Here we are regarded as appertaining to the same class as the negro, indeed sometimes these latter are treated better than we are." Li Hsi-pao deposes, "we are struck without cause; such usage would not be endured in China a single day." Chao A-ling and 14 others depose that they think the existence of a beggar in China preferable to theirs in Cuba. Ho A-chi deposes, "Chinese are treated like the black slaves. I prefer returning to China to beg, to remain here to be ground and broken." Liu Shêng-lin deposes, "although my master is good, the labour I have to perform is ten thousand times more grevious than that of China." Chang Lin-an deposes, "the men in China who suffer the extremest hardships, suffer less than those here." Li A-yao and 185 others all declare in their depositions that they desire to return to China. Ch'ên Hsio-chou deposes, "through the aid of friends I was able to redeem myself and in two years saved sufficient for the cost of my passage back. I then met certain officers who had been sent to arrest all Chinese, and I was seized, placed in prison and there forced to labour. My padrino or godfather upon this, by an outlay of $150, was permitted to bail me, and I thus avoided being again sold to the mountains as a slave, but I lost all my property." Wang Hsiang deposes, "I now possess $200; if the dépôt would grant my release I would return to China."

34. THE "PEACEFUL" PARTITION OF AFRICA

Emile Banning

The last quarter of the nineteenth century was not only a period of intensive global labor migration but also a time of renewed imperialism. The most striking example of this was the partition of Africa by European powers after 1880. In this selection from a book published in 1888, the archivist of the Belgian government presents a history of the partition for his king, Leopold II, that celebrates European "peaceful conquest." Banning writes favorably of the Berlin Conference of 1884, which he attended as a member of the Belgian delegation, and he praises Leopold's exploitation of the Congo. What does this document suggest about European attitudes toward Africa and Africans in this period? How were Europeans able to rationalize the partition of Africa? What did Banning mean by "peaceful conquest"?

Few epochs will hold a place in history comparable to that of the century which is ending. Despite some symptoms of lassitude which the contemporary generation revealed, despite the weaknesses and deceptions of which no period in the life of humanity is exempt, outstanding results and essential changes have been accumulated in all branches of activity and human thought, to the point that the mind is staggered by their weight and importance. The visible entry of Africa into the empire of civilization, the distribution of its vast territories among the nations of Europe, the initiation, under European guidance, of millions of Negroes into superior conditions of existence truly seems to be one of the most considerable revolutions of our time, one of the richest in economic and political consequences.

This activity began with the century and through three highly significant undertakings. At the head of the first figured that indefatigable mover of men and ideas who bore the name of Bonaparte. The expedition to Egypt was both a geographical and historical revelation. Since 1798 Egypt has become a European province, inseparably associated with the fortunes of the great western states. At the same time that it was disclosing the secret of its monuments and its tombs, and while their testimony was renewing our knowledge of high antiquity, the valley of the Nile became the stage of completely modern activities. The point of departure or arrival of the first important discoveries directed toward Abyssinia, the West and Meridional Sudan, Egypt was equally to become, by means of the Suez Canal, the great route of maritime navigation to the Far East.

The definitive occupation of the Cape by England in 1815 produced analogous effects, but on a smaller scale, at the extreme south of the vast African continent. The site of the Cape, which up to that time had served only as a port of call and supply, became the embryo of a colony toward the development of which were applied the resources of a great commercial power. A new base of operations was organized, and little by little its activity was felt up to the banks of the Orange and Zambesi rivers.

Beginning in 1830, the conquest of Algeria by French arms created a third center of attack, a new and powerful source of infiltration of civilizing influences. The task was bloody and laborious. Here it was not with the Negro and fetish-worshipping populations that the French clashed, but with the Arab and Moslem populations. Yet success was not long in doubt, and Africa, breached on three points of the triangle that it forms, became henceforth the object of a regularized, uninterrupted and almost always peaceful conquest.

It was toward the end of this first period of thirty years that the great voyages of exploration were organized. Begun at the end of the last century by Bruce and Mungo Park, they were continued without interruption from René Caillié and Clapperton up to Nachtigal and Stanley; and they included—only to mention the names of the most illustrious—explorations by H. Barth and Schweinfurth, Livingstone, Burton, Speke, Grant, Rohlfs and Cameron.

Up until the middle of this century, almost all of the African interior remained yet to be explored, but despite extreme difficulties and continued dangers, the exploration advanced with an extraordinary rapidity. To measure the effect of this forty-year accomplishment, contemporaries have only to recall the map of Africa that they studied in their youth.

Nevertheless, world public opinion hardly noticed this work of giants. Outside of the circle of geographic societies—and there was only a limited number of these—African questions awakened no response. The press ignored them; governments accorded them only a passing interest. But the remarkable initiative taken in 1876 by the King of the Belgians changed the entire outlook. The conference which was convened under his presidency in the month of September of that year, and the meeting at the palace of Brussels of seven of the most celebrated travellers who had just recently returned from the theater of their discoveries, struck the imagination. Both what had been done in Africa and what remained to be done was now grasped. For several years, *L'Association internationale africaine* held public attention by the expeditions in which Belgian explorers brilliantly undertook their first campaigns.

The return of Stanley in 1877, after his remarkable crossing of Equatorial Africa, gave the signal for the foundation in the following year of the Congo enterprise. From the west coast as from the east coast, deep penetrations were directed toward the interior. The last obstacles gave way before this persistent effort. A dozen years ago the central core—of a size larger by one-third than Europe—was still an immense emptiness on our maps. Today it is the very heart of the Congo Free State, from which agents trek in all directions into the vast empire by means of one of the most admirable water systems which exist on earth.

This fact, which is the expression of colossal progress in geographical science, at the same time characterizes a revolution achieved in ideas. The persevering energy of the King of the Belgians had made the African question the first order of business in Europe and kept it there. The impetus given to the imagination was general. Governments could no longer abstain; rather, it was to be more feared that certain of them would hasten precipitously to make up for lost time. Each one felt, and some among them clearly saw, that a new continent and new races were going to collaborate in the civilization of the world and basically modify the balance of universal interests.

The convocation of a conference at Berlin in 1884 by the imperial government of Germany was the result and the sanction of this movement. The six great powers of Europe, the seven other maritime states, and the United States, all took part in it. This great assembly marks precisely the point where the scientific work found its complement in political action, where national enterprise came to cooperate with individual initiative.

The Berlin Conference fulfilled a double task: it endorsed the creation, in the very heart of Equatorial Africa, of a great interior state, commercially open to all nations, but politically shielded from their competition. It also set up the bases for economic legislation which was immediately applicable to the central zone of the continent but which virtually demanded more extensive application. These regulations, inspired by the most liberal ideas and discarding all whims of selfish exploitation, will protect both the natives and the Europeans in their relations with the colonizing powers. The conference also upheld the principles— justly dear to our age—of religious and civil liberty, of loyal and peaceful competition, and it broke with the antiquated traditions of the former colonial system.

Three years have lapsed since the promulgation of the act of the Berlin Conference and already the political and economic thought which formed the bases of its clauses has been many times applied in Africa. Germany, England, France and Portugal have rivalled each other in activity in this area, while remaining faithful to the spirit of understanding and justice and to the reciprocal concessions which had dictated their common resolutions. The partition of Africa on both sides of the equator . . . was achieved peacefully, with neither trouble nor jolts, and without any of the onerous and bloody conflicts which accompanied and noticeably impeded the colonization of the two Americas. . . .

. . . The African enterprise rests on broad foundations. One can see with what vigor in action, scope in plans, and concern over their consequences all of Europe is involved. Never has the assault on a new continent been pursued by such a group nor has it been better organized in its details. Nothing of the sort happened in America or even in Australia. Where would the new world be today, what leaps forward would it have taken, if, at the end of the sixteenth century, an American conference could have done for it what the Berlin Conference has done for Africa? But the thought could never have risen. For it to have been possible and practical, the modern development of international law as well as the great progress of science and technology were necessary. The European nations had to become capable of collective action and able to place at the service of the common idea the enormous industrial and financial power of our age. From this ensued the grandiose evolution which we have witnessed and of which the glorious fruit will be the redemption of a continent and a race.

. . . The political situation which was produced in Africa by the cooperative action of the governments realized a thought which was already apparent since 1876 and which even then appeared to be the future solution of the problem. Each of the principal maritime peoples established itself in the area which best suited both its interests and its means of action. While engaging in this national activity, each of them fulfilled a social mission, spread abroad the germs of culture, created the sites for the spread of ideas, of which the rays converged on the common center. A similar plan, an identical tendency dominated them to a higher goal.

Thus the league of civilization was gradually organized in the conquest of virgin nature and heathen races. What was truly new in this conception, what has an original quality, was the role assigned to Belgium in this peaceful crusade. Belgium owes this role both to the generosity of its King and to the sympathy of the powers. If the Congo State is nowhere mentioned in the act of the Berlin Conference, it is understood in every article. It was in effect an essential idea in the general idea of which the regeneration of Africa was the object. The attack from the center is necessarily correlative to that which occurred from the diverse points of the circumference. The European states coordinated their activities with the action of the central power. Its foundation and development reveal the closest rapport with the others.

From this point of view the Congo State, in some respects, took on the aspect of an international institution: it served as the connecting link and the pivotal point for the establishments on both coasts. The efforts of the other powers were the guarantee of its success, in the same way that it cooperated in the activities of the others, endorsed their expansion, consolidated the results. All progress accomplished in the central state had its repercussions in all the colonial establishments which surround it, just as every conquest achieved in the maritime regions soon affected the interior. It is impossible to separate the two orders of activity without simultaneously compromising both. Whoever loses sight of the whole, whoever attempts to favor particular development to the detriment of general development hurts himself and condemns himself to emptiness. The theater is too narrow for anyone to isolate himself with impunity. Never on any point of the globe has the joint action of peoples appeared to the same degree as the principle and guarantee of their success. Who harms one does injury to all; who facilitates the total plan comes to the aid of each one. The Congo State will prosper or fall reciprocally with all the colonial creations which envelop it.

This was a unanimous conviction at the Berlin Conference. Experience has confirmed it with each step and will contribute more and more to center on this point the sentiment of those men who are attracted to the study of this great problem. Here is strikingly revealed the immense superiority of the modern formula of colonization over those of previous centuries. Mercantile selfishness has been replaced by the impetus of a much higher order. National interests are reconciled with universal interests in a synthesis of which the final result will be to give to the world another continent; to production, the resources of a wealth and variety scarcely glimpsed; to militant humanity, a new family whose native faculties have already caused considerable surprises and which will reserve, after a century of culture, a goodly number more for future generations.

35.   THE TOOLS OF EMPIRE
Daniel R. Headrick

The "imperialism of free trade" that characterized much European expansion from 1840 to 1860 was followed, especially after 1880, by more aggressive and popular policies calling for actual possession of colonies. The partition of Africa was one example of this change. The reasons for the "new imperialism" of military conquest and occupation have been widely debated. Marxists and socialists pointed to the financial panic of 1873, the troubled Western economies in the 1870s, shrinking domestic markets, and the need for raw materials. Others have seen the change in the growth of popular antiforeign sentiment and racism at the end of the nineteenth century.

In this essay, Daniel Headrick, a modern historian of technology, suggests that we look at the technological developments of the late nineteenth century as well. What technological innovations does he mention? How would they have made military conquest, colonization, and occupation easier?

The history of European imperialism in the nineteenth century still contains a number of paradoxes, which an understanding of technology can help elucidate. One of them is the expansion of Britain in the mid-century, a world power claiming to want no more imperial responsibilities yet reluctantly acquiring territories "in a fit of absent-mindedness." Was this really a case, as Fieldhouse put it, of "a metropolitan dog being wagged by its colonial tail"? A more appropriate metaphor might be the pseudonym Macgregor Laird used in writing to *The Spectator:* Cerberus, the many-headed dog.

For the imperialist drive did not originate from only one source. In the outposts of empire, and most of all in Calcutta and Bombay, were eager imperialists, adventurous and greedy for territory. They lacked, however, the industry to manufacture the tools of conquest. Had they been able to create the instruments appropriate to their ambitions, they might well have struck out on their own, like the settlers in the Thirteen Colonies of North America. But against Burma, China, the Middle East, and Africa they needed British technology.

In Britain, meanwhile, the politicians were at times reluctant; the lengthy delay in occupying Egypt is an example of this. But the creators of the tools of empire—people like Peacock, the Lairds, the arms manufacturers—were provisioning the empire with the equipment that the peripheral imperialists required. The result was a secondary imperialism, the expansion of British India, sanctioned, after the fact, by London.

Imperialism in the mid-century was predominantly a matter of British tentacles reaching out from India toward Burma, China, Malaya, Afghanistan, Mesopotamia, and the Red Sea. Territorially, at least, a much more impressive demonstration of the new imperialism was the scramble for Africa in the last decades of the century. Historians generally agree that from a profit-making point of view, the scramble was a dubious undertaking. Here also, technology helps explain events.

Inventions are most easily described one by one, each in its own technological and socioeconomic setting. Yet the inner logic of innovations must not blind us to the patterns of chronological coincidence. Though advances occurred in every period, many of the innovations that proved useful to the imperialists of the scramble first had an impact in the two decades from 1860 to 1880. These were the years in which quinine prophylaxis made Africa safer for Europeans; quick-firing breechloaders replaced muzzle-loaders among the forces stationed on the imperial frontiers; and the compound engine, the Suez Canal, and the submarine cable made steamships competitive with sailing ships, not only on government-subsidized mail routes, but for ordinary freight on distant seas as well. Europeans who set out to conquer new lands in 1880 had far more power over nature and over the people they encountered than their predecessors twenty years earlier had; they could accomplish their tasks with far greater safety and comfort.

Few of the inventions that affected the course of empire in the nineteenth century were indispensable; quinine prophylaxis comes closest, for it is unlikely that many Europeans would willingly have run the risks of Africa without it. The muzzle-loaders the French used in fighting Abd-el Kader could also have defeated other non-Western peoples; but it is unlikely that any European nation would have sacrificed for Burma, the Sudan, or the Congo as much as France did for Algeria.

Today we are accustomed to important innovations being so complex—computers, jet aircraft, satellites, and weapons systems are but a few examples—that only the governments of major powers can defray their research and development costs; and generally they are eager to do so. In the nineteenth century European governments were preoccupied with many things other than imperialism. Industrialization, social conflicts, international tensions, military preparedness, and the striving for a balanced budget all competed for their attention. Within the ruling circles of Britain, France, Belgium, and Germany, debates raged on the need for colonies and the costs of imperialism.

What the breechloader, the machine gun, the steamboat and steamship, and quinine and other innovations did was to lower the cost, in both financial and human terms, of penetrating, conquering, and exploiting new territories. So cost-effective did they make imperialism that not only national governments but lesser groups as well could now play a part in it. The Bombay Presidency opened the Red Sea Route; the Royal Niger Company conquered the Caliphate of Sokoto; even individuals like Macgregor Laird, William Mackinnon, Henry Stanley, and Cecil Rhodes could precipitate events and stake out claims to vast territories which later became parts of empires. It is because the flow of new technologies in the nineteenth century made imperialism so cheap that it reached the threshold of acceptance among the peoples and governments of Europe, and led nations to become empires. Is this not as important a factor in the scramble for Africa as the political, diplomatic, and business motives that historians have stressed?

All this only begs a further question. Why were these innovations developed, and why were they applied where they would prove useful to imperialists? Technological innovations in the nineteenth century are usually described in the context of the Industrial Revolution. Iron shipbuilding was part of the growing use of iron in all areas of engineering; submarine cables resulted from the needs of business and the development of the electrical industry. Yet while we can (indeed, we must) explain the invention and manufacture of specific new technologies in the context of general industrialization, it does not suffice to explain the transfer and application of these technologies to Asia and Africa. To understand the diffusion of new technologies, we must consider also the flow of information in the nineteenth century among both Western and non-Western peoples.

In certain parts of Africa, people are able to communicate by "talking drums" which imitate the tones of the human voice. Europeans inflated this phenomenon into a great myth, that Africans could speak to one another across their continent by the throbbing of tom-toms in the night. This myth of course reflected the Westerners' obsession with long-range communication. In fact, nineteenth-century Africans and Asians were quite isolated from one another and ignorant of what was happening in other parts of the world. Before the Opium War, the court of the Chinese emperor was misinformed about events in Canton and ignorant of the ominous developments in Britain, Burma, and Nigeria. People living along the Niger did not know where the river came from, nor where it went. Stanley encountered people in the Congo who had never before heard of firearms or white men. Throughout Africa, warriors learned from their own experiences but rarely from those of their neighbours.

To be sure, there were cases in which Africans or Asians adopted new technologies. Indian princes hired Europeans to train their troops. The Ethiopian Bezbiz Kasa had an English sergeant make cannons for him, while Samori Touré sent a blacksmith to learn gunsmithing from the French. Mehemet Ali surrounded himself with European engineers and officers in a crash program to modernize his country. What is remarkable about these efforts is their rarity and, in most cases, their insufficiency. In the nineteenth century, only Japan succeeded in keeping abreast of Western technological developments.

In contrast, Western peoples—whether Europeans or descendants of Europeans settled on other continents—were intensely interested in events elsewhere, technological as well as otherwise. Physicians in Africa published their findings in France and Britain. American gun manufacturers exhibited their wares in London, British experts traveled to America to study gunmaking, and General Wolseley paid a visit to the American inventor Hiram Maxim to offer suggestions. Macgregor Laird was inspired by news of events on the Niger to try out a new kind of ship. Dutch and British botanists journeyed to South America to obtain plants to be grown in Asia. Scientists in Indonesia published a journal in French and German for an international readership. The latest rifles were copied in every country and sent to the colonies for testing. The mails and cables transmitted to and from the financial centers of Europe up-to-date information on products, prices, and quantities of goods around the world. And the major newspapers, especially the London *Times*, sent out foreign correspondents and published detailed articles about events in faraway lands. Then, as now, people in the Western world were hungry for the latest news and interested in useful technological innovations. Thus what seemed to work in one place, whether iron river steamers, quinine prophylaxis, machine guns, or compound engines, was quickly known and applied in other places. In every part of the world, Europeans were more knowledgeable about events on other continents than indigenous peoples were about their neighbors. It is the Europeans who had the "talking drums."

European empires of the nineteenth century were economy empires, cheaply obtained by taking advantage of new technologies, and, when the cost of keeping them rose a century later, quickly discarded. In the process, they unbalanced world relations, overturned ancient ways of life, and opened the way for a new global civilization.

The impact of this technologically based imperialism on the European nations who engaged in it is still hotly debated. The late nineteenth and early twentieth centuries were a time of overweening national pride, of frantic, often joyful, preparations for war. The cheap victories on the imperial frontiers, the awesome power so suddenly acquired over the forces of nature and over whole kingdoms and races, were hard to reconcile with the prudence and compromises which the delicate European balance required.

The era of the new imperialism was also the age in which racism reached its zenith. Europeans, once respectful of some non-Western peoples—especially the Chinese—began to confuse levels of technology with levels of culture in general, and finally with biological capacity. Easy conquests had warped the judgment of even the scientific elites.

Among Africans and Asians the legacy of imperialism reflects their assessment of the true value of the civilization that conquered them. Christianity has had little impact in Asia, and its spread in Africa has been overshadowed by that of Islam. Capitalism, that supposed bedrock of Western civilization, has failed to take root in most Third World countries. European concepts of freedom and the rule of law have fared far worse. The mechanical power of the West has not brought, as Macgregor Laird had hoped, "the glad tidings of 'peace and good will toward men' into the dark places of the earth which are now filled with cruelty."

The technological means the imperialists used to create their empires, however, have left a far deeper imprint than the ideas that motivated them. In their brief domination, the Europeans passed on to the peoples of Asia and Africa their own fascination with machinery and innovation. This has been the true legacy of imperialism.

CHAPTER TEN

Culture and Change

36. *THE ORIGIN OF SPECIES*
Charles Darwin

Modern culture begins with Darwin and Freud. In agreement or disagreement, we are their students. Our science, the questions we ask, even much of our "common sense" reflects their work.

As often happens in cases like this, however, the thinker or work becomes a code word for shaking heads. Everyone has an opinion. Few actually read what was said.

What did Darwin say in the following excerpts from The Origin of Species, *published in 1859? Why was he writing? What occasion prompted his book? What did he think he proved? What was the difference between the idea of evolution and the idea of independent creation of species? Did he think his ideas were irreligious? Do you?*

When on board H.M.S. "Beagle," as naturalist, I was much struck with certain facts in the distribution of the organic beings inhabiting South America, and in the geological relations of the present to the past inhabitants of that continent. These facts, as will be seen in the latter chapters of this volume, seemed to throw some light on the origin of species—that mystery of mysteries, as it has been called by one of our greatest philosophers. On my return home, it occurred to me, in 1837, that something might perhaps be made out on this question by patiently accumulating and reflecting on all sorts of facts which could possibly have any bearing on it. After five years' work I allowed myself to speculate on the subject, and drew up some short notes; these I enlarged in 1844 into a sketch of the conclusions, which then seemed to me probable: from that period to the present day I have steadily pursued the same object. I hope that I may be excused for entering on these personal details, as I give them to show that I have not been hasty in coming to a decision.

My work is now (1859) nearly finished; but as it will take me many more years to complete it, and as my health is far from strong, I have been urged to publish this Abstract. I have more especially been induced to do this, as Mr. [Alfred Russel] Wallace, who is now studying the natural history of the Malay archipelago, has arrived at almost exactly the same general conclusions that I have on the origin of species. In 1858 he sent me a memoir on this subject, with a request that I would forward it to Sir Charles Lyell, who sent it to the Linnean Society, and it is published in the third volume of the Journal of that society. Sir C. Lyell and Dr. Hooker, who both knew of my work—the latter having read my sketch of 1844—honoured me by thinking it advisable to publish, with Mr. Wallace's excellent memoir, some brief extracts from my manuscripts.

This Abstract, which I now publish, must necessarily be imperfect. I cannot here give references and authorities for my several statements; and I must trust to the reader reposing some confidence in my accuracy. No doubt errors will have crept in, though I hope I have always been cautious in trusting to good authorities alone. I can here give only the general conclusions at which I have arrived, with a few facts in illustration, but which, I hope, in most cases will suffice. No one can feel more sensible than I do of the necessity of hereafter publishing in detail all the facts, with references, on which my conclusions have been grounded; and I hope in a future work to do this. For I am well aware that scarcely a single point is discussed in this volume on which facts cannot be adduced, often apparently leading to conclusions directly opposite to those at which I have arrived. A fair result can be obtained only by fully stating and balancing the facts and arguments on both sides of each question; and this is here impossible.

In considering the Origin of Species, it is quite conceivable that a naturalist, reflecting on the mutual affinities of organic beings, on their embryological relations, their geographical distribution, geological succession, and other such facts, might come to the conclusion that species had not been independently created, but had descended, like varieties, from other species. Nevertheless, such a conclusion, even if well founded, would be unsatisfactory, until it could be shown how the innumerable species inhabiting this world have been modified, so as to acquire that perfection of structure and coadaptation which justly excites our admiration. Naturalists continually refer to external conditions, such as climate, food, &c., as the only possible source of variation. In one limited sense, as we shall hereafter see, this may be true; but it is preposterous to attribute to mere external conditions, the structure, for instance, of the woodpecker, with its feet, tail, beak, and tongue, so admirably adapted to catch insects under the bark of trees. In the case of the mistletoe, which draws its nourishment from certain trees, which has seeds that must be transported by certain birds, and which has flowers with separate sexes absolutely requiring the agency of certain insects to bring pollen from one flower to the other, it is equally preposterous to account for the structure of this parasite, with its relations to several distinct organic beings, by the effects of external conditions, or of habit, or of the volition of the plant itself.

It is, therefore, of the highest importance to gain a clear insight into the means of modification and coadaptation. At the commencement of my observations it seemed to me probable that a careful study of domesticated animals and of cultivated plants would offer the best chance of making out this obscure problem. Nor have I been disappointed; in this and in all other perplexing cases I have invariably found that our knowledge, imperfect though it be, of variation under domestication, afforded the best and safest clue.

From these considerations, I shall devote the first chapter of this Abstract to Variation under Domestication. We shall thus see that a large amount of hereditary modification is at least possible; and, what is equally or more important, we shall see how great is the power of man in accumulating by his Selection successive slight variations. I will then pass on to the variability of species in a state of nature; but I shall, unfortunately, be compelled to treat this subject far too briefly, as it can be treated properly only by giving long catalogues of facts. We shall, however, be enabled to discuss what circumstances are most favourable to variation. In the next chapter the Struggle for Existence amongst all organic beings throughout the world, which inevitably follows from the high geometrical ratio of their increase, will be considered. This is the doctrine of Malthus, applied to the whole animal and vegetable kingdoms. As many more individuals of each species are born than can possibly survive; and as, consequently, there is a frequently recurring struggle for existence, it follows that any being, if it vary however slightly in any manner profitable to itself, under the complex and sometimes varying conditions of life, will have a better chance of surviving, and thus be *naturally selected*. From the strong principle of inheritance, any selected variety will tend to propagate its new and modified form.

This fundamental subject of Natural Selection will be treated at some length in the fourth chapter; and we shall then see how Natural Selection almost inevitably causes much Extinction of the less-improved forms of life, and leads to what I have called Divergence of Character. In the next chapter I shall discuss the complex and little known laws of variation. In the five succeeding chapters, the most apparent and gravest difficulties in accepting the theory will be given: namely, first, the difficulties of transitions, or how a simple being or a simple organ can be changed and perfected into a highly developed being or into an elaborately constructed organ; secondly, the subject of Instinct, or the mental powers of animals; thirdly, Hybridism, or the infertility of species and the fertility of varieties when intercrossed; and fourthly, the imperfection of the Geological Record. In the next chapter I shall consider the geological succession of organic beings throughout time; in the twelfth and thirteenth, their geographical distribution throughout space; in the fourteenth, their classification or mutual affinities, both when mature and in an embryonic condition. In the last chapter I shall give a brief recapitulation of the whole work, and a few concluding remarks.

No one ought to feel surprise at much remaining as yet unexplained in regard to the origin of species and varieties, if he make due allowance for our profound ignorance in regard to the mutual relations of the many beings which live around us. Who can explain why one species ranges widely and is very numerous, and why another allied species has a narrow range and is rare? Yet these relations are of the highest importance, for they determine the present welfare and, as I believe, the future success and modification of every inhabitant of this world. Still less do we know of the mutual relations of the innumerable inhabitants of the world during the many past geological epochs in its history. Although much remains obscure, and will long remain obscure, I can entertain no doubt, after the most deliberate study and dispassionate judgment of which I am capable, that the view which most naturalists until recently entertained, and which I formerly entertained—namely, that each species has been independently created—is erroneous. I am fully convinced that species are not immutable; but that those belonging to what are called the same genera are lineal descendants of some other and generally extinct species, in the same manner as the acknowledged varieties of any one species are the descendants of that species. Furthermore, I am convinced that Natural Selection has been the most important, but not the exclusive, means of modification.

I see no good reason why the views given in this volume should shock the religious feelings of any one. It is satisfactory, as showing how transient such impressions are, to remember that the greatest discovery ever made by man, namely, the law of the attraction of gravity, was also attacked by Leibnitz, "as subversive of natural, and inferentially of revealed, religion." A celebrated author and divine has written to me that "he has gradually learnt to see that it is just as noble a conception of the Deity to believe that He created a few original forms capable of self-development into other and needful forms, as to believe that He required a fresh act of creation to supply the voids caused by the action of His laws."

Why, it may be asked, until recently did nearly all the most eminent living naturalists and geologists disbelieve in the mutability of species? It cannot be asserted that organic beings in a state of nature are subject to no variation; it cannot be proved that the amount of variation in the course of long ages is a limited quality; no clear distinction has been, or can be, drawn between species and well-marked varieties. It cannot be maintained that species when intercrossed are invariably sterile, and varieties invariably fertile; or that sterility is a special endowment and sign of creation. The belief that species were immutable productions was almost unavoidable as long as the history of the world was thought to be of short duration; and now that we have acquired some idea of the lapse of time, we are too apt to assume, without proof, that the geological record is so perfect that it would have afforded us plain evidence of the mutation of species, if they had undergone mutation.

But the chief cause of our natural unwillingness to admit that one species has given birth to clear and distinct species, is that we are always slow in admitting great changes of which we do not see the steps. The difficulty is the same as that felt by so many geologists, when Lyell first insisted that long lines of inland cliffs had been formed, the great valleys excavated, by the agencies which we see still at work. The mind cannot possibly grasp the full meaning of the term of even a million years; it cannot add up and perceive the full effects of many slight variations, accumulated during an almost infinite number of generations.

Although I am fully convinced of the truth of the views given in this volume under the form of an abstract, I by no means expect to convince experienced naturalists whose minds are stocked with a multitude of facts all viewed, during a long course of years, from a point of view directly opposite to mine. It is so easy to hide our ignorance under such expressions as the "plan of creation," "unity of design," &c., and to think that we give an explanation when we only re-state a fact. Any one whose disposition leads him to attach more weight to unexplained difficulties than to the explanation of a certain number of facts will certainly reject the theory. A few naturalists, endowed with much flexibility of mind, and who have already begun to doubt the immutability of species, may be influenced by this volume; but I look with confidence to the future,—to young and rising naturalists, who will be able to view both sides of the question with impartiality. Whoever is led to believe that species are mutable will do good service by conscientiously expressing his conviction; for thus only can the load of prejudice by which this subject is overwhelmed be removed.

Authors of the highest eminence seem to be fully satisfied with the view that each species has been independently created. To my mind it accords better with what we know of the laws impressed on matter by the Creator, that the production and extinction of the past and present inhabitants of the world should have been due to secondary causes, like those determining the birth and death of the individual. When I view all beings not as special creations, but as the lineal descendants of some few beings which lived long before the first bed of the Cambrian system was deposited, they seem to me to become ennobled. Judging from the past, we may safely infer that not one living species will transmit its unaltered likeness to a distant futurity. And of the species now living very few will transmit progeny of any kind to a far distant futurity; for the manner in which all organic beings are grouped, shows that the greater number of species in each genus, and all the species in many genera, have left no descendants, but have become utterly extinct. We can so far take a prophetic glance into futurity as to foretell that it will be the common and widely-spread species, belonging to the larger and dominant groups within each class, which will ultimately prevail and procreate new and dominant species. As all the living forms of life are the lineal descendants of those which lived long before the Cambrian epoch, we may feel certain that the ordinary succession by generation has never once been broken, and that no cataclysm has desolated the whole world. Hence we may look with some confidence to a secure future of great length. And as natural selection works solely by and for the good of each being, all corporeal and mental endowments will tend to progress towards perfection.

It is interesting to contemplate a tangled bank, clothed with many plants of many kinds, with birds singing on the bushes, with various insects flitting about, and with worms crawling through the damp earth, and to reflect that these elaborately constructed forms, so different from each other, and dependent upon each other in so complex a manner, have all been produced by laws acting around us. These laws, taken in the largest sense, being Growth with Reproduction; Inheritance which is almost implied by reproduction; Variability from the indirect and direct action of the conditions of life, and from use and disuse: a Ratio of Increase so high as to lead to a Struggle for Life, and as a consequence to Natural Selection, entailing Divergence of Character and the Extinction of less-improved forms. Thus, from the war of nature, from famine and death, the most exalted object which we are capable of conceiving, namely, the production of the higher animals, directly follows. There is grandeur in this view of life, with its several powers, having been originally breathed by the Creator into a few forms or into one; and that, whilst this planet has gone cycling on according to the fixed law of gravity, from so simple a beginning endless forms most beautiful and most wonderful have been, and are being evolved.

37. THE FREUDIAN SLIP

Sigmund Freud

Sigmund Freud (1856–1939), the Austrian physician who founded psychoanalysis, was as influential to the development of modern ideas of human behavior as Darwin was to modern ideas of the natural world. Modern culture relies on a widespread understanding of Freudian terms—subconscious, ego, repression, sublimation, identity crisis, inferiority complex, overcompensation—that were unknown before Freud. He taught us to see our hidden, subconscious selves by studying such things as our dreams, unchecked thoughts, and unintended errors of speech. The last item, which Freud discussed in the following selection from his Psychopathology of Everyday Life *(a title we might translate as "Ordinary Crazinesses"), he called* lapsus linguae *(Latin for speech mistakes). Since the publication of this book, we know them as Freudian slips. In this selection, Freud lists a number of these slips, some of which he made himself. How do these examples support Freud's view that we hide our true selves from others? Why are these "slips" not just mistakes but revealing mistakes? Can you think of a Freudian slip that you or a friend made?*

[Examples:] . . .

(*k*) Before calling on me a patient telephoned for an appointment, and also wished to be informed about my consultation fee. He was told that the first consultation was ten dollars; after the examination was over he again asked what he was to pay, and added: "I don't like to owe money to any one, especially to doctors; I prefer to pay right away." Instead of *pay* he said *play.* His last voluntary remarks and his mistake put me on my guard, but after a few more uncalled-for remarks he set me at ease by taking money from his pocket. He counted four paper dollars and was very chagrined and surprised because he had no more money with him, and promised to send me a check for the balance. I was sure that his mistake betrayed him, that he was only *playing* with me, but there was nothing to be done. At the end of a few weeks I sent him a bill for the balance, and the letter was returned to me by the post office authorities marked "Not found." . . .

(*q*) Dr. Stekel reports about himself that he had under treatment at the same time two patients from Trieste, each of whom he always addressed incorrectly. "Good morning, Mr. Peloni!" he would say to Askoli, and to Peloni, "Good morning, Mr. Askoli!" He was at first inclined to attribute no deeper motive to this mistake, but to explain it through a number of similarities in both persons. However, he easily convinced himself that here the interchange of names bespoke a sort of boast—that is, he was acquainting each of his Italian patients with the fact that neither was the only resident of Trieste who came to Vienna in search of his medical advice.

(*r*) Two women stopped in front of a drugstore, and one said to her companion, "If you will wait a few *moments* I'll soon be back," but she said *movements* instead. She was on her way to buy some castoria for her child.

(*s*) Mr. L., who is fonder of being called on than of calling, spoke to me over the telephone from a nearby summer resort. He wanted to know when I would pay him a visit. I reminded him that it was his turn to visit me, and called his attention to the fact that, as he was the happy possessor of an automobile, it would be easier for him to call on me. (We were at different summer resorts, separated by about one half-hour's railway trip.) He gladly promised to call, and asked: "How about Labor Day (September 1st), will it be convenient for you?" When I answered affirmatively, he said, "Very well, then, put me down for *Election* Day" (November). His mistake was quite plain. He likes to visit me, but it was inconvenient to travel so far. In November we would both be in the city. My analysis proved correct.

(*t*) A friend described to me a nervous patient, and wished to know whether I could benefit him. I remarked: "I believe that in time I can remove all his symptoms by psychoanalysis, because it is a durable case," wishing to say "curable"!

(*u*) I repeatedly addressed my patient as Mrs. Smith, her married daughter's name, when her real name is Mrs. James. My attention having been called to it, I soon discovered that I had another patient of the same name who refused to pay for the treatment. Mrs. Smith was also my patient and paid her bills promptly.

(*v*) A *lapsus linguae* sometimes stands for a particular characteristic. A young woman, who is the domineering spirit in her home, said of her ailing husband that he had consulted the doctor about a wholesome diet for himself, and then added: "The doctor said that diet has nothing to do with his ailments, and that he can eat and drink what *I* want."

(*w*) I cannot omit this excellent and instructive example, although, according to my authority, it is about twenty years old. A lady once expressed herself in society—the very words show that they were uttered with fervor and under the pressure of a great many secret emotions: "Yes, a woman must be pretty if she is to please the men. A man is much better off. As long as he has *five* straight limbs, he needs no more!"

This example affords us a good insight into the intimate mechanisms of a mistake in speech by means of condensation and contamination. It is quite obvious that we have here a fusion of two similar modes of expression:

"As long as he has his four *straight limbs.*"
"As long as he has all his *five senses.*"

Or the term "straight" may be the common element of the two intended expressions:

"As long as he has his *straight* limbs."
"All five should be *straight.*"

It may also be assumed that both modes of expression—viz., those of the five senses and those of the straight five—have co-operated to introduce into the sentence about the straight limbs first a number and then the mysterious five instead of the simple four. But this fusion surely would not have succeeded if it had not expressed good sense in the form resulting from the mistake; if it had not expressed a cynical truth which, naturally, could not be uttered unconcealed, coming as it did from a woman.

Finally, we shall not hesitate to call attention to the fact that the woman's saying, following its wording, could just as well be an excellent witticism as a jocose speech-blunder. It is simply a question whether she uttered these words with conscious or unconscious intention. The behavior of the speaker in this case certainly speaks against the conscious intention, and thus excludes wit.

(*x*) Owing to similarity of material, I add here another case of speech-blunder, the interpretation of which requires less skill. A professor of anatomy strove to explain the nostril, which, as is known, is a very difficult anatomical structure. To his question whether his audience grasped his ideas he received an affirmative reply. The professor, known for his self-esteem, thereupon remarked: "I can hardly believe this, for the number of people who understand the nostril, even in a city of millions like Vienna, can be counted *on a finger*—pardon me, I meant to say *on the fingers* of a hand."

In the psychotherapeutic procedure which I employ in the solution and removal of neurotic symptoms, I am often confronted with the task of discovering from the accidental utterances and fancies of the patient the thought contents, which, though striving for concealment, nevertheless unintentionally betray themselves. In doing this the mistakes often perform the most valuable service, as I can show through most convincing and still most singular examples.

For example, patients speak of an aunt and later, without noting the mistake, call her "my mother," or designate a husband as a "brother." In this way they attract my attention to the fact that they have "identified" these persons with each other, that they have placed them in the same category, which for their emotional life signifies the recurrence of the same type. Or, a young man of twenty years presents himself during my office hours with these words: "I am the father of N. N., whom you have treated—pardon me, I mean the brother; why, he is four years older than I." I understand through this mistake that he wishes to express that, like the brother, he too, is ill through the fault of the father; like his brother, he wishes to be cured, but that the father is the one most in need of treatment. At other times an unusual arrangement of words, or a forced expression, is sufficient to disclose in the speech of the patient the participation of a repressed thought having a different motive.

Hence, in coarse as well as in finer speech disturbances, which may, nevertheles, be subsumed as "speech-blunders," I find that it is not the contact effects of the sound, but the thoughts outside the intended speech, which determine the origin of the speech-blunder, and also suffice to explain the newly formed mistakes in speech.

38. MEXICAN CINEMA

Carl J. Mora

Certain cultural artifacts come to stand as emblems for their age. Ceramics stand for Ming China, oil painting for the European Renaissance, woodblock prints for nineteenth-century Japan, and the novel for nineteenth-century Europe. For the twentieth century in Europe, the Americas, India, Egypt—almost everywhere—one thinks of film. A fu-

*sion of twentieth-century technology, mass production, and rapid move-
ment, the movies are a uniquely modern way of understanding ourselves and our world. Notice in the following selection, by a modern
film historian, how the movies came to Mexico, how film became Mexican, and how it enabled Mexicans to understand their own history and
culture. How did the centennial celebration of Mexico's independence
from Spain (1810) lead to a new revolution against the dictatorship of
Porfirio Díaz after 1910? How did Mexican filmmakers influence the revolution? How did they help create a national identity? Which parts of this
story of early Mexican film would be duplicated in other countries at
this time?*

Mexico in the 1890s was one of the *belle époque*'s success stories. Buoyed
by his country's economic progress, progress at least by the standards of
Positivism and the prevailing wisdom of the era's liberal tenets, the old
authoritarian president, *don* Porfirio Díaz, presided over a nation whose
future, like that of all Western civilization, was perceived to be bright
indeed. Mexico's international credit standing, then as now, was excellent; British, American, Spanish, French, and other European firms,
along with a number of native entrepreneurs and ranchers, built and
operated the country's railroads, extracted its mineral wealth, cultivated
its fields, herded its cattle, and managed its factories. Progress was being
achieved by taking the only effective course, that of entrusting the
economy—and the political system—to an elite of Mexican and foreign
capitalists. To this end the resources of Mexico, along with its laws and
government, had in effect been put at the disposal of entrepreneurs who
were willing to invest in the country's development—upon the guarantee
of favored treatment and assured profits.

Since Mexico was prosperous, politically stable, and a member in good
standing of progressive European civilization, it was not surprising that
the projectors and films developed and produced by Louis and Auguste
Lumière should appear in Mexico almost immediately after their popularization in Europe. Mexican audiences flocked to the *cinematográficos* as
enthusiastically as did their European and North American counter-
parts. Elsewhere in Latin America, newly opened theaters in Buenos
Aires, Rio de Janeiro, and Havana were also hard put to keep up with
the crowds that flocked to be enraptured by these early flickering
films. . . .

The very first "moving pictures" in Mexico were provided by Thomas
A. Edison's kinetoscope in January 1895; a certain John R. Roslyn invited the press to witness the novelty prior to initiating public showings.
The kinetoscope, or nickelodeon, did not prove to be very popular since
it was subject to frequent breakdowns, and the viewer had to watch the
brief show through an eyepiece. The effort to provide musical accompaniment by means of a pair of headphones through which the faint melo-

dies of a scratchy recording could be heard was also unsuccessful. The pictures themselves seemed to be largely restricted to "the contortions of a clown or the somersaults of an acrobat."

In August 1896, however, the newspapers announced the arrival of Louis and Auguste Lumière's famous invention, the *cinématographe*. Reportedly it was a Frenchman, Gabriel Vayre, who obtained authorization to set up the first projector in Mexico, at number 9 Plateros Street, today Madero Avenue, and called the location "Cinematógrafo Lumière." The Lumière projector caused an immediate sensation in the capital, and the city's residents lined up in Mexico's first movie queues to see such one-minute films as *The Card Players, Arrival of a Train, The Magic Hat,* and other such brief performances that had premiered in Paris as recently as December 1895 and were already being shown around the world.

Luis G. Urbina attended the performances at the Cinematógrafo Lumière and wrote an article about the experience, making him, in effect, Mexico's first film critic:

> The cinema is the fashion in Mexico. Its appearance has excited the capital, if the capital is considered to be limited between Peter Gay's Bar Rhum on Plateros Street, and the Escandón Palace on San Francisco Street. The new contraption has triumphed here over the kinetoscope. . . . For the moment all eyes are on the cinema.
>
> This new contraption which tries, as do its rivals, to entertain us by reproducing life, also lacks something: it lacks color. Perhaps with time it will acquire sound. . . . When fantasy, that curious dreamer, recovers from its amazement it gives thanks to Science, so abused, which Spencer has characterized as Cinderella. And there are those who still maintain that science is arid!

By December 1896 a more varied and attractive program was being offered the enthusiastic public by Vayre. The following is a typical program as advertised in the newspapers:

> Cinematógrafo Lumière. No. 9 Plateros Street. Program for Monday, December 14, 1896. 1st. Military parade in front of the Royal Palace in Madrid. 2nd. Women of the island of Tenerife supplying coal to ships of the squadron. 3rd. Parade of the Queen's Lancers. 4th. A Spanish engineer regiment en route to Cádiz to embark for the Cuban campaign. 5th. Spanish artillery in combat. 6th. Spanish infantrymen on bivouac. 7th. View of Berlin. 8th. Two Bengal tigers in the Paris zoo.

These brief views of the colonial war raging in neighboring Cuba, along with those of the Parisian tigers, bore no comparison with the newsreels that in later years were to become part and parcel of every moviegoer's experience. But such films, though intended primarily to entertain with their novelty rather than inform, pointed up the immense importance of the new medium of cinematography: Distant events in faraway countries could be captured on celluloid and reproduced on a white screen in a darkened salon. No longer would the conflict in Cuba, or the Kaiser reviewing his troops in Berlin, or the crowded streets of New York be items solely to be read about, or frozen in photographs—such events from the world's vast panorama could now be magically brought to life anywhere. These first films, obtained from the Lumière firm, brought Europe to life before Mexican audiences, but it would not be long before these audiences would see *actualidades* of their own country. The early cinema not only enabled audiences to see real-life views of foreign countries, but it also better acquainted them with their own societies.

The origins of filmmaking in Mexico are immediately associated with the name of Salvador Toscano Barragán (1872–1947), a young engineering student who was the first Mexican to open a movie salon, make films of real-life events, and create in 1898 the first of his country's "fiction films", *Don Juan Tenorio,* a one-reeler starring the popular actor Paco Gavilanes. . . .

By 1900 the cinema's popularity was solidly established and it enjoyed the loyal following of thousands. The programs still consisted of short comedy routines and acrobatics, in addition to the varied scenes of dignitaries and events in foreign countries. Thus the cinematic novelty had not yet encroached on the popularity of the traditional theater, but in the same year the latter's first real challenge arrived in the capital: the first "full-length" feature to be shown in Mexico, a French import called *The Passion of Jesus Christ,* in three reels.

In 1901, Salvador Toscano returned from Paris bringing with him a load of brand-new films and the latest Lumière projector, the *biograph.* He rented the Orrin Circus Theater and there screened his new movies, among which was probably the first bullfight ever shown on a Mexican screen, although it was either a French or Spanish *corrida.*

Between 1901 and 1904, many new cinematic salons opened throughout Mexico City. The largest cigarette manufacturer of the time, El Buen Tono, opened its own salon on the top floor of the building which housed the company offices, just across the street from the site on which the Palace of Fine Arts would shortly be erected (Juárez Avenue and San Juan de Letrán). Instead of charging admission, El Buen Tono would simply accept a certain number of its empty cigarette boxes. In January 1904, it premiered the first version, probably of French origin, of *Don Quijote de la Mancha.* It was also one of the longest films seen in Mexico up to that time, being more than 450 meters in length and lasting about forty-one minutes. . . .

Although the greatest cinematic activity was to be expected in Mexico City, provincial audiences in the other states of the extensive country were also being drawn into the new medium. Jorge Stahl (b. 1880), one of the true pioneers of the Mexican film industry, was one of the early entrepreneur showmen. His father had a hat factory in Guadalajara and young Jorge, at the age of fifteen, began a photography business. He sold it so as to acquire an Edison Kinetoscope at the St. Louis Exposition of 1904. With this machine he traveled all over the country—Guanajuato, San Luis Potosí, Chihuahua—renting theaters in these cities for one peso. Stahl recounts the following experience:

> In 1906 something curious happened to me. I opened a projection salon in Guadalajara and called it Cine Verde, with four hundred chairs and a pianola. It was a small area, but since it was the first cinema, it was the gathering place for Guadalajara society. At that time the governor was Mr. Miguel Ahumada; he sent for me a few times to tell me that that was a very dangerous locality because, in the event of a fire, a real disaster could take place. For this reason he passed various ordinances: for more doors, an evacuation route. . . . All of these things we carried out. Since the salon was always filled and people were always waiting for the second or third show . . . he says to me one day: "Listen friend Stahl, you get that cinema out of there . . . because with that nonsense you're making more money than I do as governor." He did not at all appreciate our success. And it wasn't at all difficult to fill a little locality of four hundred capacity, at twenty-five *centavos* per show. Everyone in Guadalajara was always there.

It was natural that the disadvantaged sectors of society, in Mexico and elsewhere, should respond with enthusiasm to the cinema. The developmental policies of the Díaz régime transformed Mexican society by creating the industrial infrastructure that was to make possible Mexico's economic advances after the 1940s; in the process of creating an industrial proletariat, however, a great many people were uprooted from their rural homes (now increasingly being taken over by large landholders and speculators) and forced to seek livelihood in the factories of the cities, or, starting at this early date, in the southwestern United States. Between 1810 and 1910, the population of Mexico increased 148 percent from six to fifteen million inhabitants—and the greater part of this increase was registered during the Díaz dictatorship from 1876 to 1910. This largely urban demographic growth has been generally attributed to the improvement of communications, industrialization, and the era's peace and stability. Mexico's internal and external migration prior to 1910, though significant in itself, was dwarfed by unprecedented population growth in the following decades, a growth greatly accelerated by the Revolution, and by developments in our own day. The increasingly greater visibility of the "underclasses" was already evident by 1906, and Urbina was moved to observe:

> The popular masses, uncouth and infantile, experience while sitting in front of the screen the enchantment of the child to whom the grandmother has recounted a fairy tale; but I fail to understand how, night after night, a group of people who have the obligation of being civilized can idiotize themselves at

the Salón Rojo, or in the Pathé, or the Monte Carlo, with the incessant reproduction of scenes in which the aberration, anachronisms, inverisimilitudes, are
made *ad hoc* for a public of the lowest mental level, ignorant of the most
elementary educational notions.

While Mexicans from a wide social spectrum were increasingly spending more of their leisure time at the cinema, momentous events were in
the offing. The country was approaching the centennial of Father Miguel Hidalgo y Costilla's 1810 uprising which eventually led to independence from Spain. The year 1910, however, was to bring much more to
Mexico than just a grand nationwide celebration, but the citizenry was of
course unaware of the portentous events it its future. . . .

Nineteen hundred and ten, the centennial year, arrived and Mexico
proceeded to grandly celebrate its first one hundred years of independent
existence. Military parades, official ceremonies, foreign delegations, balls,
all testified to the prosperity and respect that Mexico enjoyed in the international community. Mexican cinematographers, especially Salvador
Toscano and Enrique Rosas, dedicated themselves to capturing on celluloid the highlights of this important occasion. Many of these have been
preserved in *Memorias de un mexicano,* splendorous scenes which form an
ironic backdrop to the disaster that was shortly to overtake the *porfiriato.* *
In addition to the documentaries, the country's second commercial film
was produced in honor of the centennial: *El suplicio de Cuauhtémoc* (*The
Torture of Cuauhtémoc*) by Unión Cinematográfica, S.A., the second, albeit
short-lived, Mexican movie company (the Alva Brothers' was the first,
producing *El grito de Dolores* in 1908). Although no written sources seem to
be available regarding the film itself, its subject matter is significant in that
it "reflected the revived interest in Mexico's Indian past, also notable in
music, literature, dance, and art," prior to the Revolution.

In 1910 Francisco Madero, a wealthy Chihuahua rancher and opponent
of Díaz, issued his "Plan of San Luis Potosí," a manifesto that ignited the
widespread resentment against the government. He set November 20 as
the day on which the people should revolt against the tyrant Díaz. Even
though scattered, tiny bands of revolutionaries did launch attacks against
government installations on November 18–20, "the inability of the Díaz
government to quell these small revolutionary brush fires revealed the
hollowness behind its impressive facade." The situation steadily worsened
for the government and finally, on May 25, 1911, Díaz resigned: Madero's
call for a revolt, "essentially a colossal bluff," had succeeded.

The year 1911 was therefore rather devoid of movie news since the
public and the newspapers naturally enough had much more serious
matters to contend with. But it was not long before Mexican cinematographers were to begin bringing to the public views of the fratricidal struggle

*The regime of Porfirio Diaz.—Ed.

that was shaking the country. In 1912 the first newsreel of which there is any record curiously seemed to be reflecting a peaceful Porfirian society:

> Salón Allende. Today we inaugurate the film series entitled *Revista Nacional,* produced by the firm Navascue's y Camus. This bimonthly newsreel will show local and national events of palpitating actuality. The first film to be exhibited today shows the following events: Exhumation of the journalist *don* Trinidad Sánchez Santos, Olympic games, September 16th parade, Triumphal arches on San Francisco Avenue, Festivals of Covadonga, Disturbances in the Chamber of Deputies, Regattas in Xochimilco.

European newsreels remained very popular as Mexican audiences learned, perhaps with a sense of morbid fascination, that in the Old World the primary concern seemed to be "enlisting troops." Escapist films also increased in appeal, including the showing at the Salón Rojo of Sarah Bernhardt's *Camille;* other major films shown on capital screens in 1912 were, from Italy, *The Divine Comedy,* from France, Victor Hugo's *Les Misérables,* and in a neighborhood theater, *The Adventures of Sherlock Holmes,* which the copywriter for the advertisement, after repeatedly gallant efforts, still could not get quite right. The film's title appeared on different occasions as *Las adventuras de Charley Colms* and *Las adventuras de Shaley Colmmes.* Another odd exercise in publicity was Jacobo Granat's advertisement for films of "the centennial of Independence, in which appears the illustrious figure of General *don* Porfirio Díaz, which is enthusiastically applauded even by the ladies." The Revolution, however, was not entirely ignored on the Salón Rojo's screen: *La revolución en Chihuahua (The Revolution in Chihuahua)* aroused great interest since it showed scenes of the Madero government's military campaign against the rebel forces of Pascual Orozco in the north; musical accompaniment was provided by a military band. The Hidalgo Theater showed *La revolución en Veracruz (The Revolution in Veracruz)* which also helped to make audiences realize "the sadness of a war between brothers and the cost in lives."

The cinema was accused of fostering immorality almost from its inception and there are reports of the Federal District authorities prohibiting showings of "pornographic" films exhibiting "secrets of the *boudoir* and spasms of the bedroom." It was even said that the Pathé cinema in Irapuato, not content with projecting "immoral" films, also passed out "pornographic pamphlets." In both the capital and the provinces moralists decried the fact that on Sunday afternoons children gazed at "scenes of adultery, of crude lasciviousness, of brutal revenge, of horrifying cynicism, all skillfully projected. They saw rapine, assassinations, robberies, and suicides." The guardians of the public morality agonized over the temptations that middle-class Mexican youth might encounter in darkened screening halls, even if properly chaperoned:

Vamos al cine, mamá   (Let's go to the cinema, Mama
Mamá . . . matógrafo,   Mama . . . matograph
que eso de la "oscuridá"   Because I like the darkness
me gusta una atrocidá   very much)

The perils were not only moral but physical as well; in 1918 a certain Dr. Chacón gave a learned discourse in the Medical Academy to ophthalmologists regarding the ill effects that the cinema could cause to eyesight. Such concerns reflected an ever-growing awareness of the social impact that this new form of entertainment could have. Thus regulation came early: in 1913 the first ordinances governing the licensing and operation of movie salons in the Federal District were published. These also included safety measures designed to avoid disasters like the Acapulco fire in 1909. In addition, the regulations stipulated that all descriptive subtitles were to be written in "correct Spanish," those in any other language being prohibited unless a corresponding translation was also provided.

It was during the waning days of Madero's provisional regime that the first Italian costume drama played in Mexico. *Quo Vadis*, "indubitably the first great hit of the new form of entertainment," enjoyed a worldwide success and directed Italian filmmaking toward the lavish historical spectacular. It premiered at the Arbeu Theater in July 1913 and was billed as "the biggest event in the history of Mexico!" In November the Salón Rojo followed suit with the second Italian "superproduction," *Marc Antony and Cleopatra*, with music provided by an orchestra "formed by professors of the National Conservatory of Music."

But the make-believe carnage of ancient Rome that Mexican moviegoers enjoyed on the screen was soon to be supplanted by agonizingly authentic bloodshed in the very heart of the capital. *Porfirista* (pro-Díaz) elements in combination with some foreign business interests had been planning to topple the well-meaning but largely ineffectual Madero almost from the time he arrived in Mexico City.

On February 9, 1913, Bernardo Reyes, a Díaz supporter still smarting over the old caudillo's overthrow, and Félix Díaz, nephew of the deposed dictator, initiated a coup attempt designed to terminate the provisional government. This led to an artillery duel in the middle of Mexico City between Díaz and General Victoriano Huerta, whom Madero had ordered to put down the still-unimportant flareup. The fighting lasted from February 9 to 17 ("La Decena Trágica" or the "Tragic Ten") in which hundreds of innocent bystanders were slaughtered.

The result was that Huerta himself toppled Madero and probably arranged his assassination. Huerta's bloody assumption of power caused widespread repercussions: immediately Emiliano Zapata in Morelos and Francisco "Pancho" Villa in Chihuahua rallied to Venustiano Carranza's call for a drive to unseat the "usurper" from the presidency. In this effort, the "Constitutionalists," as the Carranza-Villa-Zapata coalition was called, had the support of the new American president, Woodrow Wilson, who could not abide Huerta. This all led to years of bloody civil war and complex political maneuverings involving principally the various Mexican factions and the United States, but also, at various times, Germany, Britain, and Japan. Meanwhile, the so-called epic Revolution forged ahead with Zapata's movement encompassing the more radical elements and Carranza's the bourgeois, reform-minded groups. Francisco Villa's host composed of northern cowboys, railroad workers, and farmers was a populist surge lacking any well-defined political or ideological thrust.

Movies of this epochal, fratricidal struggle were in great demand, and an enterprising producer sent his cameramen to film the *zapatistas* in Morelos. The result was a three-thousand-meter documentary, *Sangre hermana (Blood of Brothers)*, in which "the public could see with clarity the horrors of *zapatismo*." This film was premiered at the Lírico on February 14, 1914, and reportedly was very well attended. The advertising for it, as the above example illustrates, had to be couched in terms acceptable to Huerta's censors, but the film itself apparently displayed considerable sympathy for the revolutionary cause, and the capital's citizens through it could vent some of their hatred of the government.

In May 1914 the Salón Rojo presented a film of the "terrifying April 10 battle at San Pedro de las Colonias":

> The formidable encounter between the federal forces commanded by the heroic generals J. Refugio Velasco, De Moure, Maas, Romero, Ruiz, Jaso López, García Hidalgo, Almazán, Alvarez, Monasterio and others, with the revolutionary forces. A realistic, effective movie, without artifice, taken on the battlefield at great personal danger by an expert cinematographist to the Pathé Frères firm of Paris. The most definitive and truthful demonstration of the cruel fratricidal struggle that has caused a sea of blood to run across the soil of the tormented Mexican nation. All of the scenes are authentic, exact, as can be confirmed by the above-cited heroic generals. The heroism of the combatants and the bitterness of the struggle will accentuate in the spirit of all Mexicans the desire for unity so as to calm the anguish of our shattered nation.

Jacobo Granat's injection into his advertising of a plea for reconciliation among his countrymen seems to have gone unnoticed by the *huertistas* who, in any event, had much more serious problems on their hands than movie publicity. The basic antagonism between Wilson and Huerta had, through an involved series of events, resulted in the bombardment of Veracruz on April 21 by the United States fleet and that city's occupation by American troops.

By June, film of the event was being shown on the capital screens. The following advertisement for the Trianon Palace gives an indication of the contents of the movie along with widely shared Mexican sentiments:

> The very interesting motion picture, *The North American Invasion,* will be exhibited. Events in Veracruz. A film of actuality which reveals the iniquitous deed committed by the *yanqui* invader. The interesting scenes reproduced by the cinematographer already indicate the contrast between the active Veracruz of yesterday, of the free and sovereign Veracruz, with today's Veracruz, trampled upon by our eternal enemy. On the screen you will see all the port's social classes attending the funeral of the heroic captain Benjamín Gutiérrez, giving the lie with this act to that segment of the capitaline press that has placed in doubt the conduct of this noble city. Among the diverse scenes reproduced by this interesting movie, we will cite the following: Panoramic view of the Bay of Veracruz. San Juan de Ulúa. Mexican artillerymen. The North American squadron in combat formation facing the heroic port on the morning of April 21. The Ipiranga. The *Prairie* bombarding the Naval School. The streets of Veracruz after the combat. The neutral White Cross volunteers its service. . . . Damages caused by the bombardment . . . the invaders' camp. . . . What the *yanquis* mean by equality. Seaplanes maneuvering.

War had broken out in Europe in August 1914 and by November the first films of that conflict were shown in Mexico at the Salón Rojo, which announced that the latest views from the fighting fronts would be shown weekly. The domestic civil war continued to receive good coverage as well as sympathetic treatment for Huerta's enemies if one is to judge by some of the copy in one of Granat's advertisements for a program featuring scenes of Villa's attack on Nuevo Laredo followed by the "triumphal" entry to that border city of the "Supreme Chief of the Constitutionalist Army," Venustiano Carranza. It was described as a "national motion picture which reproduces a great historical event." Such films, which were also being shown throughout the cities and hamlets of Mexico, must have played an important role in familiarizing the citizenry with the leaders of the factions contending for power at that time. In fact, the cinemas of the republic became lively centers of political commentary as these well-known figures—Huerta, Carranza, Alvaro Obregón, Villa, Zapata, and many others—were jeered or applauded according to the public's preferences. Sometimes the audience's reaction was a good deal more volatile as in Martín Luis Guzmán's following description of movie-going Conventionists, as the supporters of Villa and Zapata were known, in Aguascalientes in 1916 watching a newsreel:

> We, nonetheless, did not see the end of the movie because something happened unexpectedly that obliged us to flee the spot we occupied just behind the screen. Don Venustiano of course was the personage who most often appeared on the screen. His appearances, increasingly more frequent, had been becoming, as was to be expected, more and more unappreciated by the

Conventionist audience. From the hissing mixed with applause on the first occasions he was seen, it progressed to frank hissing; then to hissing bordering on whistling; to open hooting, and finally to bedlam. And in that way, by stages, it finally resulted, when Carranza was seen entering Mexico City on horseback, in a hellish uproar culminating in two gunshots.

Both projectiles punctured the screen in the exact spot on which was outlined the First Chief's chest, and they struck the wall, one, half a meter above Lucio Blanco: the other, closer even, between Domínguez's head and mine.

The years between 1916 and 1920 were tumultuous ones for Mexico, but in spite of grave domestic and international problems the epic phase of the Revolution was winding down. Venustiano Carranza's provisional administration was able, through the military prowess of Obregón, to eliminate the threats from Villa and Zapata. War with the United States was narrowly averted and a new constitution promulgated in 1917, a document that in its labor, land tenure, and social welfare provisions was the most radical in the world at that time. It provided the political and juridical infrastructure that guides the country to this day, the "institutionalized Revolution," as Mexican politicians have been fond of saying these many years.

The years between 1915 and 1923 have been termed the "Golden Age" of the Mexican silent cinema, although production was extremely modest, especially if compared with the output of the major filmmaking countries, but still impressive according to Latin American standards. In this period new production companies were organized in Guanajuato and Mazatlán as well as in Mexico City, but, unlike Brazil, in which a regional filmmaking pattern was to arise, the Mexican cinema industry, like the Argentine, was soon to be centered in the capital city's environs.

39. A TOGO SCHOOL EXAMINATION, 1909

If movies have been the best educators of the twentieth century, certainly the schools might be judged a distant second. And in the early-twentieth-century world of European empires, it was the movies and schoolbooks of Europeans and Americans that increasingly instructed other peoples, in Africa, Asia, and Latin America. The following outline of a school test was administered to African students in the German West African colony of Togo in 1909. What does this test tell you about what Europeans wanted the rest of the world to know? How useful was this knowledge to young Africans? Why did the Germans ask these questions rather than others?

Saturday, 20.xi.09.

10–10½ A.M. *Calligraphy.* A passage was written on the blackboard and the pupils had to copy it.

10½–11 A.M. *Spelling.* The chairman of the commission dictated a simple passage from a short story, with which none of them were acquainted.

11–12 A.M. *Geography.* The following questions had been set as a task:

   (*a*) The large states of Europe and their capitals.

   (*b*) What are the names of Germany's most important mountains?

   (*c*) What are the names of the most important rivers in Germany and in what direction do they run?

The last question was intended to show whether the pupils could not only reproduce the names mechanically, but could also visualize a map.

3–4½ P.M. *An Essay.* The subject set was: 'What good things have the Europeans brought us?'

5½–6 P.M. *Reading.* In addition to passages known to the pupils, they had to read aloud an unfamiliar article from a little book, called "Drei Kaiserbuchlein", out of the bookshop of the North German Mission.

Monday, 22.xi.09

7½–9 A.M. *Oral Arithmetic.* The questions were asked by the teachers themselves.

10–11. *Written Arithmetic.* One question each was chosen from amongst those proposed by the school associations:

   (1) Mutliply 118.92 by 67¼ and then divide the number obtained by 3,964.

   (2) In 1906 Togo exported copra worth 8,000 marks, in 1907 11,000 marks' worth. What was the increase per cent on the export of 1907?

   (3) A labourer drinks brandy worth 0.25m a day. (*a*) How much does he pay for the brandy in a year? (*b*) How many days must he work for the brandy, if he earns 2m a day? (*c*) How many kgs of pork could he have bought with this sum, if pork costs 65 pfennige a kg?

From 11–12 and from 3–6 in the afternoon, *useful knowledge, grammar* and *translation* were examined.

Tuesday, 23.xi.09

7–8 A.M. *History.* The task set was:

The reign of emperor William I and the wars he had waged. Name those men who had specially supported his government.

From 8–11½ A.M., the examinations in translation were completed.

40. THE JAPANESE "NEW WOMAN"

Laurel Rasplica Rodd

Perhaps the most conscientious student of European ways in the first decade of the twentieth century was not a European colonial possession but independent Japan. As Japan developed a modern industrial economy, Japanese theater audiences found entertainment in a European play, and some Japanese women began to ask the same questions that women in Europe and America were beginning to ask. This selection by a modern historian reminds us again how international modern culture has become. What does this account of a brief stage in the history of Japanese feminism tell us about the international quality of modern culture? What does it tell us about the role of the media in shaping modern culture?

In November 1911, a production of Henrik Ibsen's *A Doll's House,* starring the beautiful actress Matsui Sumako (1886–1919) and directed by Shimamura Hogetsu (1871–1918), opened in Tokyo.[1] Although it was only a university production, the strong performance by Matsui and the explosive message of the play generated considerable attention from the popular press. *A Doll's House,* with its suggestion that marriage is not sacrosanct and that man's authority in the home should not go unchallenged, created an immediate sensation in a society where women had few, if any, rights.

In his review of the production, playwright Ihara Seiseien wrote that while many in the audience seemed unmoved when Nora deplored the sacrifice of wives for their husbands' honor, two women, Okada Yachiyo (sister of playwright Osanai Kaoru) and Hasegawa Shigure (herself a playwright), had pressed handkerchiefs to their eyes. Ihara recalled thinking at the time that these were "truly new women," inspired by Western theater models to reconsider women's lives.

Ihara's term "new women" (*atarashii onna*) was soon taken up by others writing about women's new roles. In particular, women journalists writing for the general-interest magazines and new women's publications that flourished in the relatively liberal era of "Taishō democracy" [1912–1926] carried the debate over the redefinition of women's roles into the public arena.[2] With the much-vaunted role of women as "good wives and

---

1. From about 1909 the Japanese new theater movement had been treating the conflicts in Japanese society, attempting to portray them in a realistic manner rather than with the traditional stylization of Kabuki, and bringing women actresses to the stage again after a three hundred year banishment.

2. Even during the era of Taishō democracy women were excluded from the political process, denied even the right to attend public meetings. Education remained conservative,

wise mothers" now held up to vigorous scrutiny by women themselves, the state lost its monopoly over gender construction in Japan.

Among those who responded during the Taishō period to the challenge to redefine women's roles were four prominent women whose backgrounds, experience, and philosophies led them to argue widely differing positions. Yosano Akiko (1878–1942) advocated a feminism grounded in equal legal, educational, and social rights and responsibilities for women. Hiratsuka Raichō (1886–1971) propounded a doctrine of motherhood that called for state protection of and special privileges for mothers. Yamakawa Kikue (1890–1980) embraced a socialist view of history that traced women's subordination to the system of private property and so set the destruction of that system as her goal. Finally, Yamada Waka (1879–1957) held a more traditional view of women as "good wives and wise mothers."[3] The debate waged among these four women in magazines and newspapers over the course of the 1910s and early 1920s introduced much of the thought and many of the writings of Western feminist thinkers, touching as it did on such crucial topics as women's role in politics and in the home, the goals of women's education, women's rights within the family and the workplace, the need for women to control their own sexuality, and—the topic that most clearly reveals the differences in these women's thought—the part government should play in supporting women in their roles as wives and mothers.

A major forum for the debate over the "new woman" was the literary magazine *Seitō* (Bluestockings), founded by Hiratsuka Raichō in September 1911 to encourage and advertise the creative talents of women. The maiden issue of *Seitō* had carried an anonymous translation of an article on Ibsen's *Hedda Gabler*, and the January 1912 issue included a supplement devoted to Matsui's performance as Nora in *A Doll's House*. The June issue carried a supplement on *Magda*, the Hermann Sudermann play, first performed in Japan in 1913, about a woman who defies her father's authority when she decides to become an opera singer. The *Seitō* articles about these plays were scholarly pieces incorporating refer-

stressing child care and the family and serving as a foundation for filial piety and national virtue. Censorship of books and the popular press was constant.

3. The term *ryōsai kenbo*, coined by Nakamura Masanao to describe a model for women's roles adapted from the nineteenth-century West (i.e., that women should provide the moral foundation of the home, educating the children and acting as "better half" to their husbands), was taken up by one branch of the Japanese women's movement, led by Hatoyama Haruko, who saw it as providing women a sphere—the home—in which they would be preeminent. It was also adopted by the Meiji government, which instituted regulations in 1898 requiring each prefecture to provide at least one high school for women, with the goal of creating "good wives, wise mothers." In the official concept, women were to be educated not to exercise power at home, but to better carry out their responsibilities as childbearers and cogs in the patriarchal family system. See Sharon Shievers, *Flowers in Salt: The Beginnings of Feminist Consciousness in Modern Japan* (Stanford: Stanford University Press, 1983), 109–13, for a discussion of the political standards for which this term became the rallying cry.

ences to both European and Japanese secondary sources. The author did not glorify Nora and Magda. Indeed, she took the position that Nora should not have abandoned her home and family for the goal of self-realization; and of Magda she wrote, "She cannot be called a true 'new woman.' "

From the beginning, however, *Seitō* was treated less as a literary than as a news event. Reporters delighted in the sensation they could cause by misreading the magazine and reporting fanciful versions of the activities of the women members of the Seitō group. Having undertaken to discuss "new women," Raichō and other members were soon being criticized as "new women who took Magda as their ideal and praised Nora," and *Seitō* was called "a nursery for Japanese Noras."

At first the Seitō members shrugged off this misrepresentation, but after two incidents involving Odake Kōkichi attracted further malicious gossip about their activities, the attacks were viewed more seriously. Odake made headlines twice. The first time was when she accepted a "five-colored liqueur" (an exotic Western drink made by floating layers of different liqueurs one upon the other) at a bar while out soliciting advertisements for the magazine, and then published a story about a "beautiful young boy" who visited Raichō after having accepted such a drink. The press spread rumors that Raichō had taken a lover. (They would have created an even greater scandal had they realized it was Odake herself who was infatuated with Raichō.) The second time was when she agreed to her uncle's proposition that she, Raichō, and Nakano Hatsue accompany him to the Yoshiwara entertainment district to learn more about the lives of prostitutes in the brothels there.

Fanned by inflammatory headlines, such as "Seitō New Women, Seeking Equal Rights with Men, Spend Night of Pleasure with Yoshiwara Prostitute," opposition to the "new women" intensified. Raichō's house was stoned, she received death threats, and many young women were pressured to resign from the group.[4] Far from being intimidated, Raichō determined to launch a serious discussion of what the real "new woman" should represent. The January 1913 issue of *Seitō*, called "On the New Woman and Other Women's Issues," featured contributions by Raichō, Itō Noe ("The Path to the New Woman"), Iwano Kiyoko ("Men and Women are Equal as Human Beings"), Katō Midori ("About the New Woman"), Ikuta Hanayo ("The Liberation of the New Woman"), and others. Raichō's contribution was a translation of Havelock Ellis's introduction to *Love and Marriage* by Ellen Key (1849–1926), which she followed with a serialized translation of the entire book. The articles examined the role of women from various perspectives, and one (attributed to

---

4. Kamichika Ichiko, a student at the Women's English Academy, was forced to dissociate herself from the group to remain in school. Later she lost a job as a teacher after her connection with the Seitō group was discovered. Many members around the country did resign.

Ōsugi Sakae's wife, Yasuko) even sardonically asserted "I Am the Old Woman," meaning a woman created by Japan's educational system and traditional method of socialization.

The February 1913 issue, which contained the focus on the "new woman and women's issues," was censored because of an article entitled "The Solution to the Woman Question" by the socialist activist Fukuda Hideko, who advocated a revolution to liberate both men and women from irrational economic and social systems created by self-interested elites. Although many of the members of Seitō were uncomfortable with the new political focus of the magazine, the leaders stood firm in their determination to air these serious matters. They were summoned by the police again when the April issue carried an article by Raichō ("To the Women of the World") that challenged the ideal of the "good wife and wise mother" and attacked the Japanese marriage system for making women yield to power, not love, and legislating against the development of affection in marriage.

Attacks on the "new women," deemed "wild talk and nonsense" by Raichō, continued. Soon other journalists entered the fray. In January 1913, *Chūō kōron* published a special issue with articles by "fifteen accomplished women," including Yosano Akiko and Raichō. The April issue countered with an article by an *Asahi* newspaper reporter entitled "Handling the New Woman." In June and July special issues dealing with the "woman question" appeared, and the magazine *Taiyō*, too, published a special number on the subject in June.

Although *Seitō* had been founded as a women's counterpart to the literary journal *Shirakaba*, and the first issue described its goal as "seeking the development of women's literature," by 1913, as the literary venture evolved into a forum for the advocacy of social and political change, the names of most of the early supporters from the literary world—among them Mori Shigeko, Hasegawa Shigure, Koganei Kimiko, and Kunikida Noriko—disappeared from the magazine. Yosano Akiko, however, continued to publish regularly in *Seitō* until it ceased publication in February 1916.

PART THREE

THE MODERN WORLD:
1914 TO THE PRESENT

Yoruba Man with Bicycle (Collection of The Newark Museum. Purchase 1977, Wallace M. Scudder Bequest Fund and The Member's Fund)

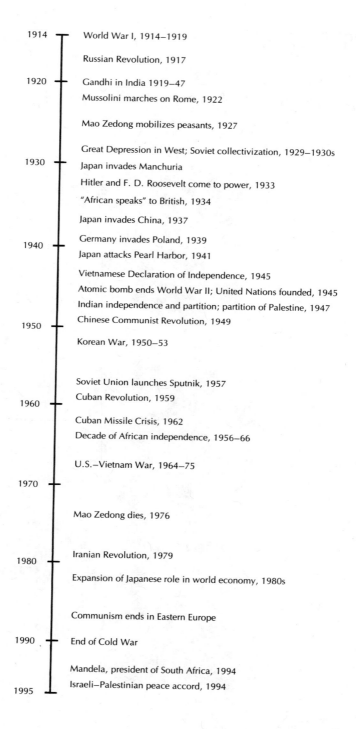

1914	World War I, 1914–1919
	Russian Revolution, 1917
1920	Gandhi in India 1919–47
	Mussolini marches on Rome, 1922
	Mao Zedong mobilizes peasants, 1927
	Great Depression in West; Soviet collectivization, 1929–1930s
1930	Japan invades Manchuria
	Hitler and F. D. Roosevelt come to power, 1933
	"African speaks" to British, 1934
	Japan invades China, 1937
1940	Germany invades Poland, 1939
	Japan attacks Pearl Harbor, 1941
	Vietnamese Declaration of Independence, 1945
	Atomic bomb ends World War II; United Nations founded, 1945
	Indian independence and partition; partition of Palestine, 1947
1950	Chinese Communist Revolution, 1949
	Korean War, 1950–53
	Soviet Union launches Sputnik, 1957
1960	Cuban Revolution, 1959
	Cuban Missile Crisis, 1962
	Decade of African independence, 1956–66
	U.S.–Vietnam War, 1964–75
1970	
	Mao Zedong dies, 1976
1980	Iranian Revolution, 1979
	Expansion of Japanese role in world economy, 1980s
	Communism ends in Eastern Europe
1990	End of Cold War
	Mandela, president of South Africa, 1994
1995	Israeli–Palestinian peace accord, 1994

CHAPTER ELEVEN

World War I and the Russian Revolution

41. WORLD WAR I IN WORLD HISTORY

L. M. Panikkar

From an Asian perspective, according to this Indian historian and diplomat, World War I was a European civil war. But the involvement of African and Asian soldiers and colonial subjects made the war a major turning point in world history. In what ways were Africans and Asians involved in the war? How did that involvement change life in the colonies? Who were perceived as the anticolonial forces of the First World War? Who were the anticolonial forces after the war?

The Great War of 1914–18 was from the Asian point of view a civil war within the European community of nations. The direct participation of Asian countries, during some stages of this conflict, was at the invitation and by the encouragement of one of the parties, the *entente* Powers, and was greatly resented by the Germans. It is necessary to emphasize this internal character of the European conflict to realize its full significance on the development of events in Asia.

. . . [A]t the beginning of the twentieth century the European nations, in the enjoyment of unprecedented economic prosperity and political prestige, remained unshakably convinced that they had inherited the earth, and that their supremacy in Asia was permanent and was something in the nature of a predetermined Divine Order. It was the age of Kipling and the white man's burden, and it seemed the manifest destiny of the white race to hold the East in fee.

In 1914, when the German invaders had reached the Marne, divisions of the Indian Army under British officers had been rushed to France and had helped at the critical moment to stem the German tide. Later, they were extensively used in the defence of the Suez Canal and the Middle East and in campaigns elsewhere in Africa. In 1917, Siam declared war on Germany. An Indo-Chinese labour force had been recruited and was working in France. On August 14, 1917, China also joined the Allies. Thus all the nations of Asia were brought into the European civil war. However, opinion in India, China and even in Japan was at the time more pro-

German than pro-Ally. In India, except among the ruling princes, there was no pro-British feeling, and public opinion rejoiced at every report of German victory and felt depressed when the Allies were winning. China declared war only with the greatest reluctance and for the express purpose of checkmating Japanese plans of aggression. In Japan itself, after the Shantung Campaign, feeling against the Allies was most marked, and a Press campaign of great virulence was conducted against Britain at the end of 1916. Actually, though the Asian countries fought on the side of the Allies, public opinion in the East looked upon the conflict as a civil war in which neither party had a claim to the friendship of the peoples of Asia, and if any party could appeal to the sympathy of Asians it was the Germanic alliance which had no tradition of Asian conquest and was allied with the chief Muslim Power, Turkey.

But the participation of Asian people in the war had far-reaching consequences. The Indian soldier who fought on the Marne came back to India with other ideas of the *Sahib* than those he was taught to believe by decades of official propaganda. Indo-Chinese Labour Corps in the South of France returned to Annam with notions of democracy and republicanism which they had not entertained before. Among the Chinese who went to France at the time was a young man named Chou En-lai, who stayed on to become a Communist and had to be expelled for activities among the members of the Chinese Labour Corps.

More important than these influences was the fact that the French and British administrations in Asia had to appeal to their subjects for moral support. To ask Indians and Indo-Chinese to subscribe to war loans for the defence of democracy and to prevent the world being overwhelmed by German *Kultur*, would have sounded as strange and callous irony unless accompanied by promises of democracy for themselves and freedom for their own cultures. When, besides subscriptions for war loans, Indians and Indo-Chinese were pressed to join up and fight to save democracy, the contradictions of the position became too obvious even for the colonial administrators. In India the demand was made openly by the nationalist leaders that prior agreement on political problems was necessary before support of the war could be considered a national programme.

Politically, a further weakening of the colonial and imperialist position came about as a result of President Wilson's declaration of fourteen points. In 1917, the doctrine of the "self-determination of peoples" had the ring of a new revelation. Whatever its effect was on the suppressed nationalities of Europe, in Asia it was acclaimed as a doctrine of liberation. As every Allied Power hastened to declare its faith in the new formula of Wilson (and it was soon raised to the position of an accepted "war aim" in the propaganda campaign against the Germans), the colonial Powers found it difficult to oppose openly or resist publicly the claims of Asian nations based on this formula. It became difficult to proclaim self-determination of people as a great ideal for the establishment of which Asian peoples should co-operate with Europeans and fight and lose their lives in distant battlefields, but which, however excellent, could not be applied to themselves. Self-government for colonial countries had thus to be accepted, and the claim to it could no longer be brushed aside as premature or stigmatized as sedition.

Apart from these political considerations economic forces generated by the war were also helping to undermine the supremacy of the West. Japan utilized the four years of war for a planned expansion of her trade in the East. German competition had been eliminated. Britain and France, engaged in a mortal struggle when their entire resources of production had to be directed towards victory, had also left the field fairly open. India gained her first major start on the industrial road and, with the strain on British economy, Indian national capital was placed in a position of some advantage. In fact the full results of the weakening of European capitalism became evident only after the war when the preeminence of London was challenged by America, and British capital, though still powerful, began to be on the defensive in India. The growth of capitalist enterprise in India, and the development of industries and participation by Indian capital in spheres so far monopolistically held by Britain, like jute [a plant fiber used in making burlap—Ed.], resulted directly from the weakening of the economic position of Britain.

Two other results of a general character may be indicated. The first, the growth of a powerful left-wing movement in the countries of Western Europe, had a direct effect on shaping events in the Eastern Empire. The Labour Party in England during the days of its growth had been closely associated with the nationalist movement in India. In fact, Ramsay MacDonald, the leader of the Socialist Party after the war, had been one of its champions from the earliest days. Similarly, Annamite nationalism had worked hand in hand with left-wing parties in France. In the period that immediately followed the war these parties had come to possess considerable influence in national affairs and, as we shall see, were instrumental in giving effect to policies which loosened the old bonds of political domination.

The second factor was, of course, the influence of the Russian Revolution. Imperialism meant something totally different after Lenin's definition of it as the last place of capitalism and his insistence that the liberation of subject peoples from colonial domination was a part of the struggle against capitalism. Also, Russia's call for and practice of racial equality, abolition of the special privileges that Tsarist Russia had acquired in Persia and China, and her acceptance, in the first flush of revolutionary enthusiasm, of the independence of countries which had been previously annexed to Russia, made it difficult for Western nations which had so long claimed to stand for liberty and progress to deny the claims of Eastern nations.

Finally, the war had accelerated the pace of movements everywhere.

For example, in India, the movement for independence which was confined to the intelligentsia in 1914 became a mass movement of immense proportions in 1919. Everywhere the case was similar. The *tempo* of events had acquired a momentum which few had foreseen and none had forecast in 1918. The war, on the world scale it was conducted in 1914–18, was in itself a great world revolution, and an impenetrable chasm had been created between the days preceding August 1914 and those following November 11, 1918.

One fact which stands out clear and illustrates this chasm in thought is the lack of faith in imperialist ideals in the period that followed the war. With the solitary exception of Churchill, there was not one major figure in any of the British parties who confessed to a faith in the white man's mission to rule. Successive Viceroys of India, Liberal, Conservative and non-party, professed publicly their adherence to the cause of Indian freedom. Secretaries of State from Edwin Montagu (1917–22) to Pethick Lawrence, including such stalwarts of Conservatism as Sir Samuel Hoare (Lord Templewood), claimed that they were working for the freedom of the Indian people and not for the maintenance of British rule. The French were no doubt more brave in their words, but the faith had gone out of them also.

Nowhere did this come out more clearly than in the treatment of China. Incidents which previously would have been dealt with sternly and for which territories and indemnities would have been exacted, were now only the subjects of a mild protest. Chiang Kai-shek's armies occupied the concessions at Hankow, and for months Hong Kong was subjected to an intensive trade boycott; these events would earlier have immediately led to a display of overwhelming naval strength. Britain in 1926 was prepared patiently to negotiate. Even the "old Church hands," who had watched with regret the sudden eclipse of European prestige, though they acted the Blimps in their clubs, never seriously felt that Western authority could be reestablished over China by the use of gunboats. There was no conviction left of the European's superiority or sense of vision.

42.   WOODROW WILSON'S FOURTEEN POINTS

Woodrow Wilson (1856–1924) was President of the United States during the First World War. He presented these "Fourteen Points" to Congress in January 1918 as a basis for a just peace treaty to end the war.

You may wish to compare these proposals with the actual peace settlement. Only points VII, VIII, X, and XIV were realized. Point IV was applied only to the defeated nations. The Versailles Treaty, which the defeated Germans were forced to sign on June 28, 1919, contained much harsher terms, including the famous "war guilt" clause (Article 231):

The Allied and Associated Governments affirm and Germany accepts the responsibility of Germany and her allies for causing all the loss and damage to which the Allied and Associated Governments and their nationals have been subjected as a consequence of the war imposed upon them by the aggression of Germany and her allies.

Why do you think there was such a gap between Wilson's ideals and the actual treaty? How might Wilson have improved on these "Fourteen Points"? Could he reasonably expect all of them to be accepted?

It will be our wish and purpose that the processes of peace, when they are begun, shall be absolutely open, and that they shall involve and permit henceforth no secret understandings of any kind. The day of conquest and aggrandizement is gone by; so is also the day of secret covenants entered into in the interest of particular Governments and likely at some unlooked-for moment to upset the peace of the world. It is this happy fact, now clear to the view of every public man whose thoughts do not still linger in an age that is dead and gone, which makes it possible for every nation whose purposes are consistent with justice and the peace of the world to avow now or at any other time the objects it has in view.

We entered this war because violations of right had occurred which touched us to the quick and made the life of our own people impossible unless they were corrected and the world secured once for all against their recurrence. What we demand in this war, therefore, is nothing peculiar to ourselves. It is that the world be made fit and safe to live in; and particularly that it be made safe for every peace-loving nation which, like our own, wishes to live its own life, determine its own institutions, be assured of justice and fair dealing by the other peoples of the world as against force and selfish aggression. All the peoples of the world are in effect partners in this interest, and for our own part we see very clearly that unless justice be done to others it will not be done to us. The program of the world's peace, therefore, is our program; and that program, the only possible program, as we see it, is this:

I. Open covenants of peace, openly arrived at, after which there shall be no private international understandings of any kind but diplomacy shall proceed always frankly and in the public view.

II. Absolute freedom of navigation upon the seas, outside territorial waters, alike in peace and in war, except as the seas may be closed in whole or in part by international action. . . .

III. The removal, so far as possible, of all economic barriers and the establishment of an equality of trade conditions among all the nations consenting to the peace and associating themselves for its maintenance.

IV. Adequate guarantees given and taken that national armaments will be reduced to the lowest point consistent with domestic safety.

V. A free, open-minded, and absolutely impartial adjustment of all colonial claims, based upon a strict observance of the principle that in determining all such questions of sovereignty the interests of the populations concerned must have equal weight with the equitable claims of the government whose title is to be determined.

VI. The Evacuation of all Russian territory and such a settlement of all questions affecting Russia as will secure the best and freest cooperation of the other nations of the world in obtaining for her an unhampered and unembarrassed opportunity for the independent determination of her own political development and national policy and assure her of a sincere welcome into the society of free nations under institutions of her own choosing; and, more than a welcome, assistance also of every kind that she may need and may herself desire. The treatment accorded Russia by her sister nations in the months to come will be the acid test of their good will, of their comprehension of her needs as distinguished from their own interests, and of their intelligent and unselfish sympathy.

VII. Belgium, the whole world will agree, must be evacuated and restored, without any attempt to limit the sovereignty which she enjoys in common with all other free nations. No other single act will serve to restore confidence among the nations in the laws which they have themselves set and determined for the government of their relations with one another. Without this healing act the whole structure and validity of international law is forever impaired.

VIII. All French territory should be freed and the invaded portions restored, and the wrong done to France by Prussia in 1871 in the matter of Alsace-Lorraine, which has unsettled the peace of the world for nearly fifty years, should be righted, in order that peace may once more be made secure in the interest of all.

IX. A readjustment of the frontiers of Italy should be effected along clearly recognizable lines of nationality.

X. The peoples of Austria-Hungary, whose place among the nations we wish to see safeguarded and assured, should be accorded the freest opportunity of autonomous development.

XI. Rumania, Serbia, and Montenegro should be evacuated; occupied territories restored; Serbia accorded free and secure access to the sea; and the relations of the several Balkan states to one another determined by friendly counsel along historically established lines of allegiance and nationality; and international guarantees of the political and economic independence and territorial integrity of the several Balkan states should be entered into.

XII. The Turkish portions of the present Ottoman Empire should be assured a secure sovereignty, but the other nationalities which are now under Turkish rule should be assured an undoubted security of life and an absolutely unmolested opportunity of autonomous development, and the Dardanelles should be permanently opened as a free passage to the ships and commerce of all nations under international guarantees.

XIII. An independent Polish state should be erected which should include the territories inhabited by indisputably Polish populations, which should be assured a free and secure access to the sea, and whose political and economic independence and territorial integrity should be guaranteed by international covenant.

XIV. A general association of nations must be formed under specific covenants for the purpose of affording mutual guarantees of political independence and territorial integrity to great and small states alike.

In regard to these essential rectifications of wrong and assertions of right we feel ourselves to be intimate partners of all the governments and peoples associated together against the Imperialists. We cannot be separated in interest or divided in purpose. We stand together until the end.

For such arrangements and covenants we are willing to fight and to continue to fight until they are achieved; but only because we wish the right to prevail and desire a just and stable peace such as can be secured only by removing the chief provocations to war, which this program does remove. We have no jealousy of German greatness, and there is nothing in this program that impairs it. We grudge her no achievement or distinction of learning or of pacific enterprise such as have made her record very bright and very enviable. We do not wish to injure her or to block in any way her legitimate influence or power. We do not wish to fight her either with arms or with hostile arrangements of trade if she is willing to associate herself with us and the other peace-loving nations of the world in covenants of justice and law and fair dealing. We wish her only to accept a place of equality among the peoples of the world,—the new world in which we now live—instead of a place of mastery.

Neither do we presume to suggest to her any alteration or modification of her institutions. But it is necessary, we must frankly say, and necessary as a preliminary to any intelligent dealings with her on our part, that we should know whom her spokesmen speak for when they speak to us, whether for the Reichstag majority or for the military party and the men whose creed is imperial domination. We have spoken now, surely in terms too concrete to admit of any further doubt or question. An evident principle runs through the whole program I have outlined. It is the principle of justice to all peoples and nationalities, and their right to live on equal terms of liberty and safety with one another, whether they be strong or weak. Unless this principle be made its foundation no part of the structure of international justice can stand. The people of the United States could act upon no other principle; and to the vindication of this principle they are ready to devote their lives, their honor, and everything that they possess. The moral climax of this the culminating and final war for human liberty has come, and they are ready to put their own strength, their own highest purpose, their own integrity and devotion to the test.

43. THE LEAGUE OF NATIONS COVENANT, 1919

The League of Nations, in which President Woodrow Wilson could not persuade the United States Congress to approve U.S. membership, was the first attempt at world government. Like the United Nations that succeeded it, the league had as many flaws as hopes. This selection includes two articles from the Covenant of the League. Article 22 concerns the mandates that the league established over the former colonies of the defeated powers in World War I (Germany, Austria, the Ottoman Empire). How consistent was this article with Wilson's 14 Points? What did this article promise the former colonies? How do you think these colonies would have responded? Article 23 shows an array of concerns for the fledgling organization but little about how such ideals might have been implemented. Should these have been concerns of the League of Nations? Should they be concerns of the United Nations? How can such ideals be realized by international law or international organizations?

ARTICLE 22

To those colonies and territories which as a consequence of the late war have ceased to be under the sovereignty of the States which formerly governed them and which are inhabited by peoples not yet able to stand by themselves under the strenuous conditions of the modern world, there should be applied the principle that the well-being and development of such peoples form a sacred trust of civilisation and that securities for the performance of this trust should be embodied in this Covenant.

The best method of giving practical effect to this principle is that the tutelage of such peoples should be entrusted to advanced nations who by reason of their resources, their experience or their geographical position can best undertake this responsibility, and who are willing to accept it, and that this tutelage should be exercised by them as Mandatories on behalf of the League.

The character of the mandate must differ according to the stage of the development of the people, the geographical situation of the territory, its economic conditions and other similar circumstances.

Certain communities formerly belonging to the Turkish Empire have reached a stage of developement where their existence as independent nations can be provisionally recognised subject to the rendering of administrative advice and assistance by a Mandatory until such time as they are able to stand alone. The wishes of these communities must be a principal consideration in the selection of the Mandatory.

Other peoples, especially those of Central Africa, are at such a stage that the Mandatory must be responsible for the administration of the territory under conditions which will guarantee freedom of conscience and religion, subject only to the maintenance of public order and morals, the prohibition of abuses such as the slave trade, the arms traffic and the liquor traffic, and the prevention of the establishment of fortifications or military and naval bases and of military training of the natives for other than police purposes and the defence of territory, and will also secure equal opportunities for the trade and commerce of other Members of the League.

There are territories, such as South-West Africa and certain of the South Pacific Islands, which, owing to the sparseness of their population, or their small size, or their remoteness from the centres of civilisation, or their geographical contiguity to the territory of the Mandatory, and other circumstances, can be best administered under the laws of the Mandatory as integral portions of its territory, subject to the safeguards above mentioned in the interests of the indigenous population.

In every case of mandate, the Mandatory shall render to the Council an annual report in reference to the territory committed to its charge.

The degree of authority, control, or administration to be exercised by the Mandatory shall, if not previously agreed upon by the Members of the League, be explicitly defined in each case by the council.

A permanent Commission shall be constituted to receive and examine the annual reports of the Mandatories and to advise the Council on all matters relating to the observance of the mandates.

ARTICLE 23

Subject to and in accordance with the provisions of international conventions existing or hereafter to be agreed upon, the Members of the League:

(a) will endeavour to secure and maintain fair and humane conditions of labour for men, women, and children, both in their own countries and in all countries to which their commercial and industrial relations extend, and for that purpose will establish and maintain the necessary international organisations;

(b) undertake to secure just treatment of the native inhabitants of territories under their control;

(c) will entrust the League with the general supervision over the execution of agreements with regard to the traffic in women and children, and the traffic in opium and other dangerous drugs;

(d) will entrust the League with the general supervision of the trade in arms and ammunition with the countries in which the control of this traffic is necessary in the common interest;

(e) will make provision to secure and maintain freedom of communications and of transit and equitable treatment for the commerce of all Members of the League. In this connection, the special necessities of the regions devastated during the war of 1914–1918 shall be borne in mind;

(f) will endeavour to take steps in matters of international concern for the prevention and control of disease.

44. STALIN'S INDUSTRIALIZATION PROGRAM AND PURGES

J. P. Nettl

Joseph Stalin (1879–1953) did not play a significant role in the Bolshevik revolution in 1917, but he was able to take advantage of Lenin's death in 1924 and secure absolute power for himself. In the 1930s Stalin turned the Communist party into a ruthless totalitarian machine. Nevertheless, in this selection a modern historian argues that some of Stalin's measures, especially industrialization, did improve Soviet life in the thirties. In what ways was Soviet life better in the 1930s than it had been in czarist times? In what ways was it worse? Was Stalinist industrialization a failure or a success? Were Stalin's Five Year Plans after 1928 more or less effective than Lenin's earlier, more "capitalist" New Economic Policy (NEP)? Why did the purges occur? What was their effect?

What was life like for ordinary people in the 1930s? The answer must be: grim and grey. If you were not a Party member for whom the present was made luminous by the logic of historical necessity and the conviction of being on the side of the future, if you were not a manager, technician or shockworker* with special privileges, the pressures must at times have seemed well-nigh intolerable. At the bottom of the process of industrialization, life is hard under any system, but even more so when all the basic received certainties of life—religion, friendship, tradition—were being questioned and changed at the same time. The myth of the good times under Lenin and NEP grew up in this period, particularly in the countryside. Some people even thought nostalgically of pre-war Russia, though of course they did not dare to say so. This was above all a period of dislocation, of movement into new regions and towns. Housing was in desperately short supply, and not high on the order of official priorities. Around many of the major cities of the Soviet Union, both in the old industrial Russia of the west and in the new towns in the centre and east, there grew a ring of improvised dwellings, often no more than holes in the ground, in which whole families crowded together. The provision of an adequate apartment was in fact one of the rewards for deserving workers and technicians, and therefore a major incentive. The hours of work were long. When they were over, social and political obligations started: meetings of factory groups or cells, trade union meetings and other activities in which Party and government plans were explained and—in an increasingly formalized manner—discussed. Informal social life virtually disappeared from the Soviet Union, for by the time all obligations of formal society had been discharged, only one's immediate family could enjoy the little energy and time that was left. Nevertheless, in spite of the fact that almost all women worked, and that the state assumed ever greater responsibilities for children, the family was the residual beneficiary; even more than in western Europe family ties were actually strengthened in this period. For every son who denounced his father to the police or the schoolteacher during the purges, a thousand failed to do so. The only successful splitters of the family in this era were the Nazis in Germany.

In general the Party was everywhere. Behind it, once the great purges began, stood the Secret Police. You learnt to trust no one. The naturally open nature of the Russians, to whom long and inconclusive conversations about the problems of life, and the offer of intimate confidences to almost complete strangers, were a normal part of life, gradually became enclosed in the new official culture of silence. The class enemy, one was constantly reminded, lurked everywhere, waiting and watching. With household names like Trotsky, Zinoviev and Bukharin [prominent Soviet

---

*"Shockworkers" were laborers who accomplished much more than the required norm. The model was Stakhanov, a coal miner who in 1931 produced 102 tons of coal with two assistants in a five-and-three-quarter hour work shift. Shockworkers in the mid-1930s ran the risk of being killed by their workmates.—Ed.

leaders whom Stalin killed—Ed.] suddenly revealed as bourgeois agents, English spies, whom could you trust? Did not Stalin call for incessant vigilance, which made surveillance of your neighbour a social duty? Whatever else the purges did, they taught the Russians the need for extreme reserve.

In the countryside things were worse, though for different reasons. The economic discrimination against agriculture made itself felt on all levels. The Communist Party made little headway among the collective farmers. Recreation, medical services, education hardly existed except on posters. The idiocy of rural life (Marx's phrase) found a grimmer realization in the Soviet Union. The depletion of the human and cultural as well as economic resources of the countryside in favour of the new industrial towns was only made worse by the absolute refusal of the leadership to acknowledge it—even though official policy was directly responsible.

Any objective evaluation of the Soviet standard of living during these years must take into account the substantial benefits supplied by the state to sections of the population who had hitherto been almost completely deprived. During the period of industrialization, there was an enormous expansion of medical and health services. Already by 1940 there were more doctors per thousand of population than in the United States, Britain, Germany or France. The system of polyclinics, whatever its medical pros and cons, certainly made access to facilities more readily available to greater numbers of people—especially since some of the sociological inhibitions which prevent people from visiting doctors were largely removed. It was in this period that relatively general sick-pay benefits were instituted, although an attempt to reduce the excessive labour turnover in the late 1930s tied these to a minimum period of service in any one enterprise. Sport became professionalized. Footballers, athletes, and above all chess players (the Russian national game *par excellence*) were induced to treat their performance as part of their plan fulfilment. Outstanding excellence was equivalent to the achievements of the shockworker in industry. More important, however, was the popularization of these events in terms of mass participation. The commitment to the performance of teams and individuals, which still marks the Soviet Union today, is thus a compound of the natural loyalties of most *aficionados* for their favourite performers with the identification of support for sporting performance as a social duty.

The system of paid holidays also dates from the mid-1930s. Naturally the facilities in no way expanded as rapidly as the demand, but the principle had at any rate been established, and was to survive as a sheet-anchor of the Soviet approach to labour problems. It is significant that recent investigations into comparative job satisfaction in the Soviet Union, on the one hand, and the United States and the West on the other, show clearly how important a part of the general attitude to work paid and organized holidays have become, and above all to what extent this institution is regarded as a fundamental and original aspect of Soviet life.

To us and our contemporaries in the Soviet Union today, preoccupied with welfare and rising standards of living, these times must in retrospect seem grim indeed. What was achieved? Let the unadorned figures speak once more. In general the year 1928, just prior to the first Five Year Plan, showed a level of industrial production very similar to the Russia of 1913 (adjusted for loss of territories after 1918). The enormous ravages of six years of foreign and civil war had been made good at last. By 1940 Soviet industrial output had trebled. The annual growth rate in these twelve years was almost 9 per cent per annum, compared to present British growth rates of less than 3 per cent. The beginning of Soviet industrialization, and the period of the first Five Year Plan, coincided with the great depression in other parts of the world, when output in the United States fell by almost a third. By 1940 the Soviet Union was a major industrial power. Yet at the same time the rate of growth, impressive as it appeared, was not significantly higher than during the recovery period of NEP from 1921 to 1927. We are therefore faced with two obvious questions, only one of which historians have really tried to answer. This concerns the means chosen to achieve full-scale industrialization in the Soviet Union. Could NEP have been continued and still have attained the levels of industrial output and the growth rates of the Stalin period? Not surprisingly historians divide ideologically over this question. Pointing to the growth rates of NEP, many Western economists and historians maintain that the system was "taking off" in any event. The partial market factors of "limited" socialism under NEP might have allocated resources more rationally, they say; there would have been more consumer goods, and more efficient use of resources. Soviet historians naturally take a contrary view. Only the absolute priority for basic industries made possible the further growth rates of the post-Second World War period, and the attainment of the superior technological sophistication of the present day. Moreover they consider the question itself largely absurd. Socialism requires this order of priorities, the transformation of the economy from individual small-scale procedures to collective and integrated large-scale production. This problem had already been discussed in the early 1920s. Only fully controlled industrialization justifies planning, and *vice versa*—only full-scale planning can solve the problems of socialist industrialization.

This leads to the second question: why was the process of industrialization in this form begun in 1928? Was it a purposeful execution of a rational and deliberate decision, or did it just happen? It is still not possible to answer this question with any real authority, but I think that within the context of a desire to accelerate production and tighten the planning process, Soviet industrialization was to a considerable extent self-generated, feeding on itself politically and economically just as collectivization had done. However much Stalin covered his actions with explanations of historical and logical inevitability, he was a far less acute theorist and thinker than Lenin. His explanations were always retrospective rather than programmatic. The squeeze on the *kulaks* [better-off peasants—Ed.] may have started as an attempt to obtain grain, but once the class-war justification for it had been articulated, a more fundamental solution to the problem developed mainly under its own steam, and this self-reinforcement was fed back up the line into the political process to become official policy. Similarly the dramatic switch from indicative planning to a full command economy became self-generating, with official explanations and justification hurrying alongside. Once the process was under way, the Soviet leaders embraced it wholeheartedly. The vision of a long next step towards socialism and finally communism opened out in the early 1930s, and transformed a series of particular policies into a fundamental philosophy.

There was one field especially to which Stalin had devoted a great deal of time and effort—Party manipulation and control. Both collectivization and the first Five Year Plan meant a greatly strengthened role for the Party, which was wholly in line with the wishes and intentions of the communist leaders. In the course of the economic upheaval the Party was to become formally integrated into Soviet life at every level—except in the agricultural countryside—in a way which hitherto had been impossible. By the time things had settled down after the purges and just before the Second World War, the Party was installed literally everywhere. Those who controlled the Party really controlled the Soviet Union rather than merely ruling it.

The great purges from 1934 to 1938 seem to be in flagrant contradiction to the demands of forced industrialization. If the Party was to lead society in its enormous production drive, it would surely need to be cohesive and united. But there are always two approaches to cohesion and unity: consensus or discipline, persuasion or terror. Stalin chose the latter alternative. Society and Party were galvanized simultaneously. Terror was applied to production. Its threat was a spur to fulfilment, and its victims were often reintegrated into the bottom of the production process as slave labourers who consumed only a fraction of what they produced—the ideal form of surplus accumulation. How then to galvanize the Party? Hitherto the struggle among the leadership in the late 1920s had had relatively little effect on the middle and lower Party levels. By 1929 the simple and gross condemnation of Trotskyism had worked its way right through, and following on the leaders the lower echelons were being purged as well—no longer because they were unsuitable, but because they were deviationists. By the mid-1930s recantation of error no longer made re-admission possible. Between 1928 and 1933 industrialization brought an influx of new recruits; the Party grew from one and a half to three and a half million members and candidates. But the numbers declined again sharply during the continuous purge of the next three years, and this time the mass purge preceded that of the élite. By the beginning of 1937 numbers were down to just below two million. The purge had got out of hand. Most important, the character of the Party was completely changed during these years; it became on average substantially younger, and though the proportion of workers or sons of workers was still overwhelming, they were themselves increasingly members of the new intelligentsia, the product of Soviet schools and Komsomol [the Party youth organization—Ed.].

By the end of 1936 a wave of arrests with and without subsequent trial was swamping the Soviet Union. The most distinguished old Bolsheviks were being arraigned and executed in batches. Perhaps a formal trial was the only concession to their rank; for every one of these, hundreds and thousands of people simply disappeared into the prisons and labour camps of the secret police and thence all too often to the grave. No one really knew how it had all started, and certainly no one knew how it was going to end. Safety of a very uncertain kind lay in denouncing others, and so the gruesome immolation went on for two years. The record, like all records of such enormity, loses its impact by the sheer quantity of well-known men who died: in August 1936 the trial of Zinoviev, Kamenev and fourteen others on capital charges, in September 1936 the suicide of Tomsky, in January 1937 the suicide of Ordzhonikidze, hitherto one of Stalin's closest collaborators (according to Khrushchev once more, he was forced to shoot himself). In June 1937 the secret trial and execution of Tukhachevsky with a galaxy of the most senior Red Army commanders—German spies all. In March 1938 the trial of Bukharin, Rykov, Yagoda and eighteen others on capital charges. Each time the arch-villain was Trotsky, grinning behind the scenes and manipulating corrupt Bolsheviks into their treacherous practices. By the time the last trial had taken place even the solid Stalinist majority of the Central Committee of 1934 had been almost wholly liquidated; the leadership of the army, of the Komsomol, and of every other major institution of the Soviet Union had been turned upside-down.

Then, quite suddenly, the fury of the terror died down to a dreadful whisper. As in the case of collectivization, the purge was rotting away the foundations of those very sectors of society which it had meant to cleanse and strengthen. The Party hierarchy was running out of replacements. In January 1938 the new Central Committee met and issued a stern warning against excesses. It was time to make an end. By December 1938 Ezhov, whose name has become notorious in Russia through the word *"Ezhovshchina"* by which the great purges are usually referred to, had quietly disappeared. The men now around Stalin, with a few exceptions, were relatively unknown: Molotov, Zhdanov, Khrushchev and Beria, Kaganovich and Mikoyan. The aftermath of the purges was in fact truly Thermidorean*: the liquidation of the secret police, a purge of the purgers. In the meantime, however, the prison population, especially of the labour camps, had swollen to the size and importance of a state within a state, and went on making its contribution to socialist accumulation. People began to wonder if the growth rate and the whole system could in fact survive without them, whether the real reason for the purges was not the need for a cheap supply of nonconsuming labour.

*"Thermidorean" means a reversal of a revolution, like that which ended the terror of the French Revolution in the month of Thermidor (July) 1794.—Ed.

CHAPTER TWELVE

Fascism, World War II, and the Holocaust

45.   THE RISE OF HITLER

Joachim C. Fest

The rise of Adolf Hitler (1889–1945), this historian shows, was not a trick sprung on the unsuspecting German people. Hitler seemed to be what many Germans (and non-Germans) wanted. Why was this? What popular yearnings did Hitler seem to satisfy? To what groups of people did he appeal? Would there have been other ways of satisfying these needs? Do these needs still exist anywhere today? Can you recognize anything of yourself in this portrait of Germany in the 1920s?

At the end of the First World War the victory of the democratic idea seemed beyond question. Whatever its weaknesses might be, it rose above the turmoil of the times, the uprisings, the dislocations, and the continual quarrels among nations as the unifying principle of the new age. For the war had not only decided a claim to power. It had at the same time altered a conception of government. After the collapse of virtually all the governmental structures of Central and Eastern Europe many new political entities had emerged out of turmoil and revolution. And these for the most part were organized on democratic principles. In 1914 there had been only three republics alongside of seventeen monarchies in Europe. Four years later there were as many republics as monarchies. The spirit of the age seemed to be pointing unequivocally toward various forms of popular rule.

Only Germany seemed to be opposing this mood of the times, after having been temporarily gripped and carried along by it. Those who would not acknowledge the reality created by the war organized into a fantastic swarm of *völkisch* (racist-nationalist) parties, clubs, and free corps. To these groups the revolution had been an act of treason; parliamentary democracy was something foreign and imposed from without, merely a synonym for "everything contrary to the German political will," or else an "institution for pillaging created by Allied capitalism."

Germany's former enemies regarded the multifarious symptoms of nationalistic protest as the response of an inveterately authoritarian people to democracy and civic responsibility. To be sure, the Germans were staggering beneath terrible political and psychological burdens: there was the shock of defeat, the moral censure of the Versailles Treaty, the loss of territory and the demand for reparations, the impoverishment and spiritual undermining of much of the population. Nevertheless, the conviction remained that a great moral gap existed between the Germans and most of their neighbours. Full of resentment, refusing to learn a lesson, this incomprehensible country had withdrawn into its reactionary doctrines, made of them a special virtue, adjured Western rationality and humanity, and in general set itself against the universal trend of the age. For decades this picture of Germany dominated the discussion of the reasons for the rise of National Socialism.

But the image of democracy victorious was also deceptive. The moment in which democracy seemed to be achieving historic fulfillment simultaneously marked the beginning of its crisis. Only a few years later the idea of democracy was challenged in principle as it had never been before. Only a few years after it had celebrated its triumph it was overwhelmed or at least direly threatened by a new movement that had sprung to life in almost all European countries.

This movement recorded its most lasting successes in countries in which the war had aroused considerable discontent or made it conscious of existing discontent, and especially in countries in which the war had been followed by leftist revolutionary uprisings. In some places these movements were conservative, harking back to better times when men were more honorable, the valleys more peaceable, and money had more worth; in others these movements were revolutionary and vied with one another in their contempt for the existing order of things. Some attracted chiefly the petty bourgeois elements, others the peasants, others portions of the working class. Whatever their strange compound of classes, interests, and principles, all seemed to be drawing their dynamic force from the less conscious and more vital lower strata of society. National Socialism was merely one variant of this widespread European movement of protest and opposition aimed at overturning the general order of things.

National Socialism rose from provincial beginnings, from philistine clubs, as Hitler scornfully described them, which met in Munich bars over a few rounds of beer to talk over national and family troubles. No one would have dreamed that they could ever challenge, let alone outdo, the powerful, highly organized Marxist parties. But the following years proved that in these clubs of nationalistic beer drinkers, soon swelled by disillusioned homecoming soldiers and proletarianized members of the middle class, a tremendous force was waiting to be awakened, consolidated, and applied.

In Munich alone there existed, in 1919, nearly fifty more or less political associations, whose membership consisted chiefly of confused remnants of the prewar parties that had been broken up by war and revolution.

They had such names as New Fatherland, Council of Intellectual Work, Siegfried Ring, Universal League, Nova Vaconia, League of Socialist Women, Free Union of Socialist Pupils, and Ostara League. The German Workers' Party was one such group. What united them all and drew them together theoretically and in reality was nothing but an overwhelming feeling of anxiety.

First of all, and most immediate, there was the fear of revolution, that *grande peur* which after the French Revolution had haunted the European bourgeoisie throughout the nineteenth century. The notion that revolutions were like forces of nature, elemental mechanisms operating without reference to the will of the actors in them, following their own logic and leading perforce to reigns of terror, destruction, killing, and chaos—that notion was seared into the public mind. That was the unforgettable experience, not Kant's belief that the French Revolution had also shown the potentiality for betterment inherent in human nature. For generations, particularly in Germany, this fear stood in the way of any practical revolutionary strivings and produced a mania for keeping things quiet, with the result that every revolutionary proclamation up to 1918 was countered by the standard appeal to law and order.

This old fear was revived by the pseudorevolutionary events in Germany and by the menace of the October Revolution in Russia. Diabolical traits were ascribed to the Reds. The refugees pouring into Munich described bloodthirsty barbarians on a rampage of killing. Such imagery had instant appeal to the nationalists. The following article from one of Munich's racist newspapers is a fair example of the fears of the period and the way these were expressed:

> Dreadful times in which Christian-hating, circumcised Asiatics everywhere are raising their bloodstained hands to strangle us in droves! The butcheries of Christians by the Jew Issachar Zederblum, alias Lenin, would have made even a Genghis Khan blush. In Hungary his pupil Cohn, alias Béla Kun, marched through the unhappy land with a band of Jewish terrorists schooled in murder and robbery, to set up, among brutal gallows, a mobile machine gallows and execute middle-class citizens and peasants on it. A splendidly equipped harem served him, in his stolen royal train, to rape and defile honorable Christian virgins by the dozen. His lieutenant Samuely has had sixty priests cruelly butchered in a single underground room. Their bellies are ripped open, their corpses mutilated, after they have been plundered to their blood-drenched skin. In the case of eight murdered priests it has been established that they were first crucified on the doors of their own churches! The very same atrocious scenes are . . . now reported from Munich.

This threat dominated Hitler's speeches of the early years. In garish colors he depicted the ravages of the "Red squads of butchers," the "murderous communists," the "bloody morass of Bolshevism." In Russia, he told his audiences, more than thirty million persons had been murdered, "partly on the scaffold, partly by machine guns and similar means, partly in veritable slaughterhouses, partly, millions upon millions, by hunger; and we all know that this wave of hunger is creeping on . . . and see that this scourge is approaching, that it is also coming upon Germany." The intelligentsia of the Soviet Union, he declared, had been exterminated by mass murder, the economy utterly smashed. Thousands of German prisoners-of-war had been drowned in the Neva or sold as slaves. Meanwhile, in Germany the enemy was boring away at the foundations of society "in unremitting, ever unchanging undermining work." The fate of Russia, he said again and again, would soon be ours! And years later, when he was already in power, he spoke again of "the horror of the Communist international hate dictatorship" that had preyed on his mind at the beginning of his career: "I tremble at the thought of what would become of our old, overcrowded continent if the chaos of the Bolshevik revolution were to be successful."

National Socialism owed a considerable part of its emotional appeal, its militancy, and its cohesion to this defensive attitude toward the threat of Marxist revolution. The aim of the National Socialist Party, Hitler repeatedly declared, "is very brief: Annihilation and extermination of the Marxist world view." This was to be accomplished by an "incomparable, brilliantly orchestrated propaganda and information organization" side by side with a movement "of the most ruthless force and most brutal resolution, prepared to oppose all terrorism on the part of the Marxists with tenfold greater terrorism." At about the same time, for similar reasons, Mussolini was founding his Fasci di combattimento. Henceforth, the new movements were to be identified by the general name of "Fascism." But the fear of revolution would not have been enough to endow the movement with that fierce energy, which for a time seemed to stem the universal trend toward democracy. After all, for many people revolution meant hope. A stronger and more elemental motivation had to be added. And in fact Marxism was feared as the precursor of a far more comprehensive assault upon all traditional ideas. It was viewed as the contemporary political aspect of a metaphysical upheaval, as a "declaration of war upon the European . . . idea of culture." Marxism itself was only the metaphor for something dreaded that escaped definition.

Anxiety was the permanent emotion of the time. It sprang from the intuition that the end of the war meant not only the end of familiar prewar Europe with its grandeur and its urge to world domination, its monarchies, and gilt-edged securities, but also the end of an era. Along with the old forms of government, the accustomed framework of life was being destroyed. The unrest, the radicalism of the politicalized masses, the disorders of revolution were interpreted as the afterpains of the war and simultaneously as harbingers of a new, strange, and chaotic age. "That is why the foundations of life quake beneath our feet."

Rarely has any age been so aware of its own transitional state. In accelerating the process, the war also created a general consciousness of it. For the first time Europe had a glimpse of what awaited it. Pessimism, so long the basic attitude of an elite minority, abruptly became the mood of the whole period.

The war had led to gigantic new forms of organization, which helped the capitalistic system attain its full development. Rationalization and the assembly line, trusts and tycoons pitilessly exposed the structural inferiority of smaller economic units.

The trend to bigness was also expressed in the extraordinary increase in cartels—from several hundred to approximately twenty-five hundred—so that in industry "only a few outsiders" remained unattached to some cartel. The number of independent businesses in the major cities had diminished by half in the thirty years before the World War. Now that war and inflation had destroyed their material base, their number dwindled more rapidly. The cruelty of the corporation, which absorbed, consumed, and dropped the individual, was felt more keenly than ever before. Fear of individual economic disaster became generalized. A considerable literature grew up around the theme that the individual's function was disappearing, that man was becoming a cog in a machine he could not understand. "In general, life seems full of dread."

This fear of a standardized, termitelike existence was expressed in the hostility to increasing urbanization, to the canyon streets and grayness of the cities, and in lamentations over the factory chimneys cropping up in quiet valleys. In the face of a ruthlessly practiced "transformation of the planet into a single factory for the exploitation of its materials and energies," belief in progress for the first time underwent a reversal. The cry arose that civilization was destroying the world, that the earth was being made into "a Chicago with a sprinkling of agriculture."

This first phase of the postwar era was characterized both by fear of revolution and anticivilizational resentments; these together, curiously intertwined and reciprocally stimulating each other, produced a syndrome of extraordinary force. Into the brew went the hate and defense complexes of a society shaken to its foundations. German society had lost its imperial glory, its civil order, its national confidence, its prosperity, and its familiar authorities. The whole system had been turned topsy-turvy, and now many Germans blindly and bitterly wanted back what they thought had been unjustly taken from them. These general feelings of unhappiness were intensified and further radicalized by a variety of unsatisfied group interests. The class of white-collar workers, continuing to grow apace, proved especially susceptible to the grand gesture of total criticism. For the industrial revolution had just begun to affect office workers and was reducing the former "non-commissioned officers of capitalism" to the status of last victims of "modern slavery." It was all the worse for them because unlike the proletarians they had never developed a class pride of their own or imagined that the breakdown of the existing order was going to lead to their own apotheosis. Small businessmen were equally susceptible because of their fear of being crushed by corporations, department stores, and rationalized competition. Another unhappy group consisted of farmers who, slow to change and lacking capital, were fettered to backward modes of production. Another group were the academics and formerly solid bourgeois who felt themselves caught in the tremendous suction of proletarianization. Without outside support you found yourself "at once despised, declassed; to be unemployed is the same as being a communist," one victim stated in a questionnaire of the period. No statistics, no figures on rates of inflation, bankruptcies, and suicides can describe the feelings of those threatened by unemployment or poverty, or can express the anxieties of those others who still possessed some property and feared the consequences of so much accumulated discontent. Public institutions in their persistent weakness offered no bulwark against the seething collective emotions. It was all the worse because the widespread anxiety no longer, as in the time of Lagarde and Langbehn, was limited to cries of woe and impotent prophecies. The war had given arms to the fearful.

The vigilante groups and the free corps that were being organized in great numbers, partly on private initiative, partly with covert government support, chiefly to meet the threat of Communist revolution, formed centers of bewildered but determined resistance to the *status quo*. The members of these paramilitary groups were vaguely looking around for someone to lead them into a new system. At first there was another reservoir of militant energies alongside the parliamentary groups: the mass of homecoming soldiers. Many of these stayed in the barracks dragging out a pointless military life, baffled and unable to say good-bye to the warrior dreams of their recent youth. In the front-line trenches they had glimpsed the outlines of a new meaning to life; in the sluggishly resuming normality of the postwar period they tried in vain to find that meaning again. They had not fought and suffered for years for the sake of this weakened regime with its borrowed ideals which, as they saw it, could be pushed around by the most contemptible of their former enemies. And they also feared, after the exalting sense of life the war had given them, the ignobility of the commonplace bourgeois world.

It remained for Hitler to bring together these feelings and to appoint himself their spearhead. Indeed, Hitler regarded as a phenomenon seems like the synthetic product of all the anxiety, pessimism, nostalgia, and defensiveness we have discussed. For him, too, the war had been education and liberation. If there is a "Fascistic" type, it was embodied in him. More than any of his followers he expressed the underlying psychological, social, and ideological motives of the movement. He was never just its leader; he was also its exponent.

His early years had contributed their share to that experience of overwhelming anxiety which dominated his intellectual and emotional constitution. That lurking anxiety can be seen at the root of almost all his statements and reactions. It had everyday as well as cosmic dimensions. Many who knew him in his youth have described his pallid, "timorous" nature, which provided the fertile soil for his lush fantasies. His "constant fear" of contact with strangers was another aspect of that anxiety, as was his extreme distrust and his compulsion to wash frequently, which became more and more pronounced in later life. The same complex is apparent in his oft-expressed fear of venereal disease and his fear of contagion in general. He knew that "microbes are rushing at me." He was ridden by the Austrian Pan-German's fear of being overwhelmed by alien races, by fear of the "locust-like immigration of Russian and Polish Jews," by fear of "the niggerizing of the Germans," by fear of the Germans' "expulsion from Germany," and finally by fear that the Germans would be "exterminated." He had the *Völkische Boebachter* print an alleged French soldier's song whose refrain was: "Germans, we will possess your daughters!" Among his phobias were American technology, the birth rate of the Slavs, big cities, "industrialization as unrestricted as it is harmful," the "economization of the nation," corporations, the "morass of metropolitan amusement culture," and modern art, which sought "to kill the soul of the people" by painting meadows blue and skies green. Wherever he looked he discovered the "signs of decay of a slowly ebbing world." Not an element of pessimistic anticivilizational criticism was missing from his imagination.

What linked Hitler with the leading Fascists of other countries was the resolve to halt this process of degeneration. What set him apart from them, however, was the manic single-mindedness with which he traced all the anxieties he had ever felt back to a single source. For at the heart of the towering structure of anxiety, black and hairy, stood the figure of the Jew: evil-smelling, smacking his lips, lusting after blonde girls, eternal contaminator of the blood, but "racially harder" than the Aryan, as Hitler uneasily declared as late as the summer of 1942. A prey to his psychosis, he saw Germany as the object of a worldwide conspiracy, pressed on all sides by Bolshevists, Freemasons, capitalists, Jesuits, all hand in glove with each other and directed in their nefarious projects by the "bloodthirsty and avaricious Jewish tyrant." *The* Jew had 75 per cent of world capital at his disposal. He dominated the stock exchanges and the Marxist parties, the Gold and Red Internationals. He was the "advocate of birth control and the idea of emigration." He undermined governments, bastardized races, glorified fratricide, fomented civil war, justified baseness, and poisoned nobility: "the wirepuller of the destinies of mankind." The whole world was in danger, Hitler cried imploringly; it had fallen "into the embrace of this octopus." He groped for images in which to make his horror tangible, saw "creeping venom," "belly-worms," and "adders devouring the nation's body." In formulating his anxiety he might equally hit on the maddest and most ludicrous phrases as on impressive or at least memorable ones. Thus he invented the "Jewification of our spiritual life," "the mammonization of our mating instinct," and "the resulting syphilization of our people." He could prophesy: "If, with the help of his Marxist creed, the Jew is victorious over the other peoples of the world, his crown will be the funeral wreath of humanity and the planet will, as it did millions of years ago, move through the ether devoid of men."

The appearance of Hitler signaled a union of those forces that in crisis conditions had great political potential. The Fascistic movements all centered on the charismatic appeal of a unique leader. The leader was to be the resolute voice of order controlling chaos. He would have looked further and thought deeper, would know the despairs but also the means of salvation. This looming giant had already been given established form in a prophetic literature that went back to German folklore. Like the mythology of many other nations unfortunate in their history, that of the Germans has its sleeping leaders dreaming away the centuries in the bowels of a mountain, but destined some day to return to rally their people and punish the guilty world. Into the twenties pessimistic literature repeatedly called up these longings, which were most effectively expressed in the famous lines of Stefan George:

> He shatters fetters, sweeps the rubble heaps
> Back into order, scourges stragglers home
> Back to eternal justice where grandeur once more is grand.
> Lord once more lord.
> Rule once more rule. He pins
> The true insigne to the race's banner.
> Through the storms and dreadful trumpet blasts
> Of reddening dawn he leads his band of liegemen
> To daylight's work of founding the New Reich.

The leader cult, viewed in terms of the "fiction of permanent warfare," was in one sense the translation of the principles of military hierarchy to political organization. The leader was the army officer lifted to superhuman heights and endowed with supernal powers. Those powers were conferred by the craving to believe and the yearning to surrender self. The tramp of marching feet on all the pavements of Europe attested to the belief in militaristic models as offering a solution to the problems of society. It was the future-minded youth in particular who were drawn to these models, having learned through war, revolution, and chaos to prize "geometrical" systems.

The same factors underlay the paramilitary aspects of the Fascistic movements, the uniforms, the rituals of saluting, reporting, standing at attention. The insigne of the movements all came down to a few basic motifs—various forms of crosses (such as the St. Olaf's cross of the Norwegian Nasjonal Samling and the red St. Andrew's cross of Portugal's National Syndicalists), also arrows, bundles of fasces, scythes. These symbols were constantly displayed on flags, badges, standards, or armbands. To some extent they were meant as defiance of the boring old bourgeois business of tailcoats and stiff collars. But primarily they seemed more in keeping with the brisk technological spirit of the age. Then, too, uniforms and military trappings could conceal social differences and bring some dash to the dullness and emotional barrenness of ordinary civilian life.

The success of Fascism in contrast to many of its rivals was in large part due to its perceiving the essence of the crisis, of which it was itself the symptom. All the other parties affirmed the process of industrialization and emancipation, whereas the Fascists, evidently sharing the universal anxiety, tried to deal with it by translating it into violent action and histrionics. They also managed to leaven boring, prosaic everyday life by romantic rituals: torchlight processions, standards, death's heads, battle cries, and shouts of *Heil,* by the "new marriage of life with danger," and the idea of "glorious death." They presented men with modern tasks disguised in the costumery of the past. They deprecated material concerns and treated "politics as an area of self-denial and sacrifice of the individual for an idea." In taking this line they were addressing themselves to deeper needs than those who promised the masses higher wages. Ahead of all their rivals, the Fascists appeared to have recognized that the Marxist or liberal conception of man as guided only by reason and material interests was a monstrous abstraction.

Thus Fascism served the craving of the period for a general upheaval more effectively than its antagonists. It alone seemed to be articulating the feeling that everything had gone wrong, that the world had been led into an impasse. That Communism made fewer converts was not due solely to its stigma of being a class party and the agency of a foreign power. Rather, Communism suffered from a vague feeling that it represented part of the wrong turn the world had taken and part of the disease it pretended it could cure. Communism seemed not the negation of bourgeois materialism but merely its obverse, not the superseding of an unjust and inadequate system, but its mirror image turned upside down.

Hitler's unshakable confidence, which often seemed sheer madness, was based on the conviction that he was the only real revolutionary, that he had broken free of the existing system by reinstating the rights of human instincts. In alliance with these interests, he believed, he was invincible, for the instincts always won out in the end "against economic motivation, against the pressure of public opinion, even against reason." No doubt the appeal to instinct brought out a good deal of human baseness. No doubt what Fascism wanted to restore was often a grotesque parody of the tradition they purported to honor, and the order they hailed was a hollow sham. But when Trotsky contemptuously dismissed the adherents of Fascistic movements as "human dust," he was only revealing the Left's characteristic ineptness in dealing with people's needs and impulses. That ineptness led to a multitude of clever errors of judgment by those who purported to understand the spirit of the age better than anyone else.

Fascism satisfied more than romantic needs. Sprung from the anxieties of the age, it was an elemental uprising in favor of authority, a revolt on behalf of order. Such paradox was its very essence. It was rebellion and subordination, a break with tradition and the sanctification of tradition, a "people's community" and strictest hierarchy, private property and social justice. But whatever the slogans it appropriated, the imperious authority of a strong state was always implied. "More than ever the peoples today have a desire for authority, guidance and order," Mussolini declared.

Mussolini spoke of the "more or less decayed corpse of the goddess Liberty." He argued that liberalism was about to "close the portals of its temple, which the peoples have deserted" because "all the political experiences of the present are antiliberal." And in fact throughout Europe, especially in the countries that had gone over to a liberal parliamentary system only after the end of the World War, there had been growing doubts of the adequacy of parliamentarism. These doubts became all the stronger the more these countries moved into the present age. There would be the feeling that the country lacked the means to meet the challenges of the transition: that the available leadership was not equal to the crisis. Witnessing the endless parliamentary disputes, the bitterness and bargaining of partisan politics, people began to long for earlier days, when rule was by decree and no one had to exercise a choice. With the exception of Czechoslovakia, the parliamentary system collapsed throughout the newly created nations of eastern and central Europe and in many of the countries of southern Europe: in Lithuania, Latvia, Estonia, Poland, Hungary, Rumania, Austria, Italy, Greece, Turkey, Spain, Portugal, and finally in Germany. By 1939 there were only nine countries with parliamentary regimes. And many of the nine, like the French Third Republic, had stabilized in a *drôle d'état*, others in a monarchy. "A fascist Europe was already a possibility."

Thus it was not the case of a single aggrieved and aggressive nation trying to impose a totalitarian pattern on Europe. The liberal age was reaching its twilight in a widespread mood of disgust and the mood manifested itself under all kinds of auspices, reactionary and progressive, ambitious and altruistic. From 1921 on, Germany had lacked a Reichstag majority that professed faith in the parliamentary system with any conviction. The ideas of liberalism had scarcely any advocates but many potential adversaries; they needed only an impetus, the stirring slogans of a leader.

46. AN OVERVIEW OF WORLD WAR II

Carter Findley and John Rothney

This brief overview of World War II by two modern historians places the conflict in a genuinely global context. When did World War II begin? How did it combine separate drives for empire? What changed the balance of the war in favor of the Allies? What is the broad significance of World War II in world history?

The habit of looking at the twentieth-century world from the perspective of European dominance is hard to shake. Even now, four decades after that dominance collapsed at the end of World War II, historians often date the war from Hitler's invasion of Poland in 1939. Americans often date the war from the Japanese attack on the U.S. fleet at Pearl Harbor on December 7, 1941. By then Britain had been fighting Germany for a year alone, while German armies overran most of Europe. Britain found an ally against Hitler only when he invaded the Soviet Union on June 22, 1941, the day the war begins in Russian history books.

For many non-Europeans, however, World War II dates from well before 1939. For the Chinese, it began in 1931 against the Japanese in Manchuria. For the Ethiopians, virtually the only Africans not under European rule, it began with the Italian invasion in 1935.

The significance of these conflicting dates is that World War II merged originally separate drives for empire into one conflict. One drive began with Hitler's war with Britain and France over Poland, the last surviving creation of the Versailles system. This last of Europe's "civil wars" became a German campaign for "living space," which culminated in a Hitlerian empire stretching across Europe.

The second drive for empire began with Japan's penetration of China. Profiting from Hitler's attack on the European colonial powers, the Japanese extended their control over a large part of the East Asian mainland and the islands of the southwest Pacific, including the Dutch East Indies and the Philippines. By the end of 1941, the German and Japanese drives for empire had converged to make World War II a conflict of continents. It pitted Europe, under Hitler's rule, against the worldwide British Empire, which also had to face much of Asia, under the dominance of Japan. Had Germany not attacked the Soviet Union, and had Japan not attacked the United States, those other two continent-sized powers might not have been drawn into the struggle. Until Hitler attacked, Stalin had adhered to the Nazi-Soviet pact of August 1939. A clear majority of U.S. citizens favored neutrality in the war until the Japanese attacked them.

Russian and American participation brought World War II to a turning point by mid-to-late 1942. Until then, the so-called Axis powers (Germany, Japan, and Italy) had achieved an unbroken series of victories. German armies surged to the northern tip of Norway, to the shores of the Greek peninsula and the Black Sea, and over much of the North African desert. The Japanese swept to the eastern frontiers of India and to the arctic fringes of North America in the Aleutian Islands.

Even in this early period, however, the Axis leaders made fateful mistakes. Hitler failed to defeat Britain. He neither invaded it nor cut its lifelines across the Atlantic and through the Mediterranean. Meanwhile, he repeated Napoleon's fatal blunder of invading Russia while Britain remained unconquered. The Japanese leaders did not join in this attack on their hereditary enemy, but tried to avert U.S. interference with their empire-building by destroying the U.S. Pacific fleet. Following the attack on Pearl Harbor, it was Hitler who declared war on the United States, not the United States on Hitler.

It was these uncoordinated Axis attacks that forced together what Churchill called the Grand Alliance of Britain, the Soviet Union, and the United States. Together, these dissimilar Allies were too strong for the Axis. Consistently victorious through most of 1942, the Axis encountered nothing but defeat thereafter. Germany and subjugated Europe had been a match for Britain, despite the troops sent by the Dominions, like Canada, Australia, and New Zealand. But the Russian war destroyed Hitler's armies, and the U.S. agreement to give priority to Germany's defeat made it certain. After mid-1942, the Americans, the British, and their allies also steadily pushed the Japanese back. When the Soviet Union, after Hitler's defeat, joined Japan's enemies in 1945, Japanese prospects became hopeless, even without the awful warning of two American nuclear attacks—the first in history and the last, so far.

Throughout the war, the Axis powers failed to cooperate effectively.

They also did not mobilize their home fronts as effectively as the Allies. Despite German rhetoric about uniting the peoples of Europe and Japanese claims to be leading an Asian crusade against imperialism, neither Germany nor Japan was able to mobilize the enthusiasm of a majority in the lands they overran. Instead their treatment of conquered peoples was marked by cruelty and greed, which inspired even civilians to abandon passivity for active resistance.

After World War I, people quickly concluded that most of the slogans for which they had fought were hollow. After World War II, the revelations of Japanese and Nazi brutality kept alive the sense that this second global conflict had been fought for a just cause. But if the war defeated evil regimes, this struggle of continents also destroyed the power of Europe as a whole and the European-dominated global system. Within a generation after 1945, even Britain, bankrupt and exhausted in victory, would grant independence to most of its Asian and African colonies. From this "end of empire" would soon emerge the Third World of countries reluctant to subordinate themselves to either the United States or the Soviet Union, the only great powers left after 1945.

Not only in the already threatening conflict of these two superpowers does the world of 1945 foreshadow the world of the 1980s. Even more intensively than in 1914–1918, the pressures of total war had expanded the powers of governments, transformed societies, and revolutionized the economies of the world. Moreover, with official encouragement, scientists had produced a weapon so incomparably deadly that thoughtful people wondered whether human beings still had a future. We still live with that unprecedented uncertainty of 1945. In this respect as in most, World War II marks the turning point of the twentieth-century world, though few people foresaw this transformation when Hitler's armies crossed the Polish border on September 1, 1939.

47. THE HOLOCAUST:
47.1. HIMMLER SPEAKS TO THE SS

Heinrich Himmler

Heinrich Himmler (1900–1945) was one of the most powerful leaders of Nazi Germany. He was the head of the SS—the Schutzstaffel, *the black-shirted elite army—which, among other responsibilities, ran the many con-*

centration camps. Hitler gave Himmler the task of implementing the "final solution of the Jewish question": the policy of killing the Jewish population of Germany and the other countries the Nazis occupied. The horror that resulted is today often referred to by the biblical word "holocaust."

The following reading consists of an excerpt from a speech Himmler gave to SS leaders on October 4, 1943. What seemed to be Himmler's concern in this speech? How does he seem able to rationalize genocide? What kind of general support for the extermination of the Jews does this excerpt suggest existed?

I also want to make reference before you here, in complete frankness, to a really grave matter. Among ourselves, this once, it shall be uttered quite frankly; but in public we will never speak of it. Just as we did not hesitate on June 30, 1934, to do our duty as ordered, to stand up against the wall comrades who had transgressed,* and shoot them, so we have never talked about this and never will. It was the tact which I am glad to say is a matter of course to us that made us never discuss it among ourselves, never talk about it. Each of us shuddered, and yet each one knew that he would do it again if it were ordered and if it were necessary.

I am referring to the evacuation of the Jews, the annihilation of the Jewish people. This is one of those things that are easily said. "The Jewish people is going to be annihilated," says every party member. "Sure, it's in our program, elimination of the Jews, annihilation—we'll take care of it." And then they all come trudging, 80 million worthy Germans, and each one has his one decent Jew. Sure, the others are swine, but this one is an A-1 Jew. Of all those who talk this way, not one has seen it happen, not one has been through it. Most of you must know what it means to see a hundred corpses lie side by side, or five hundred, or a thousand. To have stuck this out—excepting cases of human weakness—to have kept our integrity, that is what has made us hard. In our history, this is an unwritten and never-to-be-written page of glory, for we know how difficult we would have made it for ourselves if today— amid the bombing raids, the hardships and the deprivations of war—we still had the Jews in every city as secret saboteurs, agitators, and demagogues. If the Jews were still ensconced in the body of the German nation, we probably would have reached the 1916–17 stage by now.*

The wealth they had we have taken from them. I have issued a strict order, carried out by SS-Obergruppenfuhrer Pohl, that this wealth in its entirety is to be turned over to the Reich as a matter of course. We have taken none of it for ourselves. Individuals who transgress will be punished

---

*A reference to the "blood purge," in which Hitler ordered the SS to murder the leaders of the SA, a Nazi group he wished to suppress.—Ed.

*Here Himmler is apparently referring to the stalemate on Germany's western front in World War I.—Ed.

in accordance with an order I issued at the beginning, threatening that whoever takes so much as a mark of it for himself is a dead man. A number of SS men—not very many—have transgressed, and they will die, without mercy. We had the moral right, we had the duty toward our people, to kill this people which wanted to kill us. But we do not have the right to enrich ourselves with so much as a fur, a watch, a mark, or a cigarette or anything else. Having exterminated a germ, we do not want, in the end, to be infected by the germ, and die of it. I will not stand by and let even a small rotten spot develop or take hold. Wherever it may form, we together will cauterize it. All in all, however, we can say that we have carried out this heaviest of our tasks in a spirit of love for our people. And our inward being, our soul, our character has not suffered injury from it.

47.2.   TREBLINKA

Jean-François Steiner

Treblinka, in Poland, was one of several Nazi death camps. (Auschwitz was the largest camp.) In these "death factories," the Nazis murdered millions of Jews as well as many thousands of gypsies, socialists, Soviet prisoners of war, and other people. In this selection, Steiner, who lost his father at Treblinka, reveals how "rational" and "scientific" mass murder can be. How could this happen? Can it happen again?

. . . Each poorly organized debarkation [of deportees from trains arriving at Treblinka—Ed.] gave rise to unpleasant scenes—uncertainties and confusion for the deportees, who did not know where they were going and were sometimes seized with panic.

So, the first problem was to restore a minimum of hope. Lalka[1] had many faults, but he did not lack a certain creative imagination. After a few days of reflection he hit upon the idea of transforming the platform where the convoys [trains] arrived into a false station. He had the ground filled in to the level of the doors of the cars in order to give the appearance of a train platform and to make it easier to get off the trains. . . . On [a] wall Lalka had . . . doors and windows painted in gay and pleasing colors. The windows were decorated with cheerful curtains and framed by green blinds which were just as false as the rest. Each door was given a special name, stencilled at eye level: "Stationmaster," "Toilet," "Infir-

---

1. Kurt Franz, whom the prisoners called Lalka, designed the highly efficient system of extermination at Treblinka.—Ed.

mary" (a red cross was painted on this door). Lalka carried his concern for detail so far as to have his men paint two doors leading to the waiting rooms, first and second class. The ticket window, which was barred with a horizontal sign reading, "Closed," was a little masterpiece with its ledge and false perspective and its grill, painted line for line. Next to the ticket window a large timetable announced the departure times of trains for Warsaw, Bialystok, Wolkowysk, etc.... Two doors were cut into the [wall]. The first led to the "hospital," bearing a wooden arrow on which "Wolkowysk" was painted. The second led to the place where the Jews were undressed; that arrow said "Bialystok." Lalka also had some flower beds designed, which gave the whole area a neat and cheery look.

... The windows were more real than real windows; from ten yards away you could not tell the difference. The arrows were conspicuous and reassuring. The flowers, which were real, made the whole scene resemble a pretty station in a little provincial town. Everything was perfect. ...

Lalka also decided that better organization could save much time in the operations of undressing and recovery of the [deportees'] baggage. To do this you had only to rationalize the different operations, that is, to organize the undressing like an assembly line. But the rhythm of this assembly line was at the mercy of the sick, the old and the wounded, who, since they were unable to keep the pace, threatened to bog down the operation and make it proceed even more slowly than before. ... Individuals of both sexes over the age of ten, and children under ten, at a maximum rate of two children per adult, were judged fit to follow the complete circuit[2], as long as they did not show serious wounds or marked disability. Victims who did not correspond to the norms were to be conducted to the "hospital" by members of the blue commando and turned over to the Ukrainians [guards] for special treatment. A bench was built all around the ditch of the "hospital" so that the victims would fall of their own weight after receiving the bullet in the back of the head. This bench was to be used only when Kurland[3] was swamped with work. On the platform, the door which these victims took was surmounted by the Wolkowysk arrow. In the Sibylline language of Treblinka, "Wolkowysk" meant the bullet in the back of the neck or the injection. "Bialystok" meant the gas chamber.

Beside the "Bialystok" door stood a tall Jew whose role was to shout endlessly, "Large bundles here, large bundles here!" He had been nicknamed "Groysse Pack." As soon as the victims had gone through, Groysse Pack and his men from the red commando carried the bundles at a run to the sorting square, where the sorting commandos immediately took possession of them. As soon as they had gone through the

2. The "complete" circuit was getting off the train, walking along the platform through the door to the men's or women's barracks, undressing, and being led to the gas chamber "showers."—Ed.

3. Kurland was a Jew assigned to the "hospital," where he gave injections of poison to those who were too ill or crippled to make the complete circuit.—Ed.

door came the order, "Women to the left, men to the right." This moment generally gave rise to painful scenes.

While the women were being led to the left-hand barracks to undress and go to the hairdresser, the men, who were lined up double file, slowly entered the production line. This production line included five stations. At each of these a group of "reds" shouted at the top of their lungs the name of the piece of clothing that it was in charge of receiving. At the first station the victim handed over his coat and hat. At the second, his jacket. (In exchange, he received a piece of string.) At the third he sat down, took off his shoes, and tied them together with the string he had just received. (Until then the shoes were not tied together in pairs, and since the yield was at least fifteen thousand pairs of shoes per day, they were all lost, since they could not be matched up again.) At the fourth station the victim left his trousers, and at the fifth his shirt and underwear.

After they had been stripped, the victims were conducted, as they came off the assembly line, to the right-hand barracks and penned in until the women had finished: ladies first. However, a small number chosen from among the most able-bodied, were singled out at the door to carry the clothing to the sorting square. They did this while running naked between two rows of Ukrainian guards. Without stopping once they threw their bundles onto the pile, turned around, and went back for another.

Meanwhile the women had been conducted to the barracks on the left. This barracks was divided into two parts: a dressing room and a beauty salon. "Put your clothes in a pile so you will be able to find them after the shower," they were ordered in the first room. The "beauty salon" was a room furnished with six benches, each of which could seat twenty women at a time. Behind each bench twenty prisoners of the red commando, wearing white tunics and armed with scissors, waited at attention until all the women were seated. Between hair-cutting sessions they sat down on the benches and, under the direction of a *kapo* [prisoner guard] who was transformed into a conductor, they had to sing old Yiddish melodies.

Lalka, who had insisted on taking personal responsibility for every detail, had perfected the technique of what he called the "Treblinka cut." With five well-placed slashes the whole head of hair was transferred to a sack placed beside each hairdresser for this purpose. It was simple and efficient. How many dramas did this "beauty salon" see? From the very beautiful young woman who wept when her hair was cut off, because she would be ugly, to the mother who grabbed a pair of scissors from one of the "hairdressers" and literally severed a Ukrainian's arm; from the sister who recognized one of the "hairdressers" as her brother to the young girl, Ruth Dorfman, who, suddenly understanding and fighting back her tears, asked whether it was difficult to die and admitted in a small brave voice that she was a little afraid and wished it were all over.

When they had been shorn the women left the "beauty salon" double file. Outside the door, they had to squat in a particular way also specified by Lalka, in order to be intimately searched. Up to this point, doubt had been carefully maintained. Of course, a discriminating eye might have observed that . . . the smell was the smell of rotting bodies. A thousand details proved that Treblinka was not a transient camp, and some realized this, but the majority had believed in the impossible for too long to begin to doubt at the last moment. The door of the barracks, which opened directly onto the "road to heaven," represented the turning point. Up to here the prisoners had been given a minimum of hope, from here on this policy was abandoned.

This was one of Lalka's great innovations. After what point was it no longer necessary to delude the victims? This detail had been the subject of rather heated controversy among the Technicians. At the Nuremberg trials, Rudolf Höss, Commandant of Auschwitz, criticized Treblinka where, according to him, the victims knew that they were going to be killed. Höss was an advocate of the towel distributed at the door to the gas chamber. He claimed that this system not only avoided disorder, but was more humane, and he was proud of it. But Höss did not invent this "towel technique"; it was in all the manuals, and it was utilized at Treblinka until Lalka's great reform.

Lalka's studies had led to what might be called the "principle of the cutoff." His reasoning was simple: since sooner or later the victims must realize that they were going to be killed, to postpone this moment was only false humanity. The principle "the later the better" did not apply here. Lalka had been led to make an intensive study of this problem upon observing one day completely by chance, that winded victims died much more rapidly than the rest. The discovery had led him to make a clean sweep of accepted principles. Let us follow his industrialist's logic, keeping well in mind that his great preoccupation was the saving of time. A winded victim dies faster. Hence, a saving of time. The best way to wind a man is to make him run—another saving of time. Thus Lalka arrived at the conclusion that you must make the victims run. A new question had then arisen: at what point must you make the victims run and thus create panic (a further aid to breathlessness)? The question had answered itself: as soon as you have nothing more to make them do. Franz located the exact point, the point of no return: the door of the barracks.

The rest was merely a matter of working out the details. Along the "road to heaven" and in front of the gas chambers he stationed a cordon of guards armed with whips, whose function was to make the victims run, to make them rush into the gas chambers of their own accord in search of refuge. One can see that this system is more daring than the classic system, but one can also see the danger it represents. Suddenly abandoned to their despair, realizing that they no longer had anything to lose, the victims might attack the guards. Lalka was aware of this risk, but he maintained that everything depended on the pace. "It's close work," he said, "but if you maintain a very rapid pace and do not allow a single moment of hesitation, the method is absolutely without danger." There were still further elaborations later on, but from the first day, Lalka had only to pride himself on his innovation: it took no more than three quarters of an hour, by the clock, to put the victims through their last voyage, from the moment the doors of the cattle cars were unbolted to the moment the great trap doors of the gas chamber were opened to take out the bodies. Three quarters of an hour, door to door, compared to an hour and a quarter and sometimes even as much as two hours with the old system; it was a record. . . .

But let us return to the men. The timing was worked out so that by the time the last woman had emerged from the left-hand barracks, all the clothes had been transported to the sorting square. The men were immediately taken out of the right-hand barracks and driven after the women into the "road to heaven," which they reached by way of a special side path. By the time they arrived at the gas chambers the toughest, who had begun to run before the others to carry the bundles, were just as winded as the weakest. Everyone died in perfect unison for the greater satisfaction of that great Technician Kurt Franz, the Stakhanovite [model worker—Ed.] of extermination.

Since a string of twenty cars arrived at the platform every half hour, the Lalka system made it possible to fully process twelve trains of twenty cars each—or four convoys, or twenty-four thousand persons—between seven o'clock in the morning and one-fifteen in the afternoon.

The rest of the day was devoted to the sorting of the clothing in Camp Number One and the disposal of the bodies in Camp Number Two.

Transported by two prisoners on litterlike affairs, the bodies, after they were removed from the gas chambers, were carefully stacked, to save room, in immense ditches in horizontal layers, which alternated with layers of sand. In this realm, too, Lalka introduced a number of improvements.

Until the great reform, the "dentists" had extracted gold teeth and bridges from the corpses by rummaging through the big piles that accumulated during the morning in front of the trap doors of the gas chambers. It was not very efficient, as Lalka realized. Thus he got the idea of stationing a line of dentists between the gas chambers and the ditches, a veritable gold filter. As they came abreast of the dentists, the carriers of the bodies, without setting down their litters, would pause long enough for the "dentists" to examine the mouths of the corpses and extract what ever needed extracting. For a trained "dentist" the operation never required more than a minute. He placed his booty in a basin which another "dentist" came to empty from time to time. After the take had been washed in the well, it was brought to the barracks where other "dentists" sorted, cleaned and classified it.

Meanwhile, the carriers of the bodies resumed their race—all moving from one place to another was done on the double—to the ditch. Here Lalka had made another improvement: previously the body carriers had gone down and stacked their bodies themselves. Lalka, that maniac for specialization, created a commando of body stackers which never left the bottom of the ditch. When they arrived, the carriers heaved their burdens with a practiced movement, the role of personal initiative being reduced to the minimum, and returned to the trap doors of the gas chambers by a lower route, as on a gymnastic platform, so as not to disturb the upward movement. When all the corpses had been removed from the gas chambers, which was generally between noon and one o'clock, the ramp commando in charge of removal of the bodies joined the carrier commando. The burial rites lasted all afternoon and continued even into the night. Lalka had made it a rule that nobody was to go to bed until the last corpse had been stacked in its place.

47.3.   A VILLAGE IN VICHY FRANCE

Susan Zuccotti

When the Germans took Paris in the blitzkrieg, or lightning strike, of 1940, they imposed direct rule on northern France and a puppet government on the southern part of the country, led by World War I hero Marshall Philippe Pétain. Pétain governed from the old city of Vichy, about 200 miles south of Paris. After 1941, the Germans began to impose their policy of anti-Semitism on the Vichy regime, as they had done in the north, insisting that Vichy capture and imprison Jews for shipment to concentration camps. Although much of southern France complied with the order, in a high plateau just a few hours south of Vichy, an area of independent French, many of them Protestants who had long resisted Catholic Paris, refused to do the Nazis' work. In one of the towns in this area, Le Chambon-sur-Lignon, a modern historian tells how the inhabitants risked their lives to save Jewish children in their schools and Jewish families in their homes. How did the people of Le Chambon save Jews? What gave them the courage to resist the orders of their government and the Nazis? How were they so successful?

"Roughly fifty kilometers from Puy-en-Velay and about forty kilometers from Saint-Étienne, there is a little town, Le Chambon-sur-Lignon, the tiny capital of the plateau of the same name, an ancient Protestant village. There you can still find the caves where the Protestants gathered to practice their religion as well as to escape the king's dragoons." Thus begins Joseph Bass's postwar report on a remote village on a pine-studded plateau, about 960 meters above sea level, in the Massif Central west of Valence and the Rhône River. Léon Poliakov, who helped Bass hide Jews there, later described the department of Haute-Loire where Le Chambon is located as "one of the poorest and wildest regions of the Cévennes." Its Protestant inhabitants, he added, "distrust all authority, listening only to their conscience—or their pastors."

Long before Bass and Poliakov arrived there, hundreds of Jewish and non-Jewish refugees had already found their way to Le Chambon. Some had wandered into town as early as the winter of 1940–41. Most came independently at first, advised by friends or casual acquaintances of an isolated village of about 1,000 people, reputedly sympathetic. Newcomers found shelter with village families or with the roughly 2,000 peasants, most of them also Protestant, in the surrounding countryside. Others took rooms in one of more than a dozen hotels and boardinghouses in this popular summer resort area of pine forests, clear streams, and bracing air. Most were trying to escape internment, and most, needless to say, were not legally registered.

During the late spring and early summer of 1942, many foreign Jews and non-Jews released from internment camps to the care of charitable agencies also came to Le Chambon. Local institutions to care for them multiplied, openly and legally. Madeleine Barot and other young Protestant social workers of the CIMADE [a Protestant relief organization] established a family residence at the Hôtel Coteau Fleuri, outside of town. Quakers, with the help from Le Chambon's Pastor André Trocmé, funded a boardinghouse for young children. Older students joined two farm-schools operated by the Secours suisse, or moved into residences of the École Cévenol, a private Protestant secondary school slightly north of the village. Still others were welcomed at the École des roches in the village itself.

In August 1942, French police rounding up recent Jewish immigrants in the unoccupied zone did not overlook Le Chambon. They arrived in the village with three empty buses, demanding that Pastor Trocmé provide a list of resident Jews. Trocmé not only claimed ignorance, somewhat truthfully, of names and addresses but promptly sent his Protestant Boy Scouts to even the most distant farms to warn Jews to hide. Other local residents had undoubtedly already seen the approach of the police up the valley, along a road visible for miles from the Plateau. Then and later, that visibility was one secret to security in Le Chambon. Police searched the region for two or three days and returned regularly for several weeks. They apparently netted only one victim, an Austrian who was later released because he was only half-Jewish.

Jews literally poured into Le Chambon after August 1942. By this point, their presence was totally unofficial. They came with the [Jewish resistance network] Service André—[its director Joseph] Bass later reported that the pastor never hesitated to help him—and with OSE [children's aid] and other clandestine networks. Some stayed in Le Chambon only long enough to find a guide to Switzerland, but many remained, hidden with families or in boardinghouses or schools. They kept coming until, as Poliakov observed, "in some hamlets, there was not a single farm which did not shelter a Jewish family." Roughly 5,000 Jews are estimated to have been hidden among the 3,000 native residents, all of whom knew about the refugees.

In his memoirs, Poliakov describes with touching detail his arrival at a local hotel with a group of Jewish children in 1943:

> Frightened, they hovered in a corner of the room. The first peasant couple enters: "We will take a little girl between eight and twelve years old," explains the woman. Little Myriam is called: "Will you go with this aunt and uncle?" Shy and frightened, Myriam does not answer. They muffle her up in blankets and carry her to the sleigh; she leaves for the farm where she will live a healthy and simple life with her temporary parents until the end of the war. . . . In a flash, all the children were similarly housed, under the benevolent eye of Pastor Trocmé.

Who was this pastor whose name appears in every account of Le Chambon-sur-Lignon during the war? Born in Saint-Quentin in Picardy in northern France in 1901, André Trocmé studied at the Union Theological Seminary in New York City, where he met his future wife, Italian-born Magda Grilli, in 1925. A pacifist and conscientious objector, Trocmé made no secret of his beliefs after his arrival in Le Chambon in 1934. Indeed, he and Pastor Édouard Theis, the director of the École Cévenol, were equally frank after 1940 about their dislike of the Vichy regime and the racial laws. Trocmé often spoke from the pulpit about the evils of racial persecution; Theis taught the same principles at the École Cévenol. On August 15, 1942, during a visit to the village by the Vichy youth minister, Georges Lamirand, and the departmental prefect and subprefect, several older students at the school presented the officials with a letter protesting the July 16 roundup [of Jews] in Paris and expressing local support of the Jews.

Trocmé, Theis, and Roger Darcissac, the director of the public school in Le Chambon, were arrested by French police in February 1943 and held for a month. At the end of the year, the two pastors went into hiding. During that period, Theis served as a guide for CIMADE, escorting refugees to Switzerland. Magda Trocmé continued her husband's work during his absence; one scholar has judged that she was at least as important as he in saving lives. Mildred Theis kept the École Cévenol open and continued to shelter refugees. The two women had many aides. Bass remembered pastors named Poivre, Leenhardt, Jeannet, Curtet, Betrix, Vienney, and Besson from surrounding hamlets, as well as the Trocmés' good friend Simone Mairesse. Municipal officials also cooperated, if only by looking the other way. And the people of the plateau, often influenced by their outspoken pastors but guided as well by their own sense of justice, continued to protect their Jewish guests until the Liberation. Of them, Bass wrote after the war, "The conduct of the Protestant pastors and men of action of the plateau of Le Chambon deserves to be told to Jews throughout the entire world."

In considering the rescue of Jews in Le Chambon, two questions arise: why was the local population so sympathetic, and why was it so successful? To answer the first, Madeleine Barot stresses the special status of Protestants in France as a minority persecuted by Catholics. Protestants in Le Chambon still told tales of persecution around their hearths on cold winter nights and visited caves where their ancestors had hidden. The memory of persecution made them suspicious of authority, sympathetic to other minorities, and comfortable with clandestine life. In addition, many French Protestants were skeptical about the Vichy regime, in part because authoritarianism often bodes ill for minorities, but especially because, according to Barot, "Pétain dedicated France to the Virgin, and made it an intensely Catholic state." Finally, Christian anti-Semitism notwithstanding, Bible-reading Protestants of the type living around Le Chambon sometimes articulate a special affinity for the Jews, based on a shared reverence for the Old Testament and a common acceptance of God's special compact with his chosen people.

These various factors certainly did not apply to all French Protestants. Many, especially those of the assimilated and highly educated urban classes who were more removed from their historical and cultural roots, were favorably inclined toward the Vichy regime for the same economic and social reasons as their Catholic neighbors, and held the same variety of attitudes toward Jews. But Protestants around Le Chambon cherished their historic memory. That love, combined with the sturdy individualism and independence of mountain people and the leadership of a group of exceptional pastors, made Le Chambon an equally exceptional place.

But why were the rescuers of Le Chambon so successful? Admittedly, even they had their tragedies and their victims. In the spring of 1943, the Gestapo raided the École des roches, seizing many students along with their dedicated director, Daniel Trocmé, Pastor Trocmé's second cousin. Nearly all, including Daniel, died in deportation. But the Germans did not return and thus failed as miserably as the French police to find most of the Jews they knew were there. Why?

Geographic factors were important. The isolation of the area was made even more extreme by the closing of access roads in winter. Any movement on those same approach roads could be seen from the plateau. Thick forests were good for hiding. The Gestapo and the French Milice [volunteer fascist corps], busy elsewhere, were reluctant or perhaps afraid to enter a hostile area that, however dedicated by its pastor to nonviolence, was surrounded by armed Resistance fighters. Why stir up a sleeping hornets' nest? French police and gendarmes not only shared that reluctance but were also affected by local sympathies for refugees.

Two witnesses tell amusing stories. Madeleine Barot later declared of her own experience, "When the *gendarmes* in Tence [the nearest town] received an order for an arrest, they made a habit of dragging themselves along the road very visibly, of calling a halt at the café before tackling the steep ascent to the Coteau, announcing loudly that they were about to arrest some of those 'dirty Jews.' " Poliakov confirms the description, explaining that when the gendarmes received an arrest order, "they went to the [local] Hotel May and ordered a glass of wine: comfortably seated at their table, they took their papers from their satchels and spelled out 'Goldberg . . . it's about someone named Jacques Goldberg.' Unnecessary to add that when they arrived at Goldberg's domicile half an hour later, the latter was long gone." Poliakov adds that when a more serious danger approached in the form of the Gestapo or the Milice, a telephone call of warning usually preceded them from the valley.

Barot's and Poliakov's accounts both allude to the most important factor in the rescue success rate in Le Chambon—the determination of local residents to protect their guests. The people of Le Chambon lived in a state of constant alertness, with a warning system prepared. Their solidarity also made it difficult for potential informers to act. To whom could they safely leak information? Municipal authorities sympathized with the majority, as did, it appeared, many of the police. Even local censors of mail were likely to prevent a denunciation. In such a situation, a careless informer might even put himself in danger. In addition, it was psychologically more difficult for a solitary anti-Semite or opportunist to express his bile in a region where he was bucking an obvious majority. He could not so easily convince himself that he was acting as a "good and loyal Frenchman." And in any part of France—where so many individual arrests of Jews by preoccupied and understaffed local Gestapo units were prompted by denunciations—the reluctance of informers was decisive.

CHAPTER THIRTEEN

Dependence and Independence in Asia

48. INDIA:
48.1. SWARAJ

Mohandas K. Gandhi

Swaraj means "self-rule" or "independence." At least, that is its literal meaning. This selection from M. K. Gandhi's essay by that title shows that the meaning could be more complex. Gandhi began to develop his ideas of Hind Swaraj, or Indian Home Rule, when he returned from England to South Africa in 1908. An early version of this essay, published then, was reissued in its present form in 1921, two years after he returned to his birthplace, India, and again in 1938, in the last years of struggle against British rule. After Gandhi's introduction, the essay takes the form of questions and answers. The questions are posed by a presumed "reader" of Gandhi's paper. As "editor," Gandhi explains what he means. What does he mean by "swaraj"? Is it more important to him that the English leave India, or that India not become like England? What does Gandhi disapprove of in modern English civilization? What does he mean by passive resistance or soul-force (Satyagraha)? Why does he think it is preferable to violence, or body-force? What is Gandhi's attitude toward machinery? What kind of India would Gandhi have tried to create had he lived?

A WORD OF EXPLANATION

It is certainly my good fortune that this booklet of mine is receiving wide attention. The original is in Gujarati. It has a chequered career. It was first published in the columns of the *Indian Opinion* of South Africa. It was written in 1908 during my return voyage from London to South Africa in answer to the Indian school of violence and its prototype in South Africa. I came in contact with every known Indian anarchist in London. Their bravery impressed me, but I felt that their zeal was misguided. I felt that violence was no remedy for India's ills, and that her civilization required the use of a different and higher weapon for self-protection. The Satayagraha of South Africa was still an infant hardly two years old. But it had developed sufficiently to permit me to write of it with some degree of confidence. What I wrote was so much appreciated that it was published as a booklet. It attracted some attention in India. The Bombay Government prohibited its circulation. I replied by publishing its translation. I thought it was due to my English friends that they should know its contents.

In my opinion it is a book which can be put into the hands of a child. It teaches the gospel of love in place of that of hate. It replaces violence with self-sacrifice. It pits soul force against brute force. It has gone through several editions and I commend it to those who would care to read it. I withdraw nothing except one word of it, and that in deference to a lady friend.

The booklet is a severe condemnation of 'modern civilization'. It was written in 1908. My conviction is deeper today than ever. I feel that if India will discard 'modern civilization', she can only gain by doing so.

But I would warn the reader against thinking that I am today aiming at the Swaraj described therein. I know that India is not ripe for it. It may seem an impertinence to say so. But such is my conviction. I am individually working for the self-rule pictured therein. But today my corporate activity is undoubtedly devoted to the attainment of Parliamentary Swaraj in accordance with the wishes of the people of India. I am not aiming at destroying railways or hospitals, though I would certainly welcome their natural destruction. Neither railways nor hospitals are a test of a high and pure civilization. At best they are a necessary evil. Neither adds one inch to the moral stature of a nation. Nor am I aiming at a permanent destruction of law courts, much as I regard it as a 'consummation devoutly to be wished'. Still less am I trying to destroy all machinery and mills. It requires a higher simplicity and renunciation than the people are today prepared for.

The only part of the programme which is now being carried out is that of non-violence. But I regret to have to confess that even that is not being carried out in the spirit of the book. If it were, India would establish Swaraj in a day. If India adopted the doctrine of love as an active part of her religion and introduced it in her politics, Swaraj would descend upon India from heaven. But I am painfully aware that that event is far off as yet.

I offer these comments because I observe that much is being quoted from the booklet to discredit the present movement. I have even seen writings suggesting that I am playing a deep game, that I am using the present turmoil to foist my fads on India, and am making religious experiments at India's expense. I can only answer that Satyagraha is made of sterner stuff. There is nothing reserved and nothing secret in it. A portion of the whole theory of life described in *Hind Swaraj* is undoubtedly being carried into practice. There is no danger attendant upon the whole of it being practised. But it is not right to scare away people by reproducing from my writings passages that are irrelevant to the issue before the country.

Young India, January, 1921   M. K. Gandhi

WHAT IS SWARAJ?

Reader: I have now learnt what the Congress has done to make India one nation, how the Partition has caused an awakening, and how discontent and unrest have spread through the land. I would now like to know your views on Swaraj. I fear that our interpretation is not the same as yours.

Editor: It is quite possible that we do not attach the same meaning to the term. You and I and all Indians are impatient to obtain Swaraj, but we are certainly not decided as to what it is. To drive the English out of India is a thought heard from many mouths, but it does not seem that many have properly considered why it should be so. I must ask you a question. Do you think that it is necessary to drive away the English, if we get all we want?

Reader: I should ask of them only one thing, that is: "Please leave our country." If, after they have complied with this request, their withdrawal from India means that they are still in India, I should have no objection. Then we would understand that, in their language, the word "gone" is equivalent to "remained."

Editor: Well then, let us suppose that the English have retired. What will you do then?

Reader: That question cannot be answered at this stage. The state after withdrawal will depend largely upon the manner of it. If, as you assume, they retire, it seems to me we shall still keep their constitution and shall carry on the Government. If they simply retire for the asking we should have an army, etc., ready at hand. We should, therefore, have no difficulty in carrying on the Government.

Editor: You may think so; I do not. But I will not discuss the matter just now. I have to answer your question, and that I can do well by asking you several questions. Why do you want to drive away the English?

Reader: Because India has become impoverished by their Government. They take away our money from year to year. The most important posts are reserved for themselves. We are kept in a state of slavery. They behave insolently towards us and disregard our feelings.

Editor: If they do not take our money away, become gentle, and give us responsible posts, would you still consider their presence to be harmful?

Reader: That question is useless. It is similar to the question whether there is any harm in associating with a tiger if he changes his nature. Such a question is sheer waste of time. When a tiger changes his nature, Englishmen will change theirs. This is not possible, and to believe it to be possible is contrary to human experience.

Editor: Supposing we get Self-Government similar to what the Canadians and the South Africans have, will it be good enough?

Reader: That question also is useless. We may get it when when we have the same powers; we shall then hoist our own flag. As is Japan, so must India be. We must own our navy, our army, and we must have our own splendour, and then will India's voice ring through the world.

Editor: You have drawn the picture well. In effect it means this: that we want English rule without the Englishman. You want the tiger's nature, but not the tiger; that is to say, you would make India English. And when it becomes English, it will be called not Hindustan but *Englistan*. This is not the Swaraj that I want.

THE CONDITION OF ENGLAND

Reader: Then from your statement I deduce that the Government of England is not desirable and not worth copying by us.

Editor: Your deduction is justified. The condition of England at present is pitiable. I pray to God that India may never be in that plight. That which you consider to be the Mother of Parliaments is like a sterile woman and a prostitute. Both these are harsh terms, but exactly fit the case. That Parliament has not yet, of its own accord, done a single good thing. Hence I have compared it to a sterile woman. The natural condition of that Parliament is such that, without outside pressure, it can do nothing. It is like a prostitute because it is under the control of ministers who change from time to time. Today it is under Mr. Asquith, tomorrow it may be under Mr. Balfour.

Reader: As you express these views about Parliament, I would like to hear you on the English people, so that I may have your view of their Government.

Editor: To the English voters their newspaper is their Bible. They take their cue from their newspapers which are often dishonest. The same fact is differently interpreted by different newspapers, according to the party in whose interests they are edited. One newspaper would consider a great Englishman to be a paragon of honesty, another would consider him dishonest. What must be the condition of the people whose newspapers are of this type?

Reader: You shall describe it.

Editor: These people change their views frequently. It is said that they change them every seven years. These views swing like the pendulum of a clock and are never steadfast. The people would follow a powerful orator or a man who gives them parties, receptions, etc. As are the people, so is their Parliament. They have certainly one quality very strongly developed. They will never allow their country to be lost. If any person were to cast an evil eye on it, they would pluck out his eyes. But that does not mean that the nation possesses every other virtue or that it should be imitated. If India copies England, it is my firm conviction that she will be ruined.

Reader: To what do you ascribe this state of England?

Editor: It is not due to any peculiar fault of the English people, but the condition is due to modern civilization. It is a civilization only in name. Under it the nations of Europe are becoming degraded and ruined day by day.

CIVILIZATION

Reader: Now you will have to explain what you mean by civilization.

Editor: Let us first consider what state of things is described by the word "civilization". Its true test lies in the fact that people living in it make bodily welfare the object of life. We will take some examples. The people of Europe today live in better-built houses than they did a hundred years ago. This is considered an emblem of civilization, and this is also a matter to promote bodily happiness. Formerly, they wore skins, and used spears as their weapons. Now, they wear long trousers, and, for embellishing their bodies, they wear a variety of clothing, and, instead of spears, they carry with them revolvers containing five or more chambers. If people of a certain country, who have hitherto not been in the habit of wearing much clothing, boots, etc., adopt European clothing, they are supposed to have become civilized out of savagery. Formerly, in Europe, people ploughed their lands mainly by manual labour. Now, one man can plough a vast tract by means of steam engines and can thus amass great wealth. This is called a sign of civilization. Formerly, only a few men wrote valuable books. Now, anybody writes and prints anything he likes and poisons people's minds. Formerly, men travelled in waggons. Now, they fly through the air in trains at the rate of four hundred and more miles per day. This is considered the height of civilization. It has been stated that, as men progress, they shall be able to travel in airship and reach any part of the world in a few hours. Men will not need the use of their hands and feet. They will press a button, and they will have their clothing at their side. They will press another button, and they will have their newspaper. A third, and a motor-car will be in waiting for them. They will have a variety of delicately dished up food. Everything will be done by machinery. Formerly, when people wanted to fight with one another, they measured between them their bodily strength; now it is possible to take away thousands of lives by one man working behind a gun from a hill. This is civilization. Formerly, men worked in the open air only as much as they liked. Now thousands of workmen meet together and for the sake of maintenance work in factories or mines. Their condition is worse than that of beasts. They are obliged to work, at the risk of their lives, at most dangerous occupations, for the sake of millionaires. Formerly, men were made slaves under physical compulsion. Now they are enslaved by temptation of money and of the luxuries that money can buy. There are now diseases of which people never dreamt before, and an army of doctors is engaged in finding out their cures, and so hospitals have increased. This is a test of civilization. Formerly, special messengers were required and much expense was incurred in order to send letters; today, anyone can abuse his fellow by means of a letter for one penny. True, at the same cost, one can send one's thanks also. Formerly, people had two or three meals consisting of home-made bread and vegetables; now, they require something to eat every two hours so that they have hardly leisure for anything else. What more need I say? All this you can ascertain from several authoritative books. These are all true tests of civilization. And if anyone speaks to the contrary, know that he is igno-rant. This civilization takes note neither of morality nor of religion. Its votaries calmly state that their business is not to teach religion. Some even consider it to be a superstitious growth. Others put on the cloak of religion, and prate about morality. But, after twenty years' experience, I have come to the conclusion that immorality is often taught in the name of morality. Even a child can understand that in all I have described above there can be no inducement to morality. Civilization seeks to in-crease bodily comforts, and it fails miserably even in doing so. . . .

HOW CAN INDIA BECOME FREE?

Reader: I appreciate your views about civilization. I will have to think over them. I cannot take them in all at once. What, then, holding the views you do, would you suggest for freeing India?

Editor: I do not expect my views to be accepted all of a sudden. My duty is to place them before readers like yourself. Time can be trusted to do the rest. We have already examined the conditions for freeing India, but we have done so indirectly; we will now do so directly. It is a world-known maxim that the removal of the cause of a disease results in the removal of the disease itself. Similarly if the cause of India's slavery be removed, India can become free.

Reader: If Indian civilization is, as you say, the best of all, how do you account for India's slavery?

Editor: This civilization is unquestionably the best, but it is to be observed that all civilizations have been on their trial. That civilization which is permanent outlives it. Because the sons of India were found wanting, its civilization has been placed in jeopardy. But its strength is to be seen in its ability to survive the shock. Moreover, the whole of India is not touched. Those alone who have been affected by Western civilization have become enslaved. We measure the universe by our own miserable foot-rule. When we are slaves, we think that the whole uni-verse is enslaved. Because we are in an abject condition, we think that the whole of India is in that condition. As a matter of fact, it is not so, yet it is as well to impute our slavery to the whole of India. But if we bear in mind the above fact, we can see that if we become free, India is free. And in this thought you have a definition of Swaraj. It is Swaraj when we learn to rule ourselves. It is, therefore, in the palm of our hands. Do not consider this Swaraj to be like a dream. There is no idea of sitting still. The Swaraj that I wish to picture is such that, after we have once realized it, we shall endeavour to the end of our life-time to persuade others to do likewise. But such Swaraj has to be experienced, by each one for himself. One drowning man will never save another. Slaves ourselves, it would be a mere pretension to think of freeing others. Now you will have seen that it is not necessary for us to have as our goal the expulsion of the English. If the English become Indian-ized, we can accommodate them. If they wish to remain in India along with their civilization, there is no room for them. It lies with us to bring about such a state of things.

Reader: It is impossible that Englishmen should ever become Indian-ized.

Editor: To say that is equivalent to saying that the English have no humanity in them. And it is really beside the point whether they become so or not. If we keep our own house in order, only those who are fit to live in it will remain. Others will leave of their own accord. Such things occur within the experience of all of us.

Reader: But it has not occurred in history.

Editor: To believe that what has not occurred in history will not occur at all is to argue disbelief in the dignity of man. At any rate, it behoves us to try what appeals to our reason. All countries are not similarly condi-tioned. The condition of India is unique. Its strength is immeasurable. We need not, therefore, refer to the history of other countries. I have drawn attention to the fact, that, when other civilizations have suc-cumbed, the Indian has survived many a shock.

Reader: I cannot follow this. There seems little doubt that we shall have to expel the English by force of arms. So long as they are in the country we cannot rest. One of our poets says that slaves cannot even dream of happiness. We are day by day becoming weakened owing to the presence of the English. Our greatness is gone; our people look like terrified men. The English are in the country like a blight which we must remove by every means.

Editor: In your excitement, you have forgotten all we have been con-sidering. We brought the English, and we keep them. Why do you forget that our adoption of their civilization makes their presence in India at all possible? Your hatred against them ought to be transferred to their civilization. . . .

PASSIVE RESISTANCE

Reader: Is there any historical evidence as to the success of what you have called soul-force or truth-force? No instance seems to have happened of any nation having risen through soul-force. I still think that the evil-doers will not cease doing evil without physical punishment.

Editor: The poet Tulsidas has said: "Of religion, pity, or love, is the root, as egotism of the body. Therefore, we should not abandon pity so long as we are alive." This appears to me to be a scientific truth. We have evidence of its working at every step. The universe would disappear without the existence of that force. . . .

The fact that there are so many men still alive in the world shows that it is based not on the force of arms but on the force of truth or love. Therefore, the greatest and most unimpeachable evidence of the success of this force is to be found in the fact that, in spite of the wars of the world, it still lives on.

Thousands, indeed tens of thousands, depend for their existence on a very active working of this force. Little quarrels of millions of families in their daily lives disappear before the exercise of this force. Hundreds of nations live in peace. History does not and cannot take note of this fact. History is really a record of every interruption of the even working of the force of love or of the soul. Two brothers quarrel; one of them repents and re-awakens the love that was lying dormant in him; the two again begin to live in peace; nobody takes note of this. But if the two brothers, through the intervention of solicitors or some other reason take up arms or go to law—which is another form of the exhibition of brute force,—their doings would be immediately noticed in the press, they would be the talk of their neighbours and would probably go down to history. And what is true of families and communities is true of nations. There is no reason to believe that there is one law for families and another for nations. History, then, is a record of an interruption of the course of nature. Soul-force, being natural, is not noted in history.

Reader: According to what you say, it is plain that instances of this kind of passive resistance are not to be found in history. It is necessary to understand this passive resistance more fully. It will be better, therefore, if you enlarge upon it.

Editor: Passive resistance is a method of securing rights by personal suffering; it is the reverse of resistance by arms. When I refuse to do a thing that is repugnant to my conscience, I use soul-force. For instance, the Government of the day has passed a law which is applicable to me. I do not like it. If by using violence I force the Government to repeal the law, I am employing what may be termed body-force. If I do not obey the law and accept the penalty for its breach, I use soul-force. It involves sacrifice of self.

Everybody admits that sacrifice of self is infinitely superior to sacrifice of others. Moreover, if this kind of force is used in a cause that is unjust, only the person using it suffers. He does not make others suffer for his mistakes. Men have before now done many things which were subsequently found to have been wrong. No man can claim that he is absolutely in the right or that a particular thing is wrong because he thinks so, but it is wrong for him so long as that is his deliberate judgment. It is therefore meet that he should not do that which he knows to be wrong, and suffer the consequence whatever it may be. This is the key to the use of soul-force. . . .

MACHINERY

Reader: When you speak of driving out Western civilization, I suppose you will also say that we want no machinery.

Editor: By raising this question, you have opened the wound I have received. When I read Mr. Dutt's *Economic History of India*, I wept; and as I think of it again my heart sickens. It is machinery that has impoverished India. It is difficult to measure the harm that Manchester has done to us. It is due to Manchester that Indian handicraft has all but disappeared.

But I make a mistake. How can Manchester be blamed? We wore Manchester cloth and this is why Manchester wove it. I was delighted when I read about the bravery of Bengal. There were no clothmills in that presidency. They were, therefore, able to restore the original hand-weaving occupation. It is true Bengal encourages the mill-industry of Bombay. If Bengal had proclaimed a boycott of *all* machine-made goods, it would have been much better.

Machinery has begun to desolate Europe. Ruination is now knocking at the English gates. Machinery is the chief symbol of modern civilization; it represents a great sin.

The workers in the mills of Bombay have become slaves. The condition of the women working in the mills is shocking. When there were no mills, these women were not starving. If the machinery craze grows in our country, it will become an unhappy land. It may be considered a heresy, but I am bound to say that it were better for us to send money to Manchester and to use flimsy Manchester cloth than to multiply mills in India. By using Manchester cloth we only waste our money; but by reproducing Manchester in India, we shall keep our money at the price of our blood, because our very moral being will be sapped, and I call in support of my statement the very mill-hands as witnesses. And those who have amassed wealth out of factories are not likely to be better than other rich men. It would be folly to assume that an Indian Rockefeller would be better than the American Rockefeller. Impoverished India can become free, but it will be hard for any India made rich through immorality to regain its freedom. I fear we shall have to admit that moneyed men support British rule; their interest is bound up with its stability. Money renders a man helpless. The other thing which is equally harmful is sexual vice. Both are poison. A snake-bite is a lesser poison than these two, because the former merely destroys the body but the latter destroy body, mind and soul. We need not, therefore, be pleased with the prospect of the growth of the mill-industry.

Reader: Are the mills, then to be closed down?

Editor: That is difficult. It is no easy task to do away with a thing that is established. We, therefore, say that the nonbeginning of a thing is supreme wisdom. We cannot condemn mill-owners; we can but pity them. It would be too much to expect them to give up their mills, but we may implore them not to increase them. If they would be good they would gradually contract their business. They can establish in thousands of households the ancient and sacred handlooms and they can buy out the cloth that may be thus woven. Whether the mill-owners do this or not, people can cease to use machine-made goods.

Reader: You have so far spoken about machine-made cloth, but there are innumerable machine-made things. We have either to import them or to introduce machinery into our country.

Editor: Indeed, our gods even are made in Germany. What need, then, to speak of matches, pins and glassware? My answer can be only one. What did India do before these articles were introduced? Precisely the same should be done today. As long as we cannot make pins without machinery so long will we do without them. The tinsel splendour of glassware we will have nothing to do with, and we will make wicks, as of old, with home-grown cotton and use handmade earthen saucers for lamps. So doing, we shall save our eyes and money and support Swadeshi and so shall we attain Home Rule.

It is not to be conceived that all men will do all these things at one time or that some men will give up all machine-made things at once. But, if the thought is sound, we shall always find out what we can give up and gradually cease to use it. What a few may do, others will copy: and the movement will grow like the cocoanut of the mathematical problem. What the leaders do, the populace will gladly do in turn. The matter is neither complicated nor difficult. You and I need not wait until we can carry others with us. Those will be the losers who will not do it, and those who will not do it, although they appreciate the truth, will deserve to be called cowards.

Reader: What, then, of the tram-cars and electricity?

Editor: This question is now too late. It signifies nothing. If we are to do without the railways we shall have to do without the tram-cars. Machinery is like a snake-hole which may contain from one to a hundred snakes. Where there is machinery there are large cities; and where there are large cities, there are tram-cars and railways: and there only does one see electric light. English villages do not boast of any of these things. Honest physicians will tell you that where means of artificial locomotion have increased, the health of the people has suffered. I remember that when in a European town there was a scarcity of money, the receipts of the tramway company, of the lawyers and of the doctors went down and people were less unhealthy. I cannot recall a single good point in connection with machinery. Books can be written to demonstrate its evils.

Reader: Is it a good point or a bad one that all you are saying will be printed through machinery?

Editor: This is one of those instances which demonstrate that sometimes poison is used to kill poison. This, then, will not be a good point regarding machinery. As it expires, the machinery, as it were, says to us: "Beware and avoid me. You will derive no benefits from me and the benefit that may accrue from printing will avail only those who are infected with the machinery-craze."

Do not, therefore, forget the main thing. It is necessary to realize that machinery is bad. We shall then be able gradually to do away with it. Nature has not provided any way whereby we may reach a desired goal all of a sudden. If, instead of welcoming machinery as a boon, we should look upon it as an evil. It would ultimately go.

48.2. GANDHI

Jawaharlal Nehru

Mohandas Gandhi and Jawaharlal Nehru were the two most important leaders of India's national independence movement. Although they worked together and Nehru was Gandhi's choice as the first Indian prime minister, they expressed in their personalities and ideas two very different Indias. How would you describe these two Indias? Was it Gandhi's or Nehru's vision of the future that was realized? Who do you think was a better guide for India?

I imagine that Gandhiji is not so vague about the objective as he sometimes appears to be. He is passionately desirous of going in a certain direction, but this is wholly at variance with modern ideas and conditions, and he has so far been unable to fit the two, or to chalk out all the intermediate steps leading to his goal. Hence the appearance of vagueness and avoidance of clarity. But his general inclination has been clear enough for a quarter of a century, ever since he started formulating his philosophy in South Africa. I do not know if those early writings still represent his views. I doubt if they do so in their entirety, but they do help us to understand the background of his thought.

"India's salvation consists," he wrote in 1909, "in unlearning what she has learned during the last fifty years. The railways, telegraphs, hospitals, lawyers, doctors, and suchlike have all to go; and the so-called upper classes have to learn consciously, religiously, and deliberately the simple peasant life, knowing it to be a life giving true happiness." And again: "Every time I get into a railway car or use a motor bus I know that I am doing violence to my sense of what is right"; "to attempt to reform the world by means of highly artificial and speedy locomotion is to attempt the impossible."

Nehru

All this seems to me utterly wrong and harmful doctrine, and impossible of achievement. Behind it lies Gandhiji's love and praise of poverty and suffering and the ascetic life. For him progress and civilization consist not in the multiplication of wants, of higher standards of living, "but in the deliberate and voluntary restriction of wants, which promotes real happiness and contentment, and increases the capacity for service." If these premises are once accepted, it becomes easy to follow the rest of Gandhiji's thought and to have a better understanding of his activities. But most of us do not accept those premises, and yet we complain later on when we find that his activities are not to our liking.

Personally I dislike the praise of poverty and suffering. I do not think they are at all desirable, and they ought to be abolished. Nor do I appreciate the ascetic life as a social ideal, though it may suit individuals. I understand and appreciate simplicity, equality, self-control; but not the mortification of the flesh. Just as an athlete requires to train his body, I believe that the mind and habits have also to be trained and brought under control. It would be absurd to expect that a person who is given to too much self-indulgence can endure much suffering or show unusual self-control or behave like a hero when the crisis comes. To be in good moral condition requires at least as much training as to be in good physical condition. But that certainly does not mean asceticism or self-mortification.

Nor do I appreciate in the least the idealization of the simple peasant life. I have almost a horror of it, and instead of submitting to it myself I want to drag out even the peasantry from it, not to urbanization, but to the spread of urban cultural facilities to rural areas. Far from this life's giving me true happiness, it would be almost as bad as imprisonment for me. What is there in "The Man with the Hoe" to idealize over? Crushed and exploited for innumerable generations, he is only little removed from the animals who keep him company.

> Who made him dead to rapture and despair,
> A thing that grieves not and that never hopes,
> Stolid and stunned, a brother to the ox?

This desire to get away from the mind of man to primitive conditions where mind does not count, seems to me quite incomprehensible. The very thing that is the glory and triumph of man is decried and discouraged, and a physical environment which will oppress the mind and prevent its growth is considered desirable. Present-day civilization is full of evils, but it is also full of good; and it has the capacity in it to rid itself of those evils. To destroy it root and branch is to remove that capacity from it and revert to a dull, sunless, and miserable existence. But even if that were desirable it is an impossible undertaking. We cannot stop the river of change or cut ourselves adrift from it, and psychologically we who have eaten of the apple of Eden cannot forget that taste and go back to primitiveness.

It is difficult to argue this, for the two standpoints are utterly different. Gandhiji is always thinking in terms of personal salvation and of sin, while most of us have society's welfare uppermost in our minds. I find it difficult to grasp the idea of sin, and perhaps it is because of this that I cannot appreciate Gandhiji's general outlook.

49. CHINA:
49.1. THE NEW AWAKENING

Harold Isaacs

This brief selection from Harold Isaacs's The Tragedy of the Chinese Revolution, *a recent history, recalls the impact of Ch'en Tu-hsiu's* New Youth *magazine in 1915. Spirits that had risen with Sun Yat-sen's revolution in 1911, only to become depressed by its apparent failure, rose again with Ch'en's call to a new generation.*

How did Ch'en's appeal reverse traditional Confucian values? Why do you think it had such an enormous appeal?

China's economic spurt during the First World War opened all the sluices of change. Along a thousand channels new ideas, new thoughts, new aspirations found their way into the country and crashed against the dead weight of the past like mighty waves against a grounded hulk. Among the intellectuals the mood of despair and discouragement engendered by the failure of the 1911 Revolution gave way to the beginnings of a vigorous cultural renaissance which rapidly drew a whole new generation into its orbit. New leaders, new forces came to the fore. Out of the thinned ranks of the revolutionary intellectuals of 1911 emerged the figure of Ch'en Tu-hsiu, scion of an Anhwei Mandarin family, who began posing the tasks of revolt more boldly, more clearly, more courageously than anyone who had preceded him. To his side rallied the men who with him were going to make over the life of a whole generation and who in later years would enter and lead opposing armies on the battlefields of social conflict.

fight Confucianism

The task of the new generation, proclaimed Ch'en Tu-hsiu, was "to fight Confucianism, the old tradition of virtue and rituals, the old ethics and the old politics . . . the old learning and the old literature." In their place he would put the fresh materials of modern democratic thought and natural science.

> We must break down the old prejudices, the old way of believing in things as they are, before we can begin to hope for social progress [wrote Ch'en in 1915 in his magazine, *New Youth*]. We must discard our old ways. We must merge the ideas of the great thinkers of history, old and new, with our own experience, build up new ideas in politics, morality, and economic life. We must build the spirit of the new age to fit it to new environmental conditions and a new society. Our ideal society is honest, progressive, positive, free, equalitarian, creative, beautiful, good, peaceful, cooperative, toilsome, but happy for the many. We look for the world that is false, conservative, negative, restricted, inequitable, hidebound, ugly, evil, war-torn, cruel, indolent, miserable for the many and felicitous for the few, to crumble until it disappears from sight. . . .
>
> I hope those of you who are young will be self-conscious and that you will struggle. By self-consciousness I mean that you are to be conscious of the power and responsibility of your youth and that you are to respect it. Why do I think you should struggle? Because it is necessary for you to use all the intelligence you have to get rid of those who are decaying, who have lost their youth. Regard them as enemies and beasts; do not be influenced by them, do not associate with them.
>
> Oh, young men of China! Will you be able to understand me? Five out of every ten whom I see are young in age, but old in spirit. . . . When this happens to a body, the body is dying. When it happens to a society, the society is perishing. Such a sickness cannot be cured by sighing in words; it can only be cured by those who are young, and in addition to being young, are courageous. . . . We must have youth if we are to survive, we must have youth if we are to get rid of corruption. Here lies the hope for our society.

This memorable call was really the opening manifesto of the era of the second Chinese Revolution. Ch'en Tu-hsiu was a professor at the time at Peking National University, where new ideas and new impulses were stirring and where a new spirit was germinating. Ch'en's magazine was eagerly snatched up by students in every school and college in the country. When it was published, wrote one student, "it came to us like a clap of thunder which awakened us in the midst of a restless dream. . . ."

49.2.   DREAMS OF YOUTH

Lu Hsun

Lu Hsun (1881–1936) was one of China's greatest modern writers. He attended the Naval Academy at Nanking and then went to study medicine in Japan, but, as he relates here, he became increasingly distressed by China's "weak and backward" state. Literature seemed to him a more valuable pursuit. Impressed with the New Youth *magazine, he wrote his first story,* A Madman's Diary, *for* New Youth *in 1918 and then never stopped writing. While he supported the aims of the communist revolution and was hailed by Mao Tse-tung (Mao Zedong), he never became a party member.*

What made Lu Hsun turn to literature? How could literature seem more important than the Navy or medicine? What is the meaning of Lu Hsun's story of an "iron house without windows"?

When I was young I, too, had many dreams. Most of them came to be forgotten, but I see nothing in this to regret. For although recalling the past may make you happy, it may sometimes also make you lonely, and there is no point in clinging in spirit to lonely bygone days. However, my trouble is that I cannot forget completely, and these stories have resulted from what I have been unable to erase from my memory.

For more than four years I used to go, almost daily, to a pawnbroker's and to a medicine shop. I cannot remember how old I was then; but the counter in the medicine shop was the same height as I, and that in the pawnbroker's twice my height. I used to hand clothes and trinkets up to the counter twice my height, take the money proffered with contempt, then go to the counter the same height as I to buy medicine for my father who had long been ill. On my return home I had other things to keep me busy, for since the physician who made out the prescriptions was very well-known, he used unusual drugs: aloe root dug up in winter, sugarcane that had been three years exposed to frost, twin crickets, and *ardisia* . . . all of which were difficult to procure. But my father's illness went from bad to worse until he died.

I believe those who sink from prosperity to poverty will probably come, in the process, to understand what the world is really like. I wanted to go to the K—— school in N——[1] perhaps because I was in search of a change of scene and faces. There was nothing for my mother to do but to raise eight dollars for my travelling expenses, and say I might do as I pleased. That she cried was only natural, for at that time the proper thing was to study the classics and take the official examinations. Anyone who studied "foreign subjects" was looked down upon as a

---

1. The Kiangnan Naval Academy in Nanking.

fellow good for nothing, who, out of desperation, was forced to sell his soul to foreign devils. Besides, she was sorry to part with me. But in spite of that, I went to N—— and entered the K—— school; and it was there that I heard for the first time the names of such subjects as natural science, arithmetic, geography, history, drawing and physical training. They had no physiology course, but we saw woodblock editions of such works as *A New Course on the Human Body* and *Essays on Chemistry and Hygiene*. Recalling the talk and prescriptions of physicians I had known and comparing them with what I did not know, I came to the conclusion those physicians must be either unwitting or deliberate charlatans; and I began to sympathize with the invalids and families who suffered at their hands. From translated histories I also learned that the Japanese Reformation had originated, to a great extent, with the introduction of Western medical science to Japan.

These inklings took me to a provincial medical college in Japan. I dreamed a beautiful dream that on my return to China I would cure patients like my father, who had been wrongly treated, while if war broke out I would serve as an army doctor, at the same time strengthening my countrymen's faith in reformation.

I do not know what advanced methods are now used to teach microbiology, but at that time lantern slides were used to show the microbes; and if the lecture ended early, the instructor might show slides of natural scenery or news to fill up the time. This was during the Russo-Japanese War, so there were many war films, and I had to join in the clapping and cheering in the lecture hall along with the other students. It was a long time since I had seen any compatriots, but one day I saw a film showing some Chinese, one of whom was bound, while many others stood around him. They were all strong fellows but appeared completely apathetic. According to the commentary, the one with his hands bound was a spy working for the Russians, who was to have his head cut off by the Japanese military as a warning to others, while the Chinese beside him had come to enjoy the spectacle.

Before the term was over I had left for Tokyo, because after this film I felt that medical science was not so important after all. The people of a weak and backward country, however strong and healthy they may be, can only serve to be made examples of, or to witness such futile spectacles; and it doesn't really matter how many of them die of illness. The most important thing, therefore, was to change their spirit, and since at that time I felt that literature was the best means to this end, I determined to promote a literary movement. There were many Chinese students in Tokyo studying law, political science, physics and chemistry, even police work and engineering, but not one studying literature or art. However, even in this uncongenial atmosphere I was fortunate enough to find some kindred spirits. We gathered the few others we needed, and after discussion our first step, of course, was to publish a magazine, the title of which denoted that this was a new birth. As we were then rather classically inclined, we called it *Xin Sheng* (*New Life*).

When the time for publication drew near, some of our contributors dropped out, and then our funds were withdrawn, until finally there were only three of us left, and we were penniless. Since we had started our magazine at an unlucky hour, there was naturally no one to whom we could complain when we failed; but later even we three were destined to part, and our discussions of a dream future had to cease. So ended this abortive *New Life*.

Only later did I feel the futility of it all; at that time I did not really understand anything. Later I felt if a man's proposals met with approval, it should encourage him; if they met with opposition, it should make him fight back; but the real tragedy for him was to lift up his voice among the living and meet with no response, neither approval nor opposition, just as if he were left helpless in a boundless desert. So I began to feel lonely.

And this feeling of loneliness grew day by day, coiling about my soul like a huge poisonous snake. Yet in spite of my unaccountable sadness, I felt no indignation; for this experience had made me reflect and see that I was definitely not the heroic type who could rally multitudes at his call.

However, my loneliness had to be dispelled, for it was causing me agony. So I used various means to dull my senses, both by conforming to the spirit of the time and turning to the past. Later I experienced or witnessed even greater loneliness and sadness, which I do not like to recall, preferring that it should perish with me. Still my attempt to deaden my senses was not unsuccessful—I had lost the enthusiasm and fervour of my youth.

In S——[2] Hostel there were three rooms where it was said a woman had lived who hanged herself on the locust tree in the courtyard. Although the tree had grown so tall that its branches could no longer be reached, the rooms remained deserted. For some years I stayed here, copying ancient inscriptions. I had few visitors, there were no political problems or issues in those inscriptions, and my only desire was that my life should slip quietly away like this. On summer nights, when there were too many mosquitoes, I would sit under the locust tree, waving my fan and looking at the specks of sky through the thick leaves, while the caterpillars which came out in the evening would fall, icy-cold, on to my neck.

The only visitor to come for an occasional talk was my old friend Chin Hsin-yi. He would put his big portfolio down on the broken table, take off his long gown, and sit facing me, looking as if his heart was still beating fast after braving the dogs.

"What is the use of copying these?" he demanded inquisitively one night, after looking through the inscriptions I had copied.

2. Shaohsing.

"No use at all."

"Then why copy them?"

"For no particular reason."

"I think you might write something. . . ."

I understood. They were editing the magazine *New Youth*, but hitherto there seemed to have been no reaction, favourable or otherwise, and I guessed they must be feeling lonely. However I said:

"Imagine an iron house without windows, absolutely indestructible, with many people fast asleep inside who will soon die of suffocation. But you know since they will die in their sleep, they will not feel the pain of death. Now if you cry aloud to wake a few of the lighter sleepers, making those unfortunate few suffer the agony of irrevocable death, do you think you are doing them a good turn?"

"But if a few awake, you can't say there is no hope of destroying the iron house."

True, in spite of my own conviction, I could not blot out hope, for hope lies in the future. I could not use my own evidence to refute his assertion that it might exist. So I agreed to write, and the result was my first story, *A Madman's Diary*. From that time onwards, I could not stop writing. . . .

49.3   THE IMPORTANCE OF THE PEASANT PROBLEM

Mao Zedong

Chinese intellectuals like Ch'en and Lu Hsun played an important role in revolutionizing the young, especially young, middle-class students. In many ways they helped shape the thought of a new generation. One of the members of this new generation was Mao Zedong (Mao Tse-tung) (1893–1976), who began his political activity as a student in 1915. He participated in the May 4th Movement of 1919, a student protest against the decision of the Paris Peace Conference to turn German colonies over to Japan rather than China. He participated in the organization of the Chinese Communist Party in 1921, and he directed the attention of Chinese Marxists to the importance of the peasants. While Soviet Marxism had depended on the revolutionary role of the working classes, Mao showed that a Chinese revolution depended on the peasantry. In this selection from his Report on an Investigation of the Peasant Movement in Hunan *(1927), he explains why.*

What reasons does Mao give for supporting the peasants? What signs does he show of their increasing power? Who thought the peasant revolts were "terrible"? Why did Mao disagree? Why, according to Mao, did some people think the peasants were "going too far"? Was Mao right about the peasants?

During my recent visit to Hunan I made a first-hand investigation of conditions in the five counties of Hsiangtan, Hsianghsiang, Hengshan, Liling and Changsha. In the thirty-two days from January 4 to February 5, I called together fact-finding conferences in villages and county towns, which were attended by experienced peasants and by comrades working in the peasant movement, and I listened attentively to their reports and collected a great deal of material. Many of the hows and whys of the peasant movement were the exact opposite of what the gentry in Hankow and Changsha are saying. I saw and heard of many strange things of which I had hitherto been unaware. I believe the same is true of many other places, too. All talk directed against the peasant movement must be speedily set right. All the wrong measures taken by the revolutionary authorities concerning the peasant movement must be speedily changed. Only thus can the future of the revolution be benefited. For the present upsurge of the peasant movement is a colossal event. In a very short time, in China's central, southern and northern provinces, several hundred million peasants will rise like a mighty storm, like a hurricane, a force so swift and violent that no power, however great, will be able to hold it back. They will smash all the trammels that bind them and rush forward along the road to liberation. They will sweep all the imperialists, warlords, corrupt officials, local tyrants and evil gentry into their graves. Every revolutionary party and every revolutionary comrade will be put to the test, to be accepted or rejected as they decide. There are three alternatives. To march at their head and lead them? To trail behind them, gesticulating and criticizing? Or to stand in their way and oppose them? Every Chinese is free to choose, but events will force you to make the choice quickly.

GET ORGANIZED!

The development of the peasant movement in Hunan may be divided roughly into two periods with respect to the counties in the province's central and southern parts where the movement has already made much headway. The first, from January to September of last year, was one of organization. In this period, January to June was a time of underground activity, and July to September, when the revolutionary army was driving out Chao Heng-ti,* one of open activity. During this period, the member-

*Chao Heng-ti, the ruler of Hunan, was defeated by the Northern Expeditionary Army in 1926.—Ed.

ship of the peasant associations did not exceed 300,000–400,000, the masses directly under their leadership numbered little more than a million, there was as yet hardly any struggle in the rural areas, and consequently there was very little criticism of the associations in other circles. Since its members served as guides, scouts and carriers of the Northern Expeditionary Army, even some of the officers had a good word to say for the peasant associations. The second period, from last October to January of this year, was one of revolutionary action. The membership of the associations jumped to two million and the masses directly under their leadership increased to ten million. Since the peasants generally enter only one name for the whole family on joining a peasant association, a membership of two million means a mass following of about ten million. Almost half the peasants in Hunan are now organized. In counties like Hsiangtan, Hsianghsiang, Liuyang, Changsha, Liling, Ninghsiang, Pingkiang, Hsiangyin, Hengshan, Hengyang, Leiyang, Chenhsien and Anhua, nearly all the peasants have combined in the peasant associations or have come under their leadership. It was on the strength of their extensive organization that the peasants went into action and within four months brought about a great revolution in the countryside, a revolution without parallel in history.

DOWN WITH THE LOCAL TYRANTS AND EVIL GENTRY! ALL POWER TO THE PEASANT ASSOCIATIONS!

The main targets of attack by the peasants are the local tyrants, the evil gentry and the lawless landlords, but in passing they also hit out against patriarchal ideas and institutions, against the corrupt officials in the cities and against bad practices and customs in the rural areas. In force and momentum the attack is tempestuous; those who bow before it survive and those who resist perish. As a result, the privileges which the feudal landlords enjoyed for thousands of years are being shattered to pieces. Every bit of the dignity and prestige built up by the landlords is being swept into the dust. With the collapse of the power of the landlords, the peasant associations have now become the sole organs of authority and the popular slogan "All power to the peasant associations" has become a reality. Even trifles such as a quarrel between husband and wife are brought to the peasant association. Nothing can be settled unless someone from the peasant association is present. The association actually dictates all rural affairs, and, quite literally, "whatever it says, goes." Those who are outside the associations can only speak well of them and cannot say anything against them. The local tyrants, evil gentry and lawless landlords have been deprived of all right to speak, and none of them dares even mutter dissent. In the face of the peasant associations' power and pressure, the top local tyrants and evil gentry have fled to Shanghai, those of the second rank to Hankow, those of the third to Changsha and those of the fourth to the county towns, while the fifth rank and the still lesser fry surrender to the peasant associations in the villages.

"Here's ten yuan. Please let me join the peasant association," one of the smaller of the evil gentry will say.

"Ugh! Who wants your filthy money?" the peasants reply.

Many middle and small landlords and rich peasants and even some middle peasants, who were all formerly opposed to the peasant associations, are now vainly seeking admission. Visiting various places, I often came across such people who pleaded with me, "Mr. Committeeman from the provincial capital, please be my sponsor!"

In the Ching Dynasty, the household census compiled by the local authorities consisted of a regular register and "the other" register, the former for honest people and the latter for burglars, bandits and similar undesirables. In some places the peasants now use this method to scare those who formerly opposed the associations. They say, "Put their names down in the other register!"

Afraid of being entered in the other register, such people try various devices to gain admission into the peasant associations, on which their minds are so set that they do not feel safe until their names are entered. But more often than not they are turned down flat, and so they are always on tenterhooks; with the doors of the association barred to them, they are like tramps without a home or, in rural parlance, "mere trash." In short, what was looked down upon four months ago as a "gang of peasants" has now become a most honourable institution. Those who formerly prostrated themselves before the power of the gentry now bow before the power of the peasants. No matter what their identity, all admit that the world since last October is a different one.

"IT'S TERRIBLE!" OR "IT'S FINE!"

The peasants' revolt disturbed the gentry's sweet dreams. When the news from the countryside reached the cities, it caused immediate uproar among the gentry. Soon after my arrival in Changsha, I met all sorts of people and picked up a good deal of gossip. From the middle social strata upwards to the Kuomintang* right-wingers, there was not a single person who did not sum up the whole business in the phrase, "It's terrible!" Under the impact of the views of the "It's terrible!" school then flooding the city, even quite revolutionary-minded people became downhearted as they pictured the events in the countryside in their mind's

*The Nationalist Party founded in 1912 and led by Sun Yat-sen.—Ed.

eye; and they were unable to deny the word "terrible." Even quite progressive people said, "Though terrible, it is inevitable in a revolution." In short, nobody could altogether deny the word "terrible." But, as already mentioned, the fact is that the great peasant masses have risen to fulfil their historic mission and that the forces of rural democracy have risen to overthrow the forces of rural feudalism. The patriarchal-feudal class of local tyrants, evil gentry and lawless landlords has formed the basis of autocratic government for thousands of years and is the corner-stone of imperialism, warlordism and corrupt officialdom. To overthrow these feudal forces is the real objective of the national revolution. In a few months the peasants have accomplished what Dr. Sun Yat-sen wanted, but failed, to accomplish in the forty years he devoted to the national revolution. This is a marvellous feat never before achieved, not just in forty, but in thousands of years. It's fine. It is not "terrible" at all. It is anything but "terrible." "It's terrible!" is obviously a theory for combating the rise of the peasants in the interests of the landlords; it is obviously a theory of the landlord class for preserving the old order of feudalism and obstructing the establishment of the new order of democracy, it is obviously a counter-revolutionary theory. No revolutionary comrade should echo this nonsense. If your revolutionary viewpoint is firmly established and if you have been to the villages and looked around, you will undoubtedly feel thrilled as never before. Countless thousands of the enslaved—the peasants—are striking down the enemies who battened on their flesh. What the peasants are doing is absolutely right; what they are doing is fine! "It's fine!" is the theory of the peasants and of all other revolutionaries. Every revolutionary comrade should know that the national revolution requires a great change in the countryside. The Revolution of 1911 did not bring about this change, hence its failure. This change is now taking place, and it is an important factor for the completion of the revolution. . . .

50. THE VIETNAMESE DECLARATION OF INDEPENDENCE
Ho Chi Minh

One of the many results of World War II was the stirring of independence movements in the European colonies. Many of these colonies had been

conquered by Japan during the war and entertained hopes of indepen-
dence after the defeat of Japan. Vietnam was one example. In any case,
the Vietminh, the communist-Vietnamese nationalist movement, had
fought the Japanese throughout the war. They did not expect the victori-
ous Allies to turn the colony back over to France. No one then would
have imagined that independence would have to await a nine-year war
with the French followed by twenty years of war with the United States.

What seems to be Ho Chi Minh's attitude toward the United States and
France in 1945? Notice the striking similarity of the form of the declaration
to the American Declaration of Independence. Why do you suppose he
did that?

"All men are created equal. They are endowed by their Creator with certain inalienable rights; among these are Life, Liberty, and the pursuit of Happiness."

This immortal statement was made in the Declaration of Independence of the United States of America in 1776. In a broader sense, this means: All the peoples on the earth are equal from birth, all the peoples have a right to live, to be happy and free.

The Declaration of the French Revolution made in 1791 on the Rights of Man and the Citizen also states: "All men are born free and with equal rights, and must always remain free and have equal rights."

Those are undeniable truths.

Nevertheless, for more than eighty years, the French imperialists, abusing the standard of Liberty, Equality, and Fraternity, have violated our Fatherland and oppressed our fellow-citizens. They have acted contrary to the ideals of humanity and justice.

In the field of politics, they have deprived our people of every democratic liberty.

They have enforced inhuman laws; they have set up three distinct political regimes in the North, the Center and the South of Vietnam in order to wreck our national unity and prevent our people from being united.

They have built more prisons than schools. They have mercilessly slain our patriots; they have drowned our uprisings in rivers of blood.

They have fettered public opinion; they have practised obscurantism against our people.

To weaken our race they have forced us to use opium and alcohol.

In the field of economics, they have fleeced us to the backbone, impoverished our people, and devastated our land.

They have robbed us of our rice fields, our mines, our forests, and our raw materials. They have monopolized the issuing of bank-notes and the export trade.

They have invented numerous unjustifiable taxes and reduced our people, especially our peasantry, to a state of extreme poverty.

They have hampered the prospering of our national bourgeoisie; they have mercilessly exploited our workers.

In the autumn of 1940, when the Japanese Fascists violated Indochina's territory to establish new bases in their fight against the Allies, the French imperialists went down on their bended knees and handed over our country to them.

Thus, from that date, our people were subjected to the double yoke of the French and the Japanese. Their sufferings and miseries increased. The result was that from the end of last year to the beginning of this year, from Quang Tri province to the North of Vietnam, more than two million of our fellow-citizens died from starvation. On March 9, the French troops were disarmed by the Japanese. The French colonialists either fled or surrendered, showing that not only were they incapable of "protecting" us, but that, in the span of five years, they had twice sold our country to the Japanese.

On several occasions before March 9, the Vietminh League urged the French to ally themselves with it against the Japanese. Instead of agreeing to this proposal, the French colonialists so intensified their terrorist activities against the Vietminh members that before fleeing they massacred a great number of our political prisoners detained at Yen Bay and Caobang.

Notwithstanding all this, our fellow-citizens have always manifested toward the French a tolerant and humane attitude. Even after the Japanese putsch of March 1945, the Vietminh League helped many Frenchmen to cross the frontier, rescued some of them from Japanese jails, and protected French lives and property.

From the autumn of 1940, our country had in fact ceased to be a French colony and had become a Japanese possession.

After the Japanese had surrendered to the Allies, our whole people rose to regain our national sovereignty and to found the Democratic Republic of Vietnam.

The truth is that we have wrested our independence from the Japanese and not from the French.

The French have fled, the Japanese have capitulated, Emperor Bao Dai has abdicated. Our people have broken the chains which for nearly a century have fettered them and have won independence for the Fatherland. Our people at the same time have overthrown the monarchic regime that has reigned supreme for dozens of centuries. In its place has been established the present Democratic Republic.

For these reasons, we, members of the Provisional Government, representing the whole Vietnamese people, declare that from now on we break off all relations of a colonial character with France; we repeal all the international obligation that France has so far subscribed to on behalf of Vietnam and we abolish all the special rights the French have unlawfully acquired in our Fatherland.

The whole Vietnamese people, animated by a common purpose, are determined to fight to the bitter end against any attempt by the French colonialists to reconquer their country.

We are convinced that the Allied nations which at Tehran and San Francisco have acknowledged the principles of self-determination and equality of nations, will not refuse to acknowledge the independence of Vietnam.

A people who have courageously opposed French domination for more than eight years, a people who have fought side by side with the Allies against the Fascists during these last years, such a people must be free and independent.

For these reasons, we, members of the Provisional Government of the Democratic Republic of Vietnam, solemnly declare to the world that Vietnam has the right to be a free and independent country—and in fact is so already. The entire Vietnamese people are determined to mobilize all their physical and mental strength, to sacrifice their lives and property in order to safeguard their independence and liberty.

CHAPTER FOURTEEN

Dependence and Independence in Africa and the Middle East

51. AN AFRICAN SPEAKS FOR HIS PEOPLE

Parmenias Githendu Mockerie

This newspaper article written in 1934 caused many in England to question British rule in Africa. It was written by an African journalist in British-occupied Kenya while visiting England to give testimony to a British parliamentary commission investigating conditions in East Africa. According to the author, what was the impact of British rule on East Africa? How and why did the English support tribal organization and the power of chiefs?

The population of Kenya (according to recent estimates) consists of 3,000,000 Africans, 45,000 Indians, 12,000 Arabs, 17,000 Europeans; and the area of the country is approximately 225,000 square miles. Politically, the European community is organized through the activity of the European landholders, who have district associations which combine to form the Settler's Convention of Associations, whose body is represented on the Kenya Legislature by eleven elected European members. The Indian community is represented by five and the Arab by two members. The African community has no direct representation on this official body although its direct taxation to the central government is greater than that contributed by the non-Africans.

The laws of the country, most of which affect Africans, have caused them to form organizations for furthering the interests of the African community. There are two chief societies, namely, the Kikuyu Central Association, representing the Kikuyu tribe, and the Kavirondo Taxpayers' Association, organized by the Kavirondo tribe. The idea of forming African societies originated with Mr. Harry Thuku, a Kikuyu man, who in 1921 formed a society known as the East African Association. The object of the Association was to organize African men and women to protest against the reduction of wages which was introduced in 1921 by the Convention of Associations. The rate of wages was and is ten shillings a month of thirty working days of nine hours each. The proposed reduction was thirty-three and one-third percent, that is, a laborer who earned fourpence a day would only be given two pence half-penny for working on the European plantations for nine hours. The British government of Kenya during this time had passed legislation to subject all Kenya Africans over sixteen years of age to the Kipande, a system which restricted them from moving from one place to another unless they carried pass permits on their persons, and which authorized all employers of African workers to enter their wages on the permit. This system is a great hardship to the African people, and rouses anger when the holder of the permit is treated as a criminal if he forgets to carry it on his person.

The reduction in wages produced a decline in the supply of labor on the plantations, so official pressure was thought necessary to help the farmers to secure it. Forced labor was exercised through African chiefs, whose positions as civil servants were endangered if they failed to induce the requisite number of men and women to work on European plantations.

Harry Thuku, who was the leader of the East African Association, was arrested on March 15, 1922. The East African Association declared the first strike of Nairobi workers in the history of Kenya. Men and women demonstrators marched to the Nairobi police line, where their leader was confined. The demonstration was merely a protest against his arrest, and was quite harmless, because anyone who knows that the weapons of Africans are such things as sticks, would not contemplate that the demonstration could stand up against the defense force of Kenya with machine guns and rifles. Anyhow, the demonstration grew in size and instead of being dispersed peacefully, the police force was ordered to shoot down the demonstrators. The massacre was so intense that the official report admitted that twenty-five men and women were killed on the spot, but the leaders of the demonstration collected over two hundred names of persons who received bullets and died at their homes, and in addition there were many who, although they escaped death, suffered from permanent injury because they were afraid to go to hospitals to get bullets extracted; the only two hospitals in Nairobi are controlled by the government.

Mr. Harry Thuku and his two right-hand men were deported for nine years without trial. His Association was broken up when all its leaders were arrested and imprisoned. The African workers from Uganda and Tanganyika who were members of the Association discontinued their membership, and also the Kavirondo, who had been represented in the Association, were advised by the missionaries working among them to disaffiliate from the Association. The Kavirondo therefore formed their own society, the Kavirondo Taxpayers' Association, with the assistance of a British missionary. This association was formed to prevent the Kavirondo from joining the East African Association, which was supposed to contain some elements of revolution, but it stands for the principles for which Mr. Harry Thuku was deported. The Kikuyu tribe, having found that the East African Association had been deserted, formed its own organization, the Kikuyu Central Association, which has now a membership of fifteen thousand.

The Africans of Kenya have been handicapped in organizing their own societies, owing to the restrictions imposed upon them by the government. They are not allowed freedom to speak in public or freedom to hold meetings. Naturally, Africans are discontented because they find that European and Indian associations are free to hold meetings and collect funds for furthering the interests of their own organizations without interference by the government. This discrimination between races arises out of the idea that Africans are insensible to what is right and what is wrong, and must have special laws made for them. Under the Native Authority Ordinance almost any kind of restrictive rule can be made by the administration.

The Kenya Somali community, having realized the weight of restrictions laid on Africans, have requested the government to classify them with the foreign communities such as the Arab and Indian so as to exempt them from any sort of law that affects Africans. If the Somali had seen Africans enjoying the same rights of liberty as the white man and the Indian, there would be no necessity for them to request the government to classify them with the Indian community, as they are natives of Africa. The denial of freedom of association to Africans when they have no representation on the legislature of the country cannot be quietly accepted by them. The British government have pledged themselves to guard the interests of Africans in British colonies: this should mean efforts to improve their status and education. But when we come to the application of the pledge, we find it based on abstract theory.

It has been argued that the African people can be ruled through chiefs nominated by the government. This system can hardly be satisfactory to a community which had deposed the autocracy of hereditary chiefs before European colonization. The only place in East Africa where a system of hereditary chiefs was found intact during the advent of the white man was Uganda, where the common people were still under the yoke of despotic chiefs, whereas in Kenya the people had deposed them and established tribal democracy. Uganda still has hereditary kings, who nominate district chiefs, and the common people have no say in the chieftainship; but in Kenya the government nominates the chiefs, instead of allowing the African people the right of electing their own chiefs. Thus the government has introduced a foreign idea which has robbed the people of their form of democracy. Chiefs who are nominated by European officials cannot win the confidence of the people over whom they are imposed. African political associations in East Africa, having found that the government creates reactionary chiefs without the consent of the people concerned, constantly request the government to restore the right of the people to elect their chiefs. When a chief is appointed by the government, and his administration is corrupt, the people of that district are placed in an unhappy position. They cannot take legal action against him, because of fear of reprisals, and they realize that the chief would be supported by the courts in which he himself acts as judge.

Apart from the restrictions on freedom of association, the African people suffer badly from the Native Authority Ordinance, whereby a District Administrator can issue orders in his district which he executes because he acts both as administrator and as judge. It is hard for an African to find justice.

52.   UGANDA'S WOMEN

Jane Perlez

This is a recent story from the New York Times. *It describes the plight of many women in Africa. What do you see as the causes of the pain and drudgery suffered by these women? To what extent is African polygamy the problem? To what extent is the root of the problem the need for men to find work in the cities? What should be done to improve the lives of these women?*

Namutumba, Uganda—When 28-year-old Safuyati Kawuda married the man she remembers as "handsome and elegant," her husband scraped together the bride price: five goats and three chickens. The animals represented a centuries-old custom intended to compensate Mrs. Kawuda's father for losing the labor of his daughter.

In the decade since, Mrs. Kawuda has rarely seen her husband, who long ago left this hot and dusty village for a town 70 miles away. She has accepted her husband's acquisition of two other wives and has given birth to five of his 13 children.

Instead of laboring for her father she has toiled for her husband instead—hauling firewood, fetching water, digging in the fields, producing the food the family eats, and bearing and caring for the children.

Like Mrs. Kawuda, women in rural Africa are the subsistence farmers. They produce, without tractors, oxen, or even plows, more than 70 percent of the continent's food, according to the World Bank. Backbreaking hand cultivation is a job that African men consider to be demeaning "women's work." The male responsibility is generally to sell the food the women produce. But as urbanization has stepped up, men have gone to the cities in search of other jobs, leaving women like Mrs. Kawuda alone.

MANY INEQUALITIES

The discrepancy between the physical labor of women and men is accompanied by other pervasive inequalities. In the vast majority of African countries, women do not own or inherit land. Within families, boys are encouraged to go to school, girls are not. In many places, women treat wife-beating as an accepted practice. The Uganda Women's Lawyers Association recently embarked on a campaign to convince women that wife-battering is not a sign of a man's love.

Recent surveys in Africa show other significant disparities between men and women. In 10 African countries, according to the United Nations Children's Fund, women and children together make up 77 percent of the population. Yet in only 16 percent of the households in those countries do the women have the legal right to own property.

Despite calls by the United Nations for the improvement of the lives of African women and efforts by the World Bank to finance projects focused on women, little has been done to improve the dismal status of rural women, African and Western experts say. With the continent's worsening economies in the 1980's, women suffered even more.

"The poor, the majority of whom are women, have had to take on additional work burdens in order to cope with cutbacks in social services and the increased cost of living," the Weekly Review, a magazine in Kenya, reported last year.

NO EXPECTATIONS

Mrs. Kawuda has never attended school. She cannot read or write, although her husband can. She has no radio. The farthest she has been from home is Jinja, 70 miles away. She has no expectations of a better life because she has known nothing else. But her ignorance of the outside world does not stop her from knowing her life is unrelentingly tough. She knows that in her bones.

"Everything is difficult," Mrs. Kawuda said, as she bent over to hoe cassava, her bare, rough feet splattered with dark dirt. "It's more of a problem than it used to be to find firewood. If you can't find wood on the ground, you have to cut it and there is no one to help you. Digging in the fields is the most difficult. I don't like it."

Mrs. Kawuda shares her world of perpetual fatigue with her five children; her husband's second wife, Zainabu Kasoga, 27, and her four children. Her husband's third wife—"the town wife"—lives in Jinja, where the husband, 31-year-old Kadiri Mpyanku, a tea packer, spends most of his time.

When the husband visited Mrs. Kawuda on a recent weekend, he brought enough sugar for three days and a packet of beans. Mrs. Kawuda said she was dependent on him for clothes and other essentials, and money that she said he did not always have. In most households in the area, the men also live most of the time in either Jinja or Kampala, the capital.

Here in the village, 120 miles northeast of Kampala, Mrs. Kawuda and Mrs. Kasoga run a household with another woman, the wife of their husband's brother, Sayeda Naigaga, 20, and her three children.

The women live without running water or electricity in three small, mud-wall structures. In the outdoor courtyard, life grinds on: the peeling and chopping of food, eating by adults and feeding of infants, washing, bathing, weaving and the receiving of guests all take place on the orange clay ground, packed smooth by the passage of bare feet.

In the old days, Ugandan men built separate houses for each wife, but such luxuries disappeared with the collapse of the economy. Mrs. Kawuda and her five children sleep in one room of the main shelter and Mrs. Kasoga and her four children in another. When their husband is around, he shuttles between the two bedrooms.

Mrs. Kawuda is of the Bisoga tribe, the second largest in Uganda and one where polygamy is common. Sexual and marriage mores differ in various parts of Africa. The Uganda Women's Lawyers Association estimates that 50 percent of marriages in Uganda are polygamous and, according to United Nations figures, a similar percentage exists in West Africa.

In Kenya, the Government's Women's Bureau estimates that about 30 percent of the marriages are polygamous. However, because of the economic burden of keeping several wives and families, the practice is declining, the bureau says.

Often the wives in a polygamous marriage are hostile toward each other. But perhaps as a survival instinct, Mrs. Kawuda and Mrs. Kasoga are friendly, taking turns with Mrs. Naigaga to cook for the 15-member household.

Days start with the morning ritual of collecting water. For these Ugandan women, the journey to the nearest pond takes half an hour. The six-gallon cans, when full of water, are heavy on the trip home.

Digging in the fields is the most loathed of the chores, but also the one the women feel most obliged to do since the family's food supply comes from what they grow. As they work under the sun, the women drape old pieces of clothing on their heads for protection. The youngest child, 2-year-old Suniya clings to her mother's back while Mrs. Kawuda hunches over, swinging a hoe, a sight as pervasive in rural Africa as an American mother gliding a cart along the aisles of a supermarket. "Having a baby on your back is easy," Mrs. Kawuda said. "When you are eight months pregnant and digging, it is more difficult."

VISITING HUSBAND "SUPERVISES"

There was no possibility the husband would help in the fields. It was his job to "supervise," said Mrs. Kawuda, ridiculing a suggestion that he might pitch in.

When he arrived late on a recent Saturday night, Mr. Mpyanku was treated as the imperious ruler by the children, some of whom tentatively came to greet him. He was barely acknowledged by the women, who seemed a little fearful and immediately served tea.

By early Sunday morning, he had disappeared to the nearby trading post to be with his male friends. "He has gone to discuss business with his friends," Mrs. Kawuda said. "What business can I discuss with him? Will we talk to him about digging cassava?"

Mrs. Kawuda said her husband had promised not to take any more wives. "But you never know what he thinks," she said. "I can't interfere in his affairs. If I did, he would say: 'Why is she poking her nose into my affairs?' "

Fertility and children remain at the center of rural marriage in Africa. Large numbers of children improve a household's labor pool and provide built-in security for parents in old age.

Mrs. Kawuda said she wanted one more child, in the hopes of its being another boy. After that, she said, she would use an injectible form of contraceptive. It is a method popular among African rural women because it can be used without their husband's knowledge. But in reality, contraception was an abstraction to Mrs. Kawuda since she had no idea where to get it. She had never heard of condoms.

AIDS BECOMES A CONCERN

A recent concern for African women is AIDS, which like much else in their lives they seem powerless to control. Unconvinced by her husband's assurance that he is faithful to his town wife, Mrs. Kawuda said: "He can say it's all right, we need not worry. But you never know what he does in town. He fears AIDS, too. But he messes around too much."

A worldly person compared to his wives, Mr. Mpyanku speaks reasonable English and has traveled to Kenya.

He described himself as the provider of cash for the rural family. But Mr. Mpyanku's emphasis is on his own livelihood and his urban life.

He rode the most comfortable form of transportation home, a nonstop minibus from Jinja that cost about $1.50, instead of the cheaper taxi at $1. He would do the same on his return.

Yet his oldest child, a daughter, Maliyamu, 10, missed much of her schooling last year. Her report card said her $7 in school fees had not been paid. It was a cheerless sign that Mrs. Kawuda's daughter would, like her mother, remain uneducated and repeat for another generation the cycle of female poverty and punishing physical labor.

53. SOUTH AFRICA'S NELSON MANDELA

Bill Keller

This portrait of Nelson Mandela appeared in the New York Times *on May 1, 1994, as he was elected president in the first national election in which all South Africans, black and white, voted. What kind of leader is Nelson Mandela? What seem to be the most formative influences on him? Which of his experiences best prepares him for the presidency of South Africa?*

In the final months of the 27 years he spent imprisoned for subversion, Nelson Mandela resided in a warden's bungalow at Victor Verster Prison outside Cape Town, recuperating from tuberculosis and meeting secretly with state visitors.

After his release in 1990, he built a vacation home across the road from his ancestral village, an exact brick replica of the warden's house.

An interviewer later asked him what moved him to copy his jailer's house. Nostalgia for the fraternity of the prison experience? An exercise in humility? Some superhuman gesture of forgiveness?

Nothing of the kind, Mr. Mandela replied. The choice was pure pragmatism. He had grown accustomed to the floor plan. He wanted a place where he could find the bathroom at night without stumbling in the dark.

Try as admirers will to sentimentalize Mr. Mandela, the president-in-waiting of a reborn South Africa is at heart the most practical of men.

He is not unfeeling, but passion—even anger at what he has endured—does not drive him or distract him. He enjoys debate, but he is not a great philosopher or intellectual. He has principles, but he will bend them if they stand in the way of his objective—which, for the last half century, has been ending white dominion.

He has been at points in his career a militant and a moderate, an autocrat and a democrat, an economic populist and a friend of big business. And the best guess as to what he will be as the first black president of South Africa is: whatever works.

Nelson Rolihlahla Mandela was born on July 18, 1918, in Qunu, a village of mud huts, cornfields and cattle in the eroded hills of the eastern Cape.

He was born into a royal clan of the Thembu, and after his father's death the 12-year-old Nelson was raised for the chieftainship by his cousin, the acting paramount chief of the Thembu.

"It is a place where every stone, every blade of grass, every noise made by insects is part of me," he said, reminiscing during a campaign visit to his childhood home in March. "It was here that I made my first love to a young lady. So you can see how important this area is to me."

His education at a British missionary boarding school and, later, at Fort Hare University, expanded his horizons, he said, "and I therefore now no longer attach any value to any kind of ethnicity."

But almost everyone who knows Mr. Mandela traces some aspects of his character to his royal upbringing: his formal bearing, which sometimes makes him seem hard or unapproachable; his tolerance for tradition, which has helped smooth relations between the urbanized leaders of his African National Congress and the tribal authorities who still hold sway in much of rural South Africa; and a sometimes peremptory way of making decisions that seems out of step with the painstaking collective style of the movement he leads.

But his most important chiefly legacy is a regal self-confidence in his ability to win over doubters to his point of view.

PERSUASION "HIS GIFT"

As Walter Sisulu, Mr. Mandela's oldest friend, said, "His starting point is that 'I am going to persuade this person no matter what.' That is his gift. He will go to anybody, anywhere, with that confidence. Even when he does not have a strong case, he convinces himself that he has."

At Fort Hare University, where he began law studies, he fell in with Oliver Tambo, another leader-to-be of the liberation movement. The two were suspended for a student protest in 1940.

Upon returning to his native village, Mr. Mandela discovered that his family had chosen a bride for him. Finding the woman unattractive and the prospect of a career in tribal government even more so, he ran away from home and hid in the black metropolis of Soweto.

There he called on Mr. Sisulu, who ran a real estate business and was also the local kingpin of the African National Congress.

Mr. Sisulu looked upon the visitor, a towering young man with aristocratic cheekbones, utterly self-assured, and decided his prayers had been answered.

"I had no hesitation, the moment I met him, that this is the man I need," said Mr. Sisulu, now 81 and deputy president of the African National Congress. Needed for what? "For leading the African people."

Mr. Mandela took Soweto by storm. He completed his law degree and with Mr. Tambo opened the first black law partnership in South Africa. He took up amateur boxing, arising at 4 A.M. to run roadwork through Soweto. He married a nurse, Evelyn Ntoko, and had three children.

But politics came first. Impatient with the seeming impotence of the African National Congress, Mr. Mandela, Mr. Tambo, Mr. Sisulu and other restive militants organized the A.N.C. Youth League, issuing a manifesto so charged with pan-African nationalism that some of their non-black sympathizers were offended.

"This was the trend of the youth at the time," Mr. Sisulu said. Mr. Mandela, he said, was never "an extreme nationalist" or much of a revolutionary thinker at all. He was a man of action.

TAKEOVER OF THE CONGRESS

Five years after organizing the youth league, the young rebels engineered a coup and took charge of the African National Congress.

In 1961, after the police killed 69 peaceful protesters in Sharpeville, Mr. Mandela pushed the congress onto the path of armed insurrection, becoming the first commander in chief of a new guerrilla army, Spear of the Nation.

Eight months later he was arrested, but not before his cloak-and-dagger exploits had made him a figure of township legend—the "Black Pimpernel," he was called.

The legend grew with his performance as the lead defendant in the Rivonia trial, in which eight A.N.C. leaders were sentenced to life in prison for plotting sabotage against the Government. At Mr. Mandela's suggestion, the defendants admitted the charges and turned the trial into political theater. His closing words to the court are regarded as such an eloquent summary of his creed that he recited them for a tape recording that was played to crowds at his campaign rallies this year:

"I have fought against white domination, and I have fought against black domination. I have cherished the ideal of a democratic and free society in which all persons live together in harmony and equal opportunities. It is an ideal which I hope to live for and to achieve. But if needs be, it is an ideal for which I am prepared to die."

He was 44 when he entered prison. He would be 71 when he was released.

Left behind was his second wife, a medical social worker born Nomzamo Winnie Madikizela, 16 years his junior, who was in awe of the urbane township hero—and amused that to satisfy tradition he had paid her family for her in cattle.

They produced two daughters in their brief life together before he was manacled and delivered to Robben Island Prison.

For most of their marriage they would see each other only through the glass partition of the prison visiting room. Friends say that of all the feelings Mr. Mandela keeps to himself, the most painful is the remorse at having been an absentee husband and father.

Carl Niehaus, the chief spokesman for the African National Congress, recalls that Mr. Mandela phoned for him late one night and found Mrs. Niehaus at home alone. At 5 A.M. the phone rang again. It was Mr. Mandela, calling to scold his aide: "Where were you last night, and why was your wife alone that late at night?"

Robben Island Prison, six miles off Cape Town, was a university of liberation. In whispered debates conducted in the lime quarries and in written treatises circulated from cell block to cell block, the political inmates polished their ideas and developed an old-boy network that is still an important bond.

The prison, which offered plenty of racial injustices to be protested, also honed their tactics for dealing with white authority. Mr. Mandela learned Afrikaans and urged other prisoners to do the same as a way of better understanding their oppressors.

Ahmed Kathrada, another of the Rivonia defendants, said Mr. Mandela was the undisputed leader in the prison, but people took personal problems to the more approachable Walter Sisulu.

"Mandela was highly respected, highly admired," Mr. Kathrada said. "But I would not be able to say he was as loved as Sisulu was. You know that difference between a father and a leader. That was the big difference between them."

Mr. Mandela created this aura in part by refusing to show emotion. After his mother died, fellow inmates recall seeing Mr. Mandela huddled under his blanket, sobbing quietly.

He never spoke of it until last February, when several Rivonia defendants and a legion of reporters paid a campaign visit to Robben Island, and aides persuaded Mr. Mandela to dredge up the memories.

His voice husky with emotion, he described his ailing mother's last visit in 1968.

"As she left, I looked at her as she walked to the harbor," he said. "I had the feeling that I had seen her for the last time. . . . That was the case. She died. I tried to get permission from authorities to go and bury her, but they refused."

He talked on, about the death of his elder son from his first marriage— again he was not allowed to attend the funeral—and about the guards who left newspaper clippings in his cell to let him know of the persecutions his wife and children were suffering outside.

"That was very painful," Mr. Mandela said. "Of course, wounds which cannot be seen are more painful than the ones that you can see, which can be cured by a doctor. I spent a terrible time without sharing my pain with anybody."

How Mr. Mandela emerged from such experiences without any evident bitterness is the mystery that most amazes strangers.

Mr. Sisulu, who served just four months less than Mr. Mandela and is equally lacking in vengefulness, said it was simply that the non-racial philosophy of the African National Congress had trained them not to demonize their enemies.

"Bitterness does not do your cause any good," Mr. Sisulu said. "That doesn't mean you don't get angry. But you don't let it get in the way of your policy."

Pallo Jordan, an A.N.C. intellectual who heads the department of information, adds that the most vengeful South African blacks are those who cooperated with the system.

"The people who become very embittered, and become twisted, are the people who don't resist, who go along, but who recognize somewhere deep down in their being that what they are doing is destroying them and dehumanizing them," he said.

Mr. Mandela himself says prison tempered any vengeful inclinations by exposing him to sympathetic white guards who smuggled in forbidden newspapers and extra rations, and later to the leaders of the National Party Government, who approached him in hopes of opening a dialogue.

When it came to perhaps the most momentous decision of his political leadership, Mr. Mandela behaved like a tribal chief.

He seized on a prison visit by the Justice Minister, Kobie Coetsee, to open negotiations with the Government in 1986. During his campaign visit to Robben Island last February, Mr. Mandela told reporters that if he had consulted with his comrades then, their passionate hatred of the "regime" would have caused them to reject talks.

"My comrades did not have the advantages that I had of brushing shoulders with the V.I.P.'s who came here, the judges, the Minister of Justice, the Commissioner of Prisons, and I had come to overcome my own prejudice towards them," he recalled. "So I decided to present my colleagues with a fait accompli."

The negotiations edged forward, and by the end of his prison term Mr. Mandela was himself being treated as a V.I.P. When they were not driving him to the presidential residence for meetings with President F. W. de Klerk, his custodians were taking him on jaunts into town or the coast.

"The warders were bored," Mr. Mandela said. "They were looking after one prisoner. They had nothing to do. They would say, 'Mandela, we must take you to a specialist in town,' and we would go out and go all the way to Saldanha Bay." That is 60 miles up the Atlantic Coast.

Upon his release in February 1990, Mr. Mandela found that the African National Congress had changed, metastasizing into a variety of fiefs and surrogates no longer so easily susceptible to the leadership of tribal elders.

FOUR YEARS OF TALKS

The negotiations that ensued over the next four years were only partly with the Government. They also involved a laborious jawboning of his own comrades.

Mr. Mandela's style in both negotiations was the opposite of autocratic—endless, patient consultation, until passions were spent and a general consensus emerged.

The fiercest internal debate came over a proposal floated by Joe Slovo, the Communist Party chairman, to offer the white government a "sunset clause" allowing the opposition parties to share power and the civil service to keeps its jobs for five years.

Pallo Jordan was the most outspoken opponent, arguing that the inherited civil service would be a constant source of resistance to the new Government's policies.

No one doubted that Mr. Mandela favored the concession, but he declined to take a position until the issue had been exhaustively debated.

"At every step in the internal debate in the organization, he wanted me to be present," Mr. Jordan said. Finally a consensus emerged behind the plan, and it became the key to a deal with the Government. Mr. Jordan, having had his say, bowed to party discipline and to this day refuses to criticize the bargain.

For all his insistence that he is part of a "collective" that no individual should be singled out, and that the recent election campaign was really about his party's plan for governing, it is Mr. Mandela himself who embodies the aspirations of the black majority.

Early in the grueling election campaign, his campaign handlers created a format of "people's forums," in which Mr. Mandela and several other leaders fielded questions from the public.

After audiences complained, the forums were revised so that Mr. Mandela alone fielded the questions. Voters were not interested in a collective.

"On the ground, at these rallies, when Mandela comes it's 'the messiah has arrived,'" said Stanley Greenburg, a White House polling expert who has advised the A.N.C. campaign.

Some in the organization find it frightening that the new Government's credibility—its hopes of a honeymoon—depend so much on one, 75-year-old man.

Not that he seems less than durable.

He wears a hearing aid and orthopedic socks, and sometimes after a 12-hour day of campaigning he faded badly into semi-coherence. But his health and alertness generally appeared to be remarkable. He operates on four hours of sleep, and aides say they can expect phone calls from him any time bewteen 4 A.M. and 1 A.M.

The election campaign showed that he can still learn new tricks: looking into a television camera to convey warmth, curbing his didactic habit of jabbing the air with his finger, and most difficult of all, speaking to strangers about his feelings, because that is what the world expects of modern candidates.

PERSONAL LIFE OFF LIMITS

Up to a point. He refuses to talk about his personal life, rebuffing all questions about his estranged wife, Winnie, who has rebounded from a kidnapping conviction to the certainty of a seat in Parliament.

Although Mrs. Mandela has hinted at a possible reconciliation, friends of Mr. Mandela say that is unlikely. They say he has been keeping company with Graca Simbine Machel, the widow of Samora Machel, the late President of Mozambique.

For more than a year, Mr. Mandela has straddled the roles of president-in-waiting and opposition leader, of statesman and partisan.

One day he is the liberation leader, playing to keep the angry militants on his side, castigating President de Klerk for the sins of apartheid and accusing him of racist indifference to the miserable lives and violent deaths of those in the black majority.

The next day he is the patriarch, upbraiding the looters and vigilantes among his own followers.

As president he will be free to find a new balance.

In interviews during the election, he underscores the role of consensus-maker and negotiator, but the instincts of the royal upbringing remain, and some among his admirers believe that they will surface.

"I always tell these rebellious, young, undisciplined black students, when this tribal chief from the Transkei becomes president, he will not stand all this," said Dr. Nthato Motlana, a physician who has been close to the family for four decades. "He is going to say, 'You go to school, you study, you learn. This is a legitimate government, and you're going to start behaving.' Mandela, I hope, will do that.

"I am absolutely and utterly convinced that the essential ingredient of the success of this country is going to be Mandela's ability to call this country to order."

54. AFRICAN ART AND IDENTITY

Kwame Anthony Appiah

In this selection, a modern African philosopher explores the meaning of an African identity, style, or work of art in an age of global cultural interaction. Note the rich ironies in the opening discussion of an American exhibition of African art. What does the author make of the roles of the Baule artist and David Rockefeller as curators or judges for the exhibit? What do Professor Appiah and James Baldwin seem to like about Yoruba Man with a Bicycle? *(see page 227). What point is the author making about African identity?*

In 1987 the Center for African Art in New York organized a show entitled *Perspectives: Angles on African Art.* The curator, Susan Vogel, had worked with a number of "cocurators," whom I list in order of their appearance in the table of contents: Ekpo Eyo, quondam director of the Department of Antiquities of the National Museum of Nigeria; William Rubin, director of painting and sculpture at the Museum of Modern Art and organizer of its controversial Primitivism exhibit; Romare Bearden, African-American painter; Ivan Karp, curator of African ethnology at the Smithsonian; Nancy Graves, European-American painter, sculptor, and filmmaker; James Baldwin, who surely needs no qualifying glosses; David Rockefeller, art collector and friend of the mighty; Lela Kouakou, Baule artist and diviner, from Ivory Coast (this a delicious juxtaposition, richest and poorest, side by side); Iba N'Diaye, Senegalese sculptor; and Robert Farris Thompson, Yale professor and African and African-American art historian. Vogel describes the process of selection in her introductory essay. The one woman and nine men were each offered a hundred-odd photographs of "African Art as varied in type and origin and as high in quality, as we could manage" and asked to select ten for the show. Or, I should say more exactly, that this is what was offered to eight of the men. For Vogel adds, "In the case of the Baule artist, a man familiar only with the art of his own people, only Baule objects were placed in the pool of photographs." At this point we are directed to a footnote to the essay, which reads:

> Showing him the same assortment of photos the others saw would have been interesting, but confusing in terms of the reactions we sought here. Field aesthetic studies, my own and others, have shown that African informants will criticize sculptures from other ethnic groups in terms of their own traditional criteria, often assuming that such works are simply inept carvings of their own aesthetic tradition.

I shall return to this irresistible footnote in a moment. But let me pause to quote further, this time from the words of David Rockefeller, who would surely never "criticize sculptures from other ethnic groups in terms of [his] own traditional criteria," discussing what the catalog calls a "Fante female figure":

> I own somewhat similar things to this and I have always liked them. This is a rather more sophisticated version than the ones that I've seen, and I thought it was quite beautiful . . . the total composition has a very contemporary, very Western look to it. It's the kind of thing that goes very well with contemporary Western things. It would look good in a modern apartment or house.

We may suppose that David Rockefeller was delighted to discover that his final judgment was consistent with the intentions of the sculpture's creators. For a footnote to the earlier "Checklist" reveals that the Baltimore Museum of Art desires to "make public the fact that the authenticity of the Fante figure in its collection has been challenged." Indeed, work by Doran Ross suggests this object is almost certainly a modern piece introduced in my hometown of Kumasi by the workshop of a certain Francis Akwasi, which "specializes in carvings for the international market in the style of traditional sculpture. Many of its works are now in museums throughout the West, and were published as authentic by Cole and Ross" (yes, the same Doran Ross) in their classic catalog *The Arts of Ghana*.

But then it is hard to be *sure* what would please a man who gives as his reason for picking another piece (this time a Senufo helmet mask), "I have to say I picked this because I own it. It was given to me by President Houphouet Boigny of Ivory Coast." Or one who remarks, "concerning the market in African art":

> The best pieces are going for very high prices. Generally speaking, the less good pieces in terms of quality are not going up in price. And that's a fine reason for picking the good ones rather than the bad. They have a way of becoming more valuable.
>
> I like African art as objects I find would be appealing to use in a home or an office. . . . I don't think it goes with everything, necessarily—although the very best perhaps does. But I think it goes well with contemporary architecture.

There is something breathtakingly unpretentious in Mr. Rockefeller's easy movement between considerations of finance, of aesthetics, and of decor. In these responses we have surely a microcosm of the site of the African in contemporary—which is, then, surely to say, postmodern—America.

I have given so much of David Rockefeller not to emphasize the familiar fact that questions of what we call "aesthetic" value are crucially bound up with market value; not even to draw attention to the fact that this is known by those who play the art market. Rather, I want to keep clearly before us the fact that David Rockefeller is permitted to say *anything at all* about the arts of Africa because he is a *buyer* and because he is at the *center*, while Lela Kouakou, who merely makes art and who dwells at the margins, is a poor African whose words count only as parts of the commodification—both for those of us who constitute the museum public and for collectors, like Rockefeller—of Baule art. I want to remind you, in short, of how important it is that African art is a *commodity*.

But the cocurator whose choice will set us on our way is James Baldwin—the only cocurator who picked a piece that was not in the mold of the Africa of the exhibition Primitivism, a sculpture that will be my touchstone, a piece labeled by the museum *Yoruba Man with a Bicycle*. Here is some of what Baldwin said about it:

> This is something. This has got to be contemporary. He's really going to town. It's very jaunty, very authoritative. His errand might prove to be impossible. He is challenging something—or something has challenged him. He's grounded in immediate reality by the bicycle. . . . He's apparently a very proud and silent man. He's dressed sort of polyglot. Nothing looks like it fits him too well.

Baldwin's reading of this piece is, of course and inevitably, "in terms of [his] own . . . criteria," a reaction contextualized only by the knowledge that bicycles are new in Africa and that this piece, anyway, does not look anything like the works he recalls seeing from his earliest childhood at the Schomburg museum in Harlem. And his response torpedoes Vogel's argument for her notion that the only "authentically traditional" African—the only one whose responses, as she says, could have been found a century ago—must be refused a choice among Africa's art cultures because he, unlike the rest of the cocurators, who are Americans and the European-educated Africans, will use his "own . . . criteria." This Baule diviner, this authentically African villager, the message is, does not know what *we*, authentic postmodernists, now know: that the first and last mistake is to judge the Other on one's own terms. And so, in the name of this, the relativist insight, we impose our judgment that Lela Kouakou may not judge sculpture from beyond the Baule culture zone because he will—like all the other African "informants" we have met in the field—read them as if they meant to meet those Baule standards.

Worse than this, it is nonsense to explain Lela Kouakou's responses as deriving from an ignorance of other traditions—if indeed he is, as he is no doubt supposed to be, like most "traditional" artists today, if he is like, for example, Francis Akwasi of Kumasi. Kouakou may judge other artists by his own standards (what on earth else could he, could anyone, do, save make no judgment at all?), but to suppose that he is unaware that there are other standards within Africa (let alone without) is to ignore a piece of absolutely basic cultural knowledge, common to most precolonial as to most colonial and postcolonial cultures on the continent—the

piece of cultural knowledge that explains why the people we now call
"Baule" exist at all. To be Baule, for example, is, for a Baule, not to be a
white person, not to be Senufo, not to be French. The ethnic groups—
Lele Kouakou's Baule "tribe," for example—within which all African
aesthetic life apparently occurs, are . . . the products of colonial and
postcolonial articulations. And someone who knows enough to make
himself up as a Baule for the twentieth century surely knows that there
are other kinds of art.

But Baldwin's *Yoruba Man with a Bicycle* does more than give the lie to
Vogel's strange footnote; it provides us with an image of an object that
can serve as a point of entry to my theme: a piece of contemporary
African art that will allow us to explore the articulation of the postcolonial and the postmodern. *Yoruba Man with a Bicycle* is described as follows
in the catalog:

Page 124
Man with a Bicycle
Yoruba, Nigeria 20th century
Wood and paint H. 35¾ in.
The Newark Museum

The influence of the Western world is revealed in the clothes and bicycle of
this neo-traditional Yoruba sculpture which probably represents a merchant
en route to market.

And it is this word *neotraditional*—a word that is almost right—that provides, I think, the fundamental clue.

I do not know when the *Yoruba Man with a Bicycle* was made or by
whom; African art has, until recently, been collected as the property of
"ethnic" groups, not of individuals and workshops, so it is not unusual
that not one of the pieces in the Perspectives show was identified in the
"Checklist" by the name of an individual artist, even though many of
them are twentieth-century (and no one will have been surprised, by
contrast, that most of them *are* kindly labeled with the name of the
people who own the largely private collections where they now live). As a
result I cannot say if the piece is literally postcolonial, produced after
Nigerian independence in 1960. But the piece belongs to a genre that
has certainly been produced since then: the genre that is here called
neotraditional. And, simply put, what is distinctive about this genre is that
it is produced for the West.

I should qualify. Of course, many of the buyers of first instance live in
Africa, many of them are juridically citizens of African states. But African bourgeois consumers of neotraditional art are educated in the Western style, and, if they want African art, they would often rather have a
"genuinely" traditional piece—by which I mean a piece that they believe

to be made precolonially, or at least in a style and by methods that were already established precolonially. And these buyers are a minority. Most of this art, which is *traditional* because it uses actually or supposedly precolonial techniques, but is *neo*—this, for what it is worth, is the explanation I promised earlier—because it has elements that are recognizably from the colonial or postcolonial in reference, has been made for Western tourists and other collectors. . . .

For all the while, in Africa's cultures, there are those who will not see themselves as Other. Despite the overwhelming reality of economic decline; despite unimaginable poverty; despite wars, malnutrition, disease, and political instability, African cultural productivity grows apace: popular literatures, oral narrative and poetry, dance, drama, music, and visual art all thrive. The contemporary cultural production of many African societies—and the many traditions whose evidences so vigorously remain—is an antidote to the dark vision of the postcolonial novelist.

And I am grateful to James Baldwin for his introduction to the *Yoruba Man with a Bicycle*—a figure who is, as Baldwin so rightly saw, polyglot, speaking Yoruba and English, probably some Hausa and a little French for his trips to Cotonou or Cameroon; someone whose "clothes do not fit him too well." He and the other men and women among whom he mostly lives suggest to me that the place to look for hope is not just to the postcolonial novel—which has struggled to achieve the insights of a Ouologuem or Mudimbe [African novelists]— but to the all-consuming vision of this less-anxious creativity. It matters little who it was made *for;* what we should learn from is the imagination that produced it. The *Man with a Bicycle* is produced by someone who does not care that the bicycle is the white man's invention—it is not there to be Other to the Yoruba Self; it is there because someone cared for its solidity; it is there because it will take us further than our feet will take us; it is there because machines are now as African as novelists.

55. PALESTINE AND ISRAEL:
55.1. ARAB OPPOSITION TO A
STATE OF ISRAEL

After the defeat of the Ottoman Empire in World War I, the League of Nations gave Great Britain a mandate to administer the region known as

Palestine. British rule was beset by, on one hand, pressure from the Zionist movement to establish a Jewish homeland in Palestine and, on the other, pressure from Palestinian Arabs and neighboring Arab states to resist the Zionist demands. In the meantime, Zionist-inspired Jewish immigration to Palestine—mainly from Europe—continued and then increased with the rise of anti-Semitism after Hitler's coming to power in Germany in 1933. As World War II ended, the situation in Palestine worsened: both Zionist and Arab pressures intensified, with both sides resorting sometimes to violence. The horrendous experience of the Jewish people in Europe under Hitler's murderous rule naturally added to the difficulty of resolving the problem.

In November 1945 the United States and Great Britain established a commission to investigate the issue. This reading contains a portion of the Arab presentation to the commission. Why did Arabs oppose a Jewish state? What claims to Palestine did they make? Would they have accepted a nonreligious state that included Jews and Arabs? Was any compromise possible at this point? Why did the Arabs oppose the partition of Palestine?

1. The whole Arab people is unalterably opposed to the attempt to impose Jewish immigration and settlement upon it, and ultimately to establish a Jewish State in Palestine. Its opposition is based primarily upon right. The Arabs of Palestine are descendants of the indigenous inhabitants of the country, who have been in occupation of it since the beginning of history; they cannot agree that it is right to subject an indigenous population against its will to alien immigrants, whose claim is based upon a historical connection which ceased effectively many centuries ago. Moreover they form the majority of the population; as such they cannot submit to a policy of immigration which if pursued for long will turn them from a majority into a minority in an alien state; and they claim the democratic right of a majority to make its own decisions in matters of urgent national concern.

2. . . . .The entry of incessant waves of immigrants prevents normal economic and social development and causes constant dislocation of the country's life; in so far as it reacts upon prices and values and makes the whole economy dependent upon the constant inflow of capital from abroad it may even in certain circumstances lead to economic disaster. It is bound moreover to arouse continuous political unrest and prevent the establishment of that political stability on which the prosperity and health of the country depend. This unrest is likely to increase in frequency and violence as the Jews come nearer to being the majority and the Arabs a minority.

Even if economic and social equilibrium is reestablished, it will be to the detriment of the Arabs. The superior capital resources at the disposal of the Jews, their greater experience of modern economic technique and the existence of a deliberate policy of expansion and domination have already gone far toward giving them the economic mastery of Palestine. The biggest concessionary companies are in their hands; they possess a large proportion of the total cultivable land, and an even larger one of the land in the highest category of fertility; and the land they possess is mostly inalienable to non-Jews. The continuance of land-purchase and immigration, taken together with the refusal of Jews to employ Arabs on their lands or in their enterprises and the great increase in the Arab population, will create a situation in which the Arab population is pushed to the margin of cultivation and a landless proletariat, rural and urban, comes into existence. This evil can be palliated but not cured by attempts at increasing the absorptive capacity or the industrial production of Palestine; the possibility of such improvements is limited, they would take a long time to carry out, and would scarcely do more than keep pace with the rapid growth of the Arab population; moreover in present circumstances they would be used primarily for the benefit of the Jews and thus might increase the disparity between the two communities.

Nor is the evil economic only. Zionism is essentially a political movement, aiming at the creation of a state: immigration, land-purchase and economic expansion are only aspects of a general political strategy. If Zionism succeeds in its aim, the Arabs will become a minority in their own country; a minority which can hope for no more than a minor share in the government, for the state is to be a Jewish state, and which will find itself not only deprived of that international status which the other Arab countries possess but cut off from living contact with the Arab world of which it is an integral part. . . .

8. In the Arab view, any solution of the problem created by Zionist aspirations must satisfy certain conditions:

(i) It must recognize the right of the indigenous inhabitants of Palestine to continue in occupation of the country and to preserve its traditional character.

(ii) It must recognize that questions like immigration, which affect the whole nature and destiny of the country, should be decided in accordance with democratic principles by the will of the population.

(iii) It must accept the principle that the only way by which the will of the population can be expressed is through the establishment of responsible representative Government. (The Arabs find something inconsistent in the attitude of Zionists who demand the establishment of a free democratic commonwealth in Palestine and then hasten to add that this should not take place until the Jews are in a majority.)

(iv) This representative Government should be based upon the principle of absolute equality of all citizens irrespective of race and religion.

(v) The form of Government should be such as to make possible the development of a spirit of loyalty and cohesion among all elements of the community, which will override all sectional attachments. In other words it should be a Government which the whole community could regard as their own, which should be rooted in their consent and have a moral claim upon their obedience.

(vi) The settlement should recognize the fact that by geography and history Palestine is inescapably part of the Arab world; that the only alternative to its being part of the Arab world and accepting the implications of its position is complete isolation, which would be disastrous from every point of view; and that whether they like it or not the Jews in Palestine are dependent upon the goodwill of the Arabs.

(vii) The settlement should be such as to make possible a satisfactory definition within the framework of U.N.O. of the relations between Palestine and the Western Powers who possess interests in the country.

(viii) The settlement should take into account that Zionism is essentially a political movement aiming at the creation of a Jewish state and should therefore avoid making any concession which might encourage Zionists in the hope that this aim can be achieved in any circumstances.

The idea of partition and the establishment of a Jewish state in a part of Palestine is inadmissible for the same reasons of principle as the idea of establishing a Jewish state in the whole country. If it is unjust to the Arabs to impose a Jewish state on the whole of Palestine, it is equally unjust to impose it in any part of the country. Moreover, as the Woodhead Commission showed, there are grave practical difficulties in the way of partition; commerce would be strangled, communications dislocated and the public finances upset. It would also be impossible to devise frontiers which did not leave a large Arab minority in the Jewish state. This minority would not willingly accept its subjection to the Zionists, and it would not allow itself to be transferred to the Arab state. Moreover, partition would not satisfy the Zionists. It cannot be too often repeated that Zionism is a political movement aiming at the domination at least of the whole of Palestine; to give it a foothold in part of Palestine would be to encourage it to press for more and to provide it with a base for its activities. Because of this, because of the pressure of population and in order to escape from its isolation it would inevitably be thrown into enmity with the surrounding Arab states and this enmity would disturb the stability of the whole Middle East.

55.2. ISRAEL'S PROCLAMATION OF INDEPENDENCE

The Anglo-American commission failed to resolve the problem. In 1947 Britain informed the United Nations, which had replaced the League of Nations, that it could not continue indefinitely to administer Palestine. The United Nations then called for the partition of Palestine into Jewish and Arab states. On May 14, 1948, the Jews of Palestine proclaimed the independent State of Israel. The next day—when British authority officially ended—armies from the Arab nations invaded Israel. But the Arabs were defeated. At the end of the war, Israel controlled 77 percent of the former Palestine rather than the 57 percent the United Nations had allotted to a Jewish state. In the course of the war, 900,000 of the 1,300,000 Arabs who had been living in the Israeli part of Palestine became refugees.

What reasons does the document below give for the establishment of Israel? What provision does the new state seem ready to make for Palestinian Arabs? Do these differ from the rights of Jews?

The Land of Israel was the birthplace of the Jewish people. Here their spiritual, religious and national identity was formed. Here they achieved independence and created a culture of national and universal significance. Here they wrote and gave the Bible to the world.

Exiled from the Land of Israel the Jewish people remained faithful to it in all the countries of their dispersion, never ceasing to pray and hope for their return and the restoration of their national freedom.

Impelled by this historic association, Jews strove throughout the centuries to go back to the land of their fathers and regain their statehood. In recent decades they returned in their masses. They reclaimed the wilderness, revived their language, built cities and villages, and established a vigorous and ever-growing community, with its own economic and cultural life. They sought peace, yet were prepared to defend themselves. They brought the blessings of progress to all inhabitants of the country and looked forward to sovereign independence.

In the year 1897 the First Zionist Congress, inspired by Theodor Herzl's vision of the Jewish State, proclaimed the right of the Jewish people to national revival in their own country.

This right was acknowledged by the Balfour Declaration of November 2, 1917, and re-affirmed by the Mandate of the League of Nations, which gave explicit international recognition to the historic connection to the Jewish people with Palestine and their right to reconstitute their National Home.

The recent holocaust, which engulfed millions of Jews in Europe, proved anew the need to solve the problem of the homelessness and lack of independence of the Jewish people by means of the reestablishment of the Jewish State, which would open the gates to all Jews and endow the Jewish people with equality of status among the family of nations.

The survivors of the disastrous slaughter in Europe, and also Jews from other lands, have not desisted from their efforts to reach Eretz-Yisrael, in face of difficulties, obstacles and perils; and have not ceased to urge their right to a life of dignity, freedom and honest toil in their ancestral land.

In the second World War the Jewish people in Palestine made their full contribution to the struggle of the freedom-loving nations against the Nazi evil. The sacrifices of their soldiers and their war effort gained them the right to rank with the nations which founded the United Nations.

On November 29, 1947, the General Assembly of the United Nations adopted a Resolution requiring the establishment of a Jewish State in Palestine. The General Assembly called upon the inhabitants of the country to take all the necessary steps on their part to put the plan into effect. This recognition by the United Nations of the right of the Jewish people to establish their independent State is unassailable.

It is the natural right of the Jewish people to lead, as do all other nations, an independent existence in its sovereign State.

Accordingly we, the members of the National Council, representing the Jewish people in Palestine and the World Zionist Movement, are met together in solemn assembly today, the day of termination of the British Mandate for Palestine; and by virtue of the natural and historic right of the Jewish people and of the Resolution of the General Assembly of the United Nations.

We hereby proclaim the establishment of the Jewish State in Palestine, to be called Medinath Yisrael (The State of Israel).

The State of Israel will be open to the immigration of Jews from all countries of their dispersion; will promote the development of the country for the benefit of all its inhabitants; will be based on the principles of liberty, justice and peace as conceived by the Prophets of Israel; will uphold the full social and political equality of all its citizens, without distinction of religion, race, or sex; will guarantee freedom of religion, conscience, education and culture; will safeguard the Holy Places of all religions; and will loyally uphold the principles of the United Nations Charter.

The State of Israel will be ready to co-operate with the organs and representatives of the United Nations in the implementation of the Resolution of the Assembly of November 29, 1947, and will take steps to bring about the Economic Union over the whole of Palestine.

We appeal to the United Nations to assist the Jewish people in the building of its State and to admit Israel into the family of nations.

In the midst of wanton aggression [by Arab states], we yet call upon the Arab inhabitants of the State of Israel to preserve the ways of peace and play their part in the development of the State, on the basis of full and equal citizenship and due representation in all its bodies and institutions—provisional and permanent.

We extend our hand in peace, and neighbourliness to all the neighbouring states and their peoples, and invite them to cooperate with the independent Jewish nation for the common good of all. The State of Israel is prepared to make its contribution to the progress of the Middle East as a whole.

Our call goes out to the Jewish people all over the world to rally to our side in the task of immigration and development, and to stand by us in the great struggle for the fulfilment of the dream of generations for the redemption of Israel.

CHAPTER FIFTEEN

Dependence and Independence in the Americas

56. REVOLUTION AND THE INTELLECTUAL IN LATIN AMERICA

Alan Riding

The role of the writer, artist, or intellectual in Latin America is different from what it is in the United States. Intellectuals are more respected and popular than in the United States, and they are more actively concerned with political issues. Many, in fact, serve as political advisers. These are some of the conclusions of this essay. Why does this seem to be the case? What in Latin American history accounts for this difference? Has this ever been the case in the United States, or elsewhere? Under what circumstances? What other social classes play important political roles in Latin America and the United States?

While Latin American intellectuals vary from communists to supporters of the United States, the majority of them appear to be socialists. Why is this? Why are there so few supporters of a strong U.S. role in the hemisphere?

On his way from Mexico City to Stockholm to receive the 1982 Nobel Prize in Literature, and again on the way back, Gabriel García Márquez stopped over in Cuba to see his close friend and political mentor, Fidel Castro. The Colombian novelist is a frequent traveler to Havana, but these two visits took on special significance: He was emphasizing his political identification with Cuba at the moment of his greatest literary glory.

In contrast, Octavio Paz, the Mexican poet and essayist, has not visited Havana since the 1959 Cuban revolution. He once sympathized with the announced objectives of the new regime, but became disenchanted when, in his words, the revolution was "confiscated" by Marxists. He now considers the Cuban people no more fortunate than they were before the overthrow of the rightist dictatorship of Fulgencio Batista.

García Márquez and Paz live seven miles apart in Mexico City and are great admirers of each other's writing, but they are no longer close friends. Politics, their common obsession, has divided them. They have become symbols of the two opposing views in the rising political debate among Latin America's intellectuals.

At the heart of the polemic is the search for new political models for a continent viewed by the intellectuals as desperately in need of change. Latin America's writers, artists and academics look about them and see country after country locked into political systems that eliminate freedom in the name of fighting Communism—or, conversely, in the name of combating United States "imperialism." They see economic structures that condemn millions to perpetual poverty—except where leftist revolutions have brought programs of social betterment at the cost of political liberty. Positions are often expressed through sympathy for—or doubts about—Castro's Cuba, Sandinist Nicaragua and the guerrilla movements in El Salvador and Guatemala. But more complex dilemmas are also involved, confronting politics and morality, testing loyalty and honesty and raising troubling questions about justice and freedom.

What gives the debate its importance is that intellectuals exercise enormous political influence in Latin America. It is they who provide respectability to governments in power and legitimacy to revolts and revolutionary movements, they who articulate the ideas and contribute the images through which Latin Americans relate to power, they who satisfy the decidedly Latin need for a romantic and idealistic raison d'être.

Literary fame, then, has given political clout not only to García Márquez and Paz but to other writers—Jorge Luis Borges, Julio Cortázar, Carlos Fuentes and Mario Vargas Llosa among them—whose works constitute the contemporary Latin American literary boom. And their activism is emulated by hundreds of less-known intellectuals who consider themselves the political conscience of society.

Most of these intellectuals feel drawn to the left. Few are card-carrying Communists, but most of them accept García Márquez's view of the United States as the main obstacle to political and social change in Latin America. In line with this conviction, they vociferate their criticism of Washington and its right-wing allies in the hemisphere and swallow their reservations about the Cuban and Nicaraguan revolutions.

Ranged against them in the debate is a minority of intellectuals who equate dictatorships of the left and the right. For them, Cuba's Castro is as bad as Chile's Gen. Augusto Pinochet Ugarte. Yet one seldom hears them defending United States policy, and their general viewpoint seems to be one of a socialist ideal far removed from the reality of the region. The lines that divide the two camps are often blurred, and as much energy is dedicated to arguing various socialist options as to debating the merits of Marxism and capitalism.

"Why is it like this?" Mario Vargas Llosa, the Peruvian novelist, asked in a recent essay. "Why is it that instead of being basically creators and artists, writers in Peru and other Latin American countries must above all be politicians, agitators, reformers, social publicists and moralists?"

The question may be even more puzzling to people in the United States, where the political influence of writers and other intellectuals is exercised far more subtly and indirectly, and politics mainly has to do with specific issues rather than ideologies. Successive administrations in Washington have ignored the swirling debate in Latin America, or viewed it with deep suspicion, denying García Márquez and many other authors permanent visas for unrestricted entry into the United States.

There is a certain irony in this, for García Márquez, though fiercely critical of Washington's hemispheric policies, is a strong champion of United States culture. Having lived in Paris in the mid-1950's, he feels that European thought has become a prisoner of abstractions, that "the era of Sartre and Camus has long been over," and that "Americans are the literary giants of the 20th century." Acknowledging William Faulkner as his literary mentor, he holds that "there is no way one can relate to contemporary cultural life without going to the United States." All the greater, then, his frustration over the State Department's restrictive rules.

The problem, however, is not limited to American visa regulations. By holding aloof from this hidden dimension of the region's politics, the United States is passing up an opportunity to present its case to Latin America's principal opinion molders—a failure in the exercise of influence that could have large political consequences. These Latin writers are wrestling with issues—endemic poverty, human rights, chronic militarism and the conflict between left and right—that are of universal concern. Intellectuals may not be the principal actors in the Latin drama, but they define the issues. Before causes win out, it is their ideas that triumph. Nothing less than the continent's long-range political evolution may be at stake.

The Latin intellectual's position grows out of the society in which he lives. In a region characterized by weak social institutions, inadequate public education and little democratic tradition, intellectuals automatically belong to a prestigious elite. And because Latin American politics invariably revolves around personalities, men of talent are looked to for wisdom and leadership.

Taken together, the intellectuals of Latin America form a kind of unofficial parliament in which the major political events of the day are discussed, integrated into the regional agenda, or allowed to fade from the public consciousness. The Falkland Islands war of 1982 is a case in point. At the time, the intellectual community was sharply divided between those who refused to support a repressive Argentine military regime, despite their acceptance of Argentine claims to sovereignty over the islands, and those who thought that British "aggression" from across the seas required hemispheric solidarity. Yet the Falkland war never engaged the intellectuals deeply, and, less than a year later, it has left little trace in the public mind.

This kind of political eminence rarely brings wealth—few Latin writers can survive on their royalties and only García Márquez, whose books have been translated into many languages, can be called rich. But it does make writers into powerful political symbols, particularly if they have been recognized abroad, and few of today's top Latin American authors show many qualms about making full use of this power. The Mexican writer Juan Rulfo, who seems almost bashful about the renown that his novel, *Pedro Páramo*, brought him, is one of a small handful of writers who prefer to keep out of the limelight. The others usually separate their activism from their creativity and use journalism as their principal political vehicle. And they clearly feel a strong need to speak out and to be heard. It is as if they see themselves mirrored in the power structure and become hypnotized by their image.

García Márquez, at 54, remains the most active of the continent's writer-politicians, frequently to be seen in the company of world leaders from Managua to New Delhi. A stocky man with wiry hair and a mischievous smile, he clearly relishes his fame. Yet, brought up in the steamy political parlors of Colombia's Caribbean coast, he prefers, in his words, the intrigue of "secret diplomacy," as if politics were the art of whispering.

Prior to the 1979 Nicaraguan revolution, for example, he served as a secret intermediary between the Sandinists and several governments of the region. Around the same time, he privately negotiated the release of numerous political prisoners in Cuba. More recently, he has been "conspiring," as he puts it, to promote peace talks between El Salvador's warring factions.

But he has never been attracted by political office. In the late 1970's, he turned down an invitation from a coalition of leftist parties to run for the presidency of Colombia. Late last year [1982], he declined an ambassadorship offered him by Colombia's new President, Belisario Betancur. Instead, he is planning to invest his Nobel Prize money in founding a newspaper in Bogotá. "I am an emergency politician," he explains. "If I were not a Latin American, I would not be in politics. But how can the intellectual enjoy the luxury of debating the destiny of the soul when the problems are of physical survival, health, education, ignorance and so on?"

Octavio Paz, in contrast, rarely leaves his apartment on the Paseo de la Reforma, Mexico City's principal avenue. He is a gentle man, but is no less consumed by politics than García Márquez. For more than 20 years, he served as a Mexican diplomat, resigning as Ambassador to India in

1968 to protest the Mexican Army's bloody suppression of an anti-Government student movement. Now, at the age of 68, with a lifetime of political activity behind him, he prefers to sit in his book-lined study, surrounded by Asian art, and to dedicate himself to writing poetry and political and philosophical essays.

He edits the literary and political monthly Vuelta, and until recently he delivered political commentaries on Mexico's main television channel. But he sees his principal role as one of simply thinking. "Very few Latin American intellectuals of the left or the right have done much thinking," he says. "Very few. It's a serious reflection. They spout commonplaces. I don't reproach García Márquez for using his skill as a writer to defend his ideas. I reproach him because his ideas are poor. There is an enormous difference between what I do and what García Márquez does. I try to think and he repeats slogans."

As a general rule, the writers join their political activity with prolific literary output—and, at times, their books, too, have broad political impact. For example, García Márquez and the late novelists Miguel Angel Asturias and Alejo Carpentier all wrote about the phenomenon of the old-fashioned Latin American dictator—*el caudillo*—and turned him into a figure of ridicule. Many writers are so prominent as public figures—García Márquez and Paz are good examples—that they have a political following among people who have not read their books.

While they come from different countries, the writers' audience is continental, not only because they project a strong sense of a common Latin American identity but because the issues they raise are familiar throughout the region. Almost without exception, they write widely syndicated columns and give frequent interviews—more often about politics than about literature—that are read across Latin America. They frequently gather at conferences that issue sweeping declarations on world issues. And while their political opinions may be challenged, their moral authority is rarely questioned.

The phenomenon, of course, is not new to Latin America. It goes back at least as far as the symbiotic relationship between intellectuals and politics in Athens, Rome and the Renaissance courts. The leaders of the American, French and Russian revolutions were intellectuals, as were most of the political figures who brought independence in the 1960's to the European colonies in Africa and Asia. And, as recently as last month [February, 1983], President François Mitterrand of France considered it worthwhile to invite some 300 writers, artists, moviemakers, economists and philosophers from around the world to Paris for a conference splendidly entitled "Creation and Development."

Thus, the Latin American intellectual owes his role not only to the fact that so relatively few others in his society are well educated: He is also heir to a general European tradition. What distinguishes him even from the European intellectual, however, is the special tradition of dogma that he inherited from Catholic Spain and that still weighs down political thought in the hemisphere.

For three centuries after the Spanish Conquest, most Latin intellectuals came from the ranks of the clergy and observed the limitations on free thought dictated by the Spanish Inquisition. Such minimal dissent as existed could only come from within the church. Priests, for example, were the first to protest the enslavement of the Indians in colonial Mexico. Yet whatever the intellectual debate at the time, it revolved around the prevailing Catholic dogma. Priests organized Mexico's independence movement against Spain, but their troops followed the standard of the Virgin of Guadalupe. Even the Liberal Reforms that swept across Latin America in the 19th century became almost dogmatic in their anticlericalism.

This doctrinaire past facilitated the transition to Marxism following the 1917 Bolshevik revolution in Moscow. In Latin America, Marxism became the new creed and intellectuals its new priests, while the state was assigned the church's old role of organizing society. "We are the sons of rigid ecclesiastic societies," says the Mexican novelist Carlos Fuentes. "This is the burden of Latin America—to go from one church to another, from Catholicism to Marxism, with all its dogma and ritual. This way we feel protected."

Years later, in the 1960's, many Latin American Catholic priests were themselves to be drawn by Marxism in their search for answers to the continent's social ills, and the two dogmas were fused in a new category of Christian Marxists. Among most intellectuals, however, the debate remained dominated by Marxism. And today, as in the past, the political crises that regularly convulse the world of Latin America's intellectuals are essentially crises of faith, in which loyalty to the Marxist ideal is tested by the shortcomings of the Socialist reality. And, ironically, throughout this century, each generation of writers and artists has gone through its own traumatic experience, wanting to believe anew, yet finding difficulty in marrying principles with practice.

Octavio Paz was an unknown young writer when he went to Paris in the late 1930's. Like many intellectuals from the New World, he was drawn by the crusade against Fascism symbolized by the Spanish Civil War. In Paris, he came in contact with leading European intellectuals who, almost to a man, seemed entranced by the Soviet experience. "I was very influenced by Marxism," he recalls. "I was never a member of the Communist Party, but I was very close to them—first to the Stalinists and then to the Trotskyists. I also explored anarchist thought."

But like many other leftist writers, Paz was soon disillusioned by Moscow's behavior—first the expulsion of Leon Trotsky from the Soviet Union (and his subsequent murder in Mexico), then the Moscow purge trials of the 1930's, and, finally, the German-Soviet nonaggression pact of 1939. The impact of these events was felt in Communist parties throughout Latin America, provoking purges of anti-Stalinist factions that rebelled against the pro-Moscow leadership.

For Paz's generation, it was a watershed. A handful of prominent figures—including the great Mexican muralists Diego Rivera and David Alfaro Siqueiros and the late Chilean poet and Nobel laureate Pablo Neruda—remained faithful to "*el partido*," but the region's Communist parties shrank and stagnated into irrelevance. For most intellectuals, the road to the socialist Utopia no longer passed through Moscow.

But the search continued, and the warm welcome that Latin America's intelligentsia gave to the 1959 Cuban revolution reflected the anxiety of the quest. At one level, Castro's victory offered the hope that other Latin American dictators could be toppled by ragtag bands of idealistic youths. But it also seemed to deal with the "problem" of Moscow by exuding a revolutionary spirit that was the antithesis of the Soviet Union's repressive and bureaucratic form of Communism, and it confronted what most intellectuals considered to be Latin America's main problem—the need to break free of the political and economic domination of the United States. Cuba thus gave birth to a new truly Latin American dogma—*La Revolución*—that conveniently focused on Havana rather than Moscow and was dedicated largely to excoriating the "evils" of United States "imperialism."

Many writers and artists for the first time found a cause close to home with which they could identify. The Argentine novelist Julio Cortázar—a huge man who is now 68, and looks 20 years younger—had settled in Paris in the early 1950's to dedicate himself to "esthetic concerns" far removed from politics. Yet, to him, the Cuban revolution came as a kind of revelation. "I made my first trip to Havana in 1961," he recalls, "and when I saw the panorama, with all its problems, its difficulties, its contradictions, it was in some ways like being born again." Since then, politics has been an important part of his life, and he has become a fervent defender of Castro's Cuba—and, more recently, of the Nicaraguan revolution.

The Rev. Ernesto Cardenal, a poet and priest who now serves as Nicaragua's Minister of Culture, underwent a similar experience. Feeling a need to redefine his faith in more political terms, he at first found the answer in a "theology of liberation," which committed the clergy to work with the poor. But for Father Cardenal—with his long white hair and beard, his jeans and his perpetual beret, he looks more like a poet than a priest—it was his visit to Cuba in 1970 that made the crucial difference.

"It was like a second conversion," he says. "Before then, I saw myself as a revolutionary, but I had confused ideas. I was trying to find a third way, which was the Revolution of the Gospel, but then I saw that Cuba was the Gospel put into practice. And only when I converted to Marxism could I write religious poetry."

In the early years of the Cuban revolution, with Havana under constant pressure from the United States, Latin intellectuals were almost unanimous in their sympathy for the Castro regime. And even as they saw domestic freedoms evaporating in Cuba, they argued that these were "temporary" restrictions forced on the regime by "imperialism." By way of compensation, they pointed to Cuba's considerable achievements in improving the lot of the rural poor and in bringing health and education to the population.

But as Castro's repressions bit ever deeper into the cultural sphere, the mood gradually changed. An event in 1971 brought matters to a head. A Cuban poet, Heberto Padilla, was jailed for his stubbornly outspoken dissidence and was forced to make a humiliating "confession" in order to obtain his freedom. Many leading Cuban writers, including Carlos Franqui and Guillermo Cabrera Infante, had quietly opted for exile even before then, but the Padilla affair became such a scandal that most Latin intellectuals were forced to protest.

Just as the Moscow trials destroyed the leftist consensus four decades earlier, so the Padilla case shattered the concept of revolutionary infallibility for the new generation of Latin American writers and artists and raised difficult political and moral dilemmas. For Octavio Paz, by then already distanced from Cuba, the Padilla case was a morally repugnant symptom of totalitarian dictatorship. Vargas Llosa was one of those who broke with Havana over the episode. Others, such as García Márquez and Cortázar, were dismayed by the affair but saw it as a "mistake" attributable to political sectarianism, which they pledged to combat "from the inside."

"One thing that is very reproachable is that we intellectuals only define ourselves when we are affected personally," García Márquez said recently. "It was only when there were problems with intellectuals in Cuba that intellectuals began to break with Cuba, and I think this is politically immature."

The "mistake" of alienating an important group of Latin intellectuals was a surprising one for a man of Castro's evident astuteness, and he set about to undo the damage after appointing a new Minister of Culture, Armando Hart. The Casa de las Américas, Cuba's principal publishing house in the cultural field, was a particularly useful instrument, giving many young leftist writers throughout the region their first opportunity to see their work in print and organizing large conferences of intellectuals, invitations to which were seen by many as synonymous with literary recognition. By 1980, several Latin writers who had broken with Cuba over the Padilla affair had revisited the island.

But it was the extreme right in the region that contributed most to restoring the intellectuals' allegiance to Cuba. In the early 1970's, thousands of writers and academics in such countries as Brazil, Chile, Uruguay, Argentina and Bolivia were persecuted by military dictatorships and forced to flee. In exile, they received political support from Havana. And while many were not Marxists and had personal reservations about Cuba, they had no interest in criticizing their most faithful friend. Their public passions were therefore reserved exclusively for their home Governments and for the United States, which frequently supported these regimes.

Even today [1983], the Reagan Administration's continuing hostility toward Cuba serves to insure intellectual loyalty to Havana. Carlos Fuentes, who was born into a family of Mexican diplomats and has spent more of his life abroad than in Mexico, now lives in Princeton, N.J. and has not visited Cuba since 1962 because of his political differences with Castro. Yet he, too, deplores the thrust of Washington's policy, declaring: "The day the United States stops attacking Cuba, it will no longer be possible for Cuba to mobilize intellectual opinion in the region. All Latin Americans have felt they must keep silent so as not to help imperialism."

The same sense of protectiveness pervades the intellectuals' view of Nicaragua. Solidarity with the Sandinist revolution has grown in direct proportion to the rise of hostility toward the Managua regime on the part of the United States. Cortázar, García Márquez, Fuentes—even Vargas Llosa, who distinguishes between Cuba and Nicaragua—have all visited Managua at the invitation of the Sandinist leadership, and have all been sufficiently impressed by what they saw to denounce the Reagan Administration's efforts to undermine the new Government. (Their reaction has been shared, incidentally, by such European visitors as Günter Grass and Graham Greene.)

"What can we say about a country that comes out of 45 years of dictatorship?" said Fuentes after a visit to Managua last January. "It has avoided a blood bath. It has avoided a Maximum Leader. My attitude is to let these countries resolve their own problems. I'd like to ask Reagan: 'What right have you to meddle in things you don't understand?' "

When United States military units joined Honduran troops for war games close to Honduras's border with Nicaragua last month, the Sandinist Government, charging that the maneuvers were a form of hostile pressure, mobilized its own forces. But its most effective weapon, perhaps, was a delegation of intellectuals from other Latin American countries, including Cortázar and the Salvadoran poet Claribel Alegría, and even from the United States, who participated in a "peace vigil" near the Honduran border. Reporters were flown to the scene, and the word went out to the hemisphere: While the United States engaged in saber rattling, Nicaragua defended itself with a moral shield.

The readiness of the region's intellectuals to identify with Nicaragua has yet another explanation—the country's strong tradition of following the political lead of its writers. From the time of Rubén Darío, the modernist poet who made Nicaragua famous even before the world had heard of the Somoza dictatorship, Nicaragua has been a land of poets. Many, such as José Coronel Urtecho, Ernesto Cardenal and Pablo Antonio Cuadra, are famous throughout Latin America. Others served more modestly as family or village poets, enjoying as much prestige as the local doctor, teacher or priest.

It was natural, then, for the Sandinists to mobilize this talent—the protest music of Carlos Mejía Godoy as well as the poetry of rebel leaders and ordinary guerrillas—against the Somoza regime. And today, many top Sandinist officials are also writers. One of the revolutionary *comandantes*, Omar Cabezas, won an award from the Casa de las Américas for his memoirs as an insurgent. The head of the ruling junta, Daniel Ortega Saavedra, is a respected poet, while another junta member, Sergio Ramírez Mercado, is a well-known novelist. Since the revolution, some 50 poetry workshops have sprung up in the army, police and the trade unions, and even in peasant organizations.

Visiting writers are, therefore, welcomed by officials who are also fellow intellectuals. They are not unaware, of course, of the press censorship and other restrictions on political freedom that are part of the Sandinist revolution. Almost invariably, however, they blame these curbs on the harassment of Nicaragua emanating from the United States, and they point to the burst of artistic creativity since the revolution as evidence that cultural freedom survives.

There is one final irony—that this very political instability, this process of decomposition and renovation, has contributed to the richness of the region's literature. Latin America's social models may, so far, have failed, but its writers have made the failures memorable. In the end, Latin America's perceptions of itself will probably be shaped more lastingly by such books as García Márquez's *One Hundred Years of Solitude* and Paz's *The Labyrinth of Solitude* than by any political pronouncement by either author.

57. ONE HUNDRED YEARS OF SOLITUDE

Gabriel García Márquez

Colombian-born García Márquez, 1982 Nobel Prize winner, is perhaps best known for his novel One Hundred Years of Solitude. *This selection is the opening of that work. Can you see why the style has been called "magic realism"? How do you interpret the character of José Arcadio Buendía? What does the author want to suggest about inventions, Eu-*

*rope, and Latin America? What do the author's characters, settings, sto-
ries, and style suggest about Latin America?*

Many years later, as he faced the firing squad, Colonel Aureliano
Buendía was to remember that distant afternoon when his father took
him to discover ice. At that time Macondo was a village of twenty adobe
houses, built on the bank of a river of clear water that ran along a bed of
polished stones, which were white and enormous, like prehistoric eggs.
The world was so recent that many things lacked names, and in order to
indicate them it was necessary to point. Every year during the month of
March a family of ragged gypsies would set up their tents near the
village, and with a great uproar of pipes and kettledrums they would
display new inventions. First they brought the magnet. A heavy gypsy
with an untamed beard and sparrow hands, who introduced himself as
Melquíades, put on a bold public demonstration of what he himself
called the eighth wonder of the learned alchemists of Macedonia. He
went from house to house dragging two metal ingots and everybody was
amazed to see pots, pans, tongs, and braziers tumble down from their
places and beams creak from the desperation of nails and screws trying
to emerge, and even objects that had been lost for a long time appeared
from where they had been searched for most and went dragging along in
turbulent confusion behind Melquíades' magical irons. "Things have a
life of their own," the gypsy proclaimed with a harsh accent. "It's simply
a matter of waking up their souls." José Arcadio Buendía, whose unbridled imagination always went beyond the genius of nature and even
beyond miracles and magic, thought that it would be possible to make
use of that useless invention to extract gold from the bowels of the earth.
Melquíades, who was an honest man, warned him: "It won't work for
that." But José Arcadio Buendía at that time did not believe in the
honesty of gypsies, so he traded his mule and a pair of goats for the two
magnetized ingots. Úrsala Iguarán, his wife, who relied on those animals
to increase their poor domestic holdings, was unable to dissuade him.
"Very soon we'll have gold enough and more to pave the floors of the
house," her husband replied. For several months he worked hard to
demonstrate the truth of his idea. He explored every inch of the region,
even the riverbed, dragging the two iron ingots along and reciting
Melquíades' incantation aloud. The only thing he succeeded in doing
was to unearth a suit of fifteenth-century armor which had all of its
pieces soldered together with rust and inside of which there was the
hollow resonance of an enormous stone-filled gourd. When José Arcadio
Buendía and the four men of his expedition managed to take the armor
apart, they found inside a calcified skeleton with a copper locket containing a woman's hair around its neck.

In March the gypsies returned. This time they brought a telescope and
a magnifying glass the size of a drum, which they exhibited as the latest

discovery of the Jews of Amsterdam. They placed a gypsy woman at one end of the village and set up the telescope at the entrance to the tent. For the price of five reales, people could look into the telescope and see the gypsy woman an arm's length away. "Science has eliminated distance," Melquíades proclaimed. "In a short time, man will be able to see what is happening in any place in the world without leaving his own house." A burning noonday sun brought out a startling demonstration with the gigantic magnifying glass: they put a pile of dry hay in the middle of the street and set it on fire by concentrating the sun's rays. José Arcadio Buendía, who had still not been consoled for the failure of his magnets, conceived the idea of using that invention as a weapon of war. Again Melquíades tried to dissuade him, but he finally accepted the two magnetized ingots and three colonial coins in exchange for the magnifying glass. Úrsula wept in consternation. That money was from a chest of gold coins that her father had put together over an entire life of privation and that she had buried underneath her bed in hopes of a proper occasion to make use of it. José Arcadio Buendía made no attempt to console her, completely absorbed in his tactical experiments with the abnegation of a scientist and even at the risk of his own life. In an attempt to show the effects of the glass on enemy troops, he exposed himself to the concentration of the sun's rays and suffered burns which turned to sores that took a long time to heal. Over the protests of his wife, who was alarmed at such a dangerous invention, at one point he was ready to set the house on fire. He would spend hours on end in his room, calculating the strategic possibilities of his novel weapon until he succeeded in putting together a manual of startling instructional clarity and an irresistible power of conviction. He sent it to the government, accompanied by numerous descriptions of his experiments and several pages of explanatory sketches, by a messenger who crossed the mountains, got lost in measureless swamps, forded stormy rivers, and was on the point of perishing under the lash of despair, plague, and wild beasts until he found a route that joined the one used by the mules that carried the mail. In spite of the fact that a trip to the capital was little less than impossible at that time, José Arcadio Buendía promised to undertake it as soon as the government ordered him to so that he could put on some practical demonstrations of his invention for the military authorities and could train them himself in the complicated art of solar war. For several years he waited for an answer. Finally, tired of waiting, he bemoaned to Melquíades the failure of his project and the gypsy then gave him a convincing proof of his honesty: he gave him back the doubloons in exchange for the magnifying glass, and he left him in addition some Portuguese maps and several instruments of navigation. In his own handwriting he set down a concise synthesis of the studies by Monk Hermann, which he left José Arcadio so that he would be able to make use of the astrolabe, the compass, and the sextant. José Arcadio Buendía spent the long months of the rainy season shut up in a small room that he had built in the rear of the house so that no one would disturb his experiments. Having completely abandoned his domestic obligations, he spent entire nights in the courtyard watching the course of the stars and he almost contracted sunstroke from trying to establish an exact method to ascertain noon. When he became an expert in the use and manipulation of his instruments, he conceived a notion of space that allowed him to navigate across unknown seas, to visit uninhabited territories, and to establish relations with splendid beings without having to leave his study. That was the period in which he acquired the habit of talking to himself, of walking through the house without paying attention to anyone, as Úrsula and the children broke their backs in the garden, growing banana and caladium, cassava and yams, ahuyama roots and eggplants. Suddenly, without warning, his feverish activity was interrupted and was replaced by a kind of fascination. He spent several days as if he were bewitched, softly repeating to himself a string of fearful conjectures without giving credit to his own understanding. Finally, one Tuesday in December, at lunchtime, all at once he released the whole weight of his torment. The children would remember for the rest of their lives the august solemnity with which their father, devastated by his prolonged vigil and by the wrath of his imagination, revealed his discovery to them:

"The earth is round, like an orange."

Úrsula lost her patience. "If you have to go crazy, please go crazy all by yourself!" she shouted. "But don't try to put your gypsy ideas into the heads of the children." José Arcadio Buendía, impassive, did not let himself be frightened by the desperation of his wife, who, in a seizure of rage, smashed the astrolabe against the floor. He built another one, he gathered the men of the village in his little room, and he demonstrated to them, with theories that none of them could understand, the possibility of returning to where one had set out by consistently sailing east. The whole village was convinced that José Arcadio Buendía had lost his reason, when Melquíades returned to set things straight. He gave public praise to the intelligence of a man who from pure astronomical speculation had evolved a theory that had already been proved in practice, although unknown in Macondo until then, and as a proof of his admiration he made him a gift that was to have a profound influence on the future of the village: the laboratory of an alchemist.

By then Melquíades had aged with surprising rapidity. On his first trips he seemed to be the same age as José Arcadio Buendía. But while the latter had preserved his extraordinary strength, which permitted him to pull down a horse by grabbing its ears, the gypsy seemed to have been worn down by some tenacious illness. It was, in reality, the result of multiple and rare diseases contracted on his innumerable trips around the world. According to what he himself said as she spoke to José Arcadio Buendía while helping him set up the laboratory, death followed him everywhere, sniffing at the cuffs of his pants, but never deciding to give him the final clutch of its claws. He was a fugitive from all the plagues and catastrophes that had ever lashed mankind. He had survived pellagra in Persia, scurvy in the Malayan archipelago, leprosy in Alexandria, beriberi in Japan, bubonic plague in Madagascar, an earthquake in Sicily, and a disastrous shipwreck in the Strait of Magellan. That prodigious creature, said to possess the keys of Nostradamus, was a gloomy man, enveloped in a sad aura, with an Asiatic look that seemed to know what there was on the other side of things. He wore a large black hat that looked like a raven with widespread wings, and a velvet vest across which the patina of the centuries had skated. But in spite of his immense wisdom and his mysterious breadth, he had a human burden, an earthly condition that kept him involved in the small problems of daily life. He would complain of the ailments of old age, he suffered from the most insignificant economic difficulties, and he had stopped laughing a long time back because scurvy had made his teeth drop out. On that suffocating noontime when the gypsy revealed his secrets, José Arcadio Buendía had the certainty that it was the beginning of a great friendship. The children were startled by his fantastic stories. Aureliano, who could not have been more than five at the time, would remember him for the rest of his life as he saw him that afternoon, sitting against the metallic and quivering light from the window, lighting up with his deep organ voice the darkest reaches of his imagination, while down over his temples there flowed the grease that was being melted by the heat. José Arcadio, his older brother, would pass on that wonderful image as a hereditary memory to all of his descendants. Úrsula, on the other hand, held a bad memory of that visit, for she had entered the room just as Melquíades had carelessly broken a flask of bichloride of mercury.

"It's the smell of the devil," she said.

"Not at all," Melquíades corrected her. "It has been proven that the devil has sulphuric properties and this is just a little corrosive sublimate."

Always didactic, he went into a learned exposition of the diabolical properties of cinnabar, but Úrsula paid no attention to him, although she took the children off to pray. That biting odor would stay forever in her mind linked to the memory of Melquíades.

The rudimentary laboratory—in addition to a profusion of pots, funnels, retorts, filters, and sieves—was made up of a primitive water pipe, a glass beaker with a long, thin neck, a reproduction of the philosopher's egg, and a still the gypsies themselves had built in accordance with modern descriptions of the three-armed alembic of Mary the Jew. Along with those items, Melquíades left samples of the seven metals that corresponded to the seven planets, the formulas of Moses and Zosimus for doubling the quantity of gold, and a set of notes and sketches concerning the processes of the Great Teaching that would permit those who could interpret them to undertake the manufacture of the philosopher's stone. Seduced by the simplicity of the formulas to double the quantity of gold, José Arcadio Buendía paid court to Úrsula for several weeks so that she would let him dig up her colonial coins and increase them by as many times as it was possible to subdivide mercury. Úrsula gave in, as always, to her husband's unyielding obstinacy. Then José Arcadio Buendía threw three doubloons into a pan and fused them with copper filings, orpiment, brimstone, and lead. He put it all to boil in a pot of castor oil until he got a thick and pestilential syrup which was more like common caramel than valuable gold. In risky and desperate processes of distillation, melted with the seven planetary metals, mixed with hermetic mercury and vitriol of Cyprus, and put back to cook in hog fat for lack of any radish oil, Úrsula's precious inheritance was reduced to a large piece of burnt hog cracklings that was firmly stuck to the bottom of the pot.

When the gypsies came back, Úrsula had turned the whole population of the village against them. But curiosity was greater than fear, for that time the gypsies went about the town making a deafening noise with all manner of musical instruments while a hawker announced the exhibition of the most fabulous discovery of the Naciancenes. So that everyone went to the tent and by paying one cent they saw a youthful Melquíades, recovered, unwrinkled, with a new and flashing set of teeth. Those who remembered his gums that had been destroyed by scurvy, his flaccid cheeks, and his withered lips trembled with fear at the final proof of the gypsy's supernatural power. The fear turned into panic when Melquíades took out his teeth, intact, encased in their gums, and showed them to the audience for an instant—a fleeting instant in which he went back to being the same decrepit man of years past—and put them back again and smiled once more with the full control of his restored youth. Even José Arcadio Buendía himself considered that Melquíades' knowledge had reached unbearable extremes, but he felt a healthy excitement when the gypsy explained to him alone the workings of his false teeth. It seemed so simple and so prodigious at the same time that overnight he lost all interest in his experiments in alchemy. He underwent a new crisis of bad humor. He did not go back to eating regularly, and he would spend the day walking through the house. "Incredible things are happening in the world," he said to Úrsula. "Right there across the river there are all kinds of magical instruments while we keep on living like donkeys." Those who had known him since the foundation of Macondo were startled at how much he had changed under Melquíades' influence.

At first José Arcadio Buendía had been a kind of youthful patriarch who would give instructions for planting and advice for the raising of children and animals, and who collaborated with everyone, even in the physical work, for the welfare of the community. Since his house from the very first had been the best in the village, the others had been built in its image and likeness. It had a small, well-lighted living room, a dining room in the shape of a terrace with gaily colored flowers, two bedrooms, a courtyard with a gigantic chestnut tree, a well-kept garden, and a corral where goats, pigs, and hens lived in peaceful communion. The only animals that were prohibited, not just in his house but in the entire settlement, were fighting cocks.

Úrsula's capacity for work was the same as that of her husband. Active, small, severe, that woman of unbreakable nerves who at no moment in her life had been heard to sing seemed to be everywhere, from dawn until quite late at night, always pursued by the soft whispering of her stiff, starched petticoats. Thanks to her the floors of tamped earth, the unwhitewashed mud walls, the rustic, wooden furniture they had built themselves were always clean, and the old chests where they kept their clothes exhaled the warm smell of basil.

José Arcadio Buendía, who was the most enterprising man ever to be seen in the village, had set up the placement of the houses in such a way that from all of them one could reach the river and draw water with the same effort, and he had lined up the streets with such good sense that no house got more sun than another during the hot time of day. Within a few years Macondo was a village that was more orderly and hard-working than any known until then by its three hundred inhabitants. It was a truly happy village where no one was over thirty years of age and where no one had died.

Since the time of its founding, José Arcadio Buendía had built traps and cages. In a short time he filled not only his own house but all of those in the village with troupials, canaries, bee eaters, and redbreasts. The concert of so many different birds became so disturbing that Úrsula would plug her ears with beeswax so as not to lose her sense of reality. The first time that Melquíades' tribe arrived, selling glass balls for headaches, everyone was surprised that they had been able to find that village lost in the drowsiness of the swamp, and the gypsies confessed that they had found their way by the song of the birds.

That spirit of social initiative disappeared in a short time, pulled away by the fever of the magnets, the astronomical calculations, the dreams of transmutation, and the urge to discover the wonders of the world. From a clean and active man, José Arcadio Buendía changed into a man lazy in appearance, careless in his dress, with a wild beard that Úrsula managed to trim with great effort and a kitchen knife. There were many who considered him the victim of some strange spell. But even those most convinced of his madness left work and family to follow him when he brought out his tools to clear the land and asked the assembled group to open a way that would put Macondo in contact with the great inventions.

José Arcadio Buendía was completely ignorant of the geography of the region. He knew that to the east there lay an impenetrable mountain chain and that on the other side of the mountains there was the ancient city of Riohacha, where in times past—according to what he was told by the first Aureliano Buendía, his grandfather—Sir Francis Drake had gone crocodile hunting with cannons and that he repaired them and stuffed them with straw to bring to Queen Elizabeth. In his youth, José Arcadio Buendía and his men, with wives and children, animals and all kinds of domestic implements, had crossed the mountains in search of an outlet to the sea, and after twenty-six months they gave up the expedition and founded Macondo, so they would not have to go back. It was, therefore, a route that did not interest him, for it could only lead to the past. To the south lay the swamps, covered with an eternal vegetable scum, and the whole vast universe of the great swamp, which, according to what the gypsies said, had no limits. The great swamp in the west mingled with a boundless extension of water where there were soft-skinned cetaceans that had the head and torso of a woman, causing the ruination of sailors with the charm of their extraordinary breasts. The gypsies sailed along that route for six months before they reached the strip of land over which the mules that carried the mail passed. According to José Arcadio Buendía's calculations, the only possibility of contact with civilization lay along the northern route. So he handed out clearing tools and hunting weapons to the same men who had been with him during the founding of Macondo. He threw his directional instruments and his maps into a knapsack, and he undertook the reckless adventure.

During the first few days they did not come across any appreciable obstacle. They went down along the stony bank of the river to the place where years before they had found the soldier's armor, and from there they into the woods along a path between wild orange trees. At the end of the first week they killed and roasted a deer, but they agreed to eat only half of it and salt the rest for the days that lay ahead. With that precaution they tried to postpone the necessity of having to eat macaws, whose blue flesh had a harsh and murky taste. Then, for more than ten days, they did not see the sun again. The ground became soft and damp, like volcanic ash, and the vegetation was thicker and thicker, and the cries of the birds and the uproar of the monkeys became more and more remote, and the world became eternally sad. The men on the expedition felt overwhelmed by their most ancient memories in that paradise of dampness and silence, going back to before original sin, as their boots sank into pools of steaming oil and their machetes destroyed bloody lilies and golden salamanders. For a week, almost without speaking, they went ahead like sleepwalkers through a universe of grief, lighted only by the tenuous reflection of luminous insects, and their lungs were overwhelmed by a suffocating smell of blood. They could not return because the strip that they were opening as they went along would soon close up with a new vegetation that almost seemed to grow before their eyes. "It's all right," José Arcadio Buendía would say. "The main thing is not to lose our bearings." Always following his compass, he kept on guiding his men toward the invisible north so that they would be able to get out of that enchanted region. It was a thick night, starless, but the darkness was becoming impregnated with a fresh and clean air. Exhausted by the long crossing, they hung up their hammocks and slept deeply for the first time in two weeks. When they woke up, with the sun already high in the sky, they were speechless with fascination. Before them, surrounded by ferns and palm trees, white and powdery in the silent morning light, was an enormous Spanish galleon. Tilted slightly to the starboard, it had hanging from its intact masts the dirty rags of its sails in the midst of its rigging, which was adorned with orchids. The hull, covered with an armor of petrified barnacles and soft moss, was firmly fastened into a surface of stones. The whole structure seemed to occupy its own space, one of solitude and oblivion, protected from the vices of time and the habits of the birds. Inside, where the expeditionaries explored with careful intent, there was nothing but a thick forest of flowers.

The discovery of the galleon, an indication of the proximity of the sea, broke José Arcadio Buendía's drive. He considered it a trick of his whimsical fate to have searched for the sea without finding it, at the cost of countless sacrifices and suffering, and to have found it all of a sudden without looking for it, as if it lay across his path like an insurmountable object. Many years later Colonel Aureliano Buendía crossed the region again, when it was already a regular mail route, and the only part of the ship he found was its burned-out frame in the midst of a field of poppies. Only then, convinced that the story had not been some product of his father's imagination, did he wonder how the galleon had been able to get inland to that spot. But José Arcadio Buendía did not concern himself with that when he found the sea after another four days' journey from the galleon. His dreams ended as he faced that ashen, foamy, dirty sea, which had not merited the risks and sacrifices of the adventure.

"God damn it!" he shouted. "Macondo is surrounded by water on all sides."

The idea of a peninsular Macondo prevailed for a long time, inspired by the arbitrary map that José Arcadio Buendía sketched on his return from the expedition. He drew it in rage, evilly, exaggerating the difficulties of communication, as if to punish himself for the absolute lack of sense with which he had chosen the place. "We'll never get anywhere," he lamented to Úrsula. "We're going to rot our lives away here without receiving the benefits of science." That certainty, mulled over for several months in the small room he used as his laboratory, brought him to the conception of the plan to move Macondo to a better place. But that time Úrsula had anticipated his feverish designs. With the secret and implacable labor of a small ant she predisposed the women of the village against the flightiness of their husbands, who were already preparing for the move. José Arcadio Buendía did not know at what moment or because of what adverse forces his plan had become enveloped in a web of pretexts, disappointments, and evasions until it turned into nothing but an illusion. Úrsula watched him with innocent attention and even felt some pity for him on the morning when she found him in the back room muttering about his plans for moving as he placed his laboratory pieces in their original boxes. She let him finish. She let him nail up the boxes and put his initials on them with an inked brush, without reproaching him, but knowing now that he knew (because she had heard him say so in his soft monologues) that the men of the village would not back him up in his undertaking. Only when he began to take down the door of the room did Úrsula dare ask him what he was doing, and he answered with a certain bitterness. "Since no one wants to leave, we'll leave all by ourselves." Úrsula did not become upset.

"We will not leave," she said. "We will stay here, because we have had a son here."

"We have still not had a death," he said. "A person does not belong to a place until there is someone dead under the ground."

Úrsula replied with a soft firmness:

"If I have to die for the rest of you to stay here, I will die."

José Arcadio Buendía had not thought that his wife's will was so firm. He tried to seduce her with the charm of his fantasy, with the promise of a prodigious world where all one had to do was sprinkle some magic liquid on the ground and the plants would bear fruit whenever a man wished, and where all manner of instruments against pain were sold at bargain prices. But Úrsula was insensible to his clairvoyance.

"Instead of going around thinking about your crazy inventions, you should be worrying about your sons," she replied. "Look at the state they're in, running wild just like donkeys."

José Arcadio Buendía took his wife's words literally. He looked out the window and saw the barefoot children in the sunny garden and he had the impression that only at that instant had they begun to exist, conceived by Úrsula's spell. Something occurred inside of him then, something mysterious and definitive that uprooted him from his own time and carried him adrift through an unexplored region of his memory. While Úrsula continued sweeping the house, which was safe now from being abandoned for the rest of her life, he stood there with an absorbed look, contemplating the children until his eyes became moist and he dried them with the back of his hand, exhaling a deep sign of resignation.

"All right," he said. "Tell them to come help me take the things out of the boxes."

José Arcadio, the older of the children, was fourteen. He had a square head, thick hair, and his father's character. Although he had the same impulse for growth and physical strength, it was early evident that he lacked imagination. He had been conceived and born during the difficult crossing of the mountains, before the founding of Macondo, and his parents gave thanks to heaven when they saw he had no animal features.

Aureliano, the first human being to be born in Macondo, would be six years old in March. He was silent and withdrawn. He had wept in his mother's womb and had been born with his eyes open. As they were cutting the umbilical cord, he moved his head from side to side, taking in the things in the room and examining the faces of the people with a fearless curiosity. Then, indifferent to those who came close to look at him, he kept his attention concentrated on the palm roof, which looked as if it were about to collapse under the tremendous pressure of the rain. Úrsula did not remember the intensity of that look again until one day when little Aureliano, at the age of three, went into the kitchen at the moment she was taking a pot of boiling soup from the stove and putting it on the table. The child, perplexed, said from the doorway, "It's going to spill." The pot was firmly placed in the center of the table, but just as soon as the child made his announcement, it began an unmistakable movement toward the edge, as if impelled by some inner dynamism, and it fell and broke on the floor. Úrsula, alarmed, told her husband about the episode, but he interpreted it as a natural phenomenon. That was the way he always was alien to the existence of his sons, partly because he considered childhood as a period of mental insufficiency, and partly because he was always too absorbed in his fantastic speculations.

But since the afternoon when he called the children in to help him unpack the things in the laboratory, he gave them his best hours. In the small separate room, where the walls were gradually being covered by strange maps and fabulous drawings, he taught them to read and write and do sums, and he spoke to them about the wonders of the world, not only where his learning had extended, but forcing the limits of his imagination to extremes. It was in this way that the boys ended up learning that in the southern extremes of Africa there were men so intelligent and peaceful that their only pastime was to sit and think, and that it was possible to cross the Aegean Sea on foot by jumping from island to island all the way to the port of Salonika. Those hallucinating sessions remained printed on the memories of the boys in such a way that many years later, a second before the regular army officer gave the firing squad the command to fire, Colonel Aureliano Buendía saw once more that warm March afternoon on which his father had interrupted the lesson in physics and stood fascinated, with his hand in the air and his eyes motionless, listening to the distant pipes, drums, and jingles of the gypsies, who were coming to the village once more, announcing the latest and most startling discovery of the sages of Memphis.

They were new gypsies, young men and women who knew only their own language, handsome specimens with oily skins and intelligent hands, whose dances and music sowed a panic of uproarious joy through the streets, with parrots painted all colors reciting Italian arias, and a hen who laid a hundred golden eggs to the sound of a tambourine, and a trained monkey who read minds, and the multiple-use machine that could be used at the same time to sew on buttons and reduce fevers, and the apparatus to make a person forget his bad memories, and a poultice to lose time, and a thousand more inventions so ingenious and unusual that José Arcadio Buendía must have wanted to invent a memory machine so that he could remember them all. In an instant they transformed the village. The inhabitants of Macondo found themselves lost in their own streets, confused by the crowded fair.

Holding a child by each hand so as not to lose them in the tumult, bumping into acrobats with gold-capped teeth and jugglers with six arms, suffocated by the mingled breath of manure and sandals that the crowd exhaled, José Arcadio Buendía went about everywhere like a madman, looking for Melquíades so that he could reveal to him the infinite secrets of that fabulous nightmare. He asked several gypsies, who did not understand his language. Finally he reached the place where Melquíades used to set up his tent and he found a taciturn Armenian who in Spanish was hawking a syrup to make oneself invisible. He had drunk down a glass of the amber substance in one gulp as José Arcadio Buendía elbowed his way through the absorbed group that was witnessing the spectacle, and was able to ask his question. The gypsy wrapped him in the frightful climate of his look before he turned into a puddle of pestilential and smoking pitch over which the echo of his reply still floated: "Melquíades is dead." Upset by the news, José Arcadio Buendía stood motionless, trying to rise above his affliction, until the group dispersed, called away by other artifices, and the puddle of the taciturn Armenian evaporated completely. Other gypsies confirmed later on that Melquíades had in fact succumbed to the fever on the beach at Singapore and that his body had been thrown into the deepest part of the Java Sea. The children had no interest in the news. They insisted that their father take them to see the overwhelming novelty of the sages of Memphis that was being advertised at the entrance of a tent that, according to what was said, had belonged to King Solomon. They insisted so much that José Arcadio Buendía paid the thirty reales and led them into the center of the tent, where there was a giant with a hairy torso and a shaved head, with a copper ring in his nose and a heavy iron chain on his ankle, watching over a pirate chest. When it was opened by the giant, the chest gave off a glacial exhalation. Inside there was only an enormous, transparent block with infinite internal needles in which the light of the sunset was broken up into colored stars. Disconcerted, knowing that the children were waiting for an immediate explanation, José Arcadio Buendía ventured a murmur:

"It's the largest diamond in the world."

"No," the gypsy countered. "It's ice."

José Arcadio Buendía, without understanding, stretched out his hand toward the cake, but the giant moved it away. "Five reales more to touch it," he said. José Arcadio Buendía paid them and put his hand on the ice and held it for several minutes as his heart filled with fear and jubilation at the contact with mystery. Without knowing what to say, he paid ten reales more so that his sons could have that prodigious experience. Little José Arcadio refused to touch it. Aureliano, on the other hand, took a step forward and put his hand on it, withdrawing it immediately. "It's boiling," he exclaimed, startled. But his father paid no attention to him. Intoxicated by the evidence of the miracle, he forgot at that moment about the frustration of his delirious undertakings and Melquíades' body, abandoned to the appetite of the squids. He paid another five reales and with his hand on the cake, as if giving testimony on the holy scriptures, he exclaimed:

"This is the great invention of our time."

58. SLAVERY ON THE RISE IN BRAZIL

James Brooke

This is an article from the New York Times *of May 23, 1993. How has slavery returned to Brazil over a hundred years after it was outlawed there? What permits such a system to continue? Do you think Brazil is unique in this regard?*

Rolling hills cloaked in emerald green sugar cane fields lend a luxuriant air to this rural corner of Rio de Janeiro State. But, down in a creek hollow where farm workers sleep in hammocks strung in cow stalls, laborers say the alcohol distillery owner does not pay wages—only scrip redeemable for food.

Toiling from sunup to sundown for food does not fit strict definitions of slavery. But the laborers' complaints here have swelled a nationwide flood of denunciations of an upsurge of slavery in Brazil.

Brazil was the last nation in the Americas to abolish slavery, only grudgingly giving up the practice in 1888. To continue to exploit cheap labor, landowners developed means of binding laborers by forcing them to run up unpayable debts at company stores or canteens.

CHAINS MADE OF DEBT

"In the 19th century, the chains were metal," said Carlos Eduardo Barroso, a Rio de Janeiro prosecutor who is investigating labor law violations here. "Today, the chains are debt—the worker has to repay his transportation, his tools, his food."

Ever since the bite of Brazil's current recession began to be felt in 1989, documented cases of Brazilians falling victim to slavery practices have soared, from 597 in 1989 to 16,442 in 1992. The statistics are gathered by the Pastoral Land Commission, a group sponsored by the Roman Catholic Church.

"Only a fraction of cases become known," said Generosa Oliveira Silva, a coordinator of Rio's Land Commission, which is investigating the slavery allegations here.

According to the commission's definition, modern day slavery involves recruitment of workers with false promises, imprisonment for debt, and coercion to prevent workers from leaving their employers. In such situations, workers are reduced to working for food. Some workers are prevented from leaving by menacing armed foremen and others are marooned on isolated ranches, unable to find a way to leave.

"ALARMING PROPORTIONS"

"Slavery in Brazil is taking on alarming proportions," Veja, the nation's largest news weekly, warned in April. "Greater every day, slave labor is a plague that extends from the poorest regions of the country to the richest and will make Brazil enter the third millenium with one foot in the mud of the last century."

After the International Labor Organization accused Brazil in March of allowing "thousands of workers" to fall into slavery, Brazil's Labor Minister, Walter Barelli, denounced modern day forced labor as "the greatest stain in Brazilian history."

International groups have also cited Peru, Haiti and the Dominican Republic for slavery cases, but they say that Brazil appears to be the greatest offender in the Americas. In the rest of the world, India and Pakistan are often denounced for keeping as many as 35 million people in bondage because of debt.

Modern slavery in Brazil appears to take root and to flourish in rural and other isolated settings: sugar cane plantations on the Atlantic Coast and gold mines, ranches, and charcoal industries of the Amazon.

ECONOMIC DESPERATION

The recent explosion in slavery reports seems to reflect two trends: increased awareness of slavery and increased economic desperation among Brazil's rural poor.

In the Amazon, a few cases have been uncovered of foremen chaining workers at night or killing those who try to run away.

"Workers who try to escape are pursued by gunmen and returned to the estate, where they can be beaten, whipped or subject to mutilation or sexual abuse," the International Labor Organization asserted in their March report. "In 1991, 53 victims of forced labor were murdered in Brazil, but few of the accused were brought to trial or received the statutory punishment."

But most of Brazil's modern forced labor cases involve debt peonage.

RURAL WORKERS ARE LURED

Typically, labor contractors roam rural areas luring unemployed workers with promises of good wages and working conditions. But when workers arrive at the remote work camps, hundreds of miles from home, they soon discover that the bunkhouse may be no more than a plastic sheet and that they owe unpayable debts for bus transportation, meals and the use of work tools, like chain saws.

Last year, about half of Brazil's slavery complaints involved families hired to cut trees and tend charcoal furnaces in the southern Amazon state of Mato Grosso do Sul.

"They used to pay a man here his wages and then claim that he was being paid in advance for future work," said Nauci de Sousa Pires, a 62-year-old boiler assistant who has worked at the Victor Sence sugar cane alcohol company here since 1954. "More recently, they moved to the system of paying with scrip."

Increased coverage in the press about slavery, coupled with increased unionization of farm workers, appear to have contributed to the sharp jump in slavery denunciations.

VICTORY IN AWARENESS

"It's a major victory when societies stop seeing slavery as something normal," Lesley Roberts, director of Anti-Slavery International, said in a telephone interview from London, where the private group is based. Last year, the society gave its annual award for antislavery work to the Rev. Ricardo Rezende, a Brazilian priest who has received death threats for denouncing slavery on Amazon estates. While outrage over slavery is growing, the economic desperation that fuels it is also growing.

Statistics made public in April by the World Bank indicate that in the 1980's the percentage of Brazilians surviving on less than $2 a day increased from 34 percent to 41 percent.

At the same time, Brazil's income distribution, already one of the world's widest, worsened. According to Brazil's 1991 census, the poorest 10 percent of the nation's population held less than one percent of the nation's wealth. In contrast, the richest 10 percent held 49 percent of the nation's wealth.

With economic stagnation stretching into the 1990's, it has become easier for Brazil's wealthy to prey on Brazil's weak.

"With this kind of misery, people will accept any kind of offer," said Eraldo Lidio Azeredo, president of the Rio de Janeiro Farm Workers Federation, a union group. "Most workers only ask themselves: what am I going to do about my family tomorrow?"

AN EMPLOYER'S VIEW

Inside the air-conditioned offices of the Sence company, Elisa Maria Sence Barcellos, a company director and a great-granddaughter of the company founder, said in an interview: "Human relations are very important for us. We have never had a strike here."

Payment in scrip, she continued, was a temporary measure to get through a tight period for a company that has been on the verge of bankruptcy for several years.

"Every day it is more difficult to find workers," said Mrs. Barcellos, a City Councilwoman here who sees labor relations from the employers' viewpoint. "People no longer stay in the countryside; they all go to the cities and end up in those big shantytowns."

With her gold chains, designer sunglasses, fax machine and expensive cigarettes, Mrs. Barcellos seemed a world away from the cow barn half a mile down a dirt road where workers complained about being paid with paper chits.

Doralice Moreira de Souza, a 47-year-old woman with hands gnarled from years of cutting a daily quota of five tons of cane, said Mrs. Barcellos recently tried to dismiss her when she ran for a post in the farm workers' union. The new labor group was formed here as part of a nationwide effort to unionize farm workers, including those working in debt bondage, but the effort has had little success in improving working conditions for farm workers.

Looking at one of her 11 grandchildren, a 10-year-old boy named Alan, Mrs. de Souza said hopefully, "I would like him to study, so that when he grows up, he won't end up a slave like me."

CHAPTER SIXTEEN

The New World Order

59. THE COMING GOLDEN AGE OF CAPITALISM

David D. Hale

This column appeared in the Wall Street Journal *on November 7, 1991. Why does the author think the world is entering a new "golden age of capitalism"? What does he believe are the advantages and disadvantages of an increasingly integrated global market?*

The world economy is entering one of its most dramatic periods of change since the early 20th century. Since 1945, the global market economy has effectively included only about 800 million people living in 25 industrial countries, and another 400 million living in a dozen or so less developed satellite economies with large export sectors. About 80% of mankind has been living under regimes that were either communist (the Soviet Union, China, Eastern Europe), authoritarian (Africa, the Arab world) or mercantilist (Latin America, South Asia).

During the next 10 years, this 80% of mankind, about 4 billion people, will be re-entering the world marketplace for goods and capital to a far greater extent than at any time since 1914. In fact, by the year 2014, the forces of global economic integration may have produced a world similar to the one that might have emerged in the middle of the 20th century had the First World War not shattered the 19th-century global trade and investment boom.

THE RUSSIAN BREAD-BASKET

The newly marketizing economies could greatly increase the potential world supply of agricultural commodities, industrial raw materials and low-value-added manufactured goods. Before 1914, for example, Russia was the world's largest exporter of petroleum and the bread-basket of Germany. Today, its agricultural productivity is less than one-third of America's.

Similar potential—both agricultural and industrial—exists in Eastern Europe, China and Latin America. Even India could emerge as a far larger factor if it shifts from protectionism toward export-oriented policies. In the 1980s, India's 850 million people exported less than Hong Kong's 6 million.

As in the 19th century, a large rise in output from new regions of production will help restrain inflation and boost living standards of consumers in countries that import such goods. It could also, however, intensify political pressure for protection by existing producers. In the 1880s and 1890s, a boom in agricultural production knocked farm prices down. In reaction, France and Germany imposed tariffs on grain, and America's farmers supported a political movement, the Populists, that attempted to raise agricultural prices by severing the dollar's link to gold.

In the late 20th century, it is not just farmers who are threatened, but also industrial workers. Farmers could suffer from declining commodity prices as world agricultural output rises. The wages of less-skilled industrial workers could be depressed by a surge of low-cost manufactured imports. If farmers and unskilled industrial workers are not to become even more vociferous opponents of free trade than they already are, governments in the old industrial countries will have to develop remedial programs for them.

Another set of political problems could be produced by the intense competition for savings in the world financial markets of the 1990s, as the newly marketizing economies create stock and bond markets, privatize companies, gain renewed access to bank lending, and make themselves more attractive to foreign direct investment. Unless there is a rise in the global savings rate, this burst of new investment opportunities could cause world real interest rates to rise.

There are now more than 30 stock markets in the developing world with an aggregate capitalization of more than $500 billion. While two-thirds of market capitalization is concentrated in East Asia, there has been a dramatic rise of investor interest during the past 12 months in the stock markets of Latin America and South Asia. The capitalization of the Mexican stock market has mushroomed from $20 billion in 1989 to more than $80 billion.

The creation of viable capital markets in the developing countries will vastly enhance their ability to attract external saving during the 1990s. Not only will they be less dependent upon bank lending; they will also be able to tap into the huge savings pools controlled by pension funds and insurance companies in North America, Europe and Japan. Those institutions invest primarily in securitized instruments (bonds and equities) and thus could not invest in most developing countries until very recently.

The first effects of the liberal economic revolution on the world capital markets have been felt through the boom in German public spending to rebuild the former East Germany. In the 18 months since the fall of the Berlin Wall, Germany's public deficit soared to nearly 200 billion marks from 20 billion marks, and German bond yields rose from 7% to 9%. By the mid-1990s, the new capital demands of Latin America, East Asia, China and the old Soviet bloc are likely to be equal to at least one or two additional East Germanies. Whether these capital demands push interest rates sharply higher will depend upon the savings behavior of both the old industrial countries as well as the newly marketizing economies.

During the 1980s, the national saving rates of the leading industrial nations averaged only 20.4% compared to 23% in the late 1970s and 24% during the six years before the 1973 oil shock. If its saving rate were still 24%, the industrial world would have an additional $400 billion of capital available for investment.

The decline in the saving rate of the industrial countries stemmed from a sharp rise in government deficits (dis-saving) and a small decline in private saving rates. The biggest dis-savers were Japan, where the private saving rate fell from 30.3% of gross national product in the 1960s to 26.3%; France, where the government surplus fell from 4.8% of GNP to 1.4%; Germany, where the government saving rate dropped from 5.3% of GNP to 1.9%; and Italy, where the government deficit grew from 1.2% of GNP to 6.4%. The U.S. also contributed to this trend through its expanded government deficit, but the net swing in U.S. national saving was smaller than elsewhere because the U.S. entered the 1980s with the lowest saving rate in the industrial world.

Europe and Japan had high saving rates before the 1980s because their governments had introduced strongly pro-saving tax and financial regulatory policies after 1945 in order to finance postwar reconstruction. The U.S. did not feel compelled to introduce such policies and thus never experienced the surge in saving rates that occurred in the other industrial countries during the 1950s. The U.S. saving rate of 19% was one of the highest in the world before 1940, but the same rate ranked low after the war because of the sharp rise in other countries' saving rates. In Japan, the savings rate rose from an average of 12.9% between 1887 and 1936 to nearly 30% in the 1950s and 1960s. In Germany, the savings rate rose from 18% during the period 1851–1928 to nearly 24% after the war.

In the developing world, Latin America and Africa saving rates have averaged less than 20% becasue of inflation rates and tax policies that destroyed the value of financial assets. The Asian countries, by contrast, have saving rates close to 30% and have been able to finance their development domestically.

In the 1990s, market-oriented economic policies should boost saving rates in the developing countries but their investment opportunities should exceed their resources. During the next 25 years, for example, 95% of the growth in the world labor supply will occur in the developing countries, while the labor forces of Europe and Japan are projected to shrink.

Many Western politicians would prefer to ignore the reintegration problems of the old command economies. But the global economy has become too interdependent for such complacency. On the first day of the attempted coup against the Gorbachev government in the Soviet Union, the drop in values on world stock markets were greater than the total dollar value of the Soviet Union's gross national product. The losses caused by Iraq's attack on Kuwait exceed Iraq's national output even more radically.

There may be even more belligerent economic pygmies in the 1990s. Imagine, for example, the potential political risks that could be created by an independent Ukraine with nuclear weapons if it is denied access to the European agricultural market. The recent German announcement that it would support cuts in European farm subsidies suggests that Bonn understands the risks posed by economic chaos in Eastern Europe, but France continues to waffle over liberation of the European agricultural market.

GOLDEN AGE OF CAPITALISM

It may be impractical to convene a new summit conference comparable to Bretton Woods and Versailles, but there should be no doubt that the challenge facing the major industrial nations today is as great as it was in 1945 and 1918. The spread of liberal economic ideas to the third world has created the preconditions for a new golden age of capitalism—one potentially greater even than that of the 19th century.

But the creation of a benign international order will not happen automatically. It will require both the old industrial countries and the developing countries to pursue policies of altruistic self-interest by opening their markets and bolstering their saving rates. Otherwise, they will lose the opportunities for economic specialization and expanded investment created by the rebirth of a truly global market economy for the first time since 1914.

60. RIDDLE OF CHINA: REPRESSION AND PROSPERITY CAN COEXIST

Nicholas D. Kristof

This article appeared in the New York Times *on September 7, 1993. To what "riddle" does the author allude? In what ways have the Chinese people enjoyed greater prosperity in recent years? Can that be attributed to the Communist Party? To authoritarian government? To capitalist innovations? Was prosperity worth the price in political freedom and human rights?*

What is intellectually irksome about China, for anyone who values human rights, is that a Communist Party that is often brutally repressive should be so stunningly successful in raising living standards.

The party torments many of the nation's bravest and boldest thinkers, sometimes locking them up in insane asylums or imprisoning them with criminals suffering from infectious diseases. Yet at the same time, the party is presiding over one of the greatest increases in living standards in the history of the world.

The Government fights leprosy as aggressively as it attacks dissent. It inoculates infants with the same fervor with which it arrests its critics. Partly as a result, a baby born in Shanghai now has a longer life expectancy than a baby born in New York City.

ANNOYING TO DEMOCRATS

For those around the world who cherish democracy, China's success in generating prosperity and well-being is just a bit annoying—and certainly challenging to explain. It offends Western humanitarian values to think that a repressive Communist state can do more for its people than a democratic Government like India's.

Yet a Chinese woman is almost twice as likely to be literate as an Indian woman, and the risk of her baby's dying in the first year is less than half as much as in India. As a matter of priorities, many people would probably prefer a healthy baby to a meaningful vote.

"The first measure of any Government or administration is to ask, 'Is there any period in our previous history in which you would prefer to live,' " said David M. Lampton, the president of the National Committee on U.S.-China Relations. "And I think the answer for the overwhelming majority of Chinese would probably be no."

This makes moral condemnations of China much trickier than denunciations of the former East bloc, which impoverished its citizens at the same time that it repressed them. The Clinton Administration periodically complains about the Chinese Government's abusing its citizens, yet there is no question that the Communist Party is is overseeing a far greater rise in prosperity and general well-being than any Democratic or Republican administration has ever achieved in such a short time.

This is not to say that criticism of Communist repression is necessarily misguided.

"When Hitler held power, the German economy enjoyed a boom," Zhang Weiguo, a dissident journalist now living in California, noted drily. "And Japan grew very quickly during the militarist years before World War II. So we shouldn't regard economic development as our sole objective."

The point is simply that with China's economy the fastest-growing in the world, moral judgments about the Communist Party's role becomes more complex. Particularly in the Chinese countryside, the issues sometimes seem more textured, the assessments more nuanced, than they do to casual observers abroad.

From afar, it sometimes seems as if the fundamental dynamic in China is brutal repression of dissent. In reality, political dissent plays an inconsequential role in most people's lives, particularly in the countryside. Three quarters of China's population of nearly 1.2 billion lives in the villages, and it is a world of its own.

Take K. G. Sun's little village at the end of a winding dirt road in northern China. Chickens rush across the path, and a few cows and goats are tethered to the trees. It is a peaceful little place, although there was a bit of excitement in January when someone celebrated Chinese New Year by heaving a brick through the village chief's window.

Mr. Sun and the other peasants have their complaints, of course. Everyone hates the man in charge of enforcing restrictions on births, and eight different people reported him anonymously to the township when he tried to shield his son who was trying to have an extra baby.

A lean and muscular man in a ripped tank top, Mr. Sun seems to have stepped out of a painting by a Chinese Norman Rockwell. Asked his age, he says he was born in the Year of the Dog, 1958. As for his children: "I don't know which one's what age. I just know one's a 'dog' and one's a 'pig.'"

For peasants like Mr. Sun, the big grievance is corruption, including the way the village and township cadres take bribes and squander public money to live it up.

"The big officials eat big, and the little officials eat a little," a middle-aged man said, using "eat" as slang for taking bribes or misusing public funds. "And if you're not an official, you don't eat."

The peasants knew enough to be suspicious when the village chief abruptly took 12 acres of the village's best land out of production last fall and announced that a brick factory would be built on the site. The rest of the village's land was redivided so that everybody got a bit less.

FLURRY OF PROTEST LETTERS

The peasants protested, particularly when it became clear that the brick factory would be privately owned by the village chief, a police official from the county seat and a few other outsiders. The villagers wrote letters to everyone they could think of: to provincial leaders, to Prime Minister Li Peng, to People's Daily, even to The New York Times.

When an American showed up—the first Westerner ever to visit the village—the peasants delightedly poured out their complaints. Unfortunately, the village chief noticed and took his revenge.

The next day, the township police summoned the peasants who had talked to the American and subjected them to a full day of grueling interrogation. They were told that it was illegal to make contact with foreigners and that in the old days they would have been beaten to death for the offense.

The police accused them of "leaking state secrets" and suggested that they were "counterrevolutionaries." The county police have summoned the peasants for interrogations in the county seat, and officials there apparently are still deciding how to punish the villagers.

Those peasants, in other words, have plenty of reasons to be furious at the authorities. And yet one of them, interviewed later in secret, has this to say of the mood in the village:

"Overall life has gotten much better. My family eats meat maybe four or five times a week now. Ten years ago, we never had meat."

"Now the peasants can go into the cities and earn 18 yuan a day doing odd jobs," he added, referring to the equivalent of about $3.15, a munificent sum in such places. "Of course the peasants are content."

In the Chinese countryside of the 1990's, Communist Party officials often bully and cheat the peasants, yet life is getting better so rapidly that many still support the system. Most Chinese say that if the Communist Party were suddenly to announce free elections, it could count on the votes of peasants to win overwhelmingly.

The improvements are greatest in the most obscure sector of society: the poor mountain villages of central and western China where peasants still live in mud hovels and are lucky if they can send their children to elementary school for more than four or five years.

Life in those villages is still awful, but not so miserable as it used to be. Women may not give birth in clinics, but at least they are likely to have a trained midwife so that mother and infant alike have a fighting chance of surviving. Poor peasants may not be able to afford luxuries like brick houses or wrist watches or toilet paper, but at least they have enough rice so they do not have to choose which of their children to feed.

The World Bank reported in a study published this year that the proportion of Chinese living in absolute poverty—lacking decent food, housing and clothing—dropped from 220 million in 1980 to 100 million in 1990. In other words, a group of people equivalent to almost half the population of the United States can now potentially enjoy life instead of merely fight to subsist.

"What the peasants need above all is to fill their bellies," said a Chinese journalist who is often critical of the Government. "Only when they've got food to eat and a place to live will they start demanding political changes."

He cited an ancient Chinese proverb that only when men have enough to eat and a place to sleep do they run after women. The same, he said, holds for their desire for democracy.

CONSUMER ECONOMY EMERGES

One of the huge gains in the quality of life over the last 10 years is also the most difficult to quantify: the emergence of a consumer economy in which Chinese no longer have to stand in line everywhere, no longer have to wear shoes that pinch because the right sizes are unavailable, no longer have to put up with the scorn of rude shop clerks, no longer have to endure the indignity of pants that split or zippers that break.

"In a shortage economy, you always have to struggle for life; you have to struggle to get your daily necessities," said Huang Yasheng, a political scientist who grew up in Beijing and is now conducting research about China at Harvard. "It makes a tremendous difference if you can spend half an hour a day shopping instead of four or five hours."

Though Chinese no longer spend much time waiting in lines these days, no easy calculus is available to weigh that gain against the torture inflicted on Catholic priests. This reflects a broader issue. The improvements over which the Communist Party has presided tend to be in material and sometimes mundane areas, while the party's abuses touch directly upon issues of human dignity and freedom that the West says it cares most about.

The torture of a protester pressing for democracy arouses more empathy in the West than, say, the deaths of the 2,000 to 3,000 Chinese peasants who drown in floods in an average year.

One of the Communist Party's problems is a phenomenal incompetence in self-promotion. Not since coup leaders in Liberia, in West Africa, invited journalists to watch and photograph the execution of 13 ousted Cabinet ministers in 1980 has a Government shown off its worst side with such relish.

"They are incredibly inept at public relations," said John T. Kamm, a Hong Kong business consultant who has campaigned to free political prisoners.

On the other hand, what the party does well it does quietly. For instance, a comprehensive system of prenatal checkups and free maternal health care has sharply reduced the infant mortality rate over the last decade. In 1980, for every 1,000 live births, 56 babies died in their first year of life. Now only 38 die in every 1,000 live births.

That amounts to saving the lives of 378,000 babies each year. But that is a statistic, while the Government's repression is usually an anecdote— and sometimes a highly publicized one at that.

In a typical such anecdote, last month the authorities banned the country's most prominent independent labor leader, Han Dong-fang, from returning to China. The authorities had earlier imprisoned him, tortured him by running a needle through his hand, and intentionally locked him up with tuberculosis patients until he became infected himself.

WHICH IS THE REAL CHINA?

So which is the real China? Is it the nation where police deliberately expose Mr. Han to the tuberculosis that almost kills him? Or is it the country that offers free prenatal checkups and infant inoculations?

For four decades, Westerners have been debating that question. But no sooner does a consensus emerge about which is the real China than the other one emerges to confuse everyone.

In fact, it is difficult to describe either vision of China as the fundamental one. Both exist side by side, the yin and yang of the China of the 1990's.

"Both faces of China are real ones," said a Chinese woman who has ties to the leadership and yet is privately critical of the party. "You can't pick out one element and say this is the important one."

All countries and all people contain some mix of good and bad, but in China the gulf between the two sides is particularly striking. To come up with a meaningful judgment is a bit like assessing Dr. Jekyll and Mr. Hyde.

Why is it that the party tries to destroy people the way it attacks disease?

ANALYZING DENG XIAOPING

To answer that question, it helps to try to enter the mind of Deng Xiaoping and other Communist leaders. As far as anyone can make out, Mr. Deng, the paramount leader, is not just out for himself. He has genuine and profoundly held hopes for China, but these concern collective prosperity and national strength rather than individual freedom.

This is not surprising, for Chinese thinkers traditionally have emphasized the common good rather than individual rights. The expressions in Chinese for "democracy" and "freedom" were coined only 100 years ago, and terms like "human rights" have been used in a positive context by the Government for less than five years.

Mr. Deng has a desperate fear of chaos and conflict, inspired in part by his memories of the wars, famines and upheaval of the first part of this century. By some accounts Mr. Deng's father was beheaded by bandits in 1938, and two other family members were killed or driven to suicide during the Cultural Revolution that began in 1966—and that, to people like Mr. Deng, sums up the terrible price of disorder.

The combination of this mental orientation and practical experience is that Mr. Deng places a huge premium on order and that he is willing to destroy anyone who he believes might unravel it. Dissent, in his view, challenges not just the Communist Party but also China's best hope for modernization. In a talk to other leaders in 1987, he warned that if the proponents of democracy were not crushed, then China would again become simply a "dish of loose sand."

So if the price of saving China from disorder is that dissidents and their families are destroyed—or that demonstrators are mowed down by machine gun fire near Tiananmen Square—well, Mr. Deng has never been a squeamish man.

Still many young Chinese believe that Mr. Deng is making a colossal miscalculation. They see his stability as that of a pressure cooker: when the top comes off, as it must some day, the explosion will be all the greater because the lid was so tight.

In any case, one open question is how much credit the Chinese Communist Party should get for the increase in living standards. One reason China is growing so rapidly is simply that it lagged in previous decades, and furthermore the boom seems to have more to do with private initiative than with public policy.

The problem of assaying virtue is not, of course, limited to China. Even child molesters can be polite and caring 99 percent of the times, as their mothers tearfully point out at sentencing. Iraq, Libya and the former Soviet Union all raised living standards for a time, yet none got much credit for it because they were simultaneously engaging in what much of the world regarded as repulsive behavior.

On the other hand, most of China's neighbors—Taiwan and South Korea, among others—have also had their share of massacres and repression, yet the brutality gradually abated and a measure of democracy has begun to bloom in each place. In retrospect, one can make a case that the crucial historical process unfolding in each place a dozen years ago was not the torture of democracy campaigners but the emergence of a middle class that demanded and supported a more democratic system.

In the long run, then, recollections of China in the 1990's may depend on how the country develops in the coming years. If it manages to follow the East Asian model and transform itself into a prosperous and pluralistic nation along the lines of Taiwan or South Korea, then historians may regard the economic boom and the growth of a middle class as the crucial developments in China in the latter part of the 20th century.

On the other hand, if China collapses into chaos and civil war, historians are sure to find that this was predictable. They will argue that the biggest victim of the repression was ultimately the Communist Party itself, for in stifling criticism the party lost its bearings and its ability to correct itself.

FOCUSING ON REPRESSION

In that sense, repression may not be nearly as peripheral as it seems initially.

In the Soviet Union of the 1960's, for instance, dissidents were also on the fringe of society. Yet in retrospect, their voices turned out to be prophetic, and it was clearly worthwhile to focus attention on them instead of on infant mortality rates.

Repression is important in a larger sense as well: dictatorships are often more aggressive and militaristic than democracies. An authoritarian China might be more likely than a democratic one to try to "liberate" Taiwan, or "recover" Mongolia, or "secure" the South China Sea.

Mr. Zhang, the dissident journalist now living in California, suggests that in this respect the political repression, even if it directly involves only a small proportion of people, is still of crucial importance in understanding China. For all the economic strides of the last 15 years, Mr. Zhang said, the nation could lurch into chaos—or threaten its neighbors— unless the party opens up and turns to more democratic methods.

"If China develops its economy rapidly but fails to carry out political reform, there will also be a fundamental problem of safety to the international community," he warned. "In the past, we've seen the examples of Germany and Japan."

61. U.N. REPORT HIGHLIGHTS WORLDWIDE DISPARITY

Robin Wright

In this article from the Los Angeles Times, *May 16, 1993, the U.N. report lists disparities in "human development," a term meant to include economic well-being and political rights. What are some of these disparities? How serious are they? What does the U.N. recommend to alleviate them?*

Despite sweeping political, economic and social changes around the world, fewer than 10% of people worldwide now participate fully in the institutions and decisions that shape their lives, according to a new report from the United Nations.

Disparities among ethnic, gender and economic groups are stark, even in the United States, which now ranks sixth after Japan, Canada, Norway, Switzerland and Sweden on the Human Development Index that rates standards of living.

But when separated by ethnic groups, U.S. whites rank first in the world, while African Americans come in 31st, after poor Caribbean nations like Trinidad and Tobago.

Latino Americans come in 35th, after struggling former Soviet satellites like Estonia or Third World countries like South Korea—and just ahead of Chile, Russia and Malta.

"Full equality is a distant prospect in the United States," the 1993 U.N. Human Development Report says.

The infant mortality rate for blacks, for example, is more than twice as high as that for whites, while per capita income for blacks is $13,378, only 60% of the white income of $22,372. And more than half of black American children are growing up in single-parent homes, almost three times the rate among white Americans.

Yet the report cites the United States not for its inequities but for its successes and the implications for the rest of the world.

"The United States has a commendable record on human rights and affirmative action. It is an open society, with nondiscrimination written into law and a media that keeps pressure on the issue. And there have been tremendous improvements in integration since the 1960s," Mahbub ul-Haq, Pakistan's former finance and planning minister and now chief architect of the U.N. Development Program's annual report, said in an interview.

"But the United States still has grave problems, which only shows how far most other countries have to go."

Almost every country has at least one and often several underprivileged ethnic groups whose education, political access, economic opportunities and life expectancy fall seriously below the national average, the report says.

The infant mortality rate among Guatemala's Indians is 20% higher than that of the rest of the population. In South Africa, half the population, mostly whites, own 88% of all private property.

Worldwide, "exclusion, rather than inclusion, is the prevailing reality," Haq said.

But the problem is not limited to minorities. Worldwide, the majority of people are still excluded from full participation in a variety of ways.

More than a billion of the world's people—or one in every four—still languish in absolute poverty, for example, while the poorest fifth find that the richest fifth enjoy more than 150 times their income.

"For millions of people all over the world the daily struggle for survival absorbs so much of their time and energy that even if they live in democratic countries, genuine political participation is, for all practical purposes, a luxury," according to the report, which was prepared by an independent team of economists for the United Nations.

For the poor, participation in the economic system is often so limited that they can't break the cycle. In Sri Lanka, for example, the poorest 20% of the population receive less than 5% of national income.

The gap between rich and poor is also widening in several countries. Between 1970 and 1988, real income of the richest 20% of Chile's population grew by 10%, while income of the poorest 20% fell by 3%, the report says.

Participation in a country's economic life has also been blocked by the new trend in "jobless growth." Between 1960 and 1987, the economies in Germany, France and Britain more than doubled, yet their employment rates dropped.

The trend in jobless growth is even more serious in developing countries with high birthrates, which are producing legions of people but decreasing numbers of jobs, thus denying economic participation and creating political powder kegs.

The case of women offers another stark example. Although they form a majority globally, women are vastly underrepresented in political systems, occupying only about 10% of parliamentary seats and fewer than 4% of Cabinet posts, the U.N. report says.

In 1993, only six countries had female heads of government, while women still don't have the vote in several countries.

The disparities are not just in Third World countries. Japan, which ranks highest of all states in criteria making up the Human Development Index, drops to 17th when the index is adjusted for gender disparity.

In Japan, women hold only 25 of parliamentary seats. On average, Japanese women's income is a mere 51% of male earnings; only 7% of administrative and managerial jobs go to Japanese women.

Rural populations are another excluded majority. "Despite making up around two-thirds of the [world] population, they receive on average less than a quarter of the education, health, water and sanitation services," the report says.

In Bangladesh, only 4% of the rural population has access to sanitation facilities, compared to 40% of city residents—in a country with a population that is 84% rural.

"For the vast majority, achieving real participation will require a long and persistent struggle" in all areas, the report says.

"Elections are a necessary, but certainly not a sufficient, condition for democracy. Political participation is not just a casting of votes. It is a way of life."

The U.N. report also outlines five major steps to reconstruct societies and expand participation—what it calls "five new pillars of a people-centered world order." They are:

•Shift the focus of security from nations to people, from armament to development.

Changes have already begun. Since 1987, military expenditures worldwide have dropped by $240 billion, while more than 2 million armed forces members have been demobilized since the beginning of the 1990s. Defense industries are expected to cut their work forces by 25% by 1998, the report says.

But much more remains to be done. A freeze in military spending at 1990 levels over the next decade, for example, would release almost $100 billion for basic human development, it says.

•Develop new patterns of national and global governing and decentralize power, giving more authority to local governments.

New forms of government are needed because the nation state is now too small for big functions and too big for small functions. And governments still restrict power to a centralized elite. Developing states distribute only 10% or less of national spending to local authorities, while many industrial countries give only 25% to regions or towns.

•Focus new international cooperation on human needs rather than on the preference of states.

The Cold War's shadow still hovers over aid allocations as strategic importance remains a more important criterion than income, health or education.

In 1991, for example, more than half of U.S. foreign aid went to only five strategically important nations—Israel, Egypt, Turkey, the Philippines and El Salvador—while many needier countries received a small fraction of assistance.

Worldwide, twice as much bilateral aid still goes to big military spenders as to moderate spenders. In contrast, less than 7% of aid goes for human priority concerns, which should be increased to at least 20%, the report says.

•Reorient markets to serve people rather than people serving markets.

Between 1980 and 1991, almost 7,000 state-controlled enterprises were privatized worldwide. Because the process has already included mistakes, "the need to create people-friendly markets is all the greater now that so many countries have embarked on strategies of economic liberalization," the report says.

•Develop and invest in new models of development that are people-centered and sustainable environmentally.

"It has long been assumed that pursuing economic growth through increasing output would necessarily increase employment. This clearly has not happened," the report says.

Overall, the report concedes that its recommendations "call for nothing less than a revolution in our thinking."

62.   WOMEN AND POLITICS

John Harwood and Geraldine Brooks

This article appeared in the Wall Street Journal *on December 14, 1993. There have been some changes since it was written (e.g., recent defeats for women leaders in Canada and Finland) but the authors' argument still holds. Why does the United States lag behind many countries in the election of women to top offices?*

When President Clinton addressed the General Assembly this fall, so too did a parade of prominent women leaders.

Violeta Chamorro, president of Nicaragua, and Norway's prime minister, Gro Harlem Brundtland, were there, as was Begum Khaleda Zia, the prime minister of Bangladesh, who became the first Muslim woman head of state to address the General Assembly.

Suddenly, nations all over the world are choosing woman leaders. Yet the prospect of a woman being elected president of the U.S. stills seems remote. Geraldine Ferraro came the closest, in her 1984 run for vice president. But after a quarter century of modern feminism, which propelled women into public life in increasing numbers, the most powerful woman in American national politics is arguably Mr. Clinton's unelected wife, Hillary, and only after a campaign by her husband that deliberately soft-pedaled her influence and interests.

NOT THE FIRST, NOR THE SECOND

The U.S. might have been expected to break the barrier before conservative and Catholic Ireland, which elected Mary Robinson president in 1990 despite her support of abortion rights and outspoken feminism. Even three Muslim countries—Turkey, Pakistan and Bangladesh—have overcome strong religious reservations to female leadership.

Indeed, the list of nations that have or have had a woman prime minister or president now includes Western nations (Britain, France, Canada, Ireland, Portugal, Iceland), Asian nations (the Philippines), Latin American nations (Argentina, Bolivia, Nicaragua), Eastern European nations (Poland), Mideast nations (Israel, Turkey), almost the entire subcontinent region (India, Pakistan, Bangladesh, Sri Lanka) and West Indian nations (Haiti, Dutch Antilles, Dominica).

In the U.S., women have made substantial political gains over the past two decades. The number of women mayors has risen more than tenfold to 175 (out of 973 mayors of cities over 30,000 population), and women have quadrupled their ranks among state legislators to 1,517 out of 7,424. Since the 1992 election kicked off the "Year of the Woman," the number of women on Capitol Hill has nearly doubled to 54 (47 in the House, seven in the Senate, compared with 28 and two in the previous Congress). Widely divergent electorates have sent Republicans Kay Bailey Hutchinson to the Senate from Texas and Christine Todd Whitman to the New Jersey statehouse.

POLL FINDINGS

All else being equal, says Democratic pollster Celinda Lake, their gender now gives a woman a 10% boost in races for legislative seats, partly because they are less tainted by the negative feelings voters have about incumbents. But the advantage falls off sharply—nil to 3%—in races for more powerful jobs such as mayor or governor. "There's greater resistance to women the higher you go," says Irene Natividad, a political consultant and former head of the National Women's Political Caucus.

When it comes to the presidency, a 1937 Gallup survey showed that 65% of those polled said they wouldn't vote for a woman for president even if she were qualified. The last time the survey was taken, in 1987, the percentage had dropped to 12, though a differently worded Roper question in 1992 showed a 32% rejection.

The U.S. lacks some of the factors that have pushed women to power elsewhere in the world. Ancient traditions of dynastic rule, feudalism or monarchy can boost the chances of women from prominent families—even in modern electoral politics.

Some, like Pakistan's Benazir Bhutto, who was voted back to power last October, or Bangladesh's Mrs. Zia, initially came to prominence after the killing of a famous father or husband.

GENDER NOT AN ISSUE

Mrs. Zia, who had an arranged marriage, stayed at home raising her two sons as her army-officer husband rose to the presidency in 1975. On his assassination six years later, she gradually became the spokeswoman for opponents of the military government of Hussain Ershad, leading a nine-year struggle for the free elections that took place in 1991 and brought an end to years of military dominance. Surprisingly, in a devout,

85% Muslim country, gender was never a big issue. Mrs. Zia's main rival in the presidential campaign also was a woman.

"We Muslims are not as conservative and fanatical as some in the West would like to think," says Mrs. Zia. "My being a woman not only didn't hurt; I think it actually helped me win support." She believes Bangladeshis saw her self-effacing style as a welcome—and complete—contrast to the hated military dictators of the past.

The rise to power of Turkey's Tansu Ciller, a U.S.-educated economics professor who insisted her husband take her name on marriage, was even more rapid. Ms. Ciller came to politics from academia only three years before winning her party's leadership last June. Since then, she has played up her womanliness, telling the electorate: "I embrace you with a mother's love."

Ms. Ciller won the ruling True Path party's leadership partly because her economics background made her a good prospect to tackle Turkey's soaring inflation and push through the nation's flagging privatization program. The party's former leader, Suleyman Demirel, had also encouraged her political rise because he recognized his party's weakness with women voters and because Ms. Ciller offered a fresh face and a way for the party to reinvent itself. Her reinvention has gone further than perhaps Mr. Demirel intended. On becoming prime minister, she immediately sacked all but three of his former ministers.

By happenstance, Ms. Ciller became prime minister within hours of Kim Campbell's selection, for similar reasons, in Canada. (One Turkish newspaper highlighted the coincidence with the sexist headline: "Ours is Prettier.") As in Turkey, Ms. Campbell's party reached out for a leader who would offer a dramatic contrast to Brian Mulroney, whose long tenure had left voters bored and restless. Now, Ms. Ciller's political enemies already are crowing that Ms. Campbell's ignominious trouncing at the polls last October will be echoed when Turkey calls a general election in 1996. At a convention last August for former Prime Minister Mesyut Yilmaz, some delegates chanted, "Mesyut koltuga, Tansu mutfaga,"— "Mesyut back to power and Tansu back to the kitchen."

FRESH FACES HERE AT HOME

Growing hostility toward incumbents and a desire for fresh faces have been benefiting women in the U.S., as well. "It used to be that not being a member of the club hurt women. Now it helps women," says Susan Estrich, 1988 campaign manager for Michael Dukakis. Even the mostly male world of political fund-raisers and strategists is scrambling to adapt to the expanding interest in women's candidates. After Emily's List successfully pioneered fund raising for prominent Democratic women, more-established fund-raisers became less neglectful of women.

Another barrier to an eventual presidential candidacy may also now be weakening—the belief that women lack the toughness and military know-how necessary to be Commander-in-Chief. For U.S. presidents who served during the Cold War, military experience was a necessity. President Clinton, however, coming to power after the Soviet Union's collapse, got elected without having served in the armed forces. And as time goes on, the chances of contenders of either gender having military experience becomes remote.

In any case, Britain's Margaret Thatcher (the Falklands), Israel's Golda Meir (the 1973 Yom Kippur war) and India's Indira Gandhi (the decisive 1971 victory over Pakistan) have all demonstrated that women can lead their countries to war—and win.

Mr. Clinton made up for his lack of military background by homing in on the nation's desire to focus on internal concerns. Such a platform can help women, too, as polls suggest U.S. voters tend to regard women as more trustworthy and attuned to their everyday concerns, that is, the domestic side.

THE "NORMALIZATION" OF NORWAY

Norway, for example, which has few foreign-policy crises, beyond the perennial "cod wars" over fishing rights, has developed the world's most strikingly feminized political culture—although its leader, Dr. Brundtland of the Labor party, prefers to call it "normalized." In the latest national election, last September, three major parties were led by women, including the traditionalist, agrarian Center Party.

Norway started to become "normalized" in 1971. Then, aggrieved that their increasing prominence in the work force wasn't matched in politics—in 1968 women made up less than 10% of Norway's Parliament—women ran in local elections and were elected in large numbers. Sensing a chance to capture these votes at a national level, the Labor group and a smaller left-wing party made women's participation a key plank of their platforms. Labor gave 40% of candidacies to women.

Dr. Brundtland set a world record in her 1986 cabinet by filling nine of 19 ministries with women. In the current Parliament, women hold 39% of the seats. Women's equality in politics is now "a fact of life," Dr. Brundtland says, "something obvious."

While Norway is at the forefront, other European countries don't lag too far behind. France had the outspoken Edith Cresson as prime minister from 1991 to 1992 and now has Simone Veil as deputy prime minister; the German cabinet is one-fifth women. President Clinton has helped the U.S. catch up, at least at cabinet level, by appointing women to six of 22 positions.

5.2. From *The Broken Spears* by Miguel Leon-Portilla. Copyright © 1962, 1990 by Beacon Press. Reprinted by permission of Beacon Press.

6. From David Pieterzen DeVries, *Voyages from Holland to America, A.D.1632–1644*, translated from the Dutch by H. C. Murphy (New York, 1853), pp. 114–7.

7. From "Olaudah Equiano of the Niger Ibo" edited by G. I. Jones, from *Africa Remembered* by Phililp D. Curtin, ed. Madison: University of Wisconsin Press, 1967. Reprinted by permission of the publisher.

3. Commerce, Colonies, and Converts in Southeast Asia

8. From *Old World Encounters: Cross-Cultural Contacts and Exchanges in Pre-Modern Times* by Jerry H. Bentley. Copyright ©1993 by Oxford University Press, Inc. Reprinted by permission.

9. From *The Travels of Mendes Pinto* by F. Mendes Pinto, edited and translated by Rebecca D. Catz, published by The University of Chicago Press. Copyright © 1989 The University of Chicago Press. Reprinted by permission of the publisher.

10. From *The Life and Letters of St. Francis Xavier,* edited by Henry James Coleridge, 2nd edition (London: Burns and Oates, 1890).

11. From *Southeast Asia in the Age of Commerce, Volume 1: The Lands below the Winds* by Anthony Reid. Copyright © 1988 Yale University Press. Reprinted by permission of the publisher.

4. Asian Continental Empires

12. "The Late Ming Empire" is reprinted from *The Search for Modern China* by Jonathan D. Spence, by permission of W. W. Norton & Company, Inc. Copyright © 1990 by Jonathan D. Spence. *The Peony Pavillion* by Tang Xianzu. Reprinted by permission of Indiana University Press.

13. Reprinted from *The Turkish Letters of Ogier Ghiselin de Busbecq, Imperial Ambassador at Constantinople, 1554–1562,* translated by Edward S. Foster, pp. 58–62, 65–66, 109–114 (1927) by permission of Oxford University Press, Ltd.

14.1 From "Peasants Reduced to Serfdom, 1649" by Richard Hellie, trans. in Thomas Riha, ed., *Readings in Russian Civilizations,* rev. ed., Vol. 1, pp. 77–81. Chicago: The University of Chicago Press, 1969. Reprinted by permission of the publisher.

14.2. From *A Source Book for Russian History: From Early Times to 1917* by George Vernadsky, editor. New Haven: Yale University Press, 1972. Reprinted by permission of the publisher.

5. The Scientific Revolution

15. From "The Scientific Revolution in the West" by Franklin Le Van Baumer, in *Main Currents of Western Thought,* fourth edition, edited by F. Le Van Baumer. New Haven: Yale University Press, 1978. Reprinted by permission of the publisher.

16. Selections from pages 87–89, 96–99 from *A History of Their Own: Volume II, Women in Europe from Prehistory to the Present,* by Bonnie S. Anderson and Judith P. Zinsser. Copyright © by Bonnie S. Anderson and Judith P. Zinsser. Reprinted by permission of HarperCollins Publishers, Inc.

17. From the *World History Bulletin* (a publication of the World History Association, Drexel University, Philadelphia, PA), Fall/Winter 1986–7, volume 4, number 1. Permission granted by Lynda Norene Shaffer.

18. From *Sources of Japanese History,* by David John Lu, ed., Volume 1, pp. 253–255. Copyright © 1974 by McGraw-Hill, Inc. Reprinted by permission of the publisher.

6. Enlightenment and Revolution

19. From *The Philosophical Works of David Hume.* Edinburgh: A. Black & W. Tait, 1826.

20. Reprinted with the permission of Macmillan College Publishing Company from *Critique of Practical Reason,* 3/e by Immanuel Kant, trans. by Lewis White Beck. Copyright © by Macmillan College Publishing Company, Inc.

21.1. American Declaration of Independence (public domain).

21.2. Reprinted with the permission of Macmillan College Publishing Company from *A*

Documentary History of the French Revolution by John Hall Stewart, ed. Copyright © 1951 by Macmillan College Publishing Company, renewed 1979 by John Hall Stewart.

22. U.S. Bill of Rights (public domain).

23. From *Selected Writings of Bolívar* by Vincent Lecuna, comp., and Harold A. Bierck, Jr., editor, 2 volumes, pp. 175–191. New York: Colonial Press, 1951. Copyright © Banco de Venezuela.

7. Capitalism and the Industrial Revolution

24. From *Technology in World Civilization* by Arnold Pacey, pp. 128–135. Cambridge: MIT Press, 1990. Reprinted by permission of MIT Press.

25. From *The Wealth of Nations* by Adam Smith. London: Everyman's Library, J. M. Dent & Sons, Ltd., 1910.

26. From "Factory System of Production" in *The Philosophy of Manufactures* by Andrew Ure. London: Charles Knight, 1835.

27. From *Manifesto of the Communist Party* by Karl Marx and Friedrich Engels, reprinted in the Crofts Classics Series. Arlington Heights, IL: Harlan Davidson, 1955.

8. Western Economic Expansion

28. From "Imperialism of Free Trade" by John Gallagher and Ronald Robinson, in *The Economic History Review* (August 1953), 2nd Series, VI, No. 1. Basil Blackwell Ltd., 108 Cowley Road, Oxford OX4 1JF, England.

29. From *The Discovery of India* by Jawaharlal Nehru. New York: John Day Co., 1946.

30. From *Modern Asia and Africa*, edited by William H. McNeill and Mitsuko Iriye. Copyright © 1971 by Oxford University Press, Inc. Reprinted by permission.

31. From *Indians in American History*, Frederick E. Hoxie, ed., D'Arcy McNickle Center for the History of the American Indian. Harlan Davidson, Inc. Reprinted by permission of Harlan Davidson, Inc.

9. Migrations and Imperialism

32. "Labor on the Move," from *Europe and the People without a History* by Eric R. Wolf. Copyright © 1983 The Regents of the University of California Press. Reprinted by permission of the publisher.

33. From *The Cuba Commission Report: A Hidden History of the Chinese in Cuba. The Original English Language Text of 1876* (Baltimore: The Johns Hopkins University Press, 1993).

34. From *La Partage Politique de l'Afrique d'apres les transactions internationales les plus recentes, 1885 a 1888* by Emile Banning, edited and translated by Irene and Raymond Betts in *The "Scramble" for Africa*, edited by Raymond Betts. Boston: D.C. Heath and Co., 1966.

35. From *The Tools of Empire: Technology and European Imperialism in the Nineteenth Century* by Daniel R. Headrick. Copyright © 1981 by Oxford University Press, Inc. Reprinted by permission.

10. Culture and Change

36. From *The Origin of Species by Means of Natural Selection* by Charles Darwin. London: 1859. Reprinted in *Darwin*, edited by Philip Appleman. New York: Norton, 1979.

37. From "Mistakes in Speech" in *The Basic Writings of Sigmund Freud*, edited and translated by A. A. Brill, M.D. New York: The Modern Library, 1938. Copyright © Gioia B. Bernheim and Edmund R. Brill, copyright renewed 1965. Reprinted by permission.

38. From *Mexican Cinema: Reflections of a Society, 1896–1980* by Carl J. Mora. Copyright © 1982 The Regents of the University of California Press. Reprinted by permission of the publisher.

39. From *A Church Between Colonial Powers: A Study of the Church in Togo* by Hans W. Debrunner, translated by Dorothea M. Barton. London: Lutterworth Press, 1965. Copyright © 1965 The Commission on World Mission and Evangelism of the World Council of Churches.

40. From "Yosano Akiko and the Taisho Debate over the 'New Woman' " by Laurel Rasplica Rodd, in *Recreating Japanese Women, 1600–1945* edited by Gail Lee Bernstein.

11. World War I and the Russian Revolution

41. From *Asia and Western Dominance* by L. M. Panikkar. Copyright © 1953 by George Allen & Unwin Publishers, Ltd. Reprinted by permission of George Allen & Unwin Publishers, Ltd.

42. From Woodrow Wilson, *War and Peace: Presidential Messages, Addresses and Public Papers (1917–1924)*, 1, edited by Ray Stannard Baker and William E. Dodd. New York: Harper Brothers, 1927.

43. From *The League of Nations Covenant* (1919), Articles 22 and 23. Reprinted in *Colonial Rule in Africa: Readings from Primary Sources*, ed. by Bruce Fetter. (Madison: University of Wisconsin, 1979), pp. 173–175.

44. From *The Soviet Achievement* by J. P. Nettl. Copyright © 1967 Thames and Hudson. Reprinted by permission of the publisher.

12. Fascism, World War II, and the Holocaust

45. Excerpts from *Hitler* by Joachim C. Fest, translated by Clara and Richard Winston. Copyright © 1973 by Verlag Ullstein, English translation copyrights © 1974 by Harcourt Brace and Company. Reprinted by permission of Harcourt Brace and Company.

46. From Carter Vaughn Findley and John A. M. Rothney, *Twentieth-Century World*, first edition. Copyright © 1986 by Houghton Mifflin Company. Used with permission.

47.1. From Heinrich Himmler's secret speech at Posen, reprinted in *A Holocaust Reader*, edited by Lucy Dawidowicz. New York: Behrman House, 1976. Published by Behrman House, Inc., 235 Watchung Ave., West Orange, NJ 07052. Used with permission.

47.2. From *Treblinka* by Jean-François Steiner. Copyright © 1967 by Simon & Schuster, Inc. Reprinted by permission of Simon & Schuster, Inc.

47.3. Selections from pages 227–231 from *The Holocaust, the French, and the Jews* by Susan Zuccotti. Copyright © 1993 by BasicBooks, Inc. Reprinted by permission of BasicBooks, a division of HarperCollins Publishers, Inc.

13. Dependence and Independence in Asia

48.1 From *Hind Swaraj or Indian Home Rule* by M. K. Gandhi (Ahmedabad, India: Navajivan, 1938). Copyright © The Navajivan Trust, 1938. Pages 15–16, 26–27, 28, 30–31, 32–33, 58–60, 69–71, and 82–85.

48.2. From *Toward Freedom: The Autobiography of Jawaharlal Nehru* by J. Nehru. New York: John Day Company, 1942.

49.1. Reprinted from *The Tragedy of the Chinese Revolution*, second revised edition, by Harold R. Isaacs with the permission of the publishers, Stanford University Press. Copyright © 1951, 1961 by the Board of Trustees of the Leland Stanford Junior University.

49.2. From *A Call to Arms* by Lu Hsun. Beijing (Peking), 1922.

49.3. From *Report on an Investigation of the Peasant Movement in Hunan* by Mao Zedong. Beijing (Peking): Foreign Language Press, 1967.

50. From *Select Works, III* by Ho Chi Minh. Hanoi: Foreign Languages Publishing House, 1960–1962.

14. Dependence and Independence in Africa and the Middle East

51. From *An African Speaks for His People* by Parmenias Githendu Mockerie (London, 1934). Reprinted in *The African Reader: Independent Africa*, ed. by Wilfred Cartey and Martin Kilson. New York: AMS Press, 1970.

52. "Uganda's Women" by Jane Perlez, February 24, 1991. Copyrights © 1991 by The New York Times Company. Reprinted by permission.

53. "The Man for South Africa's Future," by Bill Keller, May 1, 1994. Copyright © 1994 by The New York Times Company. Reprinted by permission.

54. From *In My Father's House: Africa in the Philosophy of Culture* by Kwame Anthony Appiah. Copyright © 1992. Reprinted by permission of A. M. Heath & Company, Ltd. and Oxford University Press.

55.1. From *The Israel-Arab Reader: A Documentary History of the Middle East Conflict* by Walter Laquer and Barry Rubin, editors. Copyright © 1984 by Viking Penguin. Reprinted by permission.

55.2. From *The Israel-Arab Reader: A Documentary History of the Middle East Conflict* by Walter Laquer and Barry Rubin, editors. Copyright © 1984 by Viking Penguin. Reprinted by permission.

15. Dependence and Independence in the Americas

56. "Revolution and the Intellectual in Latin America," by Alan Riding, March 13, 1983. Copyright © 1983 by The New York Times Company. Reprinted by permission.

57. Selections from pages 11–26 from *One Hundred Years of Solitude* by Gabriel García Márquez. English translation copyright ©1970 by Harper & Row Publishers, Inc. Reprinted by permission of HarperCollins Publishers, Inc.

58. "Slavery on Rise in Brazil, as Debt Chains Workers," by James Brooke, May 23, 1993. Copyright © 1993 by The New York Times Company. Reprinted by permission.

16. The New World Order

59. "The Coming Golden Age of Capitalism" by David Hale, Nov. 7, 1991. Reprinted with permission of *The Wall Street Journal*. Copyright © 1991 Dow Jones & Company, Inc. All rights reserved.

60. "China Riddle: Life Improves Though Repression Persists," by Nicholas D. Kristof, September 7, 1993. Copyright © 1993 by The New York Times Company. Reprinted by permission.

61. From "UN Report Highlights Worldwide Disparity" by Robin Wright, May 16, 1993. Copyright © 1993 by *Los Angeles Times*. Reprinted by permission.

62. Reprinted by permission of *The Wall Street Journal*. Copyright © 1993 Dow Jones & Company, Inc. All Rights Reserved Worldwide.